The Thomas Merton Letters Series

I. THE HIDDEN GROUND OF LOVE
edited by William H. Shannon, Ph.D.

II. THE ROAD TO JOY
edited by Robert E. Daggy, Ph.D.

III. THE SCHOOL OF CHARITY
edited by Patrick Hart, O.C.S.O.

IV. THE COURAGE FOR TRUTH
edited by Christine M. Bochen, Ph.D.

The Courage for Truth

THE COURAGE FOR TRUTH

The Letters of

THOMAS MERTON

to Writers

Selected and edited by

Christine M. Bochen

Farrar · Straus · Giroux

NEW YORK

Library of Congress Cataloging-in-Publication Data
Merton, Thomas, 1915–1968.
The courage for truth : letters to writers / by Thomas Merton ;
edited by Christine M. Bochen. — 1st ed.
p.   cm.
Includes index.
1. Merton, Thomas, 1915–1968—Correspondence. 2. Poets,
American—20th century—Correspondence. 3. Authorship—Moral and
ethical aspects. 4. Ethics in literature. 5. Truth in literature.
I. Bochen, Christine M. II. Title.
PS3525.E7174Z48   1993   818'.5409—dc20   [B]   92-37078 CIP

Contents

V

Preface

Thomas Merton was born with a passion for writing. As a small child, before he could read, he loved to look at books. All his life he was a voracious reader, a compulsive notetaker, and a committed writer. When he came to the Abbey of Gethsemani in 1941, he expected he would be required to give up his writing. Fortunately, he had abbots throughout his monastic life who respected this God-given gift and wisely encouraged him to use it. Just as monasticism was the way in which Merton specified his baptismal commitment, the vocation of writing remained a significant element of his living out the monastic life.

Merton not only wrote extensively on the contemplative life but, convinced that it was accessible to everyone, managed to make *contemplation* a household word. Numberless people are grateful to him for this. Because he saw contemplation not as a separate compartment of life but as an experience that broadened life's horizons, he began in the troubled sixties to write books and articles of incisive social criticism. Merton was not a "spiritual" writer in the same way as people like Abbot Columba Marmion or Hubert Van Zeller, who were content to remain in a single genre. While he wrote with joy and generosity in the field of "spirituality," a good bit of Merton's heart always remained in the literary world he grew up in. Especially in his later years he turned to the kind of writing that had attracted him at least since the time he had been the youthful editor of the literary journal at Oakham school in England—namely, to a more creative kind of writing and to forceful and impressive literary criticism.

Merton kept in touch with "literary" people and looked forward to their visits to Gethsemani. John Yungblut, who has written some fine books on mysticism, told me of visiting the monastery in 1967 with his wife, June. He had come with the desire to discuss mysticism with the renowned monk, but in the course of their talk he made the "mistake" of telling Merton that June was writing a dissertation on Samuel Beckett.

Mysticism was quickly left behind and the theatre of the absurd became the center of attention.

Merton's correspondence with some of the outstanding men and women of letters who were his contemporaries is huge. He encouraged young writers. He felt a special affinity with writers of Latin America and wrote to many of them, especially the poets. What gives this fourth volume of the Merton correspondence its distinctive identity is the fact that in these letters we meet the "literary" Merton. If anyone wonders what kind of writing Merton would have done had he never entered the Abbey of Gethsemani, these letters offer a hint of the direction he might have taken. This is not to say that Merton doffed his monastic hood when he donned his "literary" hat. No, his life, especially in his later years, was more or less an integrated whole. Just as his literary background and interest influenced the way he wrote about spirituality (and made it so different from the work of other writers in the field), so his literary works—in a more hidden yet no less telling way—reflect and embody his spirituality.

As general editor of the Merton Letters, I want to express to Dr. Christine M. Bochen my admiration for her careful selection of letters and for the superb editing she has done, with a personal touch that enhances the readability and attractiveness of this volume.

WILLIAM H. SHANNON
General Editor

Introduction

The Courage for Truth is devoted to Thomas Merton's letters to writers. Merton's passion for writers and writing began in his youth; his autobiography, *The Seven Storey Mountain*, is filled with the names of writers he was reading—William Blake, Ernest Hemingway, Aldous Huxley, D. H. Lawrence, Gerard Manley Hopkins, Evelyn Waugh, Federico García Lorca, Jacques Maritain, and many others. There were also numerous writing efforts by Merton during his early years—a prize-winning essay on the modern novel that he wrote at the Oakham school in England; humorous pieces published in the Columbia College *Jester*; a book review in *The New York Times*; and several novels he had submitted unsuccessfully to publishers, one of which (written in 1941) was published as *My Argument with the Gestapo* in 1969. In his student years, Merton's closest friends were persons who shared his passion for things literary. Contrary to his expectations when he entered the Abbey of Gethsemani, Merton continued to write. Some of his early writing was suggested by his first abbot and served the needs of the order; other work, like his poetry, was much more his own—for example, *A Man in the Divided Sea*. With the publication of *The Seven Storey Mountain* in 1948, it was evident that the monk always was and always would be a writer.

In the three volumes of Merton's letters already published in this series, there are many addressed to writers—Daniel Berrigan, Dorothy Day, D. T. Suzuki, Erich Fromm, Mark Van Doren, Etienne Gilson, to name a few. But the present volume features letters to writers who were in a special way Merton's *literary friends*, persons who shared with Merton a passion for writing as a life work. Among these are poets, novelists, essayists, and literary critics—writers in the genres in which Merton himself wrote. These letters show Merton the writer in his element; they reveal an important dimension of this most amazing monk. Nevertheless, Merton's concern with religious experience and social issues, his relationships with family and friends, his ideas on religious renewal and monastic life—themes explored in previous volumes in the series—continue to emerge in these letters as well. In reading Merton's correspondence, we continue to encounter "the whole Merton"—monk, social critic, friend, and writer—who shares with us the details of his daily life and work. We read about his routine in the monastery and in the hermitage; about manuscripts-in-progress and the piles of mail; about the Kentucky countryside, his visits with friends, his experiments with calligraphy and photography; and about silence and solitude.

This volume covers a period of twenty years—from 1948, when Merton first wrote to Evelyn Waugh (who at the request of the London publisher had taken on the job of editing *The Seven Storey Mountain* for publication in England), to Merton's death in 1968. In this period, he corresponded with writers around the globe, developing an ever-widening circle of literary friends in Europe, the Soviet Union, and Latin America as well as in North America. Merton wrote letters to several who had already gained prominence through their work—Waugh, Maritain, Czeslaw Milosz, Boris Pasternak, James Baldwin, Walker Percy, Henry Miller, and Victoria Ocampo. But Merton also encouraged and nurtured many writers in Latin America, such as Ernesto Cardenal, and other young writers in North America.

Merton felt a natural kinship with writers. Besides sharing a common interest in poetry, new books, and fine literary magazines, Merton sensed in writers a hope for the future of humankind. Merton believed, as the title of this volume suggests, that the courage for truth was their special gift. Writing in 1964 to José Coronel Urtecho, Merton reported that he was encouraged by the "awakening of poets" in Latin America because poets "remain almost the only ones who have anything to say . . . They have the courage to disbelieve what is shouted with the greatest amount of noise from every loudspeaker; and it is this courage that is most of all necessary today." Courage is "the first thing," he wrote to Milosz, in 1960; "we [writers] need courage to dissociate ourselves from our own tribe and its conventions." This reaffirmed what Merton had said to Milosz two years earlier: "One thing I do know, is that anyone who is interested in God Who is Truth, has to break out of the ready-made shells of the 'captive' positions that offer their convenient escapes from freedom—one who loves freedom must go through the painful experience of seeking it, perhaps without success."

Speaking the truth is an obligation, a duty that requires the courage to take risks. Yet speaking the truth "sooner or later brings us into confrontation with system and power, which seek to overwhelm truth for the sake of particular interests." This is why Merton believed it is necessary that writers not be co-opted by any establishment—political or religious. That this courage to speak the truth is rooted in true freedom is evident in Merton's own life. These letters remind us that Merton spoke out boldly against war, against racism and injustice, and against all forms of human aggression and violence. Even when he was forbidden to publish on the subject of war and obeyed his superiors, he did not remain silent; he continued instead to write to his literary friends and to others. He did not hesitate to criticize his church when he saw there was more concern for the institutional structure than there was for people. Merton was never slow to say what needed to be said. "There are times," he wrote to Cardenal in 1963, "when one must speak," and Merton had great admiration for those who, like Pasternak, Milosz, and Cardenal, did speak out despite serious and even dangerous opposition.

To find the courage to speak the truth, "it is very good, almost essential, to have at one's side others with a similar determination, and one can then be guided by a common inspiration and a communion in truth," he wrote to Cardenal in 1967. Solidarity with others can be a source of "true strength," but Merton also recognized that sometimes one may have to stand alone as "a completely isolated witness." As Merton well knew, though "more difficult and dangerous . . . that too may become necessary."

The ultimate source of courage, of "fidelity to the truth," is fidelity to "the light that is in us from God." This faithfulness is in a real sense beyond us. "Perhaps the great reality of our time is this, that no one is capable of this fidelity, and all have failed in it, and that there is no hope to be looked for in any one of us. But God is faithful . . . This, I think, is the central reality." It is in this light that Merton offered advice to Pasternak, advice that he himself heeded: "Do not let yourself be disturbed too much by either friends or enemies . . . May you find again within yourself the deep life-giving silence which is genuine truth and the source of truth: for it is a fountain of life and a window into the abyss of eternity and God."

This volume is a record, in Merton's own words, of twenty years of his life as a monk and a working writer. The letters included here seemed to fall easily enough into five sections. The first section is devoted to his letters to Evelyn Waugh, which began in 1948, when the success of *The Seven Storey Mountain* made Merton feel even more keenly his isolation as a writer. Merton looked to Waugh as a fellow writer but also as a literary master who could give him the advice and criticism he needed. Waugh was more than willing to do so. There is a particular charm to these letters. Merton is eager and enthusiastic, yet modest and unassuming. The address is formal: Evelyn Waugh remains "Mr. Waugh" throughout. Yet the tone is conversational, even chatty. One can almost imagine an expression of amusement on Waugh's face as he read the letters and heard an overly enthusiastic young monk continually encouraging him to say his prayers and use the rosary.

The second section includes letters to three eminent literary figures—Jacques Maritain, Czeslaw Milosz, and Boris Pasternak. The correspondence with Maritain began in 1949; that with Milosz and Pasternak in 1958. In Maritain Merton found a kindred spirit, someone who shared his love of the Catholic intellectual tradition and especially appreciated the centrality of the contemplative experience. Merton very much admired Jacques and Raïssa Maritain; he translated Raïssa's poems and after her death encouraged Jacques in his preparation of Raïssa's *Journal* for publication. Jacques Maritain was supportive of Merton too; intervening in 1952 in Merton's behalf with an enthusiastic letter refuting the censor's view that Merton's *The Sign of Jonas* was full of "trivialities," he urged its publication. Writing to Maritain, Merton often spoke about a matter both men regarded as being of ultimate importance. In a letter of 1963 Merton says: "Dear Jacques, you are going on your journey to God. And perhaps I am too . . . There are great illusions to be got rid of, and there is a false self that has to be taken off, if it can be done. There is still much to change before I will really be living in the truth and in nothingness and in humility and without any more self-concern." These lines, and others like them, Maritain could read with full understanding and sympathy.

In Milosz, Merton found a soul mate in another sense—someone with whom he could speak about the work of a writer in a world gone mad. In a correspondence that was both congenial and intense, Milosz always wrote with a candor that Merton valued. Like few others, Milosz questioned Merton and criticized his work in ways that helped the monk to clarify his own thinking. For example, Milosz was puzzled by Merton's views on war, peace, and Christian responsibility. Responding to his criticism, Merton wrote that there were few people whose advice he respected as much as he did that of Milosz. Though he saw wisdom in what Milosz had to say, Merton explained that he was driven by conscience to speak out: "There are certain things that have to be clearly stated. I had in mind particularly the danger arising from the fact that some of the most belligerent people in this country are Christians, on the one hand fundamentalist Protestants and on the other certain Catholics. They both tend to appeal to the bomb to do a 'holy' work of destruction in the name of Christ and Christian truth. This is completely intolerable and the truth has to be stated. I cannot in conscience remain indifferent." This was an argument Milosz appreciated even if he could not share Merton's position.

Though Merton's exchange with Pasternak was brief (the Russian writer died in 1960), these letters are significant, signaling what William H. Shannon has called Merton's "return to the world." In his first letter to Pasternak, Merton wrote that he felt as if the two had "met on a deeper level of life on which individuals are not separate beings," as if they "were known to one another in God." The encounter with Pasternak affected Merton deeply and he saw in such encounters the potential for transforming the world. In 1967, writing to Pasternak's publisher Helen Wolff, Merton put it this way: "I think it is terribly important today that we keep alive the sense and possibility of a strong communion of seemingly isolated individuals in various places and cultures: eventually the foundation of true human community is there and not in the big states or institutions."

The third section contains Merton's letters to the Nicaraguan writer Ernesto Cardenal. The correspondence began in 1959, shortly after Cardenal returned to Latin America after spending two years as a novice at the Abbey of Gethsemani, and continued until Merton's death in 1968. The relationship between a novice and his master is a close one, and something of that intimacy persists in these letters, particularly the earliest ones, in which Merton appears especially solicitous and supportive. Documented in these letters is Merton's love for Latin America, its people, and its culture, a love which Cardenal nurtured by extending Merton's contacts with Latin Americans. In these letters, Merton is candid about his dissatisfactions with aspects of his life in the monastery and conveys his dream of someday moving to Latin America, going so far as to lay plans for travel in 1959. Merton again considered moving to Latin America in 1965 and joining Cardenal at his newly founded experimental community at Solentiname. Though he never went to Latin America as a monk (he had visited Cuba before he entered the monastery), Merton shared their dream of freedom and justice with Cardenal and other Latin Americans.

The breadth of Merton's contacts in Latin America is evident in the fourth section, which contains letters to writers in Argentina, Brazil, Chile, Cuba, Peru, Uruguay, Venezuela, as well as Nicaragua. The earliest of these letters were written to Pablo Antonio Cuadra, the Nicaraguan writer and editor of *La Prensa*, with whom Merton corresponded for ten years, beginning in 1958. In the sixties Merton wrote to Alceu Amoroso Lima, Esther de Cáceres, Napolean Chow, José Coronel Urtecho, Alfonso Cortés, Miguel Grinberg, Hernan Lavin Cerda, Angel Martínez, Victoria Ocampo, Nicanor Parra, Margaret Randall (then de Mondragon), Ludovico Silva, Rafael Squirru, Alejandro Vignati, and Cintio Vitier. Again and again, Merton said he "fit more naturally into Latin American culture than into that of North America." He was "convinced that the best American poetry is written in Latin America" and he believed that the "future belongs to South America, Africa, and Asia: but above all I think to South America." There was something deeply personal in Merton's sense of connection with Latin America: "In some strange way Latin America has a great deal to do with my vocation: not that I have anything to tell LA but that I have much to learn from it, and it is our vocation to learn from one another."

The last section includes a selection of letters written in the sixties to poets and writers: James Baldwin, Cid Corman, Guy Davenport, Clayton Eshleman, Lawrence Ferlinghetti, Julien Green, Henry Miller, Walker Percy, Jonathan Williams, William Carlos Williams, and Louis

Zukofsky. To some, like Baldwin, Merton wrote a letter or two. With others, like Eshleman and Zukofsky, the first letter was the beginning of a deep friendship. These letters document Merton's life and work in the last few years of his life, when he discovered and took delight in North American writers and tried his hand at the publication of a literary magazine called *Monks Pond*. That venture, undertaken in the last year of Merton's life, spawned its own flurry of correspondence, much of it "business" mail, which is not included among these letters. Still, a picture of Merton, the sometimes frenzied editor, does emerge, as well as that of the monk who has finally found, in his hermitage, the solitude and silence he longed for all his life. Generally, these later letters are shorter than the letters Merton wrote in the forties, fifties, and early sixties. Perhaps this is a sign that Merton had already said much of what he had wanted, and needed, to say.

CHRISTINE M. BOCHEN
Nazareth College of Rochester

The Courage for Truth

I

To Evelyn Waugh

It was The Seven Storey Mountain *that brought Evelyn Waugh (1903–1966) and Thomas Merton together, at first in correspondence and later in person when Waugh visited the Abbey of Gethsemani in November 1948. Waugh greatly admired Merton's autobiography after Robert Giroux, Merton's editor at Harcourt Brace and Company, sent a set of galley proofs to London, asking Waugh for an advance comment. It appeared on the dust jacket of the book's first edition: "This book may well prove to be of permanent interest in the history of religious experience." The London publisher, Tom Burns of Hollis and Carter, asked Waugh to edit the book for publication in England. In Waugh's judgment, succinct writing was not one of Merton's virtues, and he cut about twenty percent of the text "in order to adapt it to European tastes." In his foreword, Waugh noted that only "certain passages which seemed to be of purely local interest were cut out." The book was issued in 1949 under the title* Elected Silence *(taken by Waugh from a poem of Gerard Manley Hopkins).*

Merton was delighted to learn of Waugh's good opinion of the Mountain. *After addressing some of the points Waugh had raised in a letter to Giroux at Harcourt Brace, Merton turned to his "real reason" for writing to Waugh: "I need criticism the way a man dying of thirst needs water." Merton described the "difficult spot" he was in and the kinds of writing assignments his superiors had "piled up" on him.*

Merton approached Waugh as a novice might a master, which is precisely how Merton saw Waugh—as a literary master. By 1948 Evelyn Waugh was firmly established as a leading man of English letters, and he was more than willing to instruct the young monk in matters of literary style. Twenty years later, Merton concluded a reminiscence of Waugh by saying: "I never lost my great admiration of Waugh as a creative writer, though I certainly disagreed with much of his conservatism after the [Vatican] Council. But I think I understand why he felt that way—especially about Latin, etc. He would."

August 2, 1948

You will be surprised to get this but not, I hope, annoyed. Father Abbot gave me permission to write to you when I saw your letter to Harcourt Brace about *The Seven Storey Mountain.* I was especially grateful to get your reactions to the book in terms of an English audience, and it is about that and all its implications that I feel this letter ought to be written.

About my Cambridge passage, I felt the same way [as you] afterwards, thought of rewriting it. My agent [Naomi Burton], who is English, said it was okay, so I let it stand. Then every time it came up in proof I worried about it, but was too lazy to do anything definite. The book is already printed here. But I'd like to clean up that Cambridge [University] section a bit for the English edition which some people called Hollis and Carter [the publisher in London] are doing next spring. Do you think people would accuse me of duplicity in saying one thing here and another there? Anyway, I'm not as mad at Cambridge as that either. About the succinctness, perhaps the book should have been rewritten. A tremendous amount of dead wood was cut. But there was no time to go over the whole thing again. The poem ["For My Brother: Reported Missing in Action, 1943"] was the idea of the editor [Robert Giroux] at Harcourt Brace (I suppose you mean the one about my brother) and not mine. I tried to get it out but did not succeed. It is too late now, at least for the American edition. I'll probably have to go by what the English editor thinks, on that.

The real reason I write to you is not merely to rehash these little details. I am in a difficult spot here as a writer. Father Abbot [Frederic Dunne, who died Aug. 4, 1948] gives me a typewriter and says "write" and so I cover pages and pages with matter and they go to several different censors and get lost, torn up, burned, and so on. Then they get pieced together and retyped and go to a publisher who changes everything and after about four years a book appears in print. I never get a chance to discuss it with anybody and scarcely ever see any reviews and half the time I haven't the faintest idea whether the thing is good or bad or what it is. Therefore I need criticism the way a man dying of thirst needs water. Those who have any ideas in their head about writing and who can communicate with me by letter or word have so far told me that I need discipline. I know. But I don't *get* it. A man can do something for himself along those lines by paying attention and using his head, I suppose. But if you can offer me any suggestions, tell me anything I ought to read, or tell me in one or two sentences how I ought to comport myself to acquire discipline, I would be immensely grateful and you would be doing something for my soul. Because this business of writing has become intimately tied up with the whole process of my sanctification. It is an ascetic matter as much as anything else, because of the peculiar circumstances under which I write. At the moment, I may add, I am faced with a program of much writing because we have to raise money to build some new monasteries and there is a flood of vocations. Most of what I have to do concerns the Cistercian life, history, spiritual theology, biographies etc. But (be patient with me!), consider this problem: all this has suddenly piled up on me in the last two years and I find myself more or less morally obliged to continue connections with the most diverse kind of publishers. On one end of the dilemma I am writing poetry and things like that for New Directions and a wacky surrealist magazine called *Tiger's Eye* that I think I had better get out of.

In the middle is Harcourt Brace. Next year they are bringing out a book I have done about our Order and the life and so on [*The Waters of Siloe*]. Then Sheed and Ward wants something—an expansion of a pamphlet [*Cistercian Contemplatives*] I did for the monastery and which might interest you, so I'll send it along. Finally, at the other end is Bruce and Co., popular Catholic publisher in Milwaukee, and, of all things, a magazine called the *Messenger of the Sacred Heart*, which has just gone through a reform and has elevated itself above the level of *True Story* and *True Romances* to become a kind of pious *Saturday Evening Post*. But I only did one article for them . . . no more. Then *Commonweal* is always on my neck asking for things.

Frankly, I think the devil is trying to ruin me. And I am left more or less on my own in all this. I have got to find some kind of a pace that is steady and disciplined and uniform and pretty near the top of whatever I may be capable of, and stick to that . . . then if they all want to buy some of it they can.

You see by this that it is a real problem, and a spiritual one too. Of course the whole thing may change with my being taken out of this job and put on something else after I am ordained, which should come next year. We are short of men all round. But I have been bold enough to impose on your patience and your charity because I have always considered you to be about the best living writer we've got. You do not need to be told that if you read *The Seven Storey Mountain*. I think I have read *Decline and Fall* and *Vile Bodies* over more than any other book except perhaps *Ulysses*: I mean before coming here. Needless to say I am very thankful for your notice, which the publisher intends to use on the jacket of the book.

I shall certainly pray for you and hope you will pray for me too.

Waugh responded on August 13, expressing his admiration for The Seven Storey Mountain *and his hope that it would do much good. He criticized three points of content. He faulted Merton for blaming Cambridge rather than accepting the responsibility himself for having wasted opportunities at the university; he did not like Merton's criticisms of the Franciscans; and he thought that Merton "should have made it clear—tho of course quite dryly and briefly—how far your various 'love' affairs were carnal and how far purely sentimental," as if the censors would have allowed this. Then he offered the advice Merton had sought: "Why not seek to perfect it [literary work] and leave mass-production alone?"*

September 3, 1948

I cannot tell you how truly happy I am with your letter and the book you sent. Both of them have been a very great help to me. In case you think I am exaggerating, I can assure you that in a contemplative monastery where people are supposed to see things clearly it sometimes becomes very difficult to see *anything* straight. It is so terribly easy to get yourself into some kind of a rut in which you distort every issue with your own blind bad habits—for instance, rushing to finish a chapter before the bell rings and you will have to go and do something else.

It has been quite humiliating for me to find out (from [Robert] Graves and [Alan] Hodge [authors of *The Reader over Your Shoulder*, which Waugh had sent to Merton]) that my bad habits are the same as those of every other second-rate writer outside the monastery. The same haste, distraction, etc. You very charitably put it down to a supernatural attitude on my part. Yes and no. It is true that when I drop the work and go to do something else I try not to think any more about it, and to be busy with the things that are really supposed to preoccupy a contemplative. When I succeed it means that I only think about the book in hand for two hours a day, and that means a lot of loose thinking that goes through the machine and comes out on paper in something of a mess. And consequently I have to admit that much of the *Mountain* is pure first-draft writing with nothing added except a few commas. That accounts for the heaviness of the long section preceding my Baptism—in which I think the cuts should come more than anywhere else. On the whole I think my haste is just as immoral as anybody else's and comes from the same selfish desire to get quick results with a small amount of effort. In the end, the whole question is largely an ascetic one! And incidentally I would never reproach anyone like yourself with vanity for wanting to write really well! I wish I had some of your integrity.

Really I like *The Reader over Your Shoulder* very much. In the first place it is amusing. And I like their thesis that we are heading towards a clean, clear kind of prose. Really everything in my nature—and in my vocation too—demands something like that if I am to go on writing. The contemplative life demands that everything, all one's habits of thought and modes of action, should be simple and definite and free of waste[d] motion. In every department of our life, that is our biggest struggle. You would be shocked to know how much material and spiritual junk can accumulate in the corner of a monastery and in the minds of the monks. You ought to see the pigsty in which I am writing this letter. There are two big crates of some unidentified printed work the monastery wants to sell. About a thousand odd copies of ancient magazines that ought to have been sent to the Little Sisters of the Poor, a dozen atrocious-looking armchairs and piano stools that are used in the sanctuary for Pontifical Masses and stored on the back of my neck the rest of the time. Finally I am myself embedded in a small skyscraper of mixed books and magazines in which all kinds of surreal stuff is sitting on top of theology. All this is dominated by a big movie-star statue of Our Lady life-size, on a pedestal, taking up most of the room; it was spirited out of the lay-brother's choir when they varnished the floor of the Church last spring, and never found its way back.

Before I get into any more digressions I want to thank you for your offer to edit the English edition of the *Mountain*. The letter just came from Hollis and Carter and I gladly accept your offer. I was thinking that, for my own part, I could go over the book and make the corrections that occur to me and then send it along to you, to work with. As for the Cambridge business I will rewrite the whole thing if you wish. I would gladly see the whole tone of that passage changed. I am glad the book will be shorter.

I am sorry to think that I gave the impression I was looking down my nose at the Franciscans, and I hope their feelings won't be hurt. They are very nice to me. However, about the love affairs I am afraid nothing more than what is there will get past a religious censor and there is nothing that can be done about it. I had to practically move a mountain to get across that passage where Peggy Wells came back and spent the night in the same room as [Robert] Gibney and myself—and only did so by juggling it around and trying to disguise the fact that it was only a one-room apartment.

I am sending you a book of poems [*Figures for an Apocalypse*] I wrote although I am ashamed of it. If you have any good ideas about them, let me know. I have practically stopped writing verse for the moment. I also sent you a pamphlet about the monastery [*Cistercian Contemplatives*] and extracts from a magazine article in the official publication of the Order. You will find a lot of misprints made by the Belgian typesetters. Perhaps the subject matter is too technical to be really interesting but I thought you might get something out of it.

Since I last wrote to you, our Abbot died and we have a new one [Dom James Fox] who just flew away to go to the General Chapter in France. He is a very holy man and he will be glad if I extricate myself from the network of trivialities into which the magazines are trying to get me. The Vicar General of the Order [Dom Gabriel Sortais] came from France and I talked with him a lot, being his interpreter in the regular visitation of the house, and he had a lot of ideas that harmonized with yours, so definitely I shall try to keep out of useless small projects that do nothing but cause a distraction and dilute the quality of what I turn out. The big trouble is that in those two hours a day when I get at a typewriter I am always having to do odd jobs and errands, and I am getting a lot of letters from strangers too. These I hope to take care of with a printed slip telling them politely to lay off the poor monk, let the guy pray.

Hollis and Carter may want the next book I am doing for Harcourt Brace which is about the Order and our life [*The Waters of Siloe*]. Will it be all right if we shoot the proofs along to you when they come out, next spring or early summer? God forbid that I should impose on your kindness, so if you cannot read it please say so. But since you might be interested I thought I would mention it, anyway. Meanwhile I am waiting to get busy on the manuscript again.

I don't agree with Mgr. [Ronald] Knox that God isn't interested in good prose. True, it doesn't mean anything to Him *per se*, and St. Paul seems to be on Mgr. Knox's side of the argument. But I don't think that Our Lord is very pleased with preachers and writers who do their best to get the Church all mixed up. Then there is that line about the judgment meted out for every idle word. It makes me very happy to think that you are going to judge the idle words in *The Seven Storey Mountain* before God does.

Meanwhile I pray for you, and please do you also pray for me. Don't be afraid to have a great devotion to Our Lady and say the rosary a lot. Do you have any time for mental prayer? You have the gifts that grace works on and if you are not something of a contemplative already, you should be. Tell me to mind my own business—but in a way, it is my business. Anyway, God bless you, and thank you very much.

P.S. A Carthusian I write to at Parkminster [Dom Humphrey Pawsey] tells me they want to print something here to arouse at least a remote interest in a possible foundation in the U.S. If you have any connections here that would be interested in such a thing you might let me discreetly know—but discreetly. And I would pass the information on to the Carthusians.

September 22, 1948

I am very glad you went ahead with the editing of The Seven Storey Molehill. Since you have probably cut more than I would have, it will save me the useless labor to wait for the proofs & then catch the one or two lines you may have missed. I don't expect to have to add anything —I mean restore anything—unless you have cut out the fact that I was baptized & became a monk. All the rest is accidental.

Your last paragraphs interested me much. Like all people with intellectual gifts, you would like to argue yourself into a quandary that doesn't exist. Don't you see that in all your anxiety to explain how your contrition is imperfect you are expressing an instant sorrow that it is not so—and that is true contrition. After all if you are sorry because your sorrow is *not* sorrowful because of God, then you *are* sorrowful because of God, not because of yourself. Two negatives make an affirmative. All you need is to stop speculating about it, and somewhere around the second step of your analysis, make a definite act of will, and that is that. Then you will be practicing a whole lot of supernatural virtues. Above all, trust (hope). The virtue of hope is the one talented people most need. They tend to trust in themselves—and when their own resources fail then they will prefer despair to reliance on anyone else, even on God. It gives them a kind of feeling of distinction.

Really I think it might do you a lot of good & give you a certain happiness to say the Rosary every day. If you don't like it, so much the better, because then you would deliver yourself from the servitude of doing things for your own satisfaction: and that slavery to our own desires is a terrific burden. I mean if you could do it as a more or less blind act of love and homage to Our Lady, not bothering to try to find out where the attraction of the thing could possibly be hidden, and other people seem to like it. The real motive for this devotion at the moment is that the Church is very explicit: a tremendous amount depends on the Rosary & and everything depends on Our Lady. Still, if there is some reasonable difficulty I don't know about, don't feel that you *have* to try this just because someone suggests it! . . .

But things are so serious now—and values are so completely cock-eyed—that it seems to me a matter of the highest moment to get even one individual to make one more act of his free will, directing it to God in love & faith.

Everything—the whole history of our world—is hanging on such acts. Have you read St. John of the Cross? You ought to do so—he is terrific; and also he is very *clear* in spite of what people say about his difficulty. I envy you your leisure. I would be sitting on top of the Cotswolds all day long, in a trance. If you don't say many rosaries, at least please sometime say one for me. I am haunted by two ideas: solitude and poverty. I pray for you a lot, especially at Communion—& for your family. Someone told me you are doing a feature for *Life* on the Church in America. We *think* we are so much better than we are. We have a big showy front. Behind it—there is a lot of good will that loses itself in useless activity & human ambitions & display.

P.S. Once again—I am tremendously grateful for your kindness in editing the book for me. God bless you for it.

February 19, 1949

As far as I can judge, you must be back in America at the moment, finishing your articles for *Life*. So I am writing to you in New York, first of all to thank you for the preface to *Elected Silence*, a copy of which was sent to me, and which was very kind indeed, and second to assure you that the edition of *E. S.* by you is much less cut than I expected. I have not gone through it all, since Hollis and Carter said they would not have time to incorporate any corrections I might make in their edition anyway, but from what I have seen, the book is improved considerably.

I hope we are going to see those articles—and I hope you have not said anything too flattering about American Catholics. There is a fair amount of ferment, I suppose, in the Church, but I wonder how deep it goes in this country. We still need an interior life—and a few sacrifices. On the other hand I am constantly impressed by the amount of good theological writing that is coming out of France, especially from the Editions du Cerf.

New Directions is putting out a book I wrote [*Seeds of Contemplation*] and which purports to be spiritual. There is a deluxe edition of the thing, on special paper and in a box. When I was signing the colophon sheets, I reflected on the nature of the work itself and began to feel very foolish. As I progressed I was tempted to write flippant and even obscene remarks over the signature, so perhaps the whole scheme did not come from the Holy Ghost. But in any case I'll send you a copy of this book in its dressed-up edition. It is beautifully printed.

Speaking of New Directions, I told [James] Laughlin you said you had met him, and he became very agitated and made me promise to inform you that the man from New Directions whom you met was not Laughlin but one of his henchmen, a Tony Bower with whom he does not wish to be confused because he is "a character." Anyway, it was not you who told me you had met Laughlin, but I insisted that it was Laughlin you had met when you said you had had lunch with someone from New Directions. There, I hope that is settled.

Don't forget, please, that we extorted a promise that you would come back here some time.

God bless you. Say some rosaries too, if Our Lady inspires you; it is very healthy.

May 12, 1949

Thank you very much for your last letter, written before you left New York. Since then a volume of *Seeds of Contemplation* has started on its way to Gloucestershire, where I hope it will find you well and happy and will not do anything to spoil your joy. I imagine you are quite relieved to be at home and in relative peace after your American campaign. Sister Thérèse [Lentfoehr] in Milwaukee and others here and there have written in to say that they succeeded in cornering you at odd moments on your lecture tour. Which brings to mind your kind offer to look at the original ms. of *E. Silence* and perhaps incorporate unprinted passages in a second edition. I don't know if it would be worth the bother. Sister Thérèse, who is extremely kind-hearted, has a misguided notion that I am the cousin of Santa Claus and overestimates every word that I write by about seven hundred percent. Perhaps it would be just as well to let it drop, although if you really *want* to undertake this penance, you may certainly have all the necessary permission.

I have taken the liberty of dedicating our book *Waters of Siloe* to you. I do hope you will not object to having your name appear in the front matter of the history of a religious Order—and a history which is not any too well written, either. But I wished to show you some exterior token of our gratitude and sincere friendship. Besides, I felt, quite self-ishly, that the book would benefit by the presence of your name in it, and that this fact might even hoodwink some of the readers into thinking that the book had some merit.

I close assuring you that your account of the Chicago prayer wheel, or the rosary with lights, has been haunting me for months. No wonder Communism is so popular.

If you happen to be anywhere near here in two weeks, on Ascension day [May 26, 1949], or the two following, please consider yourself invited to my ordination and first low/then high mass. In any case I know you will ask Our Lady to make me a simple and holy priest.

July 30, 1949

Thank you for your letter of May 27th. I haven't seen any sign of the Ronald Knox book [*Enthusiasm*] which you mentioned yet. Perhaps it got sidetracked somewhere in the Prior's shambles.

The Month has been paying me for my effusions by sending me books. One of them was *The Loved One*. I was having a delightful time with it until the authorities discovered that it was a n-v-l and swept it away. I still have *Brideshead Revisited* here even though it is a n-v-l. (hush!) I am allowed it because it is a model for style. That was what I said, and it is absolutely true. It is beautifully done. The writing is so fine that I don't want to go on with the book at all, I just take a paragraph here and there and admire it, so that I haven't read *Brideshead* yet, either, but have just enjoyed these fragments. I hope you are not of-fended.

Waters of Siloe, which is, on the other hand, a model of downright terrible writing, partly through my fault and partly through the fault of those whose hands it passed on the way to the press, is now in print but not yet bound. Harcourt Brace will send you a copy as soon as possible, I hope. The date of publication is set for September 15th and there is already an enormous sale.

We had our centenary celebration. It only lasted one day. I learned later that one of the monks had thought up a horrible scheme for a three-day celebration, the second day of which would feature a field Mass to be attended by twenty thousand school children. The archbishop nearly fainted when he heard of it. Fortunately it never went through. I was in charge of press relations that day and sat in a press box, no less watching the field Mass as if it were a polo game. A week later someone called up on the telephone and by some mistake got me—I was the one he wanted anyway. His first question was "Do you have the rule of silence?" I said, "Who are *you*, anyway?" It turned out to be one of the reporters who had been here for the centenary. He was just trying to show off the fact that he now knew the difference between the rule of silence, which exists, and the vow of silence, which does not.

Since then it has been furiously hot here. Postulants keep arriving in great numbers, and while we all sweat in the refectory a colored novice reads to us glowing accounts of how cold is the life of the missionaries among the Eskimos. It is a book which I find very thrilling although it contains horrible passages about people eating live fish and holding their mouths with their hands to keep the fish from jumping out while being chewed.

One of the postulants we have now wears a sport shirt that is covered with pictures of fox-hunting scenes dreamed up by some genius in the Seventh Avenue ghetto of New York. Men on fat horses come whooping through the pack of hounds in every direction and I forget all about the psalms in my fascination at this curious piece of tapestry which is parked right in front of me.

If you want an idea for a novel I think I could start you on one, and find out the rest of the story. At four o'clock one morning a Negro in a dinner jacket showed up at the gate of a prim Trappist monastery in France and said he had come all the way from Haiti to join. He was not wearing a dinner jacket because of dissipation, but because he believed one ought to dress as a waiter. He signed up in the book as the official guide to the cathedral in Port-au-Prince and became a monk but I have forgotten the funny details of his short stay in the monastery. He left the Trappists and went to the Dominicans in Angers and they did not let him become a novice but put him to work in the garden. There he found out that there was a very pretty maid who worked in one of the houses overlooking the garden and he fell madly in love with her, so that whenever she appeared at the windows he began throwing kisses to her. The story immediately got around Angers that the Dominicans were throwing kisses at all the maids in all the houses around their Friary and so the man was fired. I can find out about him and about the only American postulant who entered the same monastery. He became wildly incensed at the tyranny of Trappist life and after a week in the monastery attacked the novice master with a pitchfork. He had previously rushed into the dormitory when nobody else was there and had scrawled "A Mort le Père Maître" all over the cells with chalk.

The latest rumor about me is that I am in the Vatican studying ancient manuscripts about the Cistercian Order. If you see me around London, let me know. Since Father Abbot lets me wander around in the woods by myself I am no longer so terribly bothered with the problem of solitude. Kentucky is mildly crazy but I suppose one can be a contemplative here as well as anywhere else in the world, and the easy informality of monastic life in America is probably a great improvement over the tension which I suspect exists almost everywhere in Europe. A Chinese monk was here and he gave a graphic imitation of the French monks fighting in choir over details of the chant, in his Chinese monastery. Really I think you could write a wonderful novel about Trappists and it would give you an excuse to come and stay here for six months, in hiding. We would all be glad to have you. The Abbot General gave me a good story which I am going to use myself; it is the real account of what happened to one of our Brothers who was put in a concentration camp by the Nazis and afterwards did some jobs for the Free French secret service and had some thrilling escapes from the Gestapo and whatnot. It sounds good.

There goes the bell. God bless you. I remember you at Mass and recommend you especially to Our Lady. Like everyone else in the world you are almost too shy about your religious possibilities.

On August 29, 1949, Waugh wrote to thank Merton for dedicating The Waters of Siloe *to him and offered some "technical criticisms." The arrangement of sections seemed "a little loose." Several parts seemed unnecessary altogether. And Merton was given to "pattern bombing instead of precision bombing. You scatter a lot of missiles all round the target instead of concentrating on a single direct hit." In conclusion, he wrote: "I wish I saw the faults of* The Seven Storey Mountain *disappearing and I don't."*

September 17, 1949

Thank you very much for your two letters and your very valuable advice on the two books, *Waters of Siloe* and *Seeds of Contemplation*. I heard indirectly from Hollis and Carter that you might let yourself be persuaded to edit *Waters* for the English public as you did the *Mountain*. I would have never dared to ask for such a favor but if there is any possibility of you doing it, I would be delighted at my good fortune.

Your comments on the structure of *Waters* are true. The book is now being read in the refectory and I am aware that the pattern bombing, as you call it, is even worse than in the *Mountain*. It would be a great deal tidier and better to get direct hits, as you say. Still, I know that in my spiritual reading, I am generally glad to find the same thing said over again three or four times and in three or four different ways. I think this is a characteristic of many people who try to say something about the spiritual life—not a virtue perhaps, but a characteristic fault. I am glad to have at least a fault in common with St. John of the Cross, but I agree that it would be better to get rid of it and acquire the virtue of precision instead. You know that slang is almost part of my nature. I shall, however, set myself to avoid it in at least one book, and see how it turns out. Recently, I went through a manuscript that I turned out when I thought I was being "disciplined," and the effect was horrible. It read like a literal translation from the German. My tendency is to tie myself up in knots when I get too self-conscious about what I am putting down on paper.

You console me greatly by objecting to the Prologue, which I had thrown out and which the editor demanded back. The Note is my fault, and is a hypersensitive gesture of protection against critics who have been peppering me for my notions about the contemplative life.

Having found that even in a contemplative order men resent being hustled into contemplation (especially by one who is their junior in religion!!), I am pulling in my horns and will send you the article that results. One of the censors said it consoled him.

By the way, do not think that the faults of *Waters* are due to neglect of your advice about *Mountain*. The book was finished long before *Mountain* came out and I did not have a chance to do more than wipe out a few solecisms and make other corrections of that sort in proof. I should have caught more of the clichés. The trouble with writing here is that one has few contacts with healthy modern prose, and the things you hear in the refectory do not form your style! Then I have tended to rush too much. I have burned deep in my mind a statement from Graves and Hodge that faults of style are ultimately faults of character and have moral implications. Whatever happens, the next book will come out slowly and with thought and attention. I mean the next but one. The next [*What Are These Wounds?*] is an atrocious life of a medieval stigmatic [St. Lutgarde, a thirteenth-century Trappistine]—the one which I thought was disciplined, when I was writing it. Short of rewriting I cannot seem to do anything about it. I ought to have the strength of character to refuse to let it be published at all.

In any case, I am glad to get such valuable and stimulating direction, and from one so marvelously qualified to give it. I have no difficulty in accepting you as the delegate of the Holy Ghost in this matter. By the way, I have been twisting and turning and trying to get Ward Fowler [*Modern English Usage*] from some source. Would you be annoyed if I finally turned and begged it from *you*? We have no copy in the house, and we do not have any decent (i.e. Oxford) dictionary here either. And I cap my insolence with the assurance that we would be delighted to get anything by Monsignor Knox.

In any case, God bless you. I keep you in my Mass every day and ask Our Lady to be with you and help you. Please pray for me too.

October 15, 1949

You will be amused to hear that your article on the "American Epoch in the Catholic Church" is now being read in our refectory, to the accompaniment of some obstreperous coughing by the fathers who have surnames like Flanagan. I like it very much indeed and I think you have handled the situation very well: but fortunately I had already read the article for myself. The treatment to which it is being subjected by this week's reader is atrocious. He announced, for instance, in the introductory note, that you were the author of a best-seller called *Bridgehead Revised*. Really! If they let him get so far as the voting stage (he is a novice), I assure you he gets black from me—unless he wants to change to the lay brothers. The article is well liked by everyone, even by many of the Irish. I imagine your fan mail from the latter is, however, rather hot. I remember a letter I got from a man in Peekskill, New York, for just one innocent little hint that perhaps the Irish sometimes got drunk (which you deleted from the English edition). The man said that he was positively going to send the Ancient Order of Hibernians on my trail, declared that my book has "dragged many fine men into the mire," and closed with the woeful words: "Hoping to carry this matter further." I do not know where he carried it, but no repercussions have so far reached the abbey.

I meant to say in my other letter that I appreciated your remarks about the Carthusians. The truth is, I am firmly settled here. Since God has chosen the cenobitic life for me, it is evidently what I most need and then, too, there is really an extraordinary flexibility in our life as it is being led here at the moment. Everyone is ready to accept new suggestions and ideas and we are broadening out in many ways. Did I tell you that Father Abbot now allows me to run off to the woods by myself now? It is a great help. And rather unusual, I think. Then, with the growing numbers, we have been allowed to spread out more within the enclosure itself. We used to be all cooped up in that little garden you saw. Now we can rove around the orchards during the time of spiritual reading, if we want to. So I am quite ready to believe your friend who says that the Cistercians can actually lead a more contemplative life than the Carthusians. We are certainly not hidebound and we are not overburdened with vocal prayers. And that is a burden which is heavier when the prayers are recited in private, I think.

P.S. Of course I keep you in my Mass.

January 28, 1950

It is some time since I have given an account of myself. [Tom] Burns sent a copy of Fowler and I am very grateful. I am studying it with much amusement and profit. I remember enjoying it when I dipped into it in past years. In those days I was mostly interested in his wit. That Graves and Hodge book is very helpful.

And now comes a matter that belongs to St. Benedict's fifth degree of humility. In spite of the earnest efforts of my Abbot, my agent and myself, Bruce and company is bringing forth an atrocious biography of a Cistercian stigmatic that I wrote five years ago under obedience. We did what we could to stop it but it was too late. The thing was sent to them some years ago and the contract was signed too long ago for my own good. I hope a copy of it never falls into your hands. In spite of your great forbearance, you would never forgive me. Please pray that it may not do any harm.

Did I tell you that I am now busy teaching? Perhaps not. It takes up most of my time, but it will serve to accumulate material for biographies and doctrinal studies of St. Bernard and of St. Aelred of Rievaulx. You will be pleased at the thought that I am now working slowly and thoughtfully. I like it above all because it helps me to be a monk instead of a journalist. What I am teaching is Mystical Theology. This year I am on the Cistercians. Next year we hope to have a course in Mystical Theology from Origen to St. John of the Cross. A most wonderful amount of production is being done in France, on the Fathers. Did you see that article in *The Month* on the "Return to Contemplation"?

I have long hesitated to send you a copy of the *Tears of the Blind Lions* since you do not like modern poetry, but a copy is on the way as a token of my gratitude for your great kindness in going over *Waters of Siloe*. I am eager to see what the book will be like and know it will be easier reading after your editing. I think, incidentally, that teaching will help me to get direct hits instead of spraying the whole neighborhood of my target, especially when I am trying to talk about doctrine.

In any case, please believe me to be most grateful as always, for your kindness. I remember you often at Mass, asking Our Lord to bless you and your family and your work and all that you do, that you may give Him glory and help to extend His Kingdom on earth. It is a very sobering thing to go each day to the altar to offer this tremendous Sacrifice, and one of the principal effects it has had on me has been to leave me convinced that once one has pronounced the words of the Canon there is practically nothing left worth saying—except to wait until next morning's Mass. Do not think, however, that I despise the Post-communions—or that I walk into class and stare at the young monks in silence and then walk out again in disgust.

August 12, 1950

Hollis and Carter have just sent me *Waters of Siloe*, with your kind foreword and your expert editing. It was a much more difficult piece of work for you to reshape than *Elected Silence* but I am deeply indebted to you for doing such a good job. I have no regrets at the cutting of the Prologue and am glad it went. The opening story never sat very comfortably on my conscience. The defense of my ideas about the contemplative life was quite useless, and I have done it properly, in any case, in an article for *Cross and Crown*. That was where the defense belonged.

Thank you especially for your foreword. I do not know whether the amount of books against which you warn the reader will ever be produced. I am working slowly at them and I am also teaching now. The teaching serves to accumulate material for books but does not allow me as much time for writing as I need. Your remark about life in the Scriptorium being harder is, as a matter of fact, no fancy, as I am beginning to discover after seven years of it. (My first year in the monastery was the only one when I went out every day.) However, I do get out into the fields occasionally. For the first time in eight years I have been able to do something that might reasonably be called "bathing," when I managed to fell a tree in such a way that it dropped across a stream. That made it necessary to get in the water to trim it and cut it up. Very pleasant. I shall try to get out again before they finish cutting down all the trees along that creek.

Helena looks fine, in *The Month*. I especially admire your dialogue —the most difficult thing in a historical novel, isn't it? But above all I was delighted by the witch's little song.

It has occurred to me several times that in one of my other letters I may have said something that offended you. I do hope this is not so, but if it is, I know you will forgive me. Perhaps you have had wind of that hideous book I did, on a medieval stigmatic. I can understand your being vexed at the appearance of such a thing (the publisher gave it an abominable presentation too), when you had come out on a limb to assure people that I deserved some respect. We tried to keep the thing from being printed but the idea occurred to us too late.

I think it is being printed in Ireland. I hope that you will not be splashed by the mud that may be thrown at it. But really I don't think it will reach the kind of people who really care about the difference between a good book and a bad one.

Soon I hope to be able to send you a new, short book that is coming out, called *Bread in the Wilderness*. It is about the Psalms, and I hope you will like it. It is a little technical but I hope it is not dry.

I frequently remember you at Mass, and pray Our Lord to repay you for all your kindness. It is not to me that you have been kind but to Him especially. And if my books have reached people in England and have done them any good, most of the credit goes to you. May Our Lady ever be with you and help you to do much for the glory of her Son.

P.S. Looking back at one of your letters, I found you said you were sending a volume of sermons by Mgr. Knox—I have no knowledge of their ever having arrived. About the [Père A.] Gardeil book [*La structure de l'âme et l'expérience mystique*] which you were trying to get for us: since it is so unobtainable we finally got it on microfilm. That was our only hope. But thanks very much for your efforts.

September 11, 1950

The Stromboli notepaper literally overwhelmed me. I am answering you at once to send my congratulations on the advent of Septimus and to assure you that the entire choir-novitiate here is praying for him with enthusiasm. So too am I.

Then, I enclose a monument of American Catholic endeavor. A copy of this leaflet was addressed to every priest in the community here, but was, of course, stopped by the censor. I managed to get one for your archives. It is really something, isn't it?

I am just off to the hospital, but am not especially ill. The doctors seem to think their time has come to compass me with devices. They believe that they can produce ulcers by this method: ulcers being what they intend to find. If they succeed, I shall sink back in mournful resignation at the thought that I have reached a rather unmonastic middle age.

In our Orientation course for the novices I have been working on the Desert Fathers and think they would be a wonderful subject for a book. Have you ever thought of trying it? You know the country, of course. But if you do not do it, I hope that some day I will get a chance to try. But you could do a wonderful job on them.

I must now close and tidy up, before they carry me off.

P.S. Thank you very much for the review—the first & only one I had seen. I am presuming you do not want it back as it might make this letter too heavy.

December 15, 1950

This letter has two purposes: to thank you for *Helena* and to wish you a holy Christmas—and even a merry one, although the legend is abroad that I have gone Jansenist.

Helena came when I was in the hospital. It was handed to me on the afternoon of the day when I had had three inches of bone cut out of my nose and was parked in bed with a nose full of bandages, commanded to sit up for twenty-four hours behaving in all respects like Queen Victoria. It was then that I started in on Old King Cole. I compliment you on your fidelity to the traditional picture of this King. Unfortunately your use of the famous ballad almost made me have a haemmhorage (if that is how you spell it). I am afraid that those on this side of the Atlantic who have never sung it will miss some of the nicest pages in the book.

I mentioned a legend about myself. There is another, or one that is more colorful. A certain Robert Louis, who tossed an atomic bomb on Hiroshima, I believe, entered a monastery somewhere. One day, a visitor to a slightly deaf nun in a convent hereabouts remarked: "Robert Louis has entered a monastery. He's the one who threw the atomic bomb and killed sixty thousand people." The nun let out a faint scream and rushed into the convent, returning presently with the whole community . . . "Father Louis . . . who is in the Trappist monastery . . . threw an atomic bomb . . . etc. etc." Nice reputation I have.

I beg God to bless you and all your family *a primo usque ad Septimum*. May you enjoy all the graces of Christmas. It is my intention to remember you all in my Christmas Masses. Pray for me too, please.

February 25, 1952

Many thanks for your very kind letter and for [Ronald Knox's] *Enthusiasm*. I entirely agree with your comment on the patchy character of the *Ascent [to Truth]*. It is getting to be increasingly difficult to get a book together at all, and I know very well that the chapter on "The

Problem of Unbelief" was addressed to a different "reader" than the others, while two other early chapters were originally intended for a completely different book!! I tried to drop the "Problem" chapter but the publisher wanted to keep it as bait for this apologetically minded nation. I suppose it is the one chapter that has more or less registered—at least with the clergy.

When I say that it is hard to put a book together I do not mean that I have gone to seed (although maybe as a writer I have—and perhaps it is a good thing). But I have so many other things to do now that I cannot write anything except fragmentary sentences. I am Director of the scholastics. This is very fine. I talk to them about their problems. With some of them I have an agreement that I occasionally write out cryptic ascetic sentences in the Desert Fathers tradition and slip the paper to them when they least expect it. Then they go away and think about these statements of mine. They could make a book. But I don't know if it would be a stuffy book or not. There again, you have a scattered audience.

Enthusiasm is fine. I value it highly above all as a reference book, but it is also very good reading. I promise myself to make it an arsenal if I return to writing about quietists. The Procurator General of the Carthusians [Dom Jean-Baptiste Porion] says I am too sharp on quietists and that there really are no quietists anyway. But it is to me a guarantee that the Jesuits will not be too angry with anything I say about contemplation if I drub the quietists for a few pages in every book. Besides, I have the same baleful interest in quietism that a doctor might have in chiropractors or an MFH in people who shoot foxes.

Your article on the Holy Land was read in the refectory and I thought it was the best piece of reporting you have done. I especially enjoyed the description of the Holy Sepulchre at night. Did you get any closer to the Abyssinians on the roof? Did you see the Greek monastery on the "Mountain of the Temptation"—is it still there? Did you run into anything connected with this Charbel Makhlouf in Syria? I have a piece of wood from Charles de Foucauld's hermitage in Nazareth and I am getting ready to plant it secretly in the forest here, in the hope that a small hermitage will spring up after the rains in April.

Actually, what I *am* going to do, beginning next week, is to go out to the forest with a crew of novices every day, planting some twelve thousand pine seedlings where we have been cutting a lot of timber. That, I think, is going to be very pleasant.

About *apophatic*—although it is not in the OED it does crop up in English, though in translations of French books like Mgr. Journet's *Dark Knowledge of God.* That word has, however, caused more trouble than almost anything else in the *Ascent.*

God bless you always and all your family. I keep you occasionally in my Mass.

To Paul A. Doyle

Paul A. Doyle wrote Merton requesting "information, reminiscenses, impressions, etc." related to Evelyn Waugh's visit to the Abbey of Gethsemani in 1948. Doyle was one of a group of college teachers working on the Evelyn Waugh Newsletter.

June 5, 1968

As regards the dates of Waugh's visit here (one only, in my time at least), I cannot check. I have a vague recollection that one of the days was a Sunday. Maybe that might help. I remember him telling a lot of funny stories about Arnold Lunn—he was out on the town with Lunn and played a lot of tricks on him, taking him to his (own) Club and saying in a loud voice in the lobby: "Everyone knows that the Lunns are Jews." Most of the stories are probably well-known. Told me one too of when he was in the army, in the officers' mess, drunk, spilled his drink on a commanding officer's lap, the latter told him he ought to stop drinking, to which Waugh replied: "I'm not going to renounce the habit of a lifetime to suit your personal convenience." I guess this is well-known too. He told me that he thought I would like Cambridge better if I were there now. Seemed to have a great respect for the Catholics at Cambridge (I have since got mail from them, maybe he got me on the list). He talked about liking J. F. Powers' stories—that was the first I heard of Powers. Later read him and met him. Waugh, in speaking of poetry and Tennyson, mentioned a friend of mine at Cambridge, Julian Tennyson, the great-grandson of the poet. Julian was then reading poetry in English pubs. Waugh seemed to think this a good idea. We talked a bit about the Tennysons. Also about Gloucestershire, the Cotswolds, I think Prinknash Abbey also. One thing that had especially amused him in *The Seven Storey Mountain* was the bit about the monks out in the woods chopping trees and saying "All for Jesus" at each blow of the ax. He gave an energetic imitation of what he thought this was like.

He wrote a short foreword to the English edition of *Waters of Siloe*, which he also edited. He took out quite a lot, including the prologue to the American edition, which he said was "bad art." He sent me several books, including Ward Fowler's *Modern English Usage* to improve my own style, *The Loved One* which I thought was great, *Brideshead Revisited, Helena*, and later one of the war trilogy. Also at least Graham Greene, *The Heart of the Matter*, perhaps also others. He also sent Knox's *Enthusiasm*, which he thought very good. He told me a story of Knox saying: "It seems I am the only person in the world who has not yet read *The Seven Storey Mountain*."

As to letters, I have none here, but those I received I think I passed on to Sister Thérèse for her collection of my mss. She is at 3516 West

Center Street, Milwaukee, and could probably inform you or send copies of what she has. I have no objection to your using them.

I think that's everything. I never lost my great admiration of Waugh as a creative writer, though I certainly disagreed with much of his conservatism after the Council. But I think I understand why he felt that way—especially about Latin, etc. He would.

II

*Although we are separated by great distances . . . it gives
me pleasure to speak to you as to one whom I feel to be
a kindred mind.*

MERTON TO BORIS PASTERNAK

AUGUST 22, 1958

To Jacques Maritain

*Merton first met Jacques Maritain in 1939, when Dan Walsh introduced them at
a meeting where Maritain was giving a talk on Catholic action. "I only spoke a
few conversational words to Maritain," Merton recalled in* The Seven Storey
Mountain, *"but the impression you got from this gentle, stooping Frenchman
with much gray hair was one of tremendous kindness and simplicity and godli-
ness." Looking back on his time at Columbia, Merton listed Maritain among the
writers who had "turned him on"—writers like Thomas Aquinas, St. Augustine,
Meister Eckhart, and William Blake. Maritain's influence on Merton was not
merely an academic one; Merton acknowledged that reading the works of Maritain
and Etienne Gilson was a factor in his conversion to Roman Catholicism.*

*Jacques Maritain (1882–1973) was born in Paris. In 1900 he met his wife
Raïssa Oumancoff (1883–1960), a Russian Jewish emigrée, at the Sorbonne where
both were students. They married four years later, and, in 1906, together with
Raïssa's sister Vera, they were baptized in the Roman Catholic Church; Léon
Bloy was their godfather. Conversion to Catholicism, coupled with a discovery
of Thomas Aquinas's* Summa Theologica, *shaped Jacques's and Raïssa's intellectual
and spiritual lives, initiating them as spokespersons for a new scholasticism. As
philosophers, poets, social critics, and, above all, contemplatives, they made their
mark on twentieth-century Catholicism. With Merton, they shared a commitment
to art, wisdom, and social action. Like Merton, they recognized contemplation
as the source from which all else flowed.*

Jacques Maritain's best-known books include Art and Scholasticism *(1920),*
Religion and Culture *(1930),* Integral Humanism *(1936),* Creative Intuition in
Art and Poetry *(1953),* Reflections on America *(1958), and* The Peasant of the
Garonne *(1966). Jacques and Raïssa lived in the United States for a time during
World War II and again from 1948 to 1960, while Jacques taught at Princeton.
They returned to France shortly before Raïssa's death in November 1960. After
a brief visit to the United States in 1961, Jacques took up residence with the Little*

Brothers of Jesus in Toulouse. During his last visit to the United States in 1966, he met with Merton at Gethsemani. In 1970, Jacques adopted the habit of the Little Brothers in Toulouse and, in 1971, professed religious vows. He died in Toulouse in 1973 and was buried at Kolbsheim, Alsace, in the same tomb as Raïssa.

Merton's first letter is written during a critical time in his monastic life. Driven by his intense longing for solitude, Merton found himself repeatedly tempted to leave the Trappists and to become a Carthusian. His desire to promote the establishment of the first Carthusian foundation in the United States reveals his continuing interest in the Carthusians, an interest carefully monitored by Abbot James Fox.

February 10, 1949

. . . We are preparing specially bound copies of *The Seven Storey Mountain* and a new book, *Seeds of Contemplation*, for the Holy Father.

I have already written to Mgr. [Giovanni] Montini [later Pope Paul VI], F. Paul Philippe, and Dom [Jean-Baptiste] Porion [Carthusian Procurator General] . . .

Unfortunately our Father Abbot [James Fox] would not permit me to mention the thought of a Carthusian foundation in any of these letters. He feels, naturally, that it is not the place of a simple Cistercian religious to become too active in a movement to start a Carthusian foundation. Perhaps there is not much I could do. My friend at Parkminster [Dom Humphrey Pawsey] has already spoken of my ideas to Dom Porion anyway, and he had replied that they had no men for a foundation at present but said that he was not averse to anyone discreetly sounding out prospective donors of property and so on in this country. If you happen upon any such, perhaps it might help to say a word. It would also be good to arouse interest in the Carthusians here. They are unknown. I mention them when I can in the things I write.

. . . Did you happen to see an article in the January *Thomist* about "States of Life"? I was surprised to learn that the Fathers at the Dominican house of studies had taken exception to some thoughts of mine on the active and contemplative lives—an article ["Active and Contemplative Orders," *Commonweal*, Dec. 5, 1947], which was reproduced more or less on pages 414–19 of the *Mountain*. So this article is a rebuttal. It is true that I made some careless and perhaps less correct statements about St. Thomas, but these inaccuracies were not connected with the essence of my thought and in fact I had already dropped most of them as irrelevant to the *Mountain*. My only point was that the vocation to *contemplata aliis tradere* [transmit what is experienced in contemplation to others] obviously implied the fullness of contemplation. St. Thomas says that preaching *ex plenitudine contemplationis desumitur* [is the overflow of contemplation]. I inferred that for St. Thomas the dignity of the preaching and teaching vocation was drawn not so much from the fact of preaching as from the fullness of contemplation that it implied. I therefore said that the "mixed" orders ought to be super-contemplatives, since they had to give their overflow to others . . .

This conclusion won me the accusation of trying to abolish the distinction between religious Orders. Perhaps it was a little confused. But in any case, what amused me was that the Father who wrote the article asserted that "the degree of union with God" had "nothing to do with the problem" of differentiating between vocations in the objective sense of state. I opened [Pierre] Joret's book on the Dominican life and found a whole page which said that the life of union with God marks the summit of Dominican life and also that contemplation, far from being even an intermediary end, for a Preacher, is a true end to be sought for its own sake, the highest of all ends and not just a means to the apostolate.

Father Abbot did not want me to write an article, but I wrote them a letter anyway. If you see anything in this that is a big error on my part, which I do not see, will you please let me know? I don't ask you to investigate either my article or theirs, however: you are too busy.

. . . I am swamped with work. I am trying very hard to break the ground on a book on the contemplative life [the working title was *The Cloud and the Fire*, and it was published as *The Ascent to Truth*]. It is the first try I have had at sustained theology, and I find the going rather difficult, besides which I am being constantly interrupted. I rather think Our Lord is blocking the book for the time being because He sees that it will be better later on. But really, as Sertillanges says, the life of a writer can be very grueling, and I do not hesitate to say that the severest penances I have experienced here as a Cistercian have all had to do with trying to get ideas down on paper. To be a theologian demands a severe interior asceticism, and when I find myself sighing for a life of simplicity and solitude and obscurity I wonder if, after all, I am not just seeking luxury. The other day we had the life of St. Benedict Joseph Labre in the refectory and, as usual, I came out with thoughts of myself enjoying the abjection of one despised by all etc. etc. . . . But afterwards I was forced to admit that for me sanctity is quite probably connected with books and with writing and intellectual drudgery. On the whole it is probably easier to be a tramp than a scholar.

Thank you for your kind remarks on *What Is Contemplation?*, and I especially like the term "masked contemplatives," which expresses much better what I mean. As far as I know they *are* contemplatives but they have no real way of knowing that they are because their gifts of understanding and wisdom are not strong enough to enable them to recognize their experience for what it is. They know God by experience but they can't interpret the experience. There must be very many like that even here and I think they sometimes get upset at the thought that they ought to be mystics and they are afraid that they are not.

Well, it has been a great joy and privilege for me to write to and hear from you and I hope our friendship will grow and endure . . .

July 9, 1949

Many thanks for your kind letter and your consent to write a preface for the French edition of the *Mountain* . . . The Catholic editor is a certain Abbé Omer Englebert who is to be found at a village down in my part of France, Goujounac . . . I shall write to him concerning you and tell him to get in touch with you about the preface and to take any advice you may give about the translation. They intend to cut some passages—mainly French local color, he says. Perhaps they are translating the shortened London edition of the book [*Elected Silence*, edited by Evelyn Waugh]. He is coming over here in November, he says, and I hope to discuss the job personally with him and to go over the translation myself.

Speaking of the south of France, a first-rate photographer has sent me a fine collection of pictures of some old cloisters in the corner of the Roussillon where I was born. They are Cuxa and Elne and Corneilla de Conflent and a few others. I am thinking of making an album of them and writing a preface. Do you happen to know of anything good about Romanesque architecture and particularly about the art of that section, on the Catalan border, and on the road to Compostela? I know our publishers would be enthusiastic.

. . . I am locked up in the rare book vault, all by myself, in one of the few places in the monastery where you do not hear a couple of tractors and other machines roaring at each other—but I correct myself: I can hear the new diesel monster we just bought, through the open window. It is devouring the earth where our vineyard used to be. However, Father Abbot, who is perhaps a little afraid that I may run away to the Carthusians, gave me permission to go, on occasion, into the woods and pray all alone. I found a glen that is like the Garden of Eden. In it is a beautiful little stream, and the glen echoes with the songs of solitary birds that are too shy to come near our monastery . . . Sometimes I am even tempted to desire that I had no writing to do at all, but on the whole the writing job has been a blessing because it is the one thing left that guarantees that I spend a certain part of my time alone.

That reminds me, I am revising the *Seeds of Contemplation* in which many statements are hasty and do not express my true meaning. If you have any critical suggestions I would be very grateful for them. I hope to go over the book early in August. It has been amazingly popular here, because of the *Mountain*. Forty thousand copies are in print. One of the places where it has most sold is Hollywood! That shows that one reason for the sale is mere curiosity, but Our Lady can turn all that to her advantage.

Dom Porion sent me his delightful book on the Holy Trinity and the interior life, and on every page I found echoes of my own deepest interests and preoccupations. It is a beautiful book, especially beautiful in its simplicity. I close with the assurance that I remember you in my Mass, which remains my greatest joy, and I feel that Our Lord is pouring out the love of His Heart upon all my dear friends through this Sacrifice which He has given me the privilege of offering each day for them. Liturgists would not approve of me when I say that when I get to the memento of the living I can hardly get back to business with the rest of the Canon, as the names of so many, many dear souls come to me on the tide of God's love from the depths of my heart. And I feel—with you, too—that I have all the poor worried and sensitive and fussy American intellectuals on my shoulders and that they depend in large measure upon that Mass . . .

May God bless you and Raïssa and give you solitude and happiness and tranquillity and not overwhelm you too much with apostolic labor. The other night I had a dream that I entered a Charterhouse near Strasbourg. Perhaps there is no such thing. Perhaps you have found your own Charterhouse for a few weeks at Kolbsheim. Pray for me. And when you come to America again, can't you get away for a few days to Gethsemani?

In October 1952, Maritain wrote a letter to Robert Giroux in support of the publication of The Sign of Jonas, *which had met with the disapproval of the English-language censor of the order, Dom Albert Derzelle, after the galley proofs had been produced and publicity efforts initiated. The book had already been accepted by the American censors. Maritain's letter, which was forwarded to the Abbot General, Dom Gabriel Sortais, argued cogently and forcefully on Merton's behalf.*

Father Louis, Maritain noted, writes with sincerity, simplicity, and candor and "succeeds in describing with authenticity the complexities and the phases of interior experience." The journal is "a spiritual document of singular value and singular efficacy." It draws the reader into Merton's "intimate debates": the "temptation" to seek solitude as a Carthusian, "which is one of Father Louis's crosses"; the conflict "between the work of the writer and the exigencies of the religious life"; the "liberating renunciation of 'being a poet.'" In Maritain's opinion, nothing in the journal is inappropriate; on the contrary, Merton recounts the details of daily Trappist life with "truth and delicate humor" and so aids people "in understanding the reality of the monastic existence and vocation."

Maritain easily dismisses the criticisms of the English-language censor of the order. "You tell me that the author has been reproached for these details on the ground that they are 'trivialities.' Precious trivialities, which give the book its indispensable equilibrium and authentic significance . . . Our epoch has need of books like this one . . . it is an incomparable refreshment to see such subjects treated without the common clichés and occasions or the conventional formulas . . ." The objections raised to The Sign of Jonas *he finds "utterly incomprehensible."*

Furthermore, Maritain reasons, the book is a timely "blessing" for America, which is "at a critical turning point in her spiritual evolution." Americans are experiencing a call to the interior life and Father Louis's books play an "instrumental role" in this event. "Thousands of readers are attached to him and are ready to receive from him a message which they are not disposed to hear from anyone else." The Sign of Jonas *was released and published on February 5, 1953.*

April 10, 1956

. . . Here I am Novice Master, and after all quite happy in the novitiate. It gives me a chance to return to my novitiate days and make a second *tirocinium* for myself. Not in any fake and self-conscious sense: but the novitiate is indeed a quiet and peaceful corner of the monastery. Then I have a chance to dig into Cassian (I am preparing lectures on him, and the novices are doing a translation). It does me good to talk a little about the liturgy, too. I am very interested in the psychological side of the novitiate formation. Most of our problems are in fact psychological. Questions of adaptation, the wrestling of souls with themselves and with their illusions, making themselves quite sick over it all. It seems to be quite general and I am just as good at that as anybody else, although it seems I have a harder head than the younger ones. Not as hard, though, by any means, as the old generation of Trappists. Yet they too lack something. It is not good to be insensible either!

So pray for me, dear Jacques and Raïssa. *Inops et pauper ego sum* [Needy and poor am I]. There is so much talk about being poor, but it is ghastly to be poor. Yet I suppose if I were poorer, I would be less poor . . .

October 9, 1958

. . . I am very happy with your comments about *Thoughts in Solitude*. I went through moments of anguish and doubt about this little book, which I even tried to withdraw from the publisher's hands before its publication. Then the book was published, but some people, like Dan Walsh, for instance, didn't seem to like it—on the other hand I don't think I have to please everyone. Besides, if you and Raïssa enjoyed these pages, I am sure they are good and sincere, and they are truly from myself, and are not really an offering to some self-illusion of mine. So if these pages really speak of God, this is very consoling and I thank you from the bottom of my heart. We never know whether we are on the right track when holy people think we are mistaken. But when other people just as holy—even more so—come to reassure us . . . [it makes a difference].

Yes it's true I have found an unexpected solitude here at the Novitiate. It does not mean that I don't have to talk and work with others, but that doesn't bother me. I am not always working and I have the opportunity to read in the woods or just to be there. And since the others are the Novices, it is not a distraction. Love is no distraction. If I didn't love these little ones, they could distract me. They would be an obstacle. But if I didn't love them I wouldn't love God either . . .

I will be truly happy to receive books by Louis Gardet. I read him from time to time in *Etudes Carmélitaines* as well as Olivier Lacombe. What they do is very important. There are so many serious people of good will who are interested in a non-Christian mystic precisely because they are themselves more profound and from a natural viewpoint more spiritual than even the priests whom they know—these priests who have no fear of rebutting them immediately with ready-made arguments, which though they may not realize it are cerebral and authoritarian statements, even mechanical. We must be able to feel and appreciate what it is that some people find in the Orient. I myself am very interested in Zen and I can see that it has very much to do with all that is true not only in spiritual life but in art and in life itself . . .

I am glad you have been working on your article on liturgy and contemplation. People make an effort at opposing them, and those who oppose them, in one sense or another, will never have liturgy or contemplation. Nothing is more lacking among some liturgy zealots than the liturgical sense. Can you imagine that our general chapter has just eliminated the Lenten curtain, a large drape of Oriental origin that hid the sanctuary during Lenten Masses, allegedly because it kept the monks from participating in the Masses while, in fact, the curtain *enhanced the participation* "in the mystery." What a deplorable gaff! And it's not the only one, they are more and more numerous day after day in every way, precisely because the sense of liturgy and contemplation is lacking. These people don't want liturgy but quasi-totalitarian marks of submission and "esprit de corps." Discipline, order, etc. . . .

January 30, 1960

I was distressed by the news which your December 12th letter brought me. Yes, Vera's death must have been a terrible ordeal for you —both you and Raïssa. How feeble and insignificant human words are in the face of such great mystery! Like the mystery—ever so much greater—of our salvation in Christ, it can only be understood when one is silent. So if I speak at all of you and Raïssa and Vera, it is to God that I speak . . .

I remember you and Raïssa and Vera often at Mass.

An offprint of a little article I wrote on Pasternak is on its way to you. And also my *Selected Poems*.

Pray for me also. I am experiencing, as usual, afflictions of my own. It is not a question of my choosing solitude; it is she who has chosen me.

February 22, 1960

Many thanks for your valuable little book on Liturgy and Contemplation [*Liturgie et contemplation*, coauthored with Raïssa]. I have read it with pleasure and deep agreement and am happy that you have spoken out, so clearly, on the misunderstandings and ambiguities of this pseudo-problem. It is certainly true that those who oppose one to the other are either false liturgists or false contemplatives, and it is doubly true that behind a lot of the insistence on liturgy is a purely human gregariousness. "Togetherness"—and a sort of boyscout mania for organized piety, I wonder what the reactions will be. I do not have to wonder, though. There will probably be the usual misunderstandings and recriminations.

For my own part I am soon going to revise and make additions to *Bread in the Wilderness* in which I confronted the same thing ten years ago, in a more roundabout way, and without controversy. Reading your little book will put me in the right frame of mind.

I notice that in the monastery here the emphasis on liturgy steadily grows, which is very good. But at the same time the desire for interior, contemplative prayer steadily declines. It is not merely that monks spend less time in the church—that makes no difference. But the younger ones, instead of having the deeply contemplative orientation towards silence and simplicity and being alone with God in the cloud of forgetting, seem to want to get involved in trivial and somewhat social preoccupations that tend to be sometimes utterly absurd and even disquieting. There is an arty set (that is lost in the desert from every point of view because they know nothing) and there are those who think to console one another with a kind of spurious companionableness. Then there are those who get lost in business or other projects. Etc. etc.

These things I observe. In former years I might have tried to do something about them. I do what I can of course in the place assigned to me, the novitiate. Otherwise . . . I feel more and more the paradox and mystery of my vocation, such as it is. This is my place and yet I have never felt so strongly that I have "no place" as I have felt here since becoming fully reconciled to this as "my place." My place is in reality no place, and I hesitate to act as if I were anything but a stranger anywhere, but especially here. I am an alien and a transient, and this is the last happiness that is possible to me: but a very real one. More real than all the others I thought I knew before it. Everything is alien to me and I am alien to everything, even contemplation, even writing. I have no longer a profession, although there is no getting away from the fact that in the end I have come out as a "writer," if categories count for anything.

This nameless nonentity would be pride if I did not depend on some human beings, and I depend on very many. In an obvious way on my own brothers, who tolerate me not fully aware that we are all strangers really: and then those other people here and there who are aliens too and transients and who recognize the fact like you and Raïssa—and Pasternak with whom I have exchanged one or two moving letters—and even this little Zen man [D. T.] Suzuki. Together we have tried to write something about the Desert Fathers, he from his viewpoint and I from mine, and now I am in the soup with our censors of the Order for communicating with pagans and unbelievers! Pray that we may find our way out of the woods and into print somehow reasonably.

As a piece of culminating nonsense I have obtained permission to organize three or four small groups for retreats or at any rate meetings here. There will be some Protestant theologians, professors of a nearby seminary, and some professors from a Catholic college. Small groups of not more than ten who will, it is hoped, come down for a day or two of silence and simple dialogue. I have no special natural attraction for this and have hesitated to push it, but I have felt that it ought to be done and the meetings have more or less been arranging themselves. I hope, with the help of prayer, including yours, that things will work out well. Have you any suggestions? Someone at Princeton or in the East who might be interested? . . .

April 8, 1960

I write to ask you for your advice and assistance regarding a rather important matter. Before asking your opinion, I have to explain what it is about.

Last year, having translated a part of the *Verba Seniorum* (sc. *Deserti*), I wrote to Suzuki, a Buddhist, to ask him for a short essay on the Fathers who, in many ways, resemble Zen masters. He was kind enough to write a very interesting essay on Paradise, on the contemplative life as a return to Paradise, on innocence and the "emptiness" of the wisdom of Paradise in contrast to the complications and illusions of the human science which is at once superficial and "dualist." Of course, it's Zen but it sounds a great deal like St. Augustine and St. Bernard. It was not exactly something that an unprepared reader could easily understand. Therefore I also wrote an essay containing many quotations from St. Augustine, etc. We wanted to publish both essays with the translations of the Fathers.

Then the censors of the Order intervened to prohibit this *communicatio cum infideli* [communication with an infidel]. A decision that was indeed wise from the publishing viewpoint, for the meaning of the book is no longer clear. I decided to publish the Fathers' translations alone [*The Wisdom of the Desert*], and asked our Father General [Dom Gabriel Sortais] for permission to publish my essay and Suzuki's elsewhere, in a literary review for instance. I was granted this permission. At the same time, I thought of inviting two other people, e.g., Erich Fromm and a Protestant such as Paul Tillich, to join in my conversation with Suzuki. As a matter of fact, I sent my two essays to Fromm whom I know. I think that he might be interested in the project. (He's also into "Paradise".)

Meanwhile, I submitted this new solution to our Father General. He replied that he preferred by far to see the two essays published in a Review, and, as a principle, he objected to this kind of dialogue between a member of the Order and Buddhists, Protestants, Jews and so forth in one book. He didn't *absolutely forbid* the publication of this book. What bothers him is the question of scandal and of apparent indifferentism.

As for me, I seek solely what best serves truth and souls, especially over here in the States. It seems to me that such a dialogue could do a lot of good among intellectuals. But, of course, I don't trust my own opinion or that of my publishers, who, in other respects, are adroit and well-informed. But in this case it is a non-Catholic publisher [James Laughlin of New Directions]. Would you please give me your advice and your opinion on this project? I will submit it to the Father General and he will make a decision. I think that my Father Abbot is rather in favor of this project and is ready to do his best to support it. Unfortunately I don't have any copy of the two essays. If you want them, I think the publisher can send them to you. I am sorry for bothering you but I believe this matter to be rather important and I count on your kindness . . .

P.S. I do not dare to suggest that you or Raïssa might want to get into the discussion but I would be delighted if that were possible!!

May 20, 1960

Many thanks for your kind and wise letter. I sent it on to our Father General, but meanwhile he had come to another decision, and felt that the material should not appear in book form. He does not think apparently that I have sufficiently the mind of the Church to be able to engage safely in a dialogue of this kind. We came to this decision after consulting Fr. Paul Philippe, and of course that is very good. I do not mean that Fr. Paul Philippe thinks I don't have the mind of the Church!

However, it will save a lot of work and trouble, at least. Thank you for your care in considering the matter, which I greatly appreciate.

Louis Massignon has written about the book *Maritain en notre temps* [by Henry Bars], which I have not seen. There is question of an English translation. A friend of mine and his, Herbert Mason, is suggested by Louis as a possible translator. Herbert Mason is a poet, and a good one, and I think he would be able to do a good job . . .

I am happy that P. [Louis] Bouyer and P. Régamey have come out in France with substantial support for you and Raïssa in the question of liturgy and contemplation. I hope to write an article on those general lines in a few days. There is no question that too many pseudo-liturgists are simply trying to regiment the faithful in such a way that the liturgy becomes a big, annoying, group project, an essay in "togetherness" which makes all prayer impossible. True liturgical life leads quite naturally to contemplation. There should be no problem, and there would be none if these enthusiasts did not create it . . .

June 30, 1960

I am writing this in a hospital. Nothing serious, just some tests and X rays.

The articles by Bouyer & Régamey are in *La Vie Spirituelle*. I think for April & May, or March & April. My own article was extremely reserved & since I know I would be accused of prejudice in favor of contemplation I said what could be said, & strongly, for the personal element *in liturgy*. This is of course the key to the question. My own first experience of understanding & (I spoke as one less wise) wisdom (??) was all connected with Mass & the Holy Eucharist. To me the Eucharist has always been light, illumination. Not sensible. I cannot explain this to some of my novices who try to "get" illumination & feel frustrated. This distresses me, because it should be so simply obvious that the Eucharist *is* light, union, joy. Especially light. (Of course I am in profound darkness after Mass. But without the slightest care or afterthought!!. I do not say this in the article.)

. . . I long for solitude in the woods of the monastery. Perhaps paradoxically I can find it in connection with my dialogue with non-Catholic & other intellectuals which will, I think, soon result in a small house being built apart for our meetings. When there are no meetings then I can be there alone—pray that perhaps I can even some day be there a great deal! [This building later became Merton's hermitage.]

. . . The novices will read your book on *Liturgy and Contemplation*.

I envy you in France! O lovely France. Pray for me there, anywhere, but especially at Chartres if you go there.

Victor Hammer—friend of Alexis [de Grunelin]—has meticulously printed a little book on solitude [*The Solitary Life*] for me. It represents much suffering & joy & he is sending you a copy. It is a "secret" edition—*pro manuscripto* . . .

P.S. Thanks for your words on Pasternak. I got a very touching letter from him in February. He is a chosen & Christian soul. May Christ bring him to His light.

August 17, 1960

I am shocked and pained to hear of Raïssa's painful illness and your difficult situation in Paris. I pray for you daily and remember you at Mass. Inexorably the sad things of life bear down upon us. But Christ Himself has suffered them and suffers them in us. As we drift away from the contentment of healthy and thoughtless people, and enter into the sea of perils, Christ takes hold of us. His comfort and His presence are more than health and joy. They are a greater reality. The world does not see this, and we are hardly able to believe it when we are the ones concerned. But this darkness too is a poverty which He loves in us.

Letters have come to me from Louis Massignon too, his troubles. I have got to be quite close to him with his mystery of suffering Islam, its flint-faced rejection and mad sincerity. I want to understand all the people who suffer and their beliefs and their sorrows. Especially desert people.

Pray for me too, this is a painful time for me spiritually. That I may obey God.

God bless you both. I hope Raïssa will soon be better and that you will go on to Kolbsheim. We have Victor Hammer's beautiful Crucifix, the one he did first, here in our novitiate chapel. It will be a bond with you . . .

October 10, 1960

Dear Jacques and Raïssa:

It is good to have your Paris address and to be able to send you just a word to say that I think much of you both, pray for you and suffer with you. I hope I have the modesty not to multiply phrases about suffering and Calvary at a time like this. You have entered into the great mystery of the Cross which no one comprehends and which one should speak of only in few words, and in a low tone, as it were in passing, with reverence and with fear.

All I can do then is to stand mutely by your side, and nod to you, and try to be encouraging. And my heart prays for you. The Holy One Who dwells in us prays in me for you. May He answer His own prayer to give you strength and to enrich your trial with His special grace.

Dan Walsh, himself recovering from a long sickness, is staying here with us at the Abbey and teaching some philosophy. It is good to have him here . . .

December 18, 1962

I am overwhelmed by Raïssa's *Journal*. How to put it? You must know better than I do. This document is like the sunrise, a wonder that is ordinary but if you are more attentive you find it an astounding event. I read it in solitude in the woods. Each sentence opens our heart to God. It's a book full of windows. What moves me most is that in each line I see and I hear this "child" of Proverbs 8:27–31 *"ludens in orbe terrarum"* [playing on the surface of the earth], *ludens* too in Raïssa. I dreamed a few times of this child (who the first time presented herself as a girl of the race of St. Anne) and she was sad and quiet because everyone was making fun of her strange name which was "Proverb." Also, another time on a Louisville street I saw suddenly that everyone was Proverb, without knowing it. Raïssa's words are filled with the presence and the light of this wisdom-child. She is "Proverb."

Especially she reminds me of that mystic that I love above all others, Julian of Norwich. (Raïssa even speaks of the maternal knees of God.) She has the same tone, the same candor.

I will treasure this book. To receive it is an event of significance and a very great grace. It is not only Raïssa that moves me in this book but your love for her and her love for you and your love for all your friends. This is what the Church is all about. How beautiful and simple God's plan for humankind is! That's it. Friends, who love, who suffer, who search, who see God's joy, who live in the glory of God; and all around them, the world which does not understand that it too is Proverb, which does not find the Lord's joy, which seems to seek to self-destruct, which despairs of rising above material things. That wants to destroy itself in the fire, despairing that it can soar above material things.

Thank you, dear Jacques, for this beautiful book with my name written by Raïssa's hand, on the first page. How precious this gift is to me. It will often remind me that I must be faithful to Proverb, the poor, the unknown. Pray so that I may be faithful.

Some time ago I told [John Howard] Griffin (I believe that you know him) that I wanted to translate some of Raïssa's poems that do not exist in English—beginning with the one about Chagall. Some others too, but I don't have them. Tell me who the publishers are and if you will allow me to translate and publish them, not all but about a dozen.

I noticed that Raïssa mentions a small statue from Chartres, God molding Adam. I am in the midst of studying the school of Chartres. I read with love what they say on creation. As a philosophy it is doubtless imperfect. But they were true contemplatives and poets, and their doctrine flourished on the west façade of the Cathedral. How I would like to see it now. I especially like William de Conches, whom my ancestors from Cîteaux did not like, and strongly censured. They did not know what he saw and he did express it badly. He discovered secondary causes although he spoke about them in terms that were weak and platonic. We must understand what he saw all the same . . .

December 26, 1962

. . . If I may say so, it seems to me that it would be much better not to publish this book [Raïssa's *Journal*] in its entirety for the general public.

It seems to me that even for the essence of the book it would be better to observe a scrupulous mystery. Why? Is not the book as a matter of fact true? Of course. But the truth in this form does not have many friends today. One must recognize the fact. The book would be received with respect but with flippant respect, a respect which is ashamed of its inability to love or to understand this beauty which mocks its own inner reality. We don't want that. No, we must admit that people today deny that light and that beauty; they seek other things more to their liking, more collective, more active, more totalitarian. We have to keep Raïssa's *Journal* for those who will be moved with the same love as she and you. For the others who in their way are also lovers of truth it is necessary to leave to them what they are more easily able to understand.

I do not really understand the strong reaction against contemplation—something which is so profound, so simple, so right, so traditional. Undoubtedly many people may think that contemplation is opposed to a certain form of prayer accepted in the Church. What a mistake . . . Now many people are plunging into liturgy and even into the liturgical movement, because they think that there is something dangerous in this so simple, poor and humble a reality as contemplation. Too bad. I believe it may be better to leave contemplation a little in the shadow and for those whom God Himself will attract to it, which He will do through the liturgy for sure. Do not fear.

But Raïssa's book is quite magnificent and it is a great grace in my life to be able to read it. It is so clear, so right, so true always. There certainly are things that should be read by everyone. They could be published in part, perhaps in a kind of anthology that could contain better-known pieces. A kind of "Reader."

In general I want to save the virginal purity of the book and its mystery. This it deserves. You see there are so many books right now. Publishing is a crass world and indifferent to perfection. Through a little book of my own on peace [*Peace in the Post-Christian Era*], whose publication was forbidden, I can vouch for the fact that private circulation goes much further. We need many good books of sound doctrine which circulate from hand to hand.

. . . I am sure Raïssa is praying for me in Paradise and obtains indispensable graces for me. I am greatly thankful to her and to you . . .

February 12, 1963

Thank you for your warm and wonderful letter, written the day before my birthday. It was a great joy for me to translate the poems of Raïssa, and a greater one to know that the translation had given you happiness, and to feel the warmth of your charity. Surely, in all simplicity, this is the joy and glory of Christ in His Church. This humble and great reality is far more meaningful than all the declarations of the prelates: though I do not deny that some of them have done and said great things, in the Spirit of the Lord, at the recent Council session. There is great charity in Pope John [XXIII]. But you and Raïssa have been very alive in the revival of the Church in our time, and one experiences this in contact with you.

Of course you are right about the *Journal*. It must be published. And there is no difficulty about eliminating some of the most personal passages that are really nobody's business. The book will only speak the more eloquently. I particularly like the variation between the burningly powerful personal passages and the serene, detached observations on art etc., or remarks about philosophers and writers, that come along. Your own notes are most valuable and add much. I would rather see you add to them than reduce them.

I am most struck by the suffering of Raïssa in that prolonged night and agony of hers. What can one say? One must keep deep silence in the presence of such a thing. The reason why I was doubtful about the publication of these passages is that those who know little about such things will be "scandalized" at the repetition. They are willing to accept a page of glorious suffering, but they are not able to understand that one just suffers the same way, and is miserable, for years. They do not want to know what the death of Christ in us means, and that it is not dramatic, only terrible. And they want it to be explicable. Precisely that is the terrible thing: it is without explanation.

. . . Thanks especially for *Chagall*. This is a wonderful book to have. It is a whole world in itself, full of joy and innocence, a delight and a paradise. I was so happy to find an earlier version of *Le Lac* opposite a portrait of Raïssa. I see it is after all part of the world she saw in Chagall, but I said "Dufy" because it looked like that to me at the time. In any case this is one of the most eloquent of her books, and one of which one cannot grow tired.

I am happy to think of your own *Carnet de notes* in preparation, and of the clarifications you will add to the *Journal* of Raïssa. I think that really notes and meditations from your hand at this point would be most important, and hope you will have many good ideas (you have them already) and time to write them down.

Thanks finally for the little poem about the "Glass Orchard." I have translated it and put it with the others of Raïssa, perhaps instead of the epigram against Valéry. It is more significant in itself.

I do not know who is going to publish my translations, but in any case I want to have them, with some other translations, including [César] Vallejo (one of my favorite poets) and an unknown Nicaraguan called Alfonso Cortés. I will send you a copy of my translation of his poems: what I began to say was that I want to print the translations of these few poems of Raïssa with others in my own new book of poems, which will probably come out at the beginning of next year. Is this agreeable to you? . . .

How true and frightening are the words *"le monde chrétien tombe plus bas que même Bloy ne le pensait"* [the Christian world has fallen even lower than Bloy thought]. You say this quietly and without remarks: also without exaggeration. One has a strange feeling of bewilderment in the presence of the assurance with which they themselves accept this fact, as if it were the most normal thing in the world. I do not want to bother you with a multitude of things of mine, but I am putting into the mail a mimeographed copy of my "unpublishable" book on "Peace in the Post-Christian Era." Unpublishable because forbidden by our upright and upstanding Abbot General who does not want to leave Christian civilization without the bomb to crown its history of honor. He says that my defense of peace *"fausserait le message de la vie contemplative"* [would falsify the message of the contemplative life]. The fact that a monk should be concerned about this issue is thought—by "good monks"—to be scandalous. A hateful distraction, withdrawing one's mind from Baby Jesus in the Crib. Strange to say, no one seems concerned at the fact that the crib is directly under the bomb.

Let us pray for one another and for the world, and may God be merciful to us and give us the light we so badly need, and the strength and the patience and all the other things which I, at least, lack totally. I seem to be totally drained of everything.

March 28, 1963

I am so sorry to hear that you have been ill, but I hope that the rest in bed was both enjoyable and helpful and that you are now much better. Please do not ever let letters or manuscripts of mine take up too much of your valuable time. But I am deeply touched by your kind response to the [*Thomas Merton*] *Reader*. You have read it more carefully and with greater sympathy, I believe, than a great many others. It is always to me a great consolation that you and Raïssa have always unerringly picked out the things that seemed to me to be important, in the writing I have done. Other friends, for instance, have been completely thrown off by some of my work. It is a strange thing how many people who claim to like my work are displeased with *Thoughts in Solitude*, for example. They are even quite violent about it. I am so happy that you and Raïssa attached some importance to it, because it really says more what I can and should try to say than many of the other books. In fact I feel that a lot of the writing that people say they like has really been a waste of time and paper.

Did I ever tell you how much I liked Raïssa's *Notes sur le Pater*? It is a really precious book, a perfect commentary, and so unassuming. I have quoted from the last pages in a book of mine which is to appear next year, on prayer . . .

Recently I went through your essay on Descartes carefully, and what a fine solid and permanently valuable piece it is. The translation seemed to me to be first-rate, too. One can look hard today to find something equaling that. I wanted to reread something on Descartes because I am to write an essay on [François de Salignac de La Mothe-] Fénelon, and I think that the spirituality of Fénelon, in its most exasperated and immoderate expressions, was simply a natural and normal reaction to the Cartesian reification of ideas. He wanted to get away from the imprisonment in the cogitating self and be free to love God without the medium of spurious clarities. I find Fénelon in many ways a touching and admirable person, yet not everything in his spirit is agreeable, nor through any fault of his.

Do not waste too much time on the "Peace" manuscript. I was disappointed that I was not allowed to publish it. But if you know anyone who might be interested, you can pass the copy along to them.

I will add the extra line to "Glass Orchard," and thank you for the other poem. I have no space left now in the new book, in which Raïssa will be included. The book is called *Emblems of a Season of Fury* and there are poems in it about the world today . . .

June 11, 1963

I was deeply touched by your most recent letter, and moved that you should think of writing to me when you have so many important things to do. But your letter was certainly wonderful and I want to answer it as soon as possible. I am glad you are going to Kolbsheim and hope you will have a good rest. Do not push too hard with the work, God will take care of everything, and will give you strength to do all that needs to be done. The rest is in His hands. Realize yourself to be entirely in His love and His care and worry about nothing. In these days you should be carried by Him toward your destination, and do what you do more as play than as work, which does not mean that it is not serious: for the most serious thing in the life of a Christian is play. The seriousness of Christian play is the only genuine seriousness. Our work, when it develops the seriousness of worldly accomplishment, is sad indeed, and it does nothing. But of course it is normal to work "against the clock" when one's time is clearly measured, and to feel anxiety about not finishing. But this too is part of God's play in our life, and we will see it in the end. It is like the book of Tobias, that beautiful book about God's play in the life of man, and in the troubles of man. All life is in reality the playing and dancing of the Child-God in His world, and we, alas, have not seen it and known it.

That is the real tragedy of the cold war and the nuclear weapons: the tragic false seriousness of the devil and his frenzy, his babel-building, his technology, his vulcanism. True, we must find spirituality even in this kind of context, but it is such a pitiful confusion, so full of temptations (Teilhard [de Chardin] made an attempt, and it is pitifully naïve in its confusions and its good will). But the real sorrow is this awful jigging of machines, and this construction of colossi. Do you ever see the *Scientific American*? It is really an excellent magazine, and the articles are well done, but the *advertising* is phenomenal! What naked hubris! Advertising is one of the great *loci classici* for the theology of the devil. There his hand is quite clear, with all his tropes and myths and figures and signs and all his own personal midrash.

As to the weapons: there is no question that one can make a "case" for their manufacture and stockpiling. And I suppose this is for the moment unavoidable. The problem does not really lie in the superficial realm of this immediate practical decision against that other decision. What is called into question is in actual fact the *whole moral climate of Christendom*, that is to say, all the basic assumptions, axioms and presuppositions of the world that is "post-Christian" in the sense that it has preserved the mimicry of Christian charity and the forms of Christian order without the inner reality. The tragedy of the nuclear arms is the fact that what they are destined to explode is the final empty husk of the illusion of a Christian world. And they will probably do it in the "name of Christianity." I suppose it must be so, though one must always hope that it may be otherwise. But I think that *domus nostra relinqueter nobis deserta* [our home is left a desert for us] and the heritage may be given to others. The fact remains that [President John F.] Kennedy, last October, in his very grave decision, showed that this country was definitely willing to use a real serious and proximate threat of nuclear war as an instrument in power politics. You know of course that everything was set, really, for a massive nuclear strike on Russia. Everything was ready to go, and might well have gone if Khrushchev had delayed a day longer. Now if a "Christian" country and Ruler are serious enough about it to do this when it is primarily a matter of face-saving, political maneuvering and maintaining prestige, it means that the possession of the weapons and the enormous amount of work that is going into the construction of new ones, in fact the whole gigantic structure of a completely artificial and wasteful war economy, are all centered on the possibility that a merely symbolic issue may generate a worldwide explosion. *And this is frankly accepted as right.* Not only that, but opposition is regarded as un-Christian and as a refusal of the Cross! Oh for the voice of Bloy to roar at this fantastic impiety.

If we have these weapons, and if we, as a nation, want to make a Christian use of them, we must frankly commit ourselves to the risks involved in taking serious steps toward disarmament by negotiation. But we live in an atmosphere in which the very real concept of negotiation *cannot possibly be taken seriously.* But one of the real messages of *Pacem in Terris* is that to be a Christian today one must be able to have enough confidence in the divine image in human nature to believe that there can be some vestige of truthfulness in man, and to act accordingly. For the first step is going to have to be a serious indication that we are willing to trust an enemy, even in an issue that may involve our own survival. Inability to do this means the end of our civilization. That is the problem in a nutshell.

Actually, all our trust, politically and practically, is placed in a ridiculous posture of astuteness and toughness and cleverness and "practicality," which is the most inglorious and ignominious degradation of our Western and Christian independence.

Well, enough of that. I had the great grace and favor of being able to spend five days in a hermitage, in fact six, and there is the prospect of more to come, the hermitage being in the woods near the monastery. I think that this is going to prove the solution to long-standing problems and the answer to many prayers, and it may mean that my own life will achieve some kind of final shape and meaning. Certainly I thought of you when I was praying there, and indeed you and especially Raïssa are presences there in my solitude, for I have read her *Journal* there, and that is where I keep it. It is there that I have her poems, and translated them, and there that I have read and meditated much of your own work.

Dear Jacques, you are going on your journey to God. And perhaps I am too, though I suppose my eagerness to go is partly wishful thinking, for there is yet work to be done in my own life. There are great illusions to be got rid of, and there is a false self that has to be taken off, if it can be done. There is still much to change before I will really be living in the truth and in nothingness and in humility and without any more self-concern. So when you go on your journey, take with you this thought of my need, and pray that I may be able to follow you, when the Lord wills, soon if He wills, and purified. For I want to come after you and Raïssa by the road you have taken, since our journey is in common, though we are very much alone. How good it has been to have seen His play in the friendships and influences that brought us all together in this world and this century. We will see it much more clearly *in illa die*. But meanwhile, rest at Kolbsheim, and be in joy and in light. Think of us here in the novitiate when you see the crucifix in the chapel there: we have the same rood cross, the identical one, an earlier one designed for that same chapel by Victor Hammer and done by him for the chapel. It was even taken there, and he did the whole thing over again, and brought his first cross back, so that we now have it here. It is another bond of union between us . . .

October 17, 1963

I am sorry for my long silence. Last month I was in the hospital, for nothing serious, and have been mostly in the infirmary since coming back. Hence I have not caught up with a great deal of my work and with letters.

First of all I want to thank you for the offprints of poems and short prose pieces by Raïssa from *Nova et Vetera*. I especially liked some of the statements about the poet and our time, which I have wanted to translate, but I have not yet had time. Also Julie Kernan sent me her translation of *Notes sur le Pater*. It seems to be very well done. She mentioned my writing a foreword, and I am wondering if I can. I have had to write a great deal of prefaces in the last year, and have almost reached the saturation point with that kind of thing. Yet it is such a good book and I would not want to miss a chance to say something good, again, about Raïssa. But if I do, it will have to be very short and probably not worth much. I hate to write so many statements, because in the end one is producing words that say nothing. In such a case it is far better to be silent. If I think that it would be the wrong kind of foreword, I will certainly write nothing at all.

I hope you are well, or as well as one can expect to be. Pope Paul [VI] is splendid, and I think that with great strength and wisdom he will go far beyond what anyone had hoped. We can thank God for giving us such a one.

. . . The Brothers in all the Order are stirred up and restless about many things. I do not really understand the whole problem. In Europe it comes partly from the fact that there are too few Brothers, but in this country, at least here, there have been almost too many. I do not think that in either place the Brothers' ideal is really being lived. On the contrary, what is disturbing is that people who seem to want to "solve" the problem are actually going about it in such a way that they are practically abolishing the Brothers altogether. Or at least there seems to be a real risk of it. Here all sorts of strange things are happening to the

Brothers, and things which leave the ones with genuine vocations quite bewildered. At any rate, the two novitiates, choir and brothers, have been merged, and I have them both. There are no special problems in the novitiate, as I see it. It seems that most of the trouble is likely to arise after profession. The vocations are good, and the ones who want to be Brothers are really quite genuine in their vocation. A lot of changes are being made, some helpful and others perhaps less so.

I have been thinking of Toulouse, as I have come across some rather interesting books about the Albigensians (Zoë Oldenbourg). What a tormented history that country of "mine" has, for that is "my" part of France. I love it still, and always shall. I still think of towns like Cordes with the greatest fascination . . .

November 8, 1963

Your cablegram was much appreciated, and now your letter. Thank you so much. I hate to think of you using your time and effort to write to me, but it certainly is a grace to hear from you. It was a joy for me to write the preface, and I could not resist this chance to show, once again, how much you and Raïssa have meant to me. Actually, nothing can show this. There is no way of saying such things. But at least I wanted to make some kind of gesture. And then, too, there are the rights of truth.

It is sobering to see how those who make the biggest outcry against "dogmatism," and against authoritarian positions, are themselves just as eager to condemn and to reject positions which are not agreeable to them: and do so very arbitrarily, without even troubling to understand how the opinions which they reject might actually contribute to bring out some truth in their own position. So it has been in this "Liturgy vs. Contemplation" squabble. Making a superficial appeal to a few slogans about "individualism," some of the less profound minds in the liturgical movement have decided that liturgy and contemplation are opposed and that only liturgy can survive the opposition: contemplation being inexorably rejected as "subjective." What kind of sense or meaning can there be in this verbalism?

The meaninglessness of this sort of approach is evident when one sees that these people are absolutely incapable of recognizing the true union of liturgy and contemplation when it is seen, for instance, in some of the fathers. They are just boy scouts marching off to a new activity which they think they themselves have discovered for the Church, and the salvation of the Church consists in following them.

Anyway, it seems to me that Raïssa's book on the *Pater* is perfectly set in the true context of tradition, and if the liturgical *ballila* cannot understand this, it is just too bad.

I hope *Ramparts* magazine will reach you: it has articles by John Griffin and myself on the race question and a beautiful interview of John with a Negro priest.

As for poor Jean Cocteau: I cannot have the slightest doubt of the immense mercy of God in his life. What other meaning can there be in the promise He has revealed, and in the mystery of His compassion? I can never have anything but the greatest sympathy and compassion for those who cannot manage to grapple perseveringly with the awful ambivalences created by the spectacle of *les pratiquants*. I do not see how Jean, with his temperament, his vitality, his openness to the unexpected could fit in comfortably to a context where everything is reassuring, guaranteed, imposed, safe, and just what one would expect. Alas, I am afraid that the atrocious Catholicism of the late ruling dynasty in Vietnam is the kind of Catholicism "that one would expect." No trouble about them being *pratiquants*, in life and surely in death also. Mme Nhu could be quite firm on this point, and no one would disbelieve her. And yet, with all charity, what an affront!

This is the kind of thing that makes one's heart sink. Reading the lessons from Ezechiel for the ferial days at the beginning of November moves one to the very core of one's being, and try to face the incredible horror of a Catholicism that has, as you said, gone so far beyond anything Bloy envisaged! Yet I can see it must be this way, for some inscrutable reason: and precisely for this it becomes incredible that one should seriously be tempted, as they were in the modernist crisis, to revolt against the Church. On the contrary, it is this Church, with all her wounds, her masks, and the rest, that remains in some fantastic sense "faithful" and we are faithful in her and with her, but after the manner of survivors in some awful cataclysm. The truth is, of course, that it is not so much the Church that is faithful to Christ, as Christ Who is faithful to her and faithful unto death. In this is her beauty and her strength, in spite of what sometimes appear to be the sores of the most incurable leprosy. There is nothing incurable for Christ, but only the Church has received His promises. The wounds of sin are the wounds He took upon Himself and therefore they are His wounds.

I think of you often, Jacques . . .

The following letter was published, along with other selected letters, in Seeds of Destruction *in 1964.*

December 2, 1963

I have been planning to write and thank you for the new edition of Raïssa's *Journal* which arrived, and is splendid. I will go through it again at leisure and in doing so will be near both you and her, and God too I am sure, for we can be truly near one another in Him.

Then today your deeply moving letter arrived. I have never experienced such a thing as the spiritual crisis into which the death of President Kennedy has thrown the entire nation. It is not only profound but in many ways uncanny, for it is almost an apocalyptic event, a revelation of most powerful forces of evil and of very living forces of good that try to counteract them in this nation. The incredulity of the nation was the first thing that manifested itself: I do not mean lack of faith, I mean the incapacity to realize that the President was really dead and that this had been the result of a completely evil act which was itself the product of evil in the heart of many Americans. In a word, what has shattered the nation has been the realization of the awful presence of a very well developed evil, a kind of spiritual cancer, at work in its very heart. No longer possible to situate all evil on the other side of the Iron Curtain.

At the same time, there has been in the South a frank and cynical rejoicing, not of course everywhere, but among the racists, over the death of Kennedy. A Negro priest in the South told me that Negro servants spoke of the rejoicing in the homes of racists, and their celebrations of the event. Some places in the South refused to fly flags half-mast. On the other hand I think a lot of decent men in the South have been conscience-stricken and disturbed. Kentucky is not the Deep South and hence the reaction here is that of the great part of the nation. But the shock has really been terrible for many many people who were in one way or another weak. Alcoholics have fallen back into habits they thought they had overcome, others have broken down, probably because of the fact that Kennedy as a symbol had been destroyed and they lost their strength. Or perhaps also from a sense of participation in national guilt.

The Negro priest who did the interview with Griffin in *Ramparts* by the way is having a very hard time with his bishop, who is extremely angry with him and is threatening to punish him for "defaming the Church"—that is to say, for antagonizing the Catholic racists in the South.

About these, I am learning amazing things from a young Franciscan priest who has entered our novitiate and who was stationed in Louisiana, where the local Catholics bombed their own parochial school rather than see it integrated.

I am convinced that you are right in believing that the Southern rightists are very likely behind the murder, but on the other hand it is possible that the investigation may be in many ways frustrated. The Dallas police have obviously been very negligent and stupid, if not actively accomplices, and the stories they have given out, which tend to make Oswald a Red fanatic and Ruby a well-intentioned patriot momentarily out of his mind, have been widely accepted. But will they hold water? Actually, I feel that a great part of the country *wants* to accept this version because, though evidently patched up, it fits the popular image of reality. I greatly fear that the truth is much more sordid, and hope it will be brought out.

January 9, 1964

The new year is here and the news about the Pope's visit to Palestine has been in many ways moving, both frightening and consoling. I hope much good will come of it in the long run. There is still no clear truth about the assassination of Kennedy, only a few strange rumors and the persistence of everyone wanting to accept the very simple solution that has pleased the newspapers and the Dallas police. The Kennedy family is still shattered, and I do not have much confidence in [Lyndon] Johnson as a President. I hear he was recently cavorting with the West German chancellor, dressed in cowboy hats, in signs of profound unity.

There are many things for which to thank you. For one, the *plaquette* on *Amour et amitié* is magnificent. It is totally exceptional, one of your most moving pieces of writing and full of great wisdom. I thank you warmly for writing it and sending it. The new *Journal* of course is wonderfully charged with new insights and fragments that are incomparable. It was wise indeed to bring out a new and more complete edition and I compliment you on the final success of the work. Then finally the nuns at Bethlehem (Regina Laudis) sent me a copy of *Portes de l'horizon*. That is a completely lovely book, which in any case I had known long since, for you and Raïssa sent me a copy from Princeton when it came out. But I am happy to have another copy.

It was very good of you to get the little biography of Emilie de Rodat and I am glad to have it for more or less sentimental reasons: love of the region where I once lived, up there in the Aveyron valley. I wonder if I will ever see it again? I presume it is better not to think of that: it is one of the few real sacrifices we have here. The rest do not amount to very much.

There is an ex-novice from here, studying at Amherst, who writes frequently about Cocteau, and is utterly dazzled by him. It amounts almost to worship.

For my part, though I am still a stripling compared with you, I am entering soon my fiftieth year, and want to make it a jubilee of consecration to God. To try to forget the more obvious entanglements with all that is trivial and passing, and to get more into the heart of things, from which I am so often so sadly absent. This life here has its routines and artificialities, its pretenses and its evasions, like every other form of life. We are fortunate however in that the voice of God cannot be silenced here as easily as it can in the noise of cities. Yet perhaps there are many in the cities who hear Him more clearly than we do. In any case, please pray for me. I wonder still and worry about our country. A man in the Spanish embassy in Washington, who by no means agrees with my view on nuclear war, had the strange idea of assuring me that he felt the bomb had done a great deal for America morally and spiritually. It had toned everybody up and made them more courageous. I can imagine nothing more insane, and the evidence every day certainly points to anything but a rush toward sanctity . . .

May 24, 1964

It was very good of you to ask Scribner's to send me your great newly translated book on *Moral Philosophy*. Actually it is just what I have been wanting and I am reading it with avidity. It fills an immense gap and the mere appearance of such a book draws attention to the awful poverty of most moral theology, as well as the need for totally new perspectives. I am convinced for example that it has been the lack of such thought as this that has permitted Catholic thought and law to take such absurdly legalistic and anti-human positions about things like war (though of course Pope John and some of the bishops have said what needed to be said, or have begun to). Much moral theology is simply bad moral philosophy. So your clarification is providential. If we have a good moral philosophy, who knows, perhaps someday we may get a moral theologian. (I do not want to sweep them all aside: I do like Fr. Bernard Haring.) Also I think this book is a wonderful companion volume to Raïssa's *Journal*! How is the second volume coming?

I have also been reading the big volumes of Louis Massignon's *Opera Minora*, so much more "majora" than most other people's masterpieces. They are at times completely shattering. I hope to write something about him as I now have to give an account of recent material on Islam in the magazine of the Order. I also have to report on Buddhism and Hinduism from time to time. This seems like a lot and does imply a kind of scattering of forces, but I think it will do me good and with the grace of God I can handle it. I think that one of the most crucially important subjects to investigate today is the Buddhist metaphysic of the "person," which claims to be non-personal (*anatta*) but as a matter of fact might well be something completely unique and challenging. The *anatta* idea is simply a "no" to the Hindu Atman as a pseudo-object or thought. If once one can find that on this crucial point where Buddhism and Christianity are completely opposed, they are in fact perhaps united . . . Today is the feast of the Holy Trinity, Person but not individual nature . . .

But to return to Louis Massignon: I never realized what a profound poetic mind he had; the rich poetic orchestration of his material, always inexhaustible, is something unequaled. And what spiritual implications in everything!

Dear Jacques, I hope you are well and working with joy. I wish I worked less and to better purpose . . .

September 5, 1965

It has been a terribly long time since I have written to you or heard from you, and I am not sure whether or not I ever thanked you for the *Carnets*. Perhaps I did not. But I am very delighted with them, and they form an admirable companion to Raïssa's *Journal*. Thank you very much.

Once in a while I get a little news indirectly from you. And you have perhaps been hearing that I have been ill, but this must not be taken seriously. I have just had a few minor ailments which have been troublesome but not serious.

The best news I have is that I have finally been allowed to get out of my job as novice master (though I liked the job and it was very good for me during the ten years that I had it) and am now living as a hermit in the forest near the monastery. As a matter of fact I was half a hermit ever since last October, nearly a year ago, sleeping in the hermitage and spending much of the day there when free. But now I am here all the time, only going down to the monastery for Mass and for one meal, though I do have to continue giving one conference each week to the novices and students together.

It is a very good schedule I think, and is working very well indeed. Though I am not what one would call a hermit temperament (because I am sociable and love to be with people), it does seem that this is really what God has wanted for me all along, and by His grace I am fitting into it with great peace and I think much profit. Perhaps it is a good thing I never became a Carthusian: this is a much more flexible and open regime, and I think I have things that most Carthusians would heartily envy. It is certainly wonderful to have one's own hermitage in a plot of woods where no one comes (except hunters sometimes) and to be absolutely free from the organization of a community, so that one must obey the Holy Spirit faithfully. This is both more difficult and more fruitful than merely obeying an external rule, and of course it is not possible without an internal rule too. But I find that the life organizes itself quite easily, and that it goes very smoothly, with a good balance of prayer, meditation, psalmody, active manual work, writing, reading etc. It is really quite a step forward that this has been officially recognized in the Cistercian Order as a possibility for the monks. I think it will do much for the Order. It has even been approved by the General Chapter—not my case in particular, but the general principle is admitted officially. My own case was permitted by the Abbot with the vote of his private Council.

I often think of Raïssa and so many other friends in this solitude. I feel even closer to them: to her, to P. Henrion also, and Louis Massignon, so many others . . .

September 26, 1965

I have been reading your *Carnets* [*de notes*] . . . Everything you say is quite true & even prophetic. Our mania for organization will be judged & all will be burned except love and friendship. The small groups united by genuine love will remain everywhere & the rest will go, even in monasticism. I want to quote you in the book I am writing now.

The solitary life I now lead is magnificent & all the community is happy about it, as they feel it is a grace in which they all share. I feel that too & am more united to them—I go down to concelebrate on Sundays.

Let us be united in prayer for this last & momentous [Second Vatican] Council session.

I am asking the publisher to send you my little book on Gandhi [*Gandhi on Non-Violence*].

October 6, 1965

As soon as I got your letter the other day I wrote immediately to Doubleday about Raïssa's *Journal*. As I think, the delay with Kennedy must be providential. I believe Doubleday will be very interested. A friend of mine there will like the *Journal* very much. I am just going over to Doubleday myself with the book I have just finished [*Conjectures of a Guilty Bystander*], which is itself a kind of *carnet* (rather than a Journal) but with quite a lot of poetic and descriptive stuff too.

I have kept returning to your own *Carnets* with the greatest joy. Your biography of Vera is most moving and I read it with much interest and emotion, glad to know who Vera was (is) when I had prayed for her a lot in the time of her illness. I was so moved by her interior words. There is no question that you are perfectly right in your estimate of the wonderful vocation of your "little flock." It is so evident. I bless God for it. It is a great inspiration and help to me. Vera's hope is also a huge help. Finally, your piece on the Church in Heaven is most welcome, as it reminds me how much I need my hermitage to be peopled by the angels and saints. I need their company . . . And also one needs so much to look forward to the moment of arriving among them, when their joy will be increased as well as our own, and I liked especially what you said about making new friends, or rather meeting ones who had been our friends all along, and we never knew. What a day that will be. We are so foolish and we think this earth is our home (well, it will be that after the resurrection), but there is now all the incredible nonsense that is being preached and said about a religionless religion, about total commitment to the modern secular world, etc. etc., it would make you sick if you saw it. One would think there had never been a Calvary, an Auschwitz, a Dachau . . . These poor idiots have simply determined that it is now time to be very optimistic, and the gamble succeeded, everybody likes it (Christians I mean). It is the thing. Léon Bloy would be able to say a thing or two about this rage. I am not referring to Schema 13 of course, though that has been a little naïve too. I enclose a piece of mine about the war issue, by the way, and I can readily believe the wonderful things you said of Pope Paul: he demonstrated all that at the UN the other day in his magnificent plea for peace . . .

March 7, 1966

. . . Jacques, there are moments when I feel a thousand years old, and so old that I cannot get excited about what the Church is doing. The experiments inspire in me no confidence, but the Holy Spirit will bring something out of it all, and the benefit I derive from it is a greater solitude: I see it would be completely preposterous for me to pin any hopes of mine on all the somersaults and gyrations of our *saltimbanques*, liturgical and others. Every day there is another wonderful hoopla and someone may land on his feet or perhaps on his head, and it seems to make little difference which. But they seem to survive and continue to take it all seriously, and especially they take themselves most seriously of all. If it makes them happy, I am not the one to interfere. But of course one can be sad for the objective losses: and still hope that there will be places that appreciate the true issue and do not lose their heads. The joke that has the greatest irony is that in crawling on our bellies to kiss the feet of "the world" we are after an entirely imaginary world after all: or the world that has imagined itself for us. In reality, those who remain alive and endowed with a certain intelligence in "the world" are the first to wonder at our madness. It is only non-Catholics who deplore our abandonment of Gregorian for example. As I say, I give up. I cut wood. The woods are marvelous, and last night I was watching the deer feeding in the open space near the hermitage. Through field glasses I could look right into their huge brown eyes and it seemed I could touch their big black noses with my own.

Many thanks for sending the poem to *Nova et Vetera*. I wish we took it here, but I never see it . . .

John Howard Griffin brought Jacques Maritain to Gethsemani on October 6. Maritain spoke to the community and visited Merton in his hermitage.

October 13, 1966

Thanks for your kind words and for your affection. Your short stay over here—much too short—was a grace for us all—for me in particular. Here is the book—I am sending it separately. I don't know why I hadn't given it to you. In addition, here is a new piece you might enjoy. The illustrations are by a Maryknoll priest in Japan. That's it, Jacques. Come back and see us soon. I am looking forward to hearing from you.

October 29, 1966

My letter of the other day was inadequate but I wanted to reply quickly. I have still heard nothing from Doris Dana but will expect her any time next week. I hope you are not leaving too soon.

I wrote this little poem about the *vierges étourdies* for your amusement ["Les cinq vierges"].

Do not worry about my having been in the hospital last week: only a question of some routine X rays that I have to have from time to time.

I am reading Chateaubriand's *Vie de Rancé* for the first time. It is an extraordinary piece of writing, constantly on the edge of surrealist poetry. I wonder if Jean Cocteau had ever read it. He would have been delighted with it.

November 18, 1966

Many thanks for your fine letter. I can quite understand your cry: "*A Paris j'étouffe.*" I cease to breathe easily even in Louisville and four or five hours of it are all that I can stand. I have no desire to see Paris again. There may be some mountains and woods in the world and some villages and monasteries that would attract me, but not many cities that I can think of at the moment!

I am delighted to hear that *Le paysan* [*de la Garonne*] is making his way imperturbably in that same Paris. Delighted for many reasons, for you, and because it is such a good book, and also for the Church. The fact that people are so eager for it is a sign that not all are passively accepting the superficial and confused proclamations of victory that are heard everywhere. In other words, people still sense that we have just as many problems as before and that change for the sake of change does not solve everything by magic. It also takes some thought and some work.

I have especially liked your section on philosophy. It had not occurred to me—yet it is so obvious—that the phenomenologists by and large have no sense of being. I had been reading them—no, not them, but those influenced by them—as if they *had*. That of course makes things more interesting. But of course without it they are simply a wilderness. And as for being a hermit in this age: it is very nice to be a hermit in the woods, which are not a wilderness at all but very friendly and comforting. It is much more difficult to bear with the wilderness of thought and life which is the "world" (without falling down and adoring it!) (though that would hardly seem to be much of a temptation). So if you are caught by that a little, it makes your pilgrimage more lonely and more arid. You do not need to worry about that! I am sure the book will bring light and orientation to many who need it and cannot be content to trust the press.

The "Edifying Cables" [*Cables to the Ace*] are finished and constitute a solemn anti-language which people will not know what to do with, but it does not matter.

I am delighted to hear that Doris [Dana] was baptized before you left. I had been reproaching myself for spoiling things by going to the hospital just at that time. The week after I returned I had to keep the days open for a Sufi Master from Algeria [Sidi Abdesalam] who was coming some time then: he did in fact come and turned out to be a splendid person. Spoke only Arabic but had an interpreter. A true contemplative of the highest sort, very simple and solid, like a Desert Father or someone out of the Bible, and one who has suffered much. A very pure and sober spirit, and very encouraging, he insisted that I was a "true Sufi" which made me happy. But it was a joy to have him here: he enjoyed the woods as you did. But we drank no beer.

As to Chateaubriand's *Rancé*: the writing is marvelous, with all kinds of surprises. It is a beautiful book, but of course the perspectives are a little distorted. Nevertheless that is itself part of the beauty. I read some sections of it on a tape with some poems of [René] Char, with the idea that they are somewhat alike. And some Edifying Cables too. But don't think I am making tapes. Only this one. I do not want to be a "hermit who talks on a tape recorder." Dear Jacques, let us be united in the joy of solitude and silent prayer . . .

December 20, 1966

I want to get this letter off to you right away because with Christmas my mail is getting impossible and I don't want to leave this too long: I will forget it and never give you a good report on the English ms. of Raïssa's *Journal*, by Antonia White . . .

Well, I would say that in general the translation as such seems adequate. Yet I have problems with it. First of all the general problem: the Journal itself does not read well *in English*. I am not blaming the translation. This kind of material is difficult to translate into English. What is acceptable in French becomes unacceptable in English, in many cases. For instance the use of several "alas" exclamations in a letter to the Abbot of Wisques. It weakens it in English. But no doubt this difficulty could be got around.

The specific problem, and the most important one, is the question of the contemplative vocabulary. I can see where there has been a great deal of trouble with renderings of *oraison* and *recueillement*—successive solutions have been superimposed. None of them seem to me satisfactory. The first reason is that in French these words are fairly neutral. But English renderings like "inner repose" and "God-given repose" and so on are quite different. They have a special tonality, and innuendo of values and appreciations which are not in the quiet words of the original. For instance, *repose* in English is not at all the same as *repos*. The English word has connotations of aristocratic languor and complacency which are not desirable and which add a note of almost artificiality to Raïssa's simple statements. I understand of course: the aim is to render the classic ideas of *quies contemplationis* and *hesychia*. And English words for this must be found. I would almost prefer "quietude" to "inner repose," though this has unfortunate theological resonances (quietism). The best word for *recueillement* would be, it seems to me, ABSORPTION. But in some cases I think "recollection" would be acceptable. With a little variety, then the use of "inner repose" at appropriate moments would be effective. But constant repetition of this phrase is damaging. Or so it seems to me. So too, I don't think "meditation" should be totally excluded if in the preface or in a note it could be explained that this does not necessarily mean discursive meditation. Readers familiar with non-Christian traditions, and there are many in America, would be prepared for a use of "meditation" that implied simple intuitive attention. But I think what we should do is agree on a use of terms for these important ideas and then in the preface I could clarify all that: or you could do so in notes.

This is the main problem I wanted to deal with. Later if anything else of like importance develops, I will write about it . . .

January 30, 1967

The ms. of Raïssa's *Journal* will be mailed out to Princeton in the same mail as this letter. I think your solutions for *oraison* and *recueillement* are excellent. The explanation "wordless, loving prayer" is good for *oraison*. I do wonder a little about the danger of monotony in repeating *oraison* over and over again. But you will know what to do about that. I think that "meditative absorption" and "quiet absorption" are fine for *recueillement*. Also one might say "silent absorption." Another expression I like to use is "silent awareness" or "interior awareness." In writing about prayer I like to emphasize the sense of presence, vigilance, adoring attention and so on. I think that the positive side of it needs to be emphasized when contemplation is attacked so senselessly as mere withdrawal, negation, shutting out the created world, and so on.

Jacques, I am more aware now of a really determined, concerted hostility to everything "contemplative" and "monastic." "They will think they are doing God a service when they kill all this." A real determination is to discredit in every way anything that has to do with an inner, silent, recollected, wordless form of prayer. The *Journal* will meet this great coldness and perhaps be ignored, perhaps attacked. My preface will hardly help much in this because I am already regarded with great disfavor on this account, and a preface from me, now, will no longer be an argument for the book (with these critics) but another argument against it. No doubt simple Catholics and non-Catholics do not care. I feel personally that what I have to say now is much more for those who are not in the Church than for those who are in it. My *Conjectures* is being widely read, but very much attacked by the "in group" of new Catholic thought. But the success of your *Paysan* is really a portent and a great sign for which one can be very glad indeed. I hope that it will have an effect here too. If the *Paysan* has the same kind of impact in this country, then the *Journal* too will have a far greater chance.

Ed Rice asked me to write an article on Fr. Pascal Bourgoint for *Jubilee*. I said I might be able to do this later. Can you tell me where I can get the necessary information on his early life and conversion besides of course *Les enfants terribles*? I can write to Africa for his last years. If you get a chance to set down a few words on him, I would appreciate it. But no hurry, you have your own work to do and that is much more important. Perhaps there may be an article on him in France somewhere, too? If so, please be sure that I get a copy, and I will be most grateful.

Dear Jacques, take care of yourself, and do not push too hard at the work. There is just so much that one man can do. God has certainly blessed your efforts, and He will take care of everything. He will not lose anything if you take a little rest once in a while.

April 7, 1967

I am returning the clippings and other material on Fr. Pascal, so that you will be able to get them to Jean Hugo in plenty of time for May 1. I would send you a carbon copy of my article on Fr. Pascal but the carbon is so bad you would probably have trouble reading it. Nor have I heard anything from *Jubilee* about whether or not they intend to publish it, or when. However, eventually I hope that it will be satisfactory. I can foresee that the story is going to be stereotyped in a sort of unfortunate way, as a kind of witness to the "inefficacy" of the monastic life. Actually in my opinion his vocation to the lepers is to be seen as a perfectly normal development of the monastic vocation—an individual development, a charism, which does not fit into anybody's program, and can certainly not be adduced as evidence for a superior activism of some sort. Or used validly in support of an aggressive and organized program. However, I suppose a good part of the *malentendu* comes from the fact that monasticism itself is so rigidly organized and so programmatic, in its own way. Thus we are all caught in the rivalry of programs and organizations, when all we want is to be delivered from them forever.

Here are at last a few of the pictures I took when you were here . . . One of those I took of you seems to be all right and the one of you and John [Howard Griffin] is nice.

John told me that some pictures of you and me would be in the TV documentary. I am delighted, only I asked them please not to mention the fact that they were taken in a hermitage or to mention the hermitage. That is not supposed to be part of the "news."

Well, Jacques, take care of yourself; do not work too hard. The spring days are beautiful here and I do not scruple to take a little *hesychia* in the sunlight. I keep you in my prayers. Pray for me. What is better than our prayer and our love for it? Surely it is a great gift and one which few appreciate these days, so it would seem.

August 13, 1967

I have been meaning to write for a long time, but rarely have I had such trouble answering mail as this summer. For one thing I have been rather overvisited, and for another I have been pressed for time to do at least a minimum of my work: but I am far behind with a book I am supposed to produce for the publisher next spring.

There are various reasons for this letter. The first is to send you belatedly a copy of the article on Frère Pascal. I should have sent one before publication, so that you might have suggested corrections where necessary. I hope it is not too bad. I have the feeling that the perspectives are not quite accurate, and that the mystery of such a person and such a vocation was much deeper than could even be suggested.

Then, I am sorry that you had to do so much work on the translation of *Le paysan*. If there had been anything I could have done to spare you,

I would have wanted to. But I think the only way was for John [Howard Griffin] to come over and work through it with you. That is surely best and I hope you have now finished. I do not know if John is still there, but if he is, please thank him for his good letters. I owe him two.

Thanks for your notes on Evolution from the Thomist viewpoint. I will read them carefully when I get a chance. It is a subject that I have hitherto left on the shelf, because I am hardly able to keep up with material in my own field. But one must reach a judgment on this also.

Carolyn Hammer was here yesterday, and I was happy to hear that Victor had indeed been anointed by a priest in Lexington, in the hospital, just before his death. I was able to get over and see him a couple of weeks before his last heart attack, and he seemed still very well and as alert as ever. His last little book, a kind of testament, is one of the best things he ever wrote. And of course printed (with Carolyn's help). Looking back over his work, I feel that his very best effort went into printing, including the cutting of his own type.

Carolyn also told me that things have been nicely arranged for you at Kolbsheim and that you are very well settled there. I am glad. I wish I could someday visit there, but in the matter of traveling and even going out of the monastery at all I have a superior who is extremely narrow, I regret to say.

My very best wishes to all of you at Kolbsheim, with prayers and blessings. Pray for me.

To Czeslaw Milosz

Czeslaw Milosz (1911–   ) is, in Merton's words, "one of the most important Polish poets and writers of the twentieth century." During World War II, Milosz joined the socialist resistance and wrote for the Polish underground, publishing an anthology of resistance poetry, The Invincible Song. *After the war, Milosz worked for the Polish diplomatic service in New York, Washington, and Paris before seeking political asylum in France in 1951. During the fifties, he lived in Paris and wrote a variety of works:* The Captive Mind, *probing the plight of Polish intellectuals in a repressive regime; two novels,* The Seizure of Power *and* The Issa Valley; *several volumes of poetry; and an autobiographical work,* Native Realm: A Search for Self-Definition. *Since 1960, when Milosz accepted an appointment at the University of California at Berkeley, he has lived in the United States. He has continued to be a prolific poet as well as an active promoter of Polish writers and an interpreter of the rich tradition of Polish literature. His* The History of Polish Literature *and* Postwar Polish Poetry, *published in revised editions in 1983, are essential sources for students of Polish literature. His* Collected Poems (1931–1987) *was published in 1988. Other recent publications include* The Separate Notebooks, Visions from San Francisco Bay, The Witness of Poetry *(lectures delivered at Harvard University),* Unattainable Earth, Provinces, *and* Beginning with My Streets. *Milosz's literary accomplishments have earned him many honors and prizes, especially, in 1980, the Nobel Prize for Literature.*

Merton first wrote to Milosz after reading The Captive Mind, *praising the book and raising questions about the writers Milosz anonymously named Alpha, Beta, Delta, and Gamma. Merton was eager to see more of Milosz's work and offered to assist the Polish writer in any way he could, even suggesting that he might help Milosz translate his poetry into English. From the first, admiration and honesty marked their exchange on a wide array of topics: candid critiques of each other's work; suggestions for reading; and reflections on nature and history, religion and the Church, mass media and American society. They met together twice, first in September 1964, when Milosz came to Gethsemani, and again in October 1968, when Merton met briefly with Milosz and his wife in California.*

December 6, 1958

Having read your remarkable book *The Captive Mind* I find it necessary to write to you, as without your help I am unable to pursue certain lines of thought which this book suggests. I would like to ask you a couple of questions and hope you will forgive this intrusion.

First of all I would like to say that I found your book to be one of the most intelligent and stimulating it has been my good fortune to read for a very long time. It is an important book, which makes most other books on the present state of man look abjectly foolish. I find it especially important for myself in my position as a monk, a priest and a writer. It is obvious that a Catholic writer in such a time as ours has an absolute duty to confine himself to reality and not waste his time in verbiage and empty rationalizations. Unfortunately, as I have no need to point out to you, most of us do this and much worse. The lamentable, pitiable emptiness of so much Catholic writing, including much of my own, is only too evident. Your book has come to me, then, as something I can call frankly "spiritual," that is to say, as the inspiration of much thought, meditation and prayer about my own obligations to the rest of the human race, and about the predicament of us all.

It seems to me that, as you point out, and as other writers like yourself say or imply (Koestler, Camus etc.), there *has to be* a third position, a position of integrity, which refuses subjection to the pressures of the two massive groups ranged against each other in the world. It is quite simply obvious that the future, in plain dialectical terms, rests with those of us who risk our heads and our necks and everything in the difficult, fantastic job of finding out the new position, the ever-changing and moving "line" that is no line at all because it cannot be traced out by political dogmatists. And that is the difficulty, and the challenge. I am the last in the world to pretend to know anything about it. One thing I do know, is that anyone who is interested in God Who is Truth, has to break out of the ready-made shells of the "captive" positions that offer their convenient escapes from freedom—one who loves freedom must go through the painful experience of seeking it, perhaps without success. And for my part, this letter represents a hearty peck at the inside of my own particular kind of shell, the nature and hardness of which I leave you to imagine.

First of all, I would like to get other books of yours, whether in English or in French. Or articles, anything that can help me. Tell me the names of some books, I can order them. Send me copies of articles if you have them. In exchange I will be honored to let you have any books of mine you might want.

Then, I am interested in Alpha and Beta—who are they, what are their books, and are these books available in French or English?

I would also like to know who are Gamma and Delta, naturally.

Is there anything I can do for you? It seems to me that the most obvious thing I can give you is the deep and friendly interest of a kindred mind and a will disposed for receptiveness and collaboration. And of course, my prayers. The address from which I write to you is that of a Cistercian monastery, where I have lived and worked for seventeen years as a monk and a priest. If you ever come by this way, I would be eager to have a talk with you and glad to welcome you to this house. I presume however you still live in France. You may reply to me in French or English, as you prefer.

February 28, 1959

Thanks for your splendid letter. It was delayed in reaching me by the inevitable monastic barriers and also by the annual retreat. And I have been thinking about it for a week or so. The books you said you might send have not yet arrived, but there again there are many delays. I look forward very eagerly to reading anything of yours, anything by Alpha. My German however is slow, so I cannot afford the time to read a book in German unless there is no other way of getting at it. I am sure I will enjoy *Sur les bords de l'Issa*. The few passages on Lithuania in *The Captive Mind* were striking and delightful.

I am sorry that I did not think more deeply about the trouble of heart I might cause you in writing so bluntly and glibly about *The Captive Mind*. Obviously I should have realized the many problems that would be involved. Like all the people here, I have I suppose a sort of fantastic idea of the Iron Curtain—as if people on either side of it were simply dead to each other. The abyss between Abraham's bosom and Dives in hell. From what you write in the book, Alpha would certainly react as you have said. I have a great esteem for him and shall keep him in my prayers. And I can't say I am fond of Gamma. A real Stalinist type. Beta is perhaps something new to me, and Delta is familiar. I shall certainly get hold of *The Broken Mirror*. [Lionel] Trilling I generally take with a grain of salt (I knew him at Columbia where he was a professor).

Whatever you may feel about *The Captive Mind* (and I will not presume to try to make you feel otherwise), it is certainly a book that had to be written and evidently such a book could not be written at all, unless it were written with terrible shortcomings. All were necessary, perhaps. Good will come of the suffering involved for you and for others. It is an exceptional book, in my opinion. It is one of the very few books about the writer and Communism, or about Communism itself, that has any real value as far as I can see. The rest are often just compilations of magic formulas and exorcisms, or plain platitudes. I agree with you with all my heart in feeling revulsion at the standard, superficial attitude taken by "the West" on the common, political and social level, to Russia etc. Revulsion in fact at the hypocrisy on both sides. *No one* giving a thought to human values and persons, to man's spirit, to his real destiny, to his real obligation to rebuild his world from the ground up, on the ruins of what past generations have left him. I mean no one except those who are in the middle, and who realize that they are caught between the two millstones. All the others, just helping the stones to grind, for the sake of grinding. But precisely as you say, those who are ground are coming out as clean flour.

Under separate cover I am sending you a manuscript which might be of interest to *Kultura* and which says something about the intellectual caught between tyrannies. It is called "Letter to an Innocent Bystander" and you will get it eventually by ordinary mail. I tell you in all earnestness that it is a deep need for me to at least make some kind of gesture of participation in a work like that done by *Kultura*, to try to offer something of mine that might apply to the situation. I am very happy whenever I hear of a Catholic review in Poland printing something of mine, but I feel that the things they have used are to a great extent beside the point, though that may not be true. In any case it is unbearable to me to feel that I may have let myself get too far away from the actual problems of my time in a kind of pious detachment that is an indefensible luxury. There are all sorts of complicated angles to this, though.

There is something much too mental and abstract, something too parochial about a great deal of Catholic thought and Catholic spirituality today, and this applies to the contemplatives in large measure. So much of it is all in the head. And in politics it is even worse: all the formulas, the gestures, the animosities, and the narrowness. I can easily understand your attitude though I do not know the situation. I can understand your looking for something in Simone Weil and am glad you translated her. Personally I found a great deal that rang a bell for me in *Dr. Zhivago* and I very much like [Nikolai] Berdyaev. There are people in the Orthodox Theological Institute (Institut Saint Serge) in Paris who are doing some tremendous thinking in spiritual things ([Paul] Evdokimov for instance) . . . Among the Catholics [Louis] Bouyer is writing some good things, also of course [Henri] De Lubac, [Jean] Danielou etc. And then there is [Romano] Guardini, who is splendid. I have never been able to read a line of [Paul] Claudel's big fat poems, but I like *Jeanne d'Arc au bûcher* and some of his prose, particularly about Japan. Japan is another obsession of mine. Not *Rashomon*—yet! Only Zen.

Who are the *Martiniquais* you know? [Aimé] Césaire and [Edouard] Glissant? I like their work very much, though I have had a hard time getting hold of anything by Césaire. Salute them from me!

About your poetry in English—the thought occurred to me, it may be a bad one, but it just passed through my head: why not just write out an English version of two or three short ones that you like, any kind of version, and let me try to use my ingenuity and guesswork and polish them up into versions which you could then check. This may be a crazy scheme and may not even be honest, I don't know. But to me it seems possible—at least something we might try, but of course since I know absolutely no Polish . . .

I thought of mentioning your work to Victoria Ocampo, editor of *Sur* in Buenos Aires. There must be someone down there who can translate from Polish—*Sur* would be delighted to get something by you. I will tell Victoria to write to you, as I intend to write her soon. She writes perfect French. She might want to run a Polish number of *Sur* and that would be a splendid thing. I am sure she will jump at the idea.

The main question you ask, about an agent. My agent is very good and she would certainly be delighted to help you out. She is Naomi Burton, of Curtis Brown Ltd. . . . very nice and very efficient. I highly recommend her, we are very good friends and I will mention you to her when I next write . . . I shall certainly look up Oscar de L. Milosz, who sounds very interesting. I had heard the name but no more.

Of my own work, I am sending you two packets; one of small things, *Prometheus, Monastic Peace*, and the *Tears of the Blind Lions*. Then a full-length book, *The Sign of Jonas*, and another less long, *Thoughts in Solitude*, though I fear perhaps the latter may seem to you esoteric and sterile. It is a book about which I am quite divided. It is based on notes about things to which I personally attach some importance, but these notes were revised and dressed up by me and became what I take to be a little commercial and hence false. I don't know if this is scrupulosity. The book in any case is by no means adequate. I should be interested to know very frankly if it bores you completely and seems to you to be completely alien, bourgeois etc. That would be worth knowing. The poems alas are not too good. If there is any other book of mine you hear of that you would like, I will gladly send it. Or anything I can get for you, I will send.

Milosz, life is on our side. The silence and the Cross of which we know are forces that cannot be defeated. In silence and suffering, in the heartbreaking effort to be honest in the midst of dishonesty (most of all our *own* dishonesty), in all these is victory. It is Christ in us who drives us through darkness to a light of which we have no conception and which can only be found by passing through apparent despair. Everything has to be tested. All relationships have to be tried. All loyalties have to pass through fire. Much has to be lost. Much in us has to be killed, even much that is best in us. But Victory is certain. The Resurrection is the only light, and with that light there is no error.

February 28, 1959

I realize it might seem a great impertinence to offer this ["Letter to an Innocent Bystander"] as reading for people behind the Iron Curtain, and when I wrote to you about it in my last letter I had not considered that fact. However, if it is understood that it was written for other intellectuals on *this side* of the curtain, it might not seem so inappropriate. But I should never presume to speak up, in my safe corner of the world, and try to tell people in grave danger how to be "honest." God forbid. You can use your discretion in this matter and if it is simply useless, then please return it. And tell me if it is really a piece of presumptuous complacency. I have no way of getting a real perspective otherwise.

May 21, 1959

The only trouble with receiving letters as good and full as yours, is that it is a long time before one can answer worthily. I am grateful for your fine letter, which contains so much . . .

First, your questions about the "Innocent Bystander"—I hope the fact of my not answering them has not mattered. I leave to you the choice of word for Bystander, and you have probably chosen satisfactorily. In English the special implication is that of one who stands by while a crime is being committed. I am glad you can use it in *Kultura*, but I feel ashamed of it, when I realize that it may be read by people who have a real problem. As for myself, I think the problem is still real enough for me to be able to write about it with feeling. I am more and more convinced every day that it is a religious as well as a civil obligation to be discontented with ready-made answers—no matter where they may come from. How much longer can the world subsist on institutional slogans?

Reading *The Broken Mirror*, I was moved by the sense of real kinship with most of the writers. Underneath the institutional shells which distinguish us, we have the same ardent desire for truth, for peace, for sanity in life, for reality, for sincerity. But the trouble is that our very efforts to attain these things tend to harden and make more rigid the institutional shell. And a turtle without a shell is not likely to lead a happy life, especially in a world like ours. But perhaps the trouble is that we imagine ourselves turtles. I speak here of the Polish writers in *The Broken Mirror*. I could not seem to spot any of them as Alpha, though I was looking for him. (You did not send me his book, or at any rate I did not get it.) I thought [Kazimierz] Brandys's story "The Defense of Granada" was a very good piece and of course I felt very much involved in it, it grips one's sympathies. Parts of [Wiktor] Woroszylski's "Notes for a Biography" are also very convincing and sympathetic. I liked perhaps best the notes of Jan Strzelecki. The story by Tadeusz Rozewicz seemed to me to be quite bad, like a contribution to a college-humor magazine in this country: one that we would never have published in the Columbia *Jester*. Pawel Hertz was talking about events and groups of which I know nothing, and I could not really appreciate his article. I have not yet read the other two pieces. But all in all I feel the greatest sympathy and sense of kinship with most of these writers, apart from the fact that their commitments are . . . quite alien to me. Be sure to send me Alpha's book. I think often of him, and admire him. I feel deeply for his predicament, and I pray for him. And for all the Polish writers.

Now about your own books. I suppose it is not strange that your younger earthy and cosmic self should be so sharply divided from the later political self. *Sur les bords de l'Issa* is admirably alive, rich in all kinds of archetypal material, with a deep vegetative substratum that gives it a great fertility of meanings. Your lyrical poem falls into the same category . . . this element in your being is very essential to you . . . you will not produce your greatest work without it. Its absence from *The Seizure of Power* is one of the things that makes the latter simply a routine job. Of course it is hard to see how ancient pagan naturalistic remnants from archaic Lithuanian peasant culture could be fitted into the tragic story of Warsaw. The fact is that *The Seizure of Power*, though very impressive in patches, did not seem to [hold] together well. You do not seem sure of yourself in it and your statement that you do not like the novel as a literary form by no means surprises me. Yet I think perhaps one day you may go over the same material and write a great novel. I think *The Seizure of Power* suffers from a lack of perspective, and from a natural inability to *assimilate* all the awful elements that had to go into it. One day when you have come to see it all in a unified way, it may turn out quite differently.

I am going to have to go into Simone Weil a little. My acquaintance with her is superficial. As for Providence: certainly I think the glib clichés that are made about the will of God are enough to make anyone lose his faith. Such clichés are still possible in America but I don't see how they can still survive in Europe, at least for anyone who has seen a concentration camp. For my part, I have given up my compulsive need to answer such questions neatly. It is safer and cleaner to remain inarticulate, and does more honor to God. I think the reason why we cannot see Providence at work in our world is that it is much too simple. Our notions of Providence are too complicated and too human: a question of ends and means, and why this means to this end? God wills this *for* this purpose . . . Whatever the mystery of Providence may be, I think it is more direct and more brutal in a way. But that is never evident as long as we think of God apart from the people in the concentration camp, "permitting them to be there for their own good" (time out while I vomit). Actually it is God Himself who is in the concentration camp. That is, of course, it is Christ. Not in the collective sense, but especially in the defilement and destruction of each individual soul, there is the renewal of the Crucifixion. This of course is familiar, I mean the words are familiar. People understand them to mean that a man in a concentration camp who remembers to renew his morning offering suffers like—and even, in some juridical sense, with—Christ. But the point is, whether he renews the morning offering or not, or whether he is a sinner, he *is* Christ. That this is not understood even by religious people: that it cannot be comprehended by the others, and that the last one to be able to understand it, so to speak, is "Christ" Himself . . . Providence is not *for* this hidden Christ. He Himself is His own Providence. In us. Insofar as we are Christ, we are our own Providence. The thing is then not to struggle to work out the "laws" of a mysterious force alien to us and utterly outside us, but to come to terms with what is inmost in our own selves, the very depth of our own being. No matter what our "Providence" may have in store for us, on the surface of life (and this inner Providence is not really so directly concerned with the surface of life), what is within, inaccessible to the evil will of others, is always good unless we ourselves deliberately cut ourselves off from it. As for those who are too shattered to do anything about it one way or the other, they are lifted, in pieces, into heaven and find themselves together there with no sense of how it might have been possible.

When you talk about group action you say what most concerns me, because it is something I know nothing at all about. Even as a Catholic I am a complete lone wolf, and not as independent as I might seem to be, yet not integrated in anything else either. As you say, I represent my own life. But not as I ought to. I have still too much reflected the kind of person others may have assumed I ought to be. I am reaching a happy and dangerous age when I want to smash that image above all. But that is not the kind of thing that is likely to be viewed with favor. Nor do I have any idea of what way the road will take. But as far as solidarity with other people goes, I am committed to nothing except a very simple and elemental kind of solidarity, which is perhaps without significance politically, but which is I feel the only kind which works at all. That is to pick out the people whom I recognize in a crowd and hail them and rejoice with them for a moment that we speak the same language. Whether they be Communists or whatever else they may be. Whatever they may believe on the surface, whatever may be the formulas to which they are committed. I am less and less worried by what people say or think they say: and more and more concerned with what they and I are able to be. I am not convinced that anybody is really able to say what he means any more, except insofar as he talks about himself. And even there it is very difficult. What do any of us "mean" when we talk politics?

And then Russia. I was very interested in what you said about the Russians. I am remote from all that. I have read a few books, I like Dostoevsky, and as you say there is a kind of craziness, a collective myth which strikes one as insincere. An uncharitable judgment: but perhaps there is an awful lot of old man Karamazov in all the Russians—the barefaced liar who will accuse himself of everything and mean nothing. Who just wants to talk. Yet I am very taken with Berdyaev. He is certainly too glib. His explanations and intuitions come up with a suspicious readiness, and he is always inexhaustible. But I find much less of the pseudo-mystic, or rather gnostic, in his later works. As time goes on he seems to me to get more and more solid. *The Meaning of Creation*, one of his earliest books, is one of the most fruitful, the most dangerous and the least reliable all at the same time. But a late one like *Solitude and Society* is, I think, almost perfect in its kind. As for Pasternak, of course what you say about *Zhivago* is true: he floats passively through the backwaters of history. But one does not hold it against him.

There has been an interesting attack on Pasternak by [Isaac] Deutscher, a biographer of Stalin, and a crypto-Marxist in this country. I do not mean that he is a "Communist Spy," but that he is one of those solid American intellectuals who have dimly realized the insecurity of this country, culturally, intellectually and politically, and secretly admire Russia for what they imagine to be pragmatic reasons. (It has worked.) There is, in formation, a whole body of potential "new men" in American universities and even in business circles: men without heads and without imagination, with three or four eyes and iron teeth, who are secretly in love with the concept of a vast managerial society. One day we are going to wake up and find America and Russia in bed together (forgive the unmonastic image) and realize that they were happily married all along. It is then that the rest of us are going to have to sort ourselves out and find out if there remains, for us, a little fresh air somewhere in the universe. Neither you nor I are, I think, destined to be managers. I feel much more in common with the Polish writers of *The Broken Mirror* than with an enormously large percentage of business and advertising men in this country: and they in their turn are simply another version of Dr. Faul (is he real?).

About *Prometheus*—I wonder if you interpreted it correctly? I have nothing against fire. Certainly it is the fire of the spirit: my objection is that it does not have to be stolen, and that it cannot be successfully stolen. It has been already given, and Prometheus' climb, defeat and despair are all in his own imagination. That is the tragedy. He had the fire already.

Finally, I think it is eminently good that you, especially as a Pole, are not listed as a Catholic writer pure and simple. You can do much more good that way. Categories are of very little use, and often to be clearly labeled is equivalent to being silenced.

. . . The fact that you write for Poland is not too important. What you write for Poland will be read with interest everywhere. You do not have to change your mental image of your audience. The audience will take care of itself.

All you wrote about Valka [a refugee camp near Valka] seemed to me supremely important. These are things we have to think about and write about and do something about, otherwise we are not writers but innocent (?) bystanders. Especially shameful is this business of "using" these people for a cause, and if they cannot be used, then leaving them to rot. How clear it is that on both sides they are very much the same, and that the dividing lines are not where they appear to be.

God bless you and your family. You are wise even in your insecurity, for today insecurity and wisdom are inseparable . . .

September 12, 1959

First of all thanks for Alpha's book, *Le samedi saint*. I read it with interest, and found it competent, but nothing too remarkable. I have passed it on to my publisher urging him to put it out in English, which certainly ought to be done. I note what you say about Alpha's predicament, and think of him often—remember him daily at Mass. If he were not nearly in despair there would be something the matter with him: his plight is a sign that he is at least healthy enough to react. The only thing that is to be regretted without qualification is for a man to adapt perfectly to totalitarian society. Then he is indeed beyond hope. Hence we should all be sick in some way. We should all feel near to despair in some sense, because this semi-despair is the normal form taken by hope in a time like ours. Hope without any sensible or tangible evidence on which to rest. Hope in spite of the sickness that fills us. Hope married to a firm refusal to accept any palliatives or anything that cheats hope by pretending to relieve apparent despair. And I would add, that for you especially hope must mean acceptance of limitations and imperfections and the deceitfulness of a nature that has been wounded and cheated of love and of security: this too we all feel and suffer. Thus we cannot enjoy the luxury of a hope based on our own integrity, our own honesty, our own purity of heart.

Yet on the other hand, our honesty consists in resisting the temptation to submerge our guilt in the collective deluge, and in refusing to be proud that our "hands are dirty" and making the fact a badge of adaptation and success in the totalitarian world. In the end, it comes to the old story that we are sinners, but that this is our hope because sinners are the ones who attract to themselves the infinite compassion of God. To be a sinner, to want to be pure, to remain in patient expectation of the divine mercy and above all to forgive and love others, as best we can, this is what makes us Christians. The great tragedy is that we feel so keenly that love has been twisted out of shape in us and beaten down and crippled. But Christ loves in us, and the compassion of Our Lady keeps her prayer burning like a lamp in the depths of our being. That lamp does not waver. It is the light of the Holy Spirit, invisible, and kept alight by her love for us.

Your piece in *Preuves* is very good reading, and promises that the book will be one of your very best. I am most eager to have it and to read it. The pages I have seen in the magazine are interesting and moving, and I was deeply impressed by the prophetic insights of Oscar Milosz, who seems to have been most remarkable. I too believe both in the coming destruction and in the coming resurrection of the Church and an age of worldwide Christianity. And I believe these things will happen very fast, and strangely, and without any apparent struggle on the part of men—I mean without any apparent struggle to bring about the good. Rather it will all take place against the concerted efforts of the whole human race to bring about evil and despair. The glory will belong not to man but to God.

I still do not share your scruples about writing, though lately I have been thinking of giving it up for a while, and seeking a more austere and solitary kind of existence (I go through that cycle frequently, as you have seen in *The Sign of Jonas*, but this time it is more serious). I will probably never give up writing definitively. I have just been finishing another book, *The Inner Experience**—a wider deeper view of the same thing, contemplation, with more reference to Oriental ideas. There is to me nothing but this that counts, but everything can enter into it. You are right to feel a certain shame about writing. I do too, but always too late—five years after a book has appeared I wish I had never been such a fool as to write it. But when I am writing it I think it is good. If we were not all fools we would never accomplish anything at all. As to people of good grain and bad grain, I do not have easy answers, but again I think a great deal depends on love, and that when people are loved they change. But what is happening in the world today is a wholesale collapse of man's capacity to love. He has been submerged under material concerns, and by the fantastic proliferation of men and things all around him, so that there are so many of everything that one lives in a state of constant bewilderment and fear. One cannot begin to commit himself to any definite love, because the whole game is too complex and too hazardous and one has lost all focus. So we are carried away by the whirlwind, and our children are even more helpless than we ourselves. It is the basic *help-lessness* of man coming out at the moment of his greatest power over things other than himself, that has precipitated this moral crisis. But there have always been this fear of helplessness, this impatience and panic

---

* *Merton did not publish this book-length manuscript. Selected texts have appeared in William H. Shannon's* Thomas Merton's Dark Path: The Inner Experience of a Contemplative *(1981) and Lawrence S. Cunningham's* Thomas Merton: Spiritual Master. *Individual chapters were published in* Cistercian Studies 18–19 *(1983–84).*

which makes a man want to assure himself of his power before he relaxes and allows himself to love. And so he gets carried away with his projects to remind himself that he exists, and can never allow himself to love fully—to get away from himself. Who is to blame? Everyone. The answer—the only answer I know—is that of Staretz Zossima in *The Brothers Karamazov*—to be responsible to everybody, to take upon oneself *all* the guilt—but I don't know what that means. It is romantic, and I believe it is true. But what is it? Behind it all is the secret that love has an infinite power, and its power, once released, can in an instant destroy and swallow up all hatred, all evil, all injustice, all that is diabolical. That is the meaning of Calvary. I don't expect to wake up one morning and find that I am doing this all by myself. Yet if we understood the Mass, that is what it is about; unfortunately, there is the veil of incomprehensibility suspended before the mystery by the presence and actions of the *bien-pensants* who need no mercy because they have no guilt (?). That is what we all secretly aspire to be, unfortunately, and thank God He does not allow it.

I hope you have got that last chapter satisfactorily down on paper, and if you have had to wrestle with it, it will certainly be good. The days in Red Poland would obviously be the hardest to write about, and the most important. You probably have not completely succeeded, and yet it will be excellent. By the way, Stephen Spender's wife stopped by here, and I mentioned your name. She immediately exclaimed, "Oh, *The Captive Mind.*" She is tremendously impressed with it, as is everybody. As for your friend who practiced *Ketman*,* that is certainly one form of honesty, and perhaps an admirable one. It is certainly a form of justice, and a providential kind of justice. If there is one ambition we should allow ourselves, and one form of strength, it is perhaps this kind of whole-hearted irony, to *be* a complete piece of systematic irony in the middle of the totalitarian life—or the capitalist one. And even the official religious one. But that is delicate, and thank God not yet necessary. It might be in Spain.

It gets back to the fact that we all have our game with Caesar, the Little Father who is no longer human and who therefore *ought* to be cheated, in the name of humanity. I have been reading William Blake again. His reply to Caesar seems like psychosis, but it is valid and consistent and prophetic: and involves no *Ketman* except perhaps a very little of it, on the surface, with some of his "friends" who had money but did not understand him. And this did not get into any of his writing. And I am reading Job with the novices. Maybe the Old Testament is God Himself playing *Ketman*. For me, seen in the light of Job, the Old Testament

---

* Ketman *is a term with an Arabic etymology, which in some Muslim circles means the practice of mental reservation whereby, in an unfriendly régime, one withholds the full statement of one's religious convictions. Milosz adopts the term to name the ways in which people in Eastern Europe "act" in ways that mask their views and values in order to survive in a society dominated by "the Party."*

presents no special problem. As for [Jacques] Bossuet I have always had an instinctive revulsion for everything he represents. Teilhard de Chardin I have not read.

It is a shame that you write poems that cannot be translated, but it is most important that you continue to do so. Important for you, and for poetry, and for Poland. And I think Einstein's advice was fortunate at the time, if you had simply stayed here everything might have gone to pot.*

I am sending you a couple of offprints, under separate cover. I cannot remember if I sent you the Pasternak article already. Write whenever and however you please, it is very good to have your letters and to talk with you, any time, always. I keep you in my prayers. Forgive this very rambling letter, much of which may perhaps turn out to be silly. Meanwhile I am eager to hear what you think about *Jonas*, though that is now ten years ago and I have changed a lot in many ways. Am less innocent, and what was said there quietly and gently is now coming out in a more crucial and definitive form, so that now I need many prayers. In my own way, I have the same problem that everyone has everywhere.

In his letter of February 28, 1960, Milosz challenged Merton's view of nature as expressed in The Sign of Jonas: *"Every time you speak of Nature, it appears to you as soothing, rich in symbols, as a veil or a curtain. You do not pay much attention to torture and suffering in Nature . . . I am far from wishing to convert you to Manichaeism. Only it is so that the palate of your readers is used to very strong sauces and* le Prince de ce monde *is a constant subject of their reflections. That ruler of Nature and of History . . . does not annoy you enough in your writings."*

May 6, 1960

It is a shame to make so fine a letter as your last one wait so long for an answer, and yet it is precisely the good letters that take time to answer. Yours required much thought, and I still haven't come through with anything intelligent or worthy of your wise observations.

Not that there is not plenty of resentment in me: but it is not resentment against nature, only against people, institutions and myself. I suppose this is a real defect, or rather a limitation: but actually what it amounts to is that I am in complete and deep complicity with nature, or imagine I am: that nature and I are very good friends, and console one another for the stupidity and the infamy of the human race and its civilization. We at least get along, I say to the trees, and though I am perfectly aware that the spider eats the fly, that the singing of the birds may perhaps

---

* *In 1949, when Milosz, then a member of the Polish diplomatic service in Washington, was trying to decide whether he should remain in the States, Albert Einstein advised him not to do so. "He felt that my breaking [with Poland] would be harmful for my writing (he was against exile by principle) . . ." (letter of Milosz to Merton, July 16, 1959).*

have something to do with hatred or pain of which I know nothing, still I can't make much of it. Spiders have always eaten flies and I can shut it out of my consciousness without guilt. It is the spider, not I, that kills and eats the fly. As for snakes, I do not like them much, but I can be neutral and respectful towards them, and find them very beautiful in fact, though this is a recent development. They used to strike me with terror. But they are not evil. I don't find it in myself to generate any horror for nature or a feeling of evil in it. Or myself. There, of course, there is more guilt, and shame. I do not find it at all hard to hate myself, and I am certainly not always charitable about other people; I like to flay them in words, and probably I should feel more guilty about it than I do, because here I sin, and keep on sinning.

At the same time I enjoy and respect Camus, and think I understand him. What you said about *La Chute* struck me very forcibly when I read it: it is a fine piece of Manichaean theology and very applicable to this Trappist kind of life. In fact I was able to use it to good effect, perhaps cruelly, in the spiritual direction of a narcissistic novice. But the thing of Camus that really "sends" me is the marvelous short story about the missionary who ends up as a prisoner in the city of salt. There, in a few words, you have a superb *ricanement*, in theology! And a very salutary piece for Trappists to read, because for generations we have been doing just that kind of thing. I was deeply saddened by his death. In politics I think I am very much inclined to his way of looking at things, and there is in him an honesty and a compassion which belies the toughness of his writing.

Perhaps I am capable of being more sardonic: but my life has been peculiar, and there has been enough effective evasion in it for my sardonic side to be vitiated. I have escaped so much trouble that my *ricanement* at its best is a bit adolescent. A kind of healthy shame prevents me from really using it, except in the rather silly and innocuous situations in which I slightly shock my fellow priests and religious in matters of no consequence, like sarcasm about liturgical vestments, Saint Sulpice, pious clichés and other such trivialities.

I am going to have to read Simone Weil. I know she is great and what I have read about her attracts me. Her thought as I have picked it up here and there from the remarks of others is congenial to me. But the books of hers that I have looked at so far have not appealed to me, perhaps because they were in English.

Of course, the funny thing is that I am very frequently accused, here in America and also in England, of being too Manichaean. Perhaps that is why I have obediently tried to mute the rancor that is quite often an undertone in my writing, but perhaps too it is so much of an undertone that I am the only one left who can hear it. And in the end, everyone envies me for being so happy. I do not have the impression of being especially happy, and I am in definite reaction against my surroundings:

for a "happy monk," I must admit that I certainly protest a great deal against the monastic Order, and the Order itself thinks I protest a great deal too much. But of course, it must be understood that in an institution like ours even the slightest hint of protest is already too much.

I am willing to admit that in the sight of God I do not protest enough, and that the protests I generally make are always beside the target. I have the impression that when I am indignant in print, I am always indignant about something vague and abstract, and not about something more concrete which I really hate and which I cannot recognize. It is absurd to rave vaguely about "the world" the "modern age" the "times." I suppose I will gradually get over that.

What I get back to, and here you can tell me if my examination of conscience is correct, is that in actual fact my real guilt is for being a bourgeois. I am after all the prisoner of my class, and I tell myself that I don't care if I am. One has to be prisoner of some class or other, and I might as well be what I am instead of going through the ridiculous and pharisaical pretense of being the avant-garde of a classless world. But the fact remains that I hate being a bourgeois, and hate the fact that my reaction against it is not a success: simply the bohemian reaction, I suppose, with a new twist, a religious modality.

When all this is said, I find it difficult to be sincerely bitter in the way that you describe, but also the real *ricanement* people bore me to death. I do not have much interest in Sartre, he puts me to sleep, as if he were deliberately dull: *assommant* is a much better word. He shaves me, as the French say. He beats me over the head with his dullness, though *Huis Clos* strikes me as a good and somewhat puritanical play. The other thing of his I have tried to read, *La Nausée*, is drab and stupid.

All that you have said remains unchallenged by these evasive explanations. It is quite true that I ought to speak more with the accents of my time. They are serious, they are not just a pose, the bitterness of people is not just something to be dismissed. I detest the fake optimism that is current in America, including in American religion. I shall continue to think about these things. The books of mine you have read belong however to a sort of Edenic period in my life, and what is later is more sardonic. I think the last poems will prove that statement, including the "Elegy for the Five Old Ladies."

I like the poems of Zbigniew Herbert, especially "At the Gates of the Valley." It is fine, and not just negative: there is a kind of pity in its contempt, its refusal of compassion. Do you know a few of Dylan Thomas's poems about death, including the Refusal to Mourn for a Girl Burned in an Air Raid ["A Refusal to Mourn the Death, by Fire, of a Child in London"]—that too is tremendous. I have recently been reading the poems of [Bertolt] Brecht, and until one gets to the absurd and conventional moral, the "happy ending," they too are tough and convincing. I like the one especially where the "*Vogelein schwiegen im Walde . . .*"

Why not let Zbigniew Herbert's poems be submitted to New Directions for their yearly anthology—I will copy them out and touch up the word order a bit, it might go. Let me know if you approve.

Whether or not you should come to America depends on a lot of things, but the atmosphere of this country is singularly unstimulating. Why live among lotus-eaters and conformists, and such conformists. Never was there a place where freedom was so much an illusion. But if you do come, then I would have the pleasure of talking to you down here, I hope. For that reason I hope you will come. But for the rest you will find here no imagination, nothing but people counting, counting and counting, whether with giant machines, or on their stupid fingers. All they know how to do is count. I wish you could see one good book, though, that is unknown, by my friend Robert Lax—*The Circus of the Sun*. I'll ask him to send you a review copy for *Kultura*. It is an expensive limited edition, beautifully done. Lax you would like. I have read the Bouyer book, or part of it, and it is very fine. I am interested in Protestantism now, am having some meetings with Protestant theologians, pleasant, honest and earnest men: but how serious are they I wonder. No more than Catholic theologians of the same temper and background.

What I am going to do now is send you a manuscript of a recent thing of mine, which might interest you: Notes on a "Philosophy of Solitude" [see *Disputed Questions*]. I do not say it represents anything much but it is my own authentic voice of the moment and it has had a hard time with the censors of the Order. And here is a poem too: optimistic I suppose, but it is an optimistic-*néant*. But you see, for me emptiness is fullness, not mere vacuum. But in tribute to the seriousness of this happy void I ought to make it more empty and not be so quick to say positive things about it. This I agree.

I like *Dissent* when I can get it. I will look up the Winter issue. Here in Kentucky such wild magazines come rarely. Tell Herbert that I liked his poems, and remember me to Alpha. And express to Mme Weil my admiration for Simone, on principle at least, for I have yet to give her a direct and thoughtful reading.

. . . I am very eager to see your book. When will it appear in French? And, by the way, would you please send me a couple of issues of *Kultura* with my "Letter to the Innocent Bystander" in it—I can always give it to one or two university libraries which like to collect all my stuff.

I enjoy writing to you and hearing from you in return, and believe that it is very important for both of us to correspond like this, not with any *arrière-pensée* connected with the Church, for such baldly external ways of considering spiritual things are not meaningful to me. Friendship is the first and most important thing, and is the true cement of the Church built by Christ. I am solitary enough to value any genuine contact highly, and I assure you I have not very many. There are only very few in the monastery to whom I can talk as I talk to you: there is one only here,

and he has very little to say in reply, he just listens, because he came
here young and knows nothing. But he listens intelligently. I value the
sound of your voice and appreciate highly anything that you say. Now
I must end this long letter, in order to get it started on its way to
France . . .

November 9, 1960

It was a great pleasure to get your letter of Oct. 30th and to realize
that you were actually in America. In your earlier letter you spoke of
coming to Berkeley but I did not realize that your plans were so definite.
It is a pity in one sense that you did not come to Bloomington, but certainly
Berkeley will be much better for you, and San Francisco is one of the
few cities in this country with a character of its own and some culture. I
should think that if things go well you would be wise to stay.

Certainly there are enormous problems and difficulties about the life
of an intellectual in America. There is the awful shame and revolt at being
in this continual milkshake, of being a passive, inert captive of Calypso's
Island where no one is ever tempted to think and where one just eats
and exists and supports the supermarket and the drugstore and General
Motors and the TV. Above all, there is the shame, the weakness which
makes us hesitate to associate ourselves with what has become the object
of universal scorn and hate on the part of the intellectuals in Europe. But
since courage is the first thing, maybe we need courage to dissociate
ourselves from our own tribe and its conventions, which are just a little
more subtle, a little differently poisonous, from the obvious depravation
of the lotus-eaters. In reality I think you will find here many healthy
unexploited possibilities. There are fine and honest people who really do
seek honest answers and ask to be *led* by someone. God knows, no one
with any sense wants to command an army of intellectual lotus-eaters.
And in the end one gets the feeling that as soon as anything gets serious
they will drop off and vanish into the undergrowth. One feels these people
coming at one with childlike good will, sincere curiosity, and no depth,
no earnestness except in pretense. They *seem* to want something, in fact
to want everything. But to want everything is in fact to want nothing.
One has to specify, otherwise choices are of no significance: they are not
choices.

Then in the background are the army high command and the captains
of industry. These are the serious birds, and theirs is another kind of
seriousness altogether, because they are definitely not fooling. The intellectuals, perhaps, are. The brass hats don't know exactly what they
want, but they almost know: and it is negative. They are getting tired of
being hated and want to give the world a genuine reason for hating them.
No doubt they will. Theirs is a pragmatic, unspoken pride which is all
the deeper and more incurable for being unspoken. It speaks with its

effects, for which no one claims either honor or responsibility, but they are devastating and inescapable.

So I am tempted to wonder whether you and I do not after all have some kind of responsibility toward these people who are certainly, up to a point, waiting for anything we say, and quite ready to accept it. I fear being deluded and deceived by them. Perhaps I fear it too much and this may have a lot to do with my solitude, which always anticipates defeat and frustration. But after all if we have a hearing, we ought to humbly and courageously say what we have to say, clearly, forcefully, insistently and for the glory of God's truth, not for any self-interest. And of course this means that we will *not* be pure, either. But knowing we will partly fail, we can at least try to be, and accept the consequences.

You are certainly right that the European intellectuals are guilt-ridden fools trying to go on believing in the perfect revolution somewhere. Certainly you should give it a good year, and have your say, and continue to think and meditate and read. I am sure you are on the threshold of a new development that is very important, and I am equally sure that it is better for you to be here than in France right now, though it may not be apparent just why. Simone Weil has been very good for you. I am glad you are optimistic about the Catholic thinkers and writers in this country. There is a very good Catholic poet at Oakland, a Dominican Brother, Brother Antoninus [William Everson], who also is a printer . . . Get in touch with him and say that I suggested you come to see him. I think he might be able to introduce you to some interesting people. He knows the writers in San Francisco anyway. I also suggest you go on down the coast to Monterey and Big Sur and see the Camaldolese hermitage, though this is really nothing. Just a few old hermits and some kids in shacks, but a wild, beautiful place. You can find a kind of refuge there, to think and read. There are of course a lot of writers, mostly beats, at Big Sur. People out there can tell you about it.

. . . Do you know that I have never seen *Europe Natale?** I want very much to read it. Can you send me a copy? Or shall I write to France to get it? I am not sure whether I sent you my own *Disputed Questions*. The book came out just about when you must have been coming over here and maybe it got lost in the shuffle. I am sending you another copy in a few days. I will also send you some copies of the magazine *Jubilee*, which is very good in its way, and run by good friends of mine. It would be wonderful if you did something for them, though they don't pay very much.

I know *Dissent*, and get it when I can: but that is always a bit uncertain out in this part of the country. I like it very much. I will try to get the other one you mention.

---

* *Published in 1959 as* Rodzinna Europa; *an English translation by Catherine S. Leach was published in 1965 under the title* Native Realm: A Search for Self-Definition.

You gave me some very good suggestions in the other letter. Especially about the oblique approach, through literary criticism.* I might do that, or better go at it through creative writing. I am also doing some abstract drawings at the moment. Other avenues will open up to me I am sure. Pious literature is not going to go very far, but more reflective and more fundamental things can be expressed in a variety of ways.

I would like very much to get Alpha's "Inquisition" and wish you would tell me the publisher. I think often of him and pray for him. There is no use in our being upset by weakness and sin in anyone: we are all in the same boat, and there is no point in being squeamish and repelled by it. On the contrary, as you say, it is good to feel one has companions in weakness: this can be the most healthy approach. I have certainly not come to the monastery to feel myself isolated from sin, but to bear all sins along with my own and to be, as Dostoevsky's Zossima says, responsible to everyone for everything. It is not exactly charming, and it is sometimes like being in hell . . .

I shall tell J. Laughlin of New Directions to see you when he is out there, he will certainly be interested in some Polish poets etc. He is a good sort and will give you many leads and good connections.

I have received full permission to see you any time you come this way. I hope you will come. Always be sure to let me know in plenty of time. I am very happy that you are "here" (though almost as far away as in France). Thanks again for your letters. They are a great encouragement to me. Our problems are very alike, in the professional and intellectual field at any rate . . .

March 28, 1961

It is a terribly long time since your last letter. And it was a good one too. The better they are, the longer I wait to answer them, because I am always hoping for a chance to really think about everything you say and really answer it. Because it is true that what you say affects me deeply, seeing that we are in many respects very much alike. Consequently any answer must involve the deepest in me, and that is not easy. We always seek to evade the expression of what is most important to us, in fact we are usually not able even to confront it. Haste gives us the opportunity to substitute something else for the deepest statements.

I am very glad you came to America, and have seen everything close

---

* *Reflecting on Merton's role as a writer in America, Milosz had suggested that Merton could "be useful as a guide to many people who look for something" by writing literary criticism. "Literature shows many phenomena of which people who write it are most often not conscious. Our XIXth c. poet, Norwid, used to say that poetry is no more than a percentage from contemplation, the same applies to literary criticism. Such a task would be primarily a negative one, through rejection of many values taken for granted by poets, novelists, etc. too, but also a positive one thanks to clarification" (Letter of Milosz to Merton, July 8, 1960).*

at hand. You are all too right about the sickness of this society. It is terrible and seems to get worse. I feel nothing but helplessness in my situation: I should, ideally speaking, have a wonderful perspective from which to see things in a different—a Heraclitean—light. But at the same time there is so much confusion around me and in my own self. In monasticism there is a fatal mixture of inspiration and inertia that produces an awful inarticulate guilt in anyone who does not simply bury his head in the sand. You never know when you are right and how far you can go in studying the world outside and reacting to it. There are infinite temptations, the first of which is to think that one is separate from it all and somehow "pure," while really we are full of the same poisons. Hence we fight in ourselves many of the same ambiguities. There is always the temptation to justify ourselves by condemning "the world." You are perfectly right about the "spellbound dance of paralytics." You are right too that they anesthetize themselves with the double-talk of lotus-eaters, the psychological talk: all this talk about responsibility and personalism and organization men and whatnot tends to be a part of the spell and of the dance. What is behind it? The obsession with concepts, with knowledge, with techniques, as if we were supposed to be able to manipulate everything. We have got ourselves into a complete fog of concepts and "answers." Illusory answers to illusory problems and never facing the real problem: that we have all become zombies.

This works on several levels, of course. It is quite obvious on the level of the race fanatics, but on the intellectual level it persists too. I think the Marxist psychology of bourgeois individualism is not too far wrong when it contemns the perpetual turning around and around in circles of guilt and self-analysis: as if this were capable of doing something, or exorcizing the real guilt . . . But they are in the same boat themselves, only a few stages farther back. They haven't yet got to the stage of idleness and surfeiting that will permit them to do the same thing. The poison is exactly the alienation you speak of, and it is not the individual, not society, but what comes of being an individual helpless to liberate himself from the images that society fills him with. It is a very fine picture of hell sometimes. When I see advertisements I want to curse they make me so sick, and I do curse them. I have never seen TV, that is, never watched it. Once when I did happen to pass in front of a set I saw the commercial that was on: two little figures were dancing around worshipping a roll of toilet paper, chanting a hymn in its honor. I think this is symbolic enough, isn't it? We have simply lost the ability to see what is right in front of us: things like this need no comment. What I said above does not apply to your revisionists. I don't know much about them. I know Erich Fromm is studying along those lines. Maybe there is some hope there. If there is hope anywhere, it lies somewhere in the middle between the two extremes (which in reality meet). The extremes are closer together than the "middle" which seems to be between them.

When you say I am the only one who can start something in this country, I don't know what to say. It might ideally be true. I should certainly be in such a position. It should be not too difficult to give a brief, searching glance at something like TV and then really say what one has seen. In a way I would like to. Yet I realize that the position is not so simple. For one thing, I am caught by as many nets as anybody else. It is to the interests of the Order to preserve just one kind of definite image of me, and nothing else. Lately I have been expanding on all sides beyond the limits of this approved image . . . It is not well accepted. Not that I care, but you see there would right away be very effective opposition even to so simple a matter as a study of TV and its evils. "Monks don't watch TV." And so on. For me, however, to raise this one question would mean raising an unlimited series of other questions which I am not yet prepared to face. What I would say is that if you are right, which you may be to some extent, the time is not yet ripe and I have a lot of preparing to do. I can't explain this, but I need to grow more, ripen more. My past work is nowhere near up to the level that would be required to begin something like this. My latest work is not there yet either.

Meanwhile I am going to take a vacation from writing and do a lot of reading and thinking if I can. It is really vital that I get more into the center of the real problems. I mean the real ones.

What I hope most of all is that you will be able to stop by here and that we will be able to talk. Don't worry about accommodations for your wife and children, they can be put up with friends of mine in Louisville. I do very much want to talk to you and I think it is important that we have a chance to iron out these things as it cannot be done in writing.

You are right that you would never adapt to this country. If you are out of Poland, well, you are out of it. No one knows what the future will bring. Incidentally, I don't know if I have the true picture of what is going on there but it seems to me that the flat intransigeance of the Cardinal Primate is in its own way admirable. I am not an integrist and do not want to be one, but I think the Church is right not to fool around with compromises that have no other purpose than her destruction. This at least is an honest reaction: but would that the Church reacted against the other compromises in other countries that pretend to preserve her in a way that leads only to death and to spiritual extinction, infidelity to God.

Speaking in monastic terms, of fidelity to the truth, to the light that is in us from God, that is the horror: everyone has been more or less unfaithful, and those who have seemed to be faithful have been so partially, in a way that sanctified greater evasions (the Grand Inquisitor). Perhaps the great reality of our time is this, that no one is capable of this fidelity, and all have failed in it, and that there is no hope to be looked for in any one of us. But God is faithful. It is what the Holy Week liturgy tells of His "treading the winepress by Himself." This, I think, is the central reality.

Turning back from this perspective, and looking again at the possibility of my doing something to heal the country: I don't trust myself to even begin it. There are too many ambiguities, too many hatreds, that would have to be sweated out first. I do not know if these are ever going to be sweated out in this present life. There is so much nonsense to struggle with at all times. In myself. At present I am beginning to accept this fact not with indifference but with peace and happiness because it is not as important as it seems. This, I imagine, is at least a beginning . . .

March 28, 1961

This is just an added note to the longer letter I mailed this morning. Don't be perturbed about *The Captive Mind*. It was something that had to be written, & apart from the circumstances, it stands as a very valid statement by itself, irrespective of how it may be read & how it may be used. In any case no matter what a writer does these days it can be "used" for the cold war or for other purposes. Our very existence can be "used" by somebody or other to "prove" something that suits him. Such things are largely meaningless & we are wrong to be too affected by them.

The problem is your solitude. You have isolated yourself terribly by this book & hence you feel the full weight of this isolation. But you cannot seek shelter in solidarity with your Paris friends at the moment, not openly. You can do what you want to do for the time being outside of Poland—unless I am mistaken. If you were there, that also could be used for a bad purpose & its meaning twisted & vitiated.

We have to get used to our total moral isolation. It is going to get worse. We have to regain our sense of *being*, our confidence in reality, not in words. You are what you are, & what happened to the Paris writers you recorded truthfully. It happened and it has to be said. Now go on to other things, for that is already ancient history & you cannot, & need not, change it.

Bear your solitude. It is a great pain for you & there is great strength in it if you can continue to find & accept it, which you do. The torment of doubt & self-recrimination is inevitable: only do nothing to make it worse!

June 5, 1961

Your letter is very meaningful to me. Without having anything specific to say either, I respond to it. I think we are both grasping something very important, that cannot be affirmed. I have made too many affirmations, and while I hold to them, they do not affirm what I have intended, and they cannot. I think that I have never fully reached my final choice or stated it, and that when it comes to be stated I will end up on your side, in the metaphysical torment. I have *not* coped with the basic theological questions. It only looks that way. In the depths I have more of [Charles] Péguy in me, more of Simone Weil than even I have realized, and certainly I have not let it be apparent to anyone else. There are times when I feel spiritually excommunicated. And that it is right and honest for me to be so. It is certain that my writing is not adequate and I am oppressed by the people who think that it is and who admire it as if it really answered questions. I have given the impression I had answers.

There is something wrong with the questions that are supposed to be disposed of by answers. That is the trouble with the squares. They think that when you have answers you no longer have questions. And they want the greatest possible number of answers, the smallest number of questions. The ideal is to have no more questions. Then when you have no questions you have "peace." On the other hand, the more you simply stand with the questions all sticking in your throat at once, the more you unsettle the "peace" of those who think they have swallowed all the answers. The questions cause one to be nauseated by answers. This is a healthy state, but it is not acceptable. Hence I am nauseated by answers and nauseated by optimism. There is an optimism which cheapens Christianity and makes it absurd, empties it. It is a silly, petty optimism which consists in being secure because one knows the right answers.

Sometimes the answers are beautiful and obviously right. That is the great trouble, really, not that we are stopped by answers that are inadequate. The answers are in every way apparently adequate. To grasp them and hold them is to appear to be with saints and fully embodied in the community of the saints. Yet one is nauseated by them, and cast out. One is left without answers, without comfort, without companionship, without a community. That is the thing that has finally hit me. My darkness was very tolerable when it was only dark night, something spiritually approved. But it is rapidly becoming "exterior" darkness. A nothingness in oneself into which one is pressed down further and further, until one is inferior to the entire human race and hates the inferiority. Yet clings to it as the only thing one has. Then the problem is that perhaps here in this nothingness is infinite preciousness, the presence of the God Who is not an answer, the God of Job, to Whom we must be faithful above all, beyond all. But the terrible thing is that He is *not known to others*, is incommunicable. One has no sense whatever that He is mentioned or referred to ever by anyone else; hence there is great danger that it may be the devil, for God, they say, is not at all private.

Perhaps the thing that precipitated all this was the visit to our monastery of a very good and learned monk from Europe, a scholar, full of monastic tradition, respected everywhere, an authority and quite free from all the square conventionalism. He has better answers all down the line. He has the best answers, and though I accept them intellectually something in me says "No" to them and protests against it all. I had been imagining that I could somehow fall back on these other, "better" answers. Now I see that answers are not the affair at all. The thing that shocks me is the close analogy with the workings of the party line. The ones who "know" are actually the ones with the greatest and most detached suppleness, which is theirs because they have completely committed themselves to the cause. I could have that suppleness too if I would only yield and take a certain direction, definitively: But yield what? Let go of what?

This is what I cannot do, because it seems that if I let go in this way and gained this precious suppleness I might end up by being completely unable to say anything to you, for one, and to all those like you. And the upshot of all this is that I respect your problem, your angst, your sense of inarticulateness and inferiority a thousand times more than I respect his suppleness, his clarity, his illumination, his security. He told me that I am a pessimist, and in fact he drew out all the pessimism that could possibly be latent in me by his optimism. What he was in fact telling me was not to fight. This is what I cannot do. I will multiply negatives in honor of the God of Job.

I am really glad that you are staying in this country. Your reasons are the right ones. As for the gymnastics in the Newman Hall: there again, I sometimes wonder if there is anything else in liturgy as they conceive it self-consciously? Would the liturgical movement solve your problem? I hope you run into it and tell me "no." To me, I admit, the gymnastic aspect of it gets in my hair but there is always a completely different dimension. There is the anger and sorrow of the psalms, not as offering answers, but as providing a voice for the essential nothingness in me that seems to be rejected, so that maybe I am not wrong about it after all. It is good after all to have prayers that are so replete with anger. The mystery of the Jews . . .

Away with the irrefutable proofs. Who needs them? I wish I could read some of the Polish poets who are struggling as you say with metaphysical dilemmas. I am convinced that this is the right atmosphere. *No Man Is an Island* is not a good book. It is too glib. I am sorry to have inflicted it on Poland. Did I send you *The Behavior of Titans*? You might like "Atlas [and the Fat Man"] somewhat. I am going to keep quiet for a while and I do not promise to write anything like Pascal, but I am certainly bound to stop writing pious journalism. Come when you can. Fall would be a good time. October is a nice month. November can be good, but tends to be rainy . . .

P.S. The doctrine of the immortality of the soul is not fully and really Christian. It is the whole person who is immortal. The whole mystery of the person. The hunger for mercy and justice survives and is fulfilled, if it be not sated in this life with too easy answers. Otherwise it has to be emptied in the next.

September 16, 1961

I wish I could write to you more often. To you I can talk, and begin to say what I want to say. Except that I cannot always begin before it is at once time to end. Anyway I do not think I sent you a copy of the

Auschwitz poem ["Chant to Be Used in Processions Around a Site with Furnaces"], though you may have seen it in the recent beat magazine [*Journal for the Protection of All Beings*] that City Lights Books has put out. I thought you might like this anyway, so here it is. *The Catholic Worker* also printed it, and a sect called the Mennonites picked it up; it is getting around here and there.

Certainly I have no objections to theologians and theological thought . . . I only wish that theologians were more alive and that their thought was thought. Jean Danielou was here in July and we had a couple of good conversations. He is more my style, and I get along fine with him. Yet even with him I feel there are two drawbacks: a certain reflex of ecclesiastical caution which has nothing to do with truth but only with keeping "correct" and on the right side of the authorities (to some Catholics this and this alone constitutes "truth"). The other is the fact that he writes too much and works too much and extends it all too much, so that his thought gets spread very thin. It becomes theological journalism. Very good and sound, and alive even. But not as rich and solid as it might be. Though he is very good and a charming person.

What do you think of the international situation? I wonder if the Russians will manage to make the U.S. population as a whole get so hysterical that they will wreck themselves, without benefit of bombs from abroad? In any case though I think there is a very real likelihood of war, and that the military on both sides are seriously thinking of one, even want it perhaps. If they get their wish, then . . . there might be something left of Argentina perhaps. I still think I will put my bet on this century as being the "worst of all." The nineteenth is gradually assuming a new shape in my mind. It was, at least in America, a very naïve century. The history of the Civil War is incredible. The country has never got back in touch with reality, even after two world wars. But I agree that the conquest of naturalism has been a good thing. The struggle for man to adapt himself to an anthropocentric universe is tragic: yet if he had ever really become Christian, man would see and understand his present position much better. It is because men never really understood or believed in Christ that we have reached the present position. This is not a cliché, and certainly is not meant in the sense that "men never become devout Christians." On the contrary, there have always been devout Christians, but frankly they solve no problems for anyone, least of all for the world. Christ did not die on the Cross merely so that there might be devout Christians. Incidentally I am very interested in [Erich] Fromm's new presentation of the Economic and Political Mss. of Marx in 1844 [*Marx's Concept of Man*]. It would be intriguing to really see his mind and development, if I had the time and the background. It is a bit out of my field, but anyway I read him . . .

There is no question in my mind that there is a need to integrate new questions and answers in a human universe: when I said I was fed up with answers, I meant square answers, ready-made answers, answers that ignore the question. All clear answers tend to be of this nature today, because we are so deep in confusion and grab desperately at five thousand glimmers of seeming clarity. It is better to start with a good acceptance of the dark. That in itself contains many answers in a form that is not yet worked out: one has the answers, but not the full meaning.

Anyway here is this poem and in a few days I want to send you another ms. that is a sort of statement of my position now ["A Letter to Pablo Antonio Cuadra concerning Giants"]. It was written for a poet in Nicaragua. Pablo Antonio Cuadra who by the way is running a magazine. I told him you might have something for him.

Did you say you might be coming this way in the fall? Do let us know if you can possibly make it to the Abbey . . .

January 18, 1962

Your letters are the best I think, and therefore the hardest to answer. Or rather not the hardest, but they are the ones for which one wants to reserve a good time. There is no good time. Everything is at sixes and sevens, unless one falls right through the floor of time into a kind of Zen dimension which is simple and which moves right along without reference to the nonsense of society and its institutions. Is such a thing possible?

Did that book of yours ever come out, I mean the French autobiographical one, that was supposed to be on the way two years ago? I was impatient then and still am. Your study of [Stanislaw] Brzozowski is in French or in English? I should have written to you long ago to ask if you have anything about nuclear war or catastrophe. I have been working on a collection of articles like this, including one by Lewis Mumford who has been out there with you. Did you meet him? The collection [*Breakthrough to Peace*] is now put together and ready to print, articles about nuclear war, groping for peace in some way, lashing out at the stupidity of fanatics (always very easy, for we are ourselves fanatics on occasion). But it is better than it sounds and I think it will make some sense.

I can understand how you would find the Auschwitz poem like an exercise of some sort. What else can I do? Yet I think there is no harm in doing even that much. Meanwhile I am sending a couple of things. Maybe you will like the "Song for the Death of Averroës." Do you suppose *Znak* would want one of the articles on peace? I send them anyway. There is a peace movement for such Catholics as are my close friends and think as I do; it is starting. *The Catholic Worker* is doing it, and I don't know what it will amount to. It makes sense as an act done for the sake of truth.

You don't know how well I understand what you say about not wanting to declare yourself a Catholic and wear the label, which is a political one more often than not, and which implies a certain stoical stand, and an attachment to certain institutional forms, with God far in the background. The only trouble is that this is not the meaning of the word

Catholic. It is the complete evisceration of Catholicity, but one which has been expertly and thoroughly performed by Catholics themselves. Thus I feel a certain equanimity and even smugness at the thought of my own possible excommunication. I cannot be a Catholic unless it is made quite clear to the world that I am a Jew and a Moslem, unless I am execrated as a Buddhist and denounced for having undermined all that this comfortable and social Catholicism stands for: this lining up of cassocks, this regimenting of birettas. I throw my biretta in the river. (But I don't have one.)

Friends of mine in Nicaragua are running a fine little magazine and want something of yours for it. It is called *El Pez y la Serpiente* and is mostly full of Central American poetry and art. But they want all kinds of things from everywhere. Why not send one of your poems? The one about the marmot is certainly very much their style. The editor is the one whose poems I translated in the offprint that is with the Suzuki stuff. Pablo Antonio Cuadra. I will send you an open letter I wrote with a certain amount of rage and fervor, addressed to him; it is appearing in lots of places and is probably too hot for Poland or I would offer it to *Znak*. I will send you the version appearing in England, in February . . .

Your letter sounds good and you sound contented with your *catastrophisme*. I think we have about five years in which to finish that phrase, and before that to become detached from finishing that phrase. This I really must begin, for my own part . . .

Merton's writings on war and peace did not sit well with Milosz: "I am completely puzzled by your papers on duties of a Christian and on war. Perhaps I am wrong. My reaction is emotional: no. Reasons: 1) My deep skepticism as to moral action which seems to me utopian. 2) My distrust of any peace movements, a distrust shared probably by all the Poles, as we experienced to what use various peace movements served . . . 3) Noble-sounding words turning around the obvious, because nobody would deny that the atomic war is one of the greatest evils . . . Any peace action should take into account its probable effects and not only moral duty. It is possible that every peace manifesto for every 1 person converted, throws 5 persons to the extreme right by a reaction against 'defeatism' " (Milosz's letter to Merton is undated but it was written after January 18, 1962). Later Milosz worried that he had offended Merton: "I should not have used in a hurry so harsh words speaking of your writings for peace . . . I got so used to treat any talk on peace as a part of the ritual in the Soviet bloc, as a smoke screen spread by the officialdom at celebrations, meetings etc. that my reaction is just a reflex, an emotional outburst." Milosz also questioned Merton's motivation: "I ask myself why you feel such an itch for activity? Is that so that you are unsatisfied with your having plunged too deep into contemplation and now you wish to compensate through growing another wing, so to say? And peace provides you with the only link with American young intellectuals outside? Yet activity to which you are called is perhaps different? Should you become a belated rebel, out of solidarity with rebels without a cause?" (March 14, 1962).

[Cold War Letter 56]   March 1962

There are few people whose advice I respect as much as I do yours, and whatever you say I take seriously. Hence I do not feel at all disturbed or unsettled by what you say concerning my articles about peace, because I can see the wisdom of your statements and I agree with them to a great extent.

This is one of those phases one goes through. I certainly do not consider myself permanently dedicated to a crusade for peace and I am beginning to see the uselessness and absurdity of getting too involved in a "peace movement." The chief reason why I have spoken out was that I felt I owed it to my conscience to do so. There are certain things that have to be clearly stated. I had in mind particularly the danger arising from the fact that some of the most belligerent people in this country are Christians, on the one hand fundamentalist Protestants and on the other certain Catholics. They both tend to appeal to the bomb to do a "holy" work of destruction in the name of Christ and Christian truth. This is completely intolerable and the truth has to be stated. I cannot in conscience remain indifferent. Perhaps this sounds priggish, and perhaps I am yielding to subtle temptations of self-righteousness. Perhaps too there is a great deal of bourgeois self-justification in all this. Perhaps I am just trying to make myself feel that I am still in continuous contact with the tradition of my fathers, in English history, fighting for rights and truth and so on. And so on. In other words there is a large element of myth in it all. And yet one cannot know everything and analyze everything. It seems that there may be some point in saying what I have said, and so I have said it.

You are right about the temptation to get lined up with rebels without a cause. There is something attractive and comforting about the young kids that are going off into non-violent resistance with the same kind of enthusiasm I used to have myself in the thirties for left-wing action. But this too may be a great illusion. I trust your experience.

As far as I am concerned I have just about said what I have to say. I have written four or five articles, which are gradually getting published, hailed, attacked, and causing a small stir. I may revise them all and put them together into a small book. One publisher wants such a book badly and has made an enormous offer for it. Etc. I am not going to rush into this, however.

I think that I will have to remain available to speak up from time to time about the issue in moments of critical decision, or perhaps not.

In a word, I have many doubts myself about all this. It seems to be largely self-deception. Yet to the best of my ability to judge, I feel that what I have done so far was necessary. Perhaps it was not done well.

Perhaps it was naïve. Undoubtedly I have not said the last word, nor has all that I have said been perfectly objective and well balanced. The fact that some Catholics are now angry with me is the least of my worries. I think too one of the articles may even have disturbed the President [Kennedy], and I don't want to be unfair to him. I have never aimed anything I said directly at any one person or small group.

Apart from that, however, I do think that the way people are going in this country there is growing evidence that a nuclear war is inevitable. Unless something unforeseen comes in to alter the whole picture.

Meanwhile, I enjoy the spring rains (and there have been a lot of them) and am getting ready to do my usual planting of tree seedlings for reforestation.

Keep well, and thanks for all your advice and for your understanding. I repeat that I value both.

November 11, 1963

I waited quite a while for Laughlin to send the Polish poets, and then when he sent them, having read them immediately with a great deal of pleasure, I let too much time go by, I got in a hospital and out again, and now I have forgotten all that I wanted to say about them. But in general I want to say this, that they are poets I can read, and want to read, and agree with exactly. This they have in common for me with Latin American poets. I find it difficult to keep my mind on the poets of the U.S. except one or two like William Carlos Williams, but your Polish poets fascinate me and I find myself in complete resonance with them, their moods, their irony, their austerity, their simplicity. I feel that these are really honest men speaking to me and that there is no nonsense about their poetry: it is something to be received with complete simplicity.

I like [Aleksander] Wat very much (his Breughel one is fine) but especially Zbigniew Herbert. This I think is some of the best poetry of our time, and it is about what happens. It seems to me that the poets of the U.S. seldom say anything about what happens, except to them, or what they imagine might be happening inside them. This is not enough.

Thanks for translating the "Elegy for [Ernest] Hemingway." I wonder if I could have a copy of that issue of *Kultura*, as there is someone who collects all my translations. I would appreciate it.

I am glad you have been working on [Robinson] Jeffers. I can see what would attract you in him, though I have not read him much. There is too much of him, and he is too grandiloquent for me in some ways. I have never been attracted to him much. But this is my fault and not his. Mark Van Doren likes him and I like Van Doren (one of the rare poets here I can read). Nor have I ever got into Lucretius. Personally I like Horace and Virgil, and I think Virgil is an unquestionably great one. I have always loved the *Georgics*, and Horace's *Odes*.

You talk about Polish Catholics: their right-wing function etc. This is the disturbing thing. I think of the Vietnam bunch, that was just cleaned up. One of them, Nhu, had been a student of [Emmanuel] Mounier. But he came along with strategic hamlets and fascist police and all the rest of it. Aggressive Catholicism, sure of itself, deeply involved in a power struggle, content to be purely anti-Communist, gentle to everyone but those who need it, and harsh to them: etc. This is the sickening picture that should not be everywhere, but is. Yet the Pope is not like that, John XXIII was not. Perhaps the French Catholics, in part, are not.

As for TV I still haven't seen any, and am not disposed to be content with it if I do, but I can see that you cannot go on with perpetual indignation about it. And as for keeping your fame "hot"—what for? Why do your friends object to the temperature of your fame? Perhaps because they are the kind of friends who collect famous friends. You do not have to warm them. I agree with you on your dislike of fiction and can't read most novels even when I try, but now I am well into an enormous one, [José María] Gironella's great, laconic (yet enormous) novel of the Spanish Civil War, *One Million Dead*. I think it is something everyone should read, though it starts slow and has thousands of characters.

About confession: again I understand what you mean. It is a very institutional sort of thing, especially the "Easter duty" business. But how can one confess to an institution? And what kind of forgiveness is dispensed by an organization? One puts in his bid and gets his return slip. There has to be a deeper sense of union with people, a union that is ruptured by sin. If I confess a sin it should be because I feel that the sin has divided me from you, and has hurt you, or has hurt someone here, closer to me. Or it has hurt Christ in His Body. But the devotional nonsense that tries to cover up the institutional aspect of it with ideas that sin hurts Christ in Himself, now. Nonsense. It hurts Him only in His members, or with reference to them and our common union with Him. The sins that are said to attack God directly, pride rebellion and so on, attack Him only *in myself*. They destroy His likeness in me, they cannot touch Him. Anyway the whole notion of sin is so corrupted by juridical considerations.

Still the piece I enclose is silly and not to be taken as having anything to say really about sin. Still, it has something to say about ideas of sin, and ideas which I think are wrong. But nevertheless they are quite real.

It is always very good to hear from you. Please write, I want to have your news and I will try to be better about replying myself, instead of just getting sunk in a morass of letters that are easy to answer because they say nothing.

You should not plague yourself about the superficial aspect of your relation to the Church. The deeper "truth" is much more significant and you do not see it, neither does the "Church" of those who think they have their eye on everything that goes on in the world of "souls." The Church is fortunately a mystery that is beyond the reach of bureaucracy, though sometimes one is tempted to doubt it.

December 19, 1964

Just a word to wish you the blessings of the holy season and to say I have recently written to Anne Freedgood with a statement about the anthology [*Postwar Polish Poetry*]. I had her send me proofs as I wanted to read it at leisure, and I am more convinced than ever that it is excellent. Your notes are very helpful, and your own poems are by no means the least interesting in the book. I especially like the Ghetto one ["A Poor Christian Looks at the Ghetto"]. The whole book really gives an impression of life and direction. Poland is alive, poetically, and I find that the Polish poets are people with whom I can feel myself in the greatest and most spontaneous sympathy. They speak directly to me, and I respond to them much more than I do to the poets in the U.S., or France, perhaps even England (though I do like some of the young English poets a lot). I respond to these as much as I do to some of the Latin Americans. The very young ones are quite encouraging too. Some of the surrealist stuff is better and more real than anything else that has come out of that trend.

It was very good to have you here—how long ago? [Milosz had visited Merton in September.] Since then Bro. Antoninus was here too, he is going about reading his poems, probably is back there by now, but no longer in Oakland. Back in the hills somewhere.

My new book is in print, with a lot of material on peace [*Seeds of Destruction*]. I will send you a copy if I can lay hands on an extra one . . .

March 30, 1965

Your good reflective letter of New Year's Eve was one that I appreciated very much. In fact I saved it to read in a fine wild part of the woods where I had the whole day free, and I have not forgotten it. In fact I think that we are getting to be remarkably alike in a lot of ways. Since I am now fifty, and just in general since the past few months, I am very much revising my perspectives, my relationship to the younger generation. Your own thoughts about your sons were relevant to me in many ways too, though of course I am quite remote from their problems, and yet involved in them. The novices here of course do not have the same kind of problem, most of them never having been in any sense intellectuals. Their problems are relatively simple. I have still only the vaguest understanding of the Berkeley trouble, but everything I see about it shows that it is a symptomatic and sensitive area. But from this I am really remote, I am afraid. I understand your reservations about it though, and I understand exactly what you say about the need of compassion for squares, though I must confess that I am not always perfectly sensitive to that need.

For instance: I am happy that nuns appeared in the march at Selma, I met a priest who was there and he is a fine guy, it is all right etc. But the trouble is that it is so simple that it is already ambiguous the moment it happens. This is the thing that I am up against at the moment, in my innocence of real politics: the fact that fine, simple, upright intentions, which cry out for action, become, the moment they are put into effect, ambiguous, sinister, but in a way that nobody seems to notice. Right away the ambiguities become an institution, a pattern for future actions which are more and more sinister, or rather which bog down in futilities. Wait and see. Out of it all comes murder, corruption, lying . . . I am not laying this on the poor sisters. But the fact of the South that nobody seems to pay any attention to at the moment is that nothing is being done for the sickest and most morally impoverished of them all, the Southern whites. Their stupidity and ferocity are, on the contrary, simply being driven to the extreme: of course they invite it. It would be too good not to let them ruin themselves and make fools of themselves ([George] Wallace) but in the end our blissful charity will make perfect Nazis of them. They are that already, without any of the skill of the German types.

Thus I find myself in a position where I do not identify myself with groups and I am not going to sign petitions. It would be quite absurd and most ambiguous to get myself drawn into a movement of one sort of another, and I think the monastic life is a life of liberation from movements. This is of course in many ways reprehensible and open to criticism, and it has immense disadvantages. But there you are.

Thus you see that I am not identified with the young American sub-society. I give them my sympathy, but like you I stop at the business of hating for hating's sake what is so transparently easily hated. I see, as you do, the zeal that would end with them putting the squares in camps, except that perhaps the squares will turn out smarter and put *them* in camps. Precisely the point is to be one of those for whom there can be no such solutions even implicitly.

As for the new liturgy: there are people around I suppose who would be ready to assassinate, morally, anyone who admitted that he did not like English in the liturgy. I am not saying I like it or don't like it. We have some of the readings in English in the High Mass, and that is ok except the translations are terribly trite. But when I find monks wanting to throw out Latin altogether I hesitate. After all, our Latin liturgy is pretty good and very solid. It may not be exciting but it stands firm and holds up for year after year, and the chant is, as far as I am concerned, inexhaustibly good. I defy them to replace that with anything one-tenth as good.

As to being in the know about dope in the spiritual life: I have made a couple of attempts to get information, but it was singularly uninformative. I would not be able to experiment with the stuff myself and would not want to, so in the end there is another area where I have nothing left but yawns. And I suppose that means another bond with the youth of the day has slipped.

And as to Zen, well, it might just turn out that my Zen had nothing to do with theirs, I don't know.

Thus your thoughtful letter has helped me to admit that I am not all that attached to the younger generation. All I know is that I sympathize with them and am open to them, but living in the woods as I do more and more, how can I pretend that I really know them? I have come around a corner, as you have, and I simply feel that there is so much of significance simply in my own living and doing or not doing such work as I do or don't do, that there is no further reason to imagine having an identity that is made up of relationship with new movements.

Still, it is true I do write for pacifist publications, and I send you a review of a book about Simone Weil* I did recently . . .

January 5, 1968

It is a long time since I have heard from you. In fact three years ago to the day I remember enjoying your last letter which I took with me for a full day out in the wilds across the valley here.

I hope you are still to be found at the same address. What I want to ask is this: can you send me a few translations of young Polishpoets for a little magazine [*Monks Pond*] I am starting? The magazine will be free, literary and will also include texts from Asian religions and other interesting areas. I would love to have something Eastern European, for example a bit of your own reminiscences if available in English, or anything of yours and anything from the Polishpoets. Why I keep spelling that as one word is a mystery to me.

How have you been? Let us hear some news of you! Hope you are well . . .

March 15, 1968

Let me reassure you. There was absolutely nothing wounding in your letter. Anything you may be tempted to think about the Church, I think myself, and much more so as I am in constant contact with all of it. The boy scout atmosphere, the puerile optimism about the "secular city" and all the pathetic maneuvers to be accepted by the "world"—I see all this and much more. And I also get it from the other side. Conservative Catholics in Louisville are burning my books because I am opposed to the Vietnam war. The whole thing is ridiculous. I do think however that some of the young priests have a pathetic honesty and sincerity which is very moving. Beyond that, I have nothing to say. And I have a thick skin. You can say absolutely nothing about the Church that can shock me. If I stay with the Church it is out of a disillusioned love, and with a realization that I myself could not be happy outside, though I have no guarantee of being happy inside either. In effect, my "happiness" does not depend on any institution or any establishment. As for you, you are part of my

---

* *Merton's review of Jacques Cabaud's* Simone Weil, a Fellowship in Love *was originally published in* Peace News *and was reprinted as "Pacifism and Resistance in Simone Weil" in* Faith and Violence.

"Church" of friends who are in many ways more important to me than the institution.

So don't worry about your letter, or anything else of the sort.

I have been meaning to send you a copy of my magazine, which, as you will see, is concerned with nonorthodoxies, whether poetic or religious. If you can think of anything that would fit into it, please send me something.

Take care of yourself. Peace and joy.

July 1, 1968

I'm fighting my way through another issue [Fall 1968] of my magazine, and am consoled by the quality of so much good stuff. I want to use your "Sentences." May I please?

July 29, 1968

The Penguin selection of [Zbigniew] Herbert is splendid. A very fine book. I keep being impressed by his work. Was he in this country this spring? I seem to have heard something of it. I'd have liked to meet him.

Anyway: I'd like to reprint a group of seven or eight of the little prose poems that are around pp. 63ff. This will be in my fourth and last issue of *Monks Pond*. I could also perhaps do a short note on ZH. However, if you also have one or two unpublished translations of Herbert that you could spare—that would be good, and would save me from just a section of reprints. I don't like to reprint anything that has been done in this country, and Penguin really is American as well as English. But Herbert is fine.

I might be in California in October—whizzing through SF very briefly. I don't like to stay in any city more than a few hours. Are you going to be around? Could we get together in a SF restaurant for lunch? (I don't want to come to Berkeley particularly, it's off my route [but I can if necessary]. I'm heading up the coast to our nuns near Eureka.) Let me know and perhaps we can arrange something.

P.S. Please let me know about permission to use the bits from Penguin.

Darjeeling
November 21, 1968

I have been in India about a month & have met quite a few interesting people. Seen monasteries, temples, lamas, paintings, jungles—not to mention the arch-city of Calcutta. Quite an experience. I will be going on soon to Ceylon & Indonesia. Hope you are both well. It was good to see you in SF.

To Boris Pasternak

Boris Leonidovich Pasternak was born in Moscow in 1890. His father was a painter, his mother a concert pianist. As a youth, Boris Pasternak studied music in the hope of becoming a composer; at twenty, he turned his attention to the study of law at Moscow University before going to Germany to study philosophy. During World War I he returned to Moscow where, because of an old injury, he worked in a factory. His first volume of poetry, Twin in the Clouds, *was published in 1914; the second,* My Sister, Life, *appeared in 1922. During the thirties, when Pasternak wrote little, he translated poetry, including Shakespearean plays, into Russian.* Dr. Zhivago, *Pasternak's best-known work, was first accepted, then rejected, by the State Publishing House. It appeared in an Italian translation in 1957 and in an English translation in 1958. When Pasternak was awarded the Nobel Prize for Literature in 1958, he was expelled from the Soviet Writers' Union and labeled a traitor. He refused to accept the Nobel Prize and continued to live in a writers' colony until his death in May 1960.*

Merton first wrote to Pasternak in August 1958, before reading Dr. Zhivago, *and spoke of his deep kinship with the Russian: "It is as if we met on a deeper level of life on which individuals are not separate beings . . . it is as if we were known to one another in God." He sent Pasternak a copy of* Prometheus: A Meditation. *Pasternak replied in September with an enthusiasm that matched Merton's, finding the latter's letter "wonderfully filled with kindred thoughts." Merton's second letter, expressing great admiration for* Dr. Zhivago, *was written on the day Pasternak was awarded the Nobel Prize for Literature. Merton described his dream of Proverb, whom he likened to Lara.*

August 22, 1958

Although we are separated by great distances and even greater barriers it gives me pleasure to speak to you as to one whom I feel to be a kindred mind. We are both poets—you a great one and I a very minor one. We share the same publisher in this country—New Directions. At least for our poetry; for your prose work is appearing under the Pantheon imprint and mine appears in another house.

I have not yet had the pleasure of reading your recent autobiography although I am familiar with the earlier one, *Safe Conduct,* by which I was profoundly impressed. It may surprise you when I say, in all sincerity, that I feel much more kinship with you, in your writing, than I do with most of the great modern writers in the West. That is to say that I feel that I can share your experience more deeply and with a greater intimacy and sureness, than that of writers like [James] Joyce whom I nevertheless so well like and understand. But when you write of your youth in the Urals, in Marburg, in Moscow, I feel as if it were my own experience, as if I were you. With other writers I can share ideas, but you seem to communicate something deeper. It is as if we met on a deeper level of life on which individuals are not separate beings. In the language familiar to me as a Catholic monk, it is as if we were known to one another in God. This is a very simple and to me obvious expression for something quite normal and ordinary, and I feel no need to apologize for it. I am convinced that you understand me perfectly. It is true that a person always remains a person and utterly separate and apart from every other person. But it is equally true that each person is destined to reach with others an understanding and a unity which transcend individuality, and Russian tradition describes this with a concept we do not fully possess in the West—*sobornost.*

It gives me pleasure to send you under separate cover a kind of prose poem or meditation on *Prometheus,** which has been privately printed near here recently. At least you will like the handsome printing. I hope the book reaches you. I am writing to you in your village home near Moscow—of which I happened to read in an English magazine. If you get this letter, and not the book, I hope you will let me know. I will try again.

It is my intention to begin learning Russian in order to try to get into Russian literature in the original. It is very hard to get much in the way of translations. I would much prefer to read you in Russian, though it will probably be a long time before I am able to do so. What I have read of modern Russian poets in translation is to me very stimulating. I have no difficulty in admitting a certain lassitude and decadence in much Western literature. I like [Vladimir] Mayakovsky and also I am very much interested in [Velimir] Khlebnikov (is that how you spell it?). What do you think of him? [Aleksandr] Blok of course I find very interesting. What about the new poets? Are there some good ones? Whom do you recommend? Do you know of the many very fine poets there have been in Latin America? I am particularly fond of a great Negro poet of Brazil, Jorge de Lima. [Pablo] Neruda, of Chile, is probably well known in the USSR and I presume you know him.

My dear Pasternak, it is a joy to write to you and to thank you for your fine poetry and your great prose. A voice like yours is of great importance for all mankind in our day—so too is a voice like that of [Dmitry] Shostakovich. The Russian leaders do not perhaps realize to the full how important and how great you are for Russia and for the world. Whatever may lie ahead for the world, I believe that men like yourself and I hope myself also may have the chance to enter upon a dialogue that will really lead to peace and to a fruitful age for man and his world. Such peace and fruitfulness are spiritual realities to which you already have access, though others do not.

---

* Prometheus: A Meditation, *printed in a limited edition of one hundred fifty copies by Margaret I. King Library Press in Lexington, Kentucky, under the supervision of Victor and Carolyn Hammer.*

These are the realities which are important. In the presence of these deeper things, and in witness of them, I clasp your hand in deep friendship and admiration. You are in my prayers and I beg God to bless you.

Pasternak replied on September 27, 1958, thanking Merton for the "congenial" letter, which seemed to him "wonderfully filled with kindred thoughts as having been written half by myself." On October 3, 1958, Pasternak wrote again to thank Merton for Prometheus.

October 23, 1958

What a great joy it was to receive your two letters. It has given me much food for thought, this bare fact of the communication between us: at a time when our two countries are unable to communicate with one another seriously and sincerely, but spend millions communicating with the moon . . . No, the great business of our time is this: for one man to find himself in another one who is on the other side of the world. Only by such contacts can there be peace, can the sacredness of life be preserved and developed and the image of God manifest itself in the world.

Since my first letter to you I have obtained and read the book [*Dr. Zhivago*] published by Pantheon, and it has been a great and rewarding experience. First of all it has astounded me with the great number of sentences that I myself might have written, and in fact perhaps have written. Just one example at random: I am bringing out a book on sacred art in which one of the theses is practically this: "All genuine art resembles and continues the Revelation of St. John." This is to me so plain and so obvious that as a result I have seriously questioned the claim of the Renaissance to have produced much genuinely religious art . . . But enough of the small details.

The book is a world in itself, a sophiological world, a paradise and a hell, in which the great mystical figures of Yurii and Lara stand out as Adam and Eve and though they walk in darkness walk with their hand in the hand of God. The earth they walk upon is sacred because of them. It is the sacred earth of Russia, with its magnificent destiny which remains hidden for it in the plans of God. To me the most overwhelmingly beautiful and moving passage is the short, tranquil section in the Siberian town where Yurii lying in the other room listens through the open door to the religious conversation of Lara and the other woman. This section is as it were the "eye" of a hurricane—that calm center of whirlwind, the emptiness in which is truth, spoken in all its fullness, in quiet voice, by lamplight. But it is hard to pick out any one passage. All through the book great waves of beauty break over the reader like waves of a newly discovered sea. Through you I have gained a great wondering love for the Urals (here I cannot accept your repudiation of the earlier books, where I first discovered this). The train journey to the east is magnificent. The exciting and rich part about the partisans is very interesting. Of course, I find in the book too little of Uncle Nikolai and his ideas—this is my only complaint and perhaps it is unjust, for his ideas speak in everything that happens.

Am I right in surmising that the ideas in this book run closely parallel to those in [Vladimir] Soloviev's *Meaning of Love?* There is a great similarity. Both works remind us to fight our way out of complacency and realize that all our work remains yet to be done, the work of transformation which is the work of love, and love alone. I need not tell you that I also am one who has tried to learn deeply from Dostoevsky's Grand Inquisitor, and I am passionately convinced that this is the most important of all lessons for our time. It is important here, and there. Equally important everywhere.

Shall I perhaps tell you how I know Lara, where I have met her? It is a simple enough story but obviously I do not tell it to people—you are the fourth who knows it, and there seems to be no point in a false discreetness that might restrain me from telling you since it is clear that we have so much in common.

One night I dreamt that I was sitting with a very young Jewish girl of fourteen or fifteen, and that she suddenly manifested a very deep and pure affection for me and embraced me so that I was moved to the depths of my soul. I learned that her name was "Proverb," which I thought very simple and beautiful. And also I thought: "She is of the race of Saint Anne." I spoke to her of her name, and she did not seem to be proud of it, because it seemed that the other young girls mocked her for it. But I told her that it was a very beautiful name, and there the dream ended. A few days later when I happened to be in a nearby city [Louisville], which is very rare for us, I was walking alone in the crowded street and suddenly saw that everybody was Proverb and that in all of them shone her extraordinary beauty and purity and shyness, even though they did not know who they were and were perhaps ashamed of their names— because they were mocked on account of them. And they did not know their real identity as the Child so dear to God who, from before the beginning, was playing in His sight all days, playing in the world.

Thus you are initiated into the scandalous secret of a monk who is in love with a girl, and a Jew at that! One cannot expect much from monks these days. The heroic asceticism of the past is no more.

I was so happy that you liked the best parts of *Prometheus*, and were able to tell me so. The other day I sent you a folder with some poems which I do not recommend as highly spiritual, but perhaps you might like them as poems. Yet I do not insist on this division between spirituality and art, for I think that even things that are not patently spiritual if they come from the heart of a spiritual person are spiritual. That is why I do not take you too seriously when you repudiate your earlier writings. True, they have not attained the stature of the latest great work, but they contain many seeds of it. I am deeply moved for instance by the florist's cellar in *Safe Conduct* which, like everything else in life, is symbolic. You yourself have said it!

I shall try to send you a book of mine, *The Sign of Jonas*, which is autobiographical and has things in it about the monastic life which might interest you. Perhaps New Directions can send you one or another book of my verse, but my poems are not very good.

So now I bring this letter to a close. It is a joy to write to you, and to hear from you. I continue to keep you in my prayers, and I remember you every day at Mass. Especially I shall say for you one of my Christmas Masses: on that day we have three Masses and one of them may be applied for our own intentions. Usually we have to say Mass for some stranger. But one of my Christmas Masses will be a special present for you. I was going to say a Mass on All Souls' Day (Nov. 2) for all your friends who had died especially in all the troubles recounted in the book. I was not able to arrange this, but I will do so some other time, I do not know when. I will try to drop you a line and let you know.

Meanwhile, then, with every blessing, I clasp your hand in warm friendship, my dear Pasternak. May the Most Holy Mother of God obtain for your soul light and peace and strength, and may her Holy Child be your joy and your protection at all times.

December 15, 1958

For a long time I have been holding my breath in the midst of the turmoil of incomparable nonsense that has surrounded your name in every part of the world. It has been a tremendous relief to hear from you indirectly [through John Harris, see *The Hidden Ground of Love*, edited by William H. Shannon, pp. 384–85] and to learn that things are once again beginning to regain some semblance of sanity. You, like Job, have been surrounded not by three or four misguided comforters, but by a whole world of madmen, some of them reproaching you with reproaches that have been compliments, others complimenting you with compliments that have been reproaches, and seemingly very few of them have understood one word of what you have written. For what could be more blind and absurd than to make a political weapon, for one side or the other, out of a book that declares clearly the futility and malignity of tendencies on every side which seek to destroy man in his spiritual substance? Perhaps it is the destiny of every free man to bring out, like a poultice, the folly and the putrescence of our world: but such a vocation is not always pleasant.

One of the first things I did when I heard about the Nobel affair was to write a letter to [Aleksei] Surkov of the Writers' Union declaring that I spoke for all those who were fully aware that your book was not a political pamphlet and was not intended to be taken as such, and that it was a great work of art of which Soviet Russia should have the sense to be proud. I do not know if it did any good. Incidentally, since we have here no newspapers or radios, it was quite "accidental" or rather providential that I heard so much about the case so soon.

I do not know what the latest developments may be. If the question of making *Dr. Zh.* into a movie in America should arise and become an issue with you over there, I would strongly advise that you attach no importance to any movie but rather that you should, if the case arises to make a decision, rather *oppose* yourself to it. The movies here are quite bad, and I have always firmly resisted any attempt to use one of my books in a film. If a refusal on this point, by you, would aid your position with your government, then I would advise making such a refusal. Of course, remember I am perhaps not the wisest judge. But certainly a Hollywood production of *Dr. Zh.* would do more harm than good in every respect.

I have indeed been praying for you, and so have my young novices, young and pure souls, who know of you and who have been touched by your wonderful poem on Christ in the Garden of Gethsemani ["Garden of Gethsemane"]. We shall continue our prayers.

Do not let yourself be disturbed too much by either friends or enemies. I hope you will clear away every obstacle and continue with your writing on the great work that you surely have in store for us. May you find again within yourself the deep life-giving silence which is genuine truth and the source of truth: for it is a fountain of life and a window into the abyss of eternity and God. It is the wonderful silence of the winter night in which Yurii sat up in the sleeping house and wrote his poems while the wolves howled outside: but it is an inviolable house of peace, a fortress in the depths of our being, the virginity of our soul where, like the Blessed Mary, we give our brave and humble answer to life, the "Yes" which brings Christ into the world.

I cannot refrain from speaking to you of Abraham, and his laughter and prostration when he was told by God that he, a hundred years old, should be the father of a great nation and that from his body, almost dead, would come life to the whole world. The peak of liberty is in his laughter, which is a resurrection and a sacrament of the resurrection, the sweet and clean folly of the soul who has been liberated by God from his own nothingness. Here is what Philo of Alexandria has said about it:

"To convict us, so often proud and stiff-necked at the smallest cause, Abraham falls down (Genesis 17:17) and straightaway laughs with the laughter of the soul: mournfulness in his face but smiles in his mind where joy vast and unalloyed has made its lodging. For the sage who receives an inheritance of good beyond his hope, these two things were simultaneous, to fall and to laugh. He falls as a pledge that the proved nothingness of his mortal being keeps him from boasting. He laughs because God alone is good and the giver of great gifts that make strong his piety. Let created being fall with mourning in its face: it is only what nature demands, so feeble of footing, so sad of heart in itself. Then let it be raised up by God and laugh, for God alone is its support and joy."

I wish you this laughter in any sorrow that may touch your life.

Kurt W. [Wolff] has sent me the *Essai autobiographique* [written as the introduction to *A Sketch for an Autobiography* and published separately in 1958] and I am reading it with great pleasure. In my turn I am sending you a book of mine, also autobiographical in character, called *The Sign of Jonas*. It may take a little time to get there. New Directions may also send you a small volume of my poems, of which I am by no means proud.

I am learning Russian now, a little at a time, and later on I would be grateful if you would help me to get a few good simple books in Russian on which to practice—some good easy prose, and some poems. Is there a Russian book of saints? Someone has suggested that perhaps the legends of Sts. Evgraf, Lara, etc. might throw light on your characters. But anyway, I know nothing of the Russian saints except of course for Seraphim of Sarov. I am very interested in the struggle between St. Nilus and Joseph of Volotsk—you can easily imagine why.

I hope this letter will reach you by Christmas, and it will bring you my blessings and my prayers and my deep affection, for the Holy Feast. My second Christmas Mass is for your intentions and for your family: and I will feast with you spiritually in the light of the Child of God Who comes shyly and silently into the midst of our darkness and transforms the winter night into Paradise for those who, like the Shepherds and the humble Kings, come to find Him where no one thinks of looking: in the obviousness and poverty of man's ordinary everyday life.

Pasternak last wrote to Merton on February 7, 1960, acknowledging Merton's gift of the privately printed Christmas book, Nativity Kerygma. *Merton published the letter in* Disputed Questions *as a "Postscript to 'The Pasternak Affair,' " noting that it reflected "the titanic inner struggle which the poet was waging to keep his head above water—no longer because of political pressure but because of the almost infinite complications of his life itself, as a result of his celebrity." Though Pasternak expressed deep frustration, he ended on a positive note: "I shall rise, you will see it. I finally will snatch myself and suddenly deserve and recover again your wonderful confidence . . . " In a postscript, he urged Merton not to write to him: "The next turn to renew the correspondence will be mine."*

To Aleksei Surkov

Following the announcement that Pasternak was to receive the Nobel Prize for Literature, Merton wrote to Aleksei Surkov, the head of the Soviet Writers' Union, to protest their expulsion of Pasternak.

October 29, 1958

I am writing this letter to you today as a sincere friend of literature wherever it may be found, including Russia. I write to you assuming that you are, as I am, interested in the future of man. I assume that we both attach supreme importance to basic human values, in spite of the diversity in the means which we take to protect them. I am aware that for you literature and politics are inseparable. For me, however, I can assure you that this letter has nothing political about it. I am a notoriously, and conspicuously, non-political author. It is probably for this reason that you know little or nothing about me. I am counting on this fact, however, to write an objective and unprejudiced letter about a matter of great importance to us both, and to our respective nations.

But lest you too readily assume that I have some unconscious political bias, I can assure you that I do not find it hard to believe that the capitalist system may sometime evolve into something else, and I will not grieve if it does so. I am passionately opposed to every form of violent aggression in war, revolution or police terrorism, no matter who may exercise this aggression, and no matter for what "good" ends. I am a man dedicated entirely to peace and to justice, and to the rights of man whether as a citizen, a worker, or, in this case, as a *writer*.

I speak to you in the name of those innumerable Western intellectuals who have waited for years with keen hopeful sympathy to read some great work that might come out of Russia. I speak to you as one who has the most sincere admiration for the Russian literary heritage, in all its extreme richness. But I also speak to you as one who has been repeatedly disappointed by the failure of modern Russian writers to fulfill the tremendous expectations aroused by the great writers of the past.

It was therefore with great joy, and deep respect for Russia, that I and so many like me were able to hail the recent work of Boris Pasternak which burst upon us full of turbulent and irrepressible life, giving us a deeply moving picture of the heroic sufferings of the Russian nation and its struggles, sacrifices and achievements. That this work received the Nobel Prize certainly cannot have been a merely political trick. It is the expression of the sincere and unprejudiced admiration of the world for a Russian genius worthy to inherit the preeminence of the great Tolstoy.

What makes you think that we in the West are eager to seize upon those scattered passages which show Communism in a not too favorable light? Have we not heard much stronger things than this said by Khrushchev himself about Stalin in the Twentieth Party Congress of 1956? Was it not natural that when Pasternak heard such things said, he felt that it would be permissible to him to say much less, and in a much more indirect way, himself?

Pasternak indicates in this book that in the early days of the Revolution there was much senseless brutality. But if you silence Pasternak by violence *now*, are you not giving overwhelming evidence that what he attributed to the early days is still there today? I hardly see how you can avoid condemning yourselves in condemning Pasternak, because he obviously wrote this book with the conviction that tyranny and brutality had come to an end. If you condemn him, and prove him wrong, what does that mean?

If your government is strong and prosperous, what does it have to fear from anything said by Pasternak about the early days of the Revolution? If you silence him it will only be interpreted as a sign of insecurity and weakness. In 1956, the whole world hoped that at last freedom and prosperity would come to reward the long hard years of bitter sacrifice made by the supremely generous Russian nation under Stalin. *Dr. Zhivago* was written with nothing else but this hope in mind. That you condemn the book and its author means that this hope has proved to be a tragic illusion, and that the darkness is settling once again deeper than ever. In condemning Pasternak, you are condemning yourselves and are condemning Russia. If Pasternak suffers unjust and violent retribution for his well-intentioned work, the whole world will feel bitter sorrow for Russia. If Pasternak is punished unjustly when, in good faith, he simply followed the lead of the highest officials in the Party, and spoke out as they did, then it will be a proof that the Soviet system cannot survive where free speech is allowed, and consequently that the Soviet system is committed by its very nature to unrelieved despotism for as long as it may exist.

Are you Communists unable to see how this great book has glorified Russia? Can you not understand that this book will make the whole world love and admire the Russian people and nation, and venerate them for the superb heroism with which they have borne the burdens laid upon them by history? If you punish Pasternak it is because you do not love Russia, do not love mankind, but seek only the limited interests of the political minority.

I had asserted that this would not be a political letter, and yet I find that these last statements have a political nature. You will call them lies. *Please believe that I would be the first man in the world to rejoice if it were proven to me that these statements were false.* I beg you to give me some such proof. I will be delighted to embrace it and to proclaim it. But if Boris Pasternak is beaten down and persecuted for his work, I can never accept any "proof" you might wish to offer. The best proof will be if Pasternak is left free!

You may be offended by the things I have felt it necessary to write. And yet I write to you as a friend, not as an enemy, not as one who hates you. For the Russian nation I have the greatest and most sincere love, and an unbounded admiration. For the present Leaders of Russia I feel no hatred, and no fear, but only sorrow.

In closing, I had thought momentarily that I might challenge you to publishing this letter in *Pravda* along with your arguments against it. Would such a thing be possible in Russia? It would be possible here!

To Helen Wolff

News of Pasternak continued to reach Merton through his friends, John Harris, in England, and Helen Wolff, publisher at Pantheon Books, which brought out Dr. Zhivago in the U.S. Even after Pasternak's death, Merton and Wolff continued to speak of the writer who was for them a paradigm of courage. Merton's letters to Wolff are also filled with exchanges about a common passion: books. While she was at Pantheon and later when she moved to Harcourt Brace, Wolff kept Merton informed about works in progress, frequently sending him newly published books.

April 14, 1959

I owe you a whole variety of letters. And first of all I am grateful for all the news of Pasternak . . . Has anything materialized, to help him financially?

Thank you for your kind words about *The Secular Journal*. It is a very youthful book, but perhaps there are some worthwhile pages in it. I am glad it has come out now, this is a good time for it.

Thank you also for *I Remember*. You have presented it very attractively, and I am delighted to find in it the notes on translating Shakespeare which are a very important addition. I have not been able to read them yet, I am saving them for a moment in which I can give them thought. With Pasternak one does not just read things in a rush. He puts himself so generously into everything, even and especially his letters—to strangers. I have not heard any more from him, but the quotes from his letters to Miriam Rogers etc. are most illuminating. I also received some news about him indirectly from a person to whom he writes in England [John Harris]—but this was before February 11th.

I hear that he wrote a personal account of the whole Nobel Prize affair and what he had to go through. Perhaps by this time it has got out of Russia though I would fear the consequences if it were published.

With the address you sent me I contacted [D. T.] Suzuki, he replied immediately very interested in the texts from the Desert Fathers, and agreeing that they had very much of a Zen flavor about them. I have sent him the whole ms. [*The Wisdom of the Desert*] and think he will write a preface. This is a very interesting little project, and one that will be quite fruitful, I believe. I feel a great sympathy for and kinship with Suzuki, one reaches immediately a complete and deep understanding with him, and in a very direct way. He set down some thoughts of his on Christianity which were quite remarkable, though I think they might scare a few conventional theologians out of their wits. Yet his thoughts are very much like those of the Greek Fathers, and very deep. I shall be delighted to have his book from the Bollingen Foundation [*Zen and Japanese Culture*]. Everything he writes is to me very interesting and important. He is a great man.

As the moment draws near for you and Kurt [Wolff] to take off for Switzerland I am at the same time sorry and glad. Glad for your sake, and sorry for ours. What is to become of Pantheon Books? I am glad at least that you will continue your publishing from there . . .

Great excitement: . . . A statue that has been done for us by a sculptor in Ecuador [Jaime Andrade] has just arrived. I will tell you more about it later. God bless you, and all the best of wishes.

Wolff invited Merton to submit an essay for a volume on Pasternak's Dr. Zhivago: *"No such book should appear without an essay by you . . ." (Wolff to Merton, Apr. 27, 1959).*

May 8, 1959

. . . I want my good wishes and this present to arrive with you in Zurich, and to assure you that I am with you in spirit and in affection, and follow you with my prayers. This article ["Boris Pasternak and the People with Watch Chains"] is not yet a full study of Pasternak's Christian symbolism by any means, it only prepares the ground. I have however added three pages that give it point. I intend to go much deeper into the question later when I have been through his book more carefully again. In the meantime, I do hope this will be satisfactory for the wonderful volume, and I am deeply touched that you have asked me. This is all censored so there are no more obstacles from our end. Please let me know if it is satisfactory. I look forward to the publication of the Volume with the greatest anticipation, and with my whole heart I join in this homage of friendship for a great man who has moved us all so deeply and helped us open our eyes with him and see the light of wisdom in our chaotic world. I hope someday he will see this article of mine and will feel that I have to some extent grasped his meaning and followed him.

Certainly I feel that the Christian poetry and literature of our time must abandon static and outworn concepts and utter their praise of Christ in intuitions that are dynamic and in full movement. Such is Pasternak's vision of reality, a reality which must be caught as it passes, reality which must carry us away with it. If we pause even for a moment to formulate abstractions we will have lost life as it goes by. *Timeo Jesum transeuntem et non revertentem* (I fear Jesus will go by and will not come back—as St. Augustine says). This is the very vision of reality we have in the *I Ching*.

How great is this cosmic temple of God in which we live, great though blackened by the smoke of our conflicts! Have no anxiety for Kurt. There is a far greater dimension to his life than that which is limited by a few years. Let him walk always with his head in the stars. And all of us the same . . .

How happy I am that [C. G.] Jung is doing an autobiography, and that Kurt is working with him. I recently read Jung's *The Undiscovered*

Self and want to say how much I enjoyed it and agreed with it. He is one of the rare men who are helping us rediscover the true shape of our life, and the true validity of our symbols.

. . . Thank you for all the news of Pasternak in your last letter and please give him my love. I intend to write to him later in the summer . . .

P.S. There are some semi-political passages in the article—cut them & *edit them* as you please!

On June 5, 1959, Helen Wolff wrote that Pasternak did not want Pantheon to publish a volume of literary essays about Zhivago. *Pasternak had been put off by the "Joycean symbol-hunting" in Edmund Wilson's article in* The Nation *and "evidently Pasternak did not want to enter posterity as the author of just one book." Wolff enclosed a copy of Pasternak's letter to his American and German publishers and said she would copy "those parts [of Merton's essay] that are not offensive to the censor" and send them to Pasternak.*

June 22, 1959

. . . The letter from Pasternak was most refreshing. I was glad to hear that he repudiated the exaggerations of Edmund Wilson and Co. They were getting to be much too precisely pedantic. Though I can see that there is some foundation for the general view they take. But when it gets down to the etymological details of family names . . . I can well understand Pasternak's protests. I hope he doesn't feel I have taken too many liberties with his symbols myself. I am perhaps too eager to see them as religious: but I do not mean that they are religious in a narrow or institutional sense. I am not trying to claim him for a social group. I do believe he is very fundamentally Christian in the broad and prophetic sense that is vital today.

Certainly it seems wiser not to erect at once a monument to *Zhivago.* I am glad you sent him my article and hope he will have something good to say about it. The other one on the Pasternak Affair ["The Pasternak Affair in Perspective"] will have to be published later though I am no authority on that by any means. This one ["Boris Pasternak and the People with Watch Chains"] is in *Jubilee* for July and I will send you a copy when I have one.

Here is a manuscript, as yet not fully finished, which Kurt and you might enjoy. It is a new departure for me, and I think also it might interest Jung. I am incidentally very glad to hear his Autobiography is being written. I was deeply impressed by his *Undiscovered Self,* and recommend it to people as one of the most understanding apologies for religion I have read for a long time. In fact one of the only ones, because as a rule I don't waste my time reading apologetics.

. . . Soon I hope to send you something more—the Desert Fathers' book. The big edition, with Suzuki's essay [*Zen and the Birds of Appetite*], is a long way off. I haven't heard from him. By the way please be sure to tip me off on anything new about Zen that is good. The last big Bollingen [Foundation] book [D. T. Suzuki's *Zen and Japanese Culture*] was tremendous . . .

November 16, 1959

It is a long time since I was pleasantly surprised by your letter from Washington Square—amid the ruins. It was good to hear from you directly, and then again indirectly from J. Laughlin who saw you both at Locarno, or Ticino rather. I suppose he told you about the Desert Fathers' book that is being designed by Mardersteig at Verona. Suzuki finally came through with a very neat and provoking little article in which he suddenly takes a kind of original Patristic Christian stance of his own, very delightful and inspiring. Though there is always that elusive Buddhist quality, and so much that one should not even try to pin down. It is all in the book, which I hope you shall see early next year. [Suzuki's essay was not published in *The Wisdom of the Desert*. See letter to Jacques Maritain, dated April 8, 1960.]

I am distressed to hear that the article never got through to Pasternak. I should have been happy to think he had read it. Another, a rather more foolish one ["The Pasternak Affair in Perspective"], which is only an amplification of the first one I wrote last year, is coming out some time. I will send it but it has a lot of semi-political material and I suppose it would never get through to him. There would be no point in sending it through except perhaps to have him correct the errors. I am always glad of some little fragment of news about him, and think of him often. I pray for him every day at Mass, and hope later to send him my collected poems, or rather selected poems [*Selected Poems of Thomas Merton*], which New Directions is now busy with.

. . . This is an age of deep spiritual winter, in which everything is quite cold and the leaves and birds are all gone. We have ice to walk on instead of water, but that is the only advantage. And like you I believe we should never minimize suffering and try to explain it away, especially with seemingly religious rationalizations and clichés . . .

How is the Jung biography coming along? I was in the hospital lately and read there *The Secret of the Golden Flower* [eighth-century Chinese work for which Jung had written a foreword and commentary], which is a beautiful and wise book, and highly civilized. If you ever have anything to say about "Atlas and the Fat Man," I would be glad to hear it . . .

All blessings to you and Kurt, and through you to Pasternak. Give him my love. I shall write when I have something intelligent to say. I presume ordinary letters are still reaching him . . .

January 4, 1960

. . . Your letter brought me the happy and satisfying news that my article had finally reached BP and that he was pleased with it. I am very glad. It is perfectly all right to go ahead and have it published in Germany and I hope you have not waited for my reply before going ahead and doing so. The other Pasternak article is on its way to you in two copies by sea mail. I still have not written to him, telling myself that he is swamped with mail. But I did send him the *Nativity Kerygma* which I think you received last year—in fact I remember that you liked it. I hope he received it . . .

As soon as I get some copies of my *Selected Poems*, which New Directions has brought out, I will send one to you and one to Pasternak.

Very best wishes to you and Kurt for the New Year. Here is a rather vague-looking picture of me—I thought perhaps you would like to have it. Call it a New Year's present, or something to remind you of a distant friend who always likes to hear from you, and especially about BP—and Jung, and everything.

I hope the year will be blessed and fruitful. I keep you both in my prayers and Masses, and remember Pasternak at Mass every morning without fail. I heard there was a possibility of his coming to Florence for some kind of Peace congress next summer: but I know how much such rumors are worth.

February 19, 1960

Many thanks for the picture of Kurt. It is indeed a face ennobled by the hardships of life, and a spiritual one. I shall keep it before me to remind me of you both. In fact this week I have had it posted on the novitiate bulletin board, as I do when I have someone special for the novices to pray for.

Our bulletin board is really quite interesting. I try to make it so, in any case. I have had several good articles from *Encounter* on it, including one this week on the decline of the English language in American universities. Someone sent me a French magazine with some fine pictures of monasteries, and I even put up occasional cartoons from *The New Yorker* when I think they have some point for us, and when I happen to come by such things (which is rarely).

Kurt this week is in good company on the board—he is next to a large signed photograph of John XXIII, which quite bowled me over—and there is also a charming picture of the wife and children of an English schoolmaster [John Harris] through whom Pasternak reached me with some news over a year ago, and with whom I have not ceased to correspond.

That brings me to great news—a fine letter from Pasternak himself arrived just the other day. But it tells the story of his struggles with an immense correspondence and his inability to get to his work. I am not replying directly, it would only burden him. But as you must be always writing to him with solid reasons, I hope in one of the letters you will include a little word from me thanking him and saying how glad I was to hear from him. Though he does not want me to send him things, I think I will try to send him my *Selected Poems*. Did I send you these? Perhaps not. I can hardly remember when I send things out and when not. Do please let me know if you have not received them thus far.

I have also had a letter again from Laurens Van der Post who is close to Jung and whom I consider a very remarkable person and writer. He is an African explorer, though that is no right word. He is a kind of philosopher of Africa, with deep wisdom. Africa! She needs a philosopher at such a time as this and the whole world needs a philosophy of the Dark Continent. The next twenty years are going to show this very plainly . . .

June 9, 1960

Thank you for the thoughtful letter in which you wrote to me of Pasternak and of the end of his story on earth. Oddly this has come just at the moment when, in preparing for book [*Disputed Questions*] publication the two essays on him that I wrote, I have a chance to round out the whole story and pay some kind of definitive tribute to his greatness as a man and as a poet. I do not feel that I have begun to be capable of doing so, and the words I have written seem to me to be foolish and superficial. In the presence of such a story one feels helpless.

In our world where words have been multiplied without meaning, emptied of meaning, and in which gestures and actions are all to a great extent false, one is ashamed to try to speak of someone so genuine and so deeply honest. In the long run I think the simple, heartfelt expressions of his Russian friends, on the day of his funeral, convey what man can attempt to convey in such a situation.

Your quotation from [Charles] Péguy is certainly very true. He died not only of his whole life but of everybody's whole life. We are so involved together in everything that happens everywhere—for good and for evil.

What stands out more and more, and what will continue to grow on us, is his sense of life: infinite life, eternal life. Hence his sense of resurrection. His sense of working actively and consciously, in a dedicated way, toward the accomplishment of the greatest mystery: the mystery so great that it must be a scandal to all. The impossible mystery of the resurrection, and the new creation. Of all the writers of our time, including all those who are most consciously and explicitly Christian, Pasternak is the one who had the deepest sense of this central Christian mystery. I would say that for the majority of conventional Christians what to him was a primary fact remained a scandal, something they had put out of their consciousness, in order to reduce their religion to ethical proprieties only.

Pasternak could approach this mystery with the confidence of the poet who is at home with symbols. His love gave the symbols great power and his vocation in the end was prophetic in a sense that has been granted to few religious men in our time.

Farrar Straus wants to reprint in the book of essays [*Disputed Questions*] Pasternak's last letter to me, which is nothing extraordinary, but warm and lively as usual. I have hesitated about it, but I suppose it would be all right, and it can give further confirmation of the true picture of the man in all his simplicity, warmth and generosity. What a great thing it has been for all of us to have been in contact with him. And to remain in contact with him, for I have no doubt that we do . . .

July 23, 1960

Today I have finally been able to squeeze some of the wonderful unpublished material about Pasternak into the book: only in the appendix, but better that way than not at all. Besides, it is a short appendix and perhaps more people will read it, after they have bogged down in the middle of the long article. I regret that the editors did not see fit to divide it up into numbered sections as I myself desired. It goes for fifty pages with barely a break. Most readers will have given up long before then: unless I can count on their exceptional devotion to B.P.

Really the pictures of the funeral floored me. They were tremendous, and a very moving witness to the love of the Russian people for the poet and prophet that has been given them—the only one in an age so dry of prophetic inspiration, and so full of the accents of false prophecy. It was just like Zhivago, except for the wonderful silent crowd filing through the trees and over the footbridge. Everywhere people are saying that they still feel Pasternak close to them. He is a great and eloquent witness of the resurrection and of immortality. We will never come to an end in wondering at his gifts and in loving his memory.

I have been working on "Atlas" too: he is to be in a book called *The Behavior of Titans* (New Directions) with various other pieces. I know "Atlas" is not polished and some of it is heavy and gratuitously provoking in some ways. But I intend it all that way. It is supposed to be crude, with flashes of depth and delicacy, then more heavy crudeness. It is untrimmed and largely unformed, but I think the rawness of the raw material in it will have an effect of its own. In a word it is primitive. The other things in the book are, some of them, a little more subtle. Yet I like "Atlas" best of the things in that book, I believe . . .

I have been reading a lot of Chinese philosophy and am falling completely under the spell of Classic Chinese thought so much so that I am strongly tempted to learn at least a few basic ideograms and how to handle them so that I can be to some extent independent of a translation which can be for me just a starter, rather than the whole story.

Chuang Tzu particularly I love. But of course Confucius also and his followers of the early days. It takes a lot of thought to penetrate through the translation of the mind of the original, I mean to get anywhere near that mind. The fact that we in the West have really ignored this for so long is terrible. But I can imagine the excitement of the first Jesuits in

China who pounced on all those things and began to translate them into Latin.

I have read some of the [Ezra] Pound translations published by New Directions, and of course am often suspicious of him, and yet he often has brilliant and helpful insights. Also he does not hesitate to tell you something about the ideograms as he understands them. I love Chinese calligraphy.

I hope the waters of the lake are bluer than ever, and that the sun on the mount is clear, and that there are many flowers all around you. How is the Jung autobiography coming along? What else is new, that is good?

September 5, 1960

. . . The new book with the Pasternak material greatly expanded is now out and as soon as possible I want to get a copy to you. You might like some of the other things in it, particularly I think you and Kurt will appreciate the essay on solitude ["Philosophy of Solitude"]. Victor Hammer did a smaller version [*The Solitary Life*] of this on his private press. Did he send it to you I wonder? . . .

How are you both? I think of you often and keep you in my prayers. The grinding ruggedness of our lives in varying degrees of loneliness may sometimes seem grim but really I don't think we would ever settle for an exchange with the comfortable vacuity that seems to be the alternative. We should be proud of our vocation to the unusual, the lonely and the absurd (for it really has meaning).

October 28, 1961

It was so good to hear from you again. I am especially glad you are with Harcourt Brace. They are now doing a [*Thomas*] *Merton Reader* and I think it will be not bad. At least the editor [Thomas P. McDonnell] has been down here & I have worked on it with him. He has been willing to listen to my ideas about it so I suppose that is why I am content. Really I do think it will manage to say many things that would not otherwise be said. I have even added little bits of new material & we have dug up some old things that had gone out of print . . .

I am happy you read the Notes on Solitude ["Philosophy of Solitude"] in a good environment. I consider that to be one of the things I most wanted to say, & really, having said that, there is little I want to add. Except that the world situation seems to require some very plain statements about our moral duty in the unfolding of the apocalypse. So am writing a few things along those lines, but not a book.

I am happy to hear from you & Kurt. You are perfectly right about the need to do things with delight. I have a delightful hermitage now, it's fine for work and even for serious study & just a place to meditate & be at peace & realize the nearness of Paradise. What else is there?

Wolff invited Merton to write a "spiritual introduction" to a selection of letters of François de Salignac de La Mothe-Fénelon, published in a volume entitled Fénelon: Letters of Love and Counsel, *selected and translated by John McEwen.*

February 16, 1963

By all means send the Fénelon. I like him very much & would like to try an introduction. I will almost certainly be able to do it if I am not too rushed. So I look forward to receiving the manuscript . . .

May 13, 1963

Finally I have finished your Fénelon preface, and I have taken my time. Also I have enjoyed it, and gone into it thoroughly I think. I may even make a few additions if time permits, and send them along . . .

In writing about Fénelon I decided to mimeograph some texts from him on peace, and made use of a couple of passages that were in the ms. of the letters. I am not planning to publish this, though it may perhaps be printed somewhere like *The Catholic Worker*. So I hope I have your permission to do this. By sea mail I am sending a few copies of this mimeographed thing. There are all sorts of possibilities in Fénelon.

What I like most about the Letters is that the spiritual and especially the problematic aspect is not overemphasized, but his ordinary relations are brought out. He is a most important and interesting figure and one needs to see him in full perspective. I do hope that the preface helps to do this. In fact I have made it rather an "introductory essay" as you will see, and not just a preface saying my what a fine book.

How are you and Kurt? I bet Switzerland must be awfully pretty now. We have had a dry spring and as a result a lot of the trees that have flowers in April just failed to bloom altogether. The weather is always quite peculiar. I suppose it is natural to assume that the atomic tests may have something to do with it, but still it may not be altogether improbable.

. . . Unfortunately I am now in a position where I am not allowed to publish on the issue of war and peace. Isn't that absurd? Especially when the Encyclical [John XXIII's *Pacem in Terris*] has come out with exactly what I had been saying. It is wearying to have to work in a great slow moving structure like this, but . . . I hope we make it through these next years. Pope John certainly knows what the problems are, but still too few of the Cardinals realize it. However, what matters is the laymen even more than the cardinals. So little time left in which to wake up completely.

March 3, 1964

Your letter reached me back in January and since then I have heard you are with us again. It is good to have you back, and I hope that everything is settling down well and that you are profitably busy with good books to publish. I look forward to seeing Fénelon come along later in the spring. One feels close to such a man. I am having something of the same kind of trouble since it is now absolutely impossible for me to open my mouth in public about the bomb or to write a word about it, against it. I suppose if I were writing for it . . . I won't say that. But anyway, I am in trouble there, and it is galling, humbling, sickening and I suppose in the long run it is salutary. I often see how meaningless one's life can be, and one's work. The meaning is deep in the meaninglessness itself. But the meaning does not turn out to be very comforting either. Far from it.

Don't let me burden you with lamentations. But again, I think of Pasternak. And Kurt has much to suffer, you also. We all do . . .

Among her husband's papers, Helen Wolff found a draft of a letter Kurt Wolff had written to Merton. She sent it to Merton.

April 17, 1964

Probably I have not yet answered your letter with the note of Kurt about the anthology of mystical texts. It would be a fascinating project and one I would not mind doing some time, but it would have to be a very long-term undertaking and I cannot commit myself to it now, now least of all. Things have been very busy and complicated for me, and my publishing situation is in a terrible tangle. It would be absolutely irrational for me even to think of undertaking a book for another publisher at this moment. Yet as I go on reading I can surely keep it in mind, and perhaps some day one can consider it.

Now as to the books you have sent. [Wlodzimierz] Odojewski's *Dying Day* is a fascinating and sometimes beautiful book in its strange way. What is most of all surprising is that such a "subjective" book comes from behind the Iron Curtain, though I suppose that this should surprise us least of all. The stifling atmosphere of socialist realism would make such a book imperative. And of course it is a very real picture of the hot, breathless, obsessive, imprisoned life of the spirit in the socialist world: again not too essentially different from the frustrations in our own square society, though we are better able to breathe. On the whole I think this is a very telling piece of work and rather brilliantly done, especially the dream parts. If you are in contact with him or if anyone is, please tell him how much I have liked his book and how much I compliment him on it.

That [Piotr] Rawicz [*Blood from the Sky*]. It is magnificently horrible, and I am terribly impressed by it. There is a sort of limitlessness and lawlessness, a total madness about it which makes it a strangely sober statement in the end, so that one takes everything very seriously. It is neither honest nor possible to complain of a single line. He has the right to say anything he likes and be heard, because even the most extravagant thing he can say is far short of the truth, and what he is talking about has awful religious implications. So thanks for both these books . . .

Thanks especially for the little Pasternak poem. It is just right for me at the moment. Do keep in touch and send anything that seems right. I thought the [Konstantin] Paustovsky book, by the way, was a very great piece of work and find him wonderful to read. It is splendid. If people only read it, it might do a lot for peace and good sense, because it would make Russia a human reality instead of a spook to throw bombs at.

The spring is coming our way and is very pure still, and joyous. This week has been a good one for work. I have been doing something on Gandhi, which I hope will see the light. One lives in hopes . . .

July 5, 1965

Some time ago I received the new Odojewski novel, and I was waiting to read it before thanking you, so that I might say something about it. Unfortunately I still haven't got around to it. Somehow my taste for novels is not very active, and I have so many other things I must read soon, for my own work. But when I do read it, I will report on it.

Meanwhile your new catalogue has come in, and there are a couple of things in it that do concern me more intimately, so that I would like to review them. First the one on the *Zen Koan* [by Isshu Miura and Ruth F. Sasaki]. I am charged now with reporting on all non-Christian mysticism and so on for the magazine of our Order, so I hope I can be put on a list for habitually receiving such books. Then also the new [Joseph] Pieper, on "Festivity" [*In Tune with the World: A Theory of Festivity*] which looks fine, and which, if I do not review, I will certainly be referring to and perhaps quoting. Actually I will most probably review it . . .

August 28, 1966

Thanks very much indeed for sending me Konrad Lorenz's book *On Aggression*. I am enjoying it very much. It is a clear, persuasive, urbane treatment of a vitally important topic. I admire it most of all as an example of the humane wisdom we can expect from some of our scientists. I wish that many more of them would come forward and give us such timely lessons in such engaging language. I am very grateful to Dr. Lorenz for his ideas.

There is one point where I slightly disagree: he chides Heraclitus on page 95 for his famous remark that "war is the father of all things," then he goes on to add that if he had said "conflict" the statement might be more acceptable. Heraclitus is not easy to understand but I am quite sure that what he meant here was precisely conflict. He was a great dialectical thinker and also, incidentally, the kind who would probably have enjoyed a book like this. I have an essay on Heraclitus ["Herakleitos the Obscure"] which might interest Dr. Lorenz and induce a lasting contrition, if you think I ought to send it to him. What do you suggest?

You are very good to remember me. I am now living in the woods as a hermit and depend much on interesting books, both for my work and for my life in general, so do not hesitate to send along things that are worthwhile . . .

August 11, 1967

It was a happy surprise to get your letter back in June. I often think of you and wonder how you are. I was glad to hear you had found some good in the Cold War Letters. Really, it is surprising how these mimeographed things these days find their way around to those who may like them and need them. I am always a little awed by the fact. Actually, this collection is something I had almost forgotten I had written. It is comforting to think that you have shared them and have read them in the moments of thoughtfulness which are so precious. Thank you.

I am just working through the terrible account of the Auschwitz Trials (Frankfurt) in view of an essay. Yes, the sickness seems awful, and there is no reason whatever to say that what happened at Auschwitz could not happen in other countries, the U.S. included. Vietnam is not exactly an indication of pure benevolence, though for some reason the official image Washington tries to present is that of benefactors of the human race . . .

I wonder if you would enjoy the little commentary on Camus's *Plague* that I wrote, in view of a pamphlet [*Albert Camus's* The Plague]? I am in any case sending a copy along, and may perhaps add one or two other out-of-the-way items. Since you are so kind and seem to like these things, you encourage me to share them, knowing of course that you will put them aside for the appropriate time—or for no time at all if they do not suit you.

P.S. Do you know we lost Victor Hammer a month or so ago? A very fine and wonderful friend. His last little book is a real gem. I am going to talk to his wife about perhaps publishing a collection of his writings. Are you publishing the Pasternak letters [*Letters to Georgian Friends*] you mentioned? I certainly hope so.

In October 1967 Helen Wolff invited Merton to write an essay which she hoped to send out with advance copies of Pasternak's letters. It was fitting, she noted, that the essay be written "by a literary figure who would command respect and whom Pasternak would have wished to see associated with his work." Merton gladly accepted the invitation and wrote "Pasternak's Letters to Georgian Friends."

November 2, 1967

Many thanks for your letter and I am happy that you should think of me as someone appropriate to write the booklet you suggest about Pasternak. Although I have been saying no to the little side jobs lately, I certainly hope I can make an exception for him. I continue to admire him and revere him so much and never cease to feel close to him. I think it is terribly important today that we keep alive the sense and possibility of a strong communion of seemingly isolated individuals in various places and cultures: eventually the foundation of true human community is there and not in the big states or institutions.

I do have much work on hand, and all I need to do is to get sick and everything will be thrown into turmoil. But I think I can at least tentatively promise you what you want by the end of January and I look forward to seeing the proofs of the Letters as soon as you have them.

Lately I have been drawn into some absorbing work on the cargo cults and other apocalyptic movements which spring up here and there and everywhere. In the light of what I have found out, it is much easier to understand the Black Power movement as well as the Cultural Revolution in China. I think there is here something of key importance— and something with which our leaders are apparently completely out of touch. One must learn to "read" the meaning of these things! At any rate it is most interesting to try.

Do keep me in mind, please, if you publish anything in this field or anything about Indians, especially Mexican. I am not only "reporting" on such material but using it in a long poem [*The Geography of Lograire*] which is growing and evolving all the time. Perhaps an apocalypse of our age!!

January 8, 1968

I have finished the piece on the Pasternak Letters and have enjoyed writing it. However it may take me a little time to have it typed up, but I hope to get it into your hands in a couple weeks. Very cold here now —Russian winter! I hope you are well . . .

January 19, 1968

Here is my piece on the Pasternak letters. It is longer than we at first planned but I assume that does not make much difference. I felt it was worthwhile to develop some of the deep ideas that people might not otherwise find in the letters. They are really quite remarkable. It is always a joy to get in contact with a mind as rich and as free as was that of Pasternak.

When is the book due to appear?

As I understand it, this piece is to be printed separately as a kind of pamphlet. I would be most happy to have a couple of dozen copies of it and perhaps more, if you can spare them. I can always use such things to send out to people who send me things. That is not a very literate sentence but I am laid up with the flu and snowed in. I am slowly recovering the ability to think straight but have not quite got all the way. I just wanted to get this into an envelope and I'll mail it when I can.

January 26, 1968

I was glad to get your letter & to know the Pasternak piece was OK. It is certainly all right with me if the *Times* wants to use it.

Merton's essay "Pasternak's Letters to Georgian Friends" was not published until 1978, when it appeared in The New Lazarus Review.

III

*[Ernesto] has an unequaled gift of getting poetry out of
the confusion and pathos of the modern world, without
being bitter about it.*
MERTON TO JOSÉ CORONEL URTECHO,
JUNE 30, 1965

To Ernesto Cardenal

*In a letter to the Argentinian poet Miguel Grinberg, Thomas Merton observed
that Ernesto Cardenal "will be one of the most significant spiritual voices in the
two Americas" (June 21, 1963). Cardenal, born in 1925 in Granada, Nicaragua,
studied Spanish literature at the University of Mexico and American literature
at Columbia University; he lived in Europe for two years before returning in
1952 to Nicaragua, where he took part in the resistance movement to topple the
dictatorship of Somoza García. Cardenal remembered the unsuccessful April
Conspiracy of 1954 in one of the cantos of his long poem* La Hora O ["Zero
Hour"], *which is regarded as a classic in revolutionary literature.*

*In 1957, following a "radical religious conversion," Cardenal entered the
Abbey of Gethsemani, where Thomas Merton was his novice master. Cardenal
remembers that "it was an incredible privilege to be instructed by this great
master of mysticism who for so many years had been my master through his
books." When Cardenal met with Merton "for spiritual guidance," Merton "would
ask about Nicaragua, Somoza, the poets of Nicaragua, the Nicaraguan countryside, poets from other parts of Latin America, other dictators." There was a lesson
for Cardenal in Merton's questions: "At first I thought I'd have to renounce
everything when I entered the Trappist order—my books, my interest in my
country, in politics and the dictatorship of Latin America, in Nicaraguan politics,
in Somoza, in everything. And Merton made me see that I didn't have to renounce
anything" (see* Merton by Those Who Knew Him Best, *edited by Paul Wilkes).
For Merton, it was an opportunity to delve deeply into Latin American life and
culture, a subject in which he was already widely read.*

*The notes Cardenal made during his stay at Gethsemani served as the basis
for a set of lyrics, which he published as* Gethsemani, Ky. *After leaving the
monastery for health reasons in 1959, Cardenal studied for the priesthood and
was ordained in 1965. That year he founded Nuestra Señora de Solentiname [Our
Lady of Solentiname], a lay monastery like that which he and Merton had dis-*

cussed. The campesinos' dialogues on Sunday Gospel readings have been pub-
lished as El Evangelio en Solentiname *(1975). After the monastery was destroyed*
by Somoza in 1977, Cardenal became chaplain for the Sandinista National Lib-
eration Front, which overthrew Somoza in 1979. With his appointment as Minister
of Culture in the Sandinista government, Cardenal extended his efforts nationwide
to encourage the people's creative work in poetry and crafts.

Though some have been perplexed by the story of the contemplative turned
revolutionary, the pacifist who came to accept violence as inevitable and necessary,
Cardenal himself sees a consistency in his life story. In an interview with Margaret
Randall, published in Risking a Somersault in the Air: Conversations with Nicaraguan Poets, *Cardenal said: "I always thought my life had been a coherent line,*
set forth by God, a series of experiences that may seem crazy and disconnected
to many: burying myself in a Trappist monastery, then twelve years on an island
in Solentiname (where many also thought it was a waste of time, a place unknown
even inside *Nicaragua), and then the revolution, my exile (which meant traveling*
around the world doing solidarity work for my country), and finally this very
bureaucratic job as Minister of Culture, with its round of voyages since the victory
. . . As Minister of Culture, for the most part I've had to renounce my vocation
as a poet. Yet it all seems like a single mission to me: the total silence of the
Trappist novitiate, when you communicate only through sign language, the iso-
lation of Solentiname, and the agitated activity of these trips, before and after
the revolution. Everything up to now has been a preparation helping me give
myself to this cause." He expresses a similar thought in the poem "Epistle to José
Coronel Urtecho": "They've told me I talk only about politics now. / It's not about
politics but about Revolution / which for me is the same thing as the kingdom of
God." For Cardenal all of life is the stuff of poetry. In addition to the books
noted above, Cardenal's published works include Oración por Marilyn Monroe,
y otros poemas *(1965),* Salmos *(1967),* Homenaje a los indios americanos *(1969),*
Vida en el amor *(1970), and* En Cuba *(1972).*

Merton first wrote to Cardenal in August 1959, shortly after Cardenal left
Gethsemani. From the beginning the tone of Merton's letters is intimate and
solicitous: he is still somewhat the novice master with Cardenal, encouraging
spiritual growth and risk, supporting the seminary student in his work, and
sharing joy in the foundation at Solentiname. But Merton's letters are also self-
revelatory: Merton shares with Cardenal his longing for an alternative to Geth-
semani and its "big-institution monasticism," his "hunger for a more peaceful,
more solitary, less rigid existence," his passion for Latin America, and his special
interest in its Indian culture as well as his dream of one day going to Latin
America.

August 17, 1959

. . . I was relieved to hear you had finally arrived, because I thought
interiorly that the plan would very probably not be quite as simple as it
looked on paper. Certainly when it was expected that you would reach
Mexico City from San Antonio in eight hours, I knew it was impossible.

And so you had two days in New Orleans: they must indeed have been miserable. I think the weariness of the journey and the other effects of your leaving here, with the inevitable let-down, must have been chiefly responsible for your sadness. I know of course how you would feel, and it was to be expected.

You came here under ideal conditions, and everything was of a nature to make you happy and give you peace. You had given yourself completely to God without afterthought and without return, and He on His part had brought you to a place where the life was unexpectedly easy and pleasant and where everything went along quite smoothly for you. Hence in reality the first real Cross you met with, in your response to God's call, was the necessity to *leave* this monastery, under obedience, after having been told that it was not God's will for you to stay here.

You must not regard this as the end of your vocation, or as a break in the progress of your soul towards God. On the contrary, it is an entirely necessary step and is part of the vital evolution of your vocation. It is a step in your spiritual maturity, and that is why it is difficult for you. Certainly it would have been pleasant to remain in the state of almost passive irresponsibility here—that is one of the qualities and one of the vices of this monastery: everything is geared to keep one passive and, in a certain sense, infantile. This is from a certain point of view excellent, and it can quickly bring many souls into a state of detachment and peace which favors a certain interior life. But unfortunately also the peculiar circumstances of this monastery prevent real spiritual growth. Underneath the superficial and somewhat false good humor, with its façade of juvenile insouciance, lie the deep fear and anxiety that come from a lack of real interior life. We have the words, the slogans, the notions. We cultivate the pageantry of the monastic life. We go in for singing, ritual, and all the externals. And ceremonies are very useful in dazzling the newcomer, and keeping him happy for a while. But there seems to be a growing realization that for a great many in the community this is all a surface of piety which overlies a fake mysticism and a complete vacuity of soul. Hence the growing restlessness, the rebellions, the strange departures of priests, the hopelessness which only the very stubborn can resist, with the aid of their self-fabricated methods of reassurance.

Your own interior life was perfectly genuine. God gave you many graces and brought you close to Himself, and perhaps you would never have come so close to Him anywhere else. For these last two years, Gethsemani was ideal for you, and you must regard it as a great grace that God brought you here. It is something that has changed the whole direction of your life. But at the same time if you had remained here, the general spirit of unrest in the community and the growing fear of falsity which have disturbed so many of our best vocations and made them leave, would have reached you too. And by that time you would have been professed, and in a very difficult position.

The fact that you were in danger of developing a stomach ulcer was a warning sign of the very painful and harmful experiences that would have awaited you if you had stayed here, and I assure you that the happiness you had known in the novitiate would not have lasted long.

What next? You must wait patiently, prayerfully, and in peace. No one can say yet whether you should enter another monastery. I do not know if you will be happy in the choir anywhere, since you do not sing. I advise you not to think too much about whether or not you are happy. You will never again reduplicate the feeling of happiness which you had here, because it is not normal to do so. You would not have known such happiness even if you had remained. Your life now will be serious and even sad. This is as it should be. We have no right to escape into happiness that most of the world cannot share. This is a very grim and terrible century, and in it we must suffer sorrow and responsibility with the rest of the world. But do not think that God is less close to you now. I am sure you are closer to Him, and are on the path to a new and strange reality. Let Him lead you.

J. Laughlin tells me that he is publishing my translation of your Drake poem ["Drake in the Southern Sea"] in the New Directions annual. Along with some poems of Pablo [Antonio Cuadra]. [Robert] Lax will be glad to hear that *The Circus [of the Sun]* is being printed in Mexico . . .

I have little time now, so I will finish and write you again later. Keep me posted, and let me know when you enter at Cuernavaca [Benedictine Monastery of the Resurrection in Mexico]. I told the novices your message, that the world was unlivable, and they received it with awe . . .

Please give my best regards to Dom Gregorio [Lemercier, O.S.B., Superior at Cuernavaca], and say I pray for him and for his monastery. Your description of it sounded very beautiful . . .

September 12, 1959

Not only have I received two good letters from you but a charming one also from your dear Grandmother thanking me for helping you, etc. I can see indirectly from her letter and from what she says people say of you that your stay at Gethsemani made a very great difference in your life and that you have changed and developed remarkably. It is my own experience that God did much work in your soul when you were here and I believe He will continue to carry on this good work, all the more so when you are passive and quiet and content to let Him work without desiring to see anything that He is doing. I am very pleased to hear that your stomach is better . . . It may happen that trouble in the stomach may come when you are evolving toward a change or a new step—when a new phase of your life is beginning to come into being. When the step is made, the stomach will be quiet.

Both Dom Gregorio and I agree that it is utterly providential that the Jesuit Fathers have offered you hospitality in their seminary and will educate you for the priesthood without charge. This is another evident sign of God's love for you, and with all peace and joy you should accept it, with no anxiety and care about where or how you will exercise this priesthood when the time comes. Simply receive the necessary education and seminary training, with great humility and love, and do not fear the effects of a different kind of formation. If for some reason it is insisted upon that you behave officially as a Jesuit-formed spirit, let your conformity with the party line make contact with only such men as [Jean-Pierre De] Caussade, [Jean-Nicolas] Grou, Lallemente, etc. who are all strong on peace, passivity, abandonment, and not aggressive or systematic at all. But I am sure any director will recognize in you the value of your tendency to silence, childlikeness and peace.

The pieces of ceramic work returned from St. Meinrad and the larger crucifix is definitely one of your very best works. It came out a deep brick red, and has a very heavenly and spiritual joy about it which I like greatly. I am having Fr. Gerard put it on a walnut Cross and it will hang here in our room. I will have a picture taken of it if I can. The other smaller pieces are all good. Should I try to send you any of them?

Dom G. showed me pictures of the church of the monastery at Cuernavaca and it is certainly very interesting and effective. I should imagine that saying Mass there with the roof open to heaven must be a wonderful experience. His visit here was a great success and we had some good talks. It is good to find someone who agrees so completely with one's views on the monastic life. I am sure your stay there will be very profitable and that it will carry you forward, far beyond what you reached when you were here. Gethsemani is a very limited place, in its way. The Holy Spirit is certainly working here, but there comes a point where further development is frustrated or impossible and where truth becomes seriously falsified. Of course I suppose that is true wherever human institutions are found.

Your poems about Gethsemani [*Gethsemani, Ky.*] are very effective and have a special meaning for anyone who knows the scene and the incidents. The simplest ones are the best—for instance the little song "*Hay un rumor de tractores . . .*" and the other one about the smell of the earth in the spring in Nicaragua, and the ones that bring to mind contrasts and comparisons with Nicaragua. The one about the snow is very effective: perhaps it is the best . . . I think you are right in saying that these are less good than the ones you wrote before coming here. Certainly they have less power. But they should be what they are, simple and quiet and direct. And with that charming Chinese brevity. On the other hand your poems in the *Revista de la Literatura* are splendid. They constitute some of the few really good political poems I have read—they have the quality, and even more, that the left-wing poets had in the thirties. They are powerful and arresting and I am very happy with them. I wish I knew more about the background and the story. I think they are clearly your best poems.

I have been reading some more of [Jorge] Carrera Andrade and think I will have to translate some of them. He is very good.

Stephen Spender's wife came through here and we had a very fine conversation together. She is a splendid person, very interested in religion, liturgy, St. John of the Cross, Yoga, etc. etc. I told her about Corn Island [an island off the coast of Nicaragua where Cardenal and Merton thought about founding a monastery] and she was enthusiastic. I have had no information about it though, and do not know whether the Bishop will stop by to talk about it . . .

I shall keep Gonzolo in my prayers and Masses. It is dangerous work but I hope it will be fruitful. I think you must all go a little slow, and don't depend too much on [Fidel] Castro. I think he is a little out of his depth and there is danger that he may make decisions and gestures that have no basis in reality, in order to salvage something of his own position which will be more and more menaced. Take it easy. There is great danger that the revolution in Nicaragua may serve as nothing but a cat's paw for the Communists. Let *them* get burnt. However, I cannot claim to know the political situation.

I value and appreciate your prayers. Keep them up. I am sure God will hear them. I have great confidence in the future, though I do not know exactly what will come out. I think there is considerable hope of a really constructive answer and solution to everything. More later . . .

October 8, 1959

Though the extant copy of much of this letter is cut off at the right margin and therefore incomplete, it is possible to reconstruct the gist of the letter. Merton had received "good news" from Dom Gregorio Lemercier; it seemed to him that the dispensation permitting Merton to leave Gethsemani would be granted. Though Merton did not yet know whether or not Rome had contacted Abbot James Fox, who was at the time hospitalized in Bardstown, Merton was taking the opportunity to write "a conscience matter" letter detailing his plans for traveling to Mexico via Albuquerque, New Mexico, where he could look at Indian pueblos and perhaps "make a kind of retreat in the desert." He wondered about what papers he would need (passport, visa, tourist card) and alerted Cardenal that he would be sending packages of books, from time to time, to be held for his arrival. One "small trial" was his health (Merton had been hospitalized for an operation in mid-October). Sickness, he noted, could be providential, slowing down a man when he was about to turn an important corner. This move was "such a wonderful opportunity" to "realize in actual fact" the simplicity of the monastic life, get away from "all the artificiality," and find the ideal in true purity and solitude. To the typed letter, Merton added this note in his own hand.

How are you? I have not heard anything from you since Dom Gregorio brought your poems. I am wondering if a letter of yours has failed to reach me. If you answer this one, it had better be conscience matter. Let me know any other hints or suggestions you think will be useful. When traveling in Mexico perhaps I ought simply to dress as a layman.

I will need prayers in the next two or three weeks as the struggle with Father Abbot [James Fox] may be quite difficult though there is nothing he can do now, at least as far as I am concerned . . .

St. Anthony Hospital, Louisville
October 17, 1959

I am in the hospital for a few days, but it is only question of a minor operation, and everything seems to be all right. I hope to be fully recovered in a day or two.

So far there is no indication that Father Abbot has heard anything from Rome. At least he has not said anything to me about it, and his attitude does not indicate that he feels upset about anything. I should be very surprised if he had heard from Rome, & at the same time I presume that nothing will be done until he is consulted. Hence I may have to wait quite a long time. But it is worth being patient about.

Before I came to the hospital I got all the Carmelite nuns at the Louisville Carmel to pray for this intention. I also had the happiness of saying their proper Mass of St. Teresa on the Feast day—which was the day of my operation. I am sure their prayers will be very powerful.

[D. T.] Suzuki is finally sending his preface to my Desert Fathers' book. It has not arrived yet but it should be very interesting. I am very happy about it.

Naturally I look forward very much to coming to Mexico, and continue every day to pray that this venture may be successful for the glory of God. One must expect obstacles & difficulties but there seem to be so many indications that this is God's will & I trust He will bring it to completion in His own way. I look forward to hearing news from you when Dom Gregorio returns from Rome. I am very pleased that his requests were successful and that Cuernavaca is now established as a Priory.

. . . I am expecting to return to the monastery tomorrow or the day after. There is no special news at Gethsemani—everything is as usual. There are very few new postulants, but Fr. Robert made his profession on October 4th.

October 24, 1959

I got your letter of the 17th safely yesterday when I returned from the hospital, so everything is ok. Father Abbot left this morning for California and will return before November 1st. Things are evidently going to move quite slowly, but I have every hope of success, but I have not the slightest idea what is taking place. But that is very well. The thing is in the hands of God and we must let Him work it out as He pleases. Certainly our prayers are being answered, in due season. The only thing that surprises me is that so far nothing difficult or unpleasant has occurred, and somewhere along the line there is going to be a hard and nerve-racking obstacle to negotiate, in the very difficult rupture that will have to made with Gethsemani and with its Father Abbot. That is what I most dread and feel will be most difficult, because of all the personal ties and even obligations that exist. This is what . . . will now require the most prayers and the greatest help of the Holy Spirit. A work of God can often and usually does demand a complete uprooting that is extremely painful and disconcerting, and which requires great fidelity in the one called to do the work. The difficulty comes in the darkness and possibility of doubt, in the mystical risk involved. I am very glad that the danger and the risk appear very clearly to me, and I am resolved to be faithful in this risk and not cling to the security of the established position I have here. But I dread going off with imprecations hurled after me, and being treated as a traitor, etc. This must not be allowed to affect things so much that I become influenced by it. Yesterday I had a very fine long conversation with the Prioress of the Louisville Carmel [Mother Angela Collins] who is a fine person and who has her nuns praying for our project. But we will all have to be very determined and struggle without discouragement, trusting in God and accepting difficulty and delay.

That brings me to the question of your own health. I certainly do not think that the stomach trouble you had here will necessarily be an obstacle to your entering the seminary, and I would not let it become an obstacle by worrying about it. The reason for your leaving here was that this life puts an exceptional pressure on one who tends to have ulcers: but seminary life is closer to normal and it would hardly burden you more than an ordinary life would. You will doubtless always be molested with stomach trouble in one form or other so I would just make the best of it, do not let it deter you from undertaking the things that are for God's glory; accept the handicap He has willed for you and take the normal care of your health that will enable you to support the work you have to do.

Pablo Antonio's letter contains a lot of wisdom, and I agree with him that a place like Ometepe has about it all the elements that are called for in a contemplative foundation that is to play a really vital role in Latin American culture and society. It will take a little time before we might be ready for Ometepe but that is the kind of thing that really makes sense. Corn Island has natural advantages, but that is all. I feel, as does Pablo Antonio, that one must also be rooted in the Indian and Latin cultural complex in a very definite way. Besides that, the Bishop of Bluefields [Carthusian Bishop Matthew A. Niedhammer], when he finally got around to replying to my second letter, became very timorous and told me that he could not take me unless I were actually *sent* by my Superiors. My explanation of this is that I sent the letter to him open, with permission of Father Abbot, and Father Abbot evidently enclosed a letter of his own which put the fear of God into the good bishop and told him, in no uncertain terms, to steer clear of anyone who wanted to leave Gethsemani. The bishop really sounded frightened . . .

I will certainly let you know when I can hope to come to Mexico and it would be wonderful to look at the city and its environs together. I shall want to see all the best things and meet your friends. It will be necessary for me to really soak in the atmosphere of Mexico and get thoroughly acclimatized, though naturally I am not looking for a lot of hectic social life. But it is certainly a duty to become quietly and gradually really a part of the nation and of its life and not simply be a gringo tourist. I just want to look and learn and be quietly receptive for a very long time, and become integrated in the whole cultural atmosphere of the city and the nation. Above all I hope no one will expect me to come as a kind of celebrity with something to say and a part to play, because that would be very harmful to the whole project. Everything should be done quietly and discreetly, for very many reasons—first of all for my own personal and spiritual good, and secondly for the success and right working of the plan. Because it is very important that no publicity be given to the fact that I have left Gethsemani and the Order, but that even those who know about it should understand it simply as a normal leave of absence. Later when the new venture begins, it will make itself understood on its own terms. Above all nothing must be said about new or special projects, and the worst thing that could happen would be for me to be surrounded by eager inquirers and prospective postulants ready to join a "new Order." That would be fatal . . .

I shall take your advice about wearing plain secular clothes. I don't even want to wear black. If I don't look like a priest, at least I don't want to look like a Jehovah's Witness. But of course it all depends what I can get. The suitcase they gave me, to take to the hospital, fell open in the middle of a street in Louisville and I was scrambling around to put books, shirts etc. back in. It was raining, too . . .

My regards to Dom Gregorio—he will have received the letter from you and one I wrote the last day at the hospital. I still am not sure whether the indult is to be sent to him or to me—or both. The simplest would be, if he gets the original, to send me a photostat. But he doubtless has thought out what he intends to do, and I leave the whole thing in his hands and those of God. When I told the Carmelite Prioress how Dom G. had come here and proposed his plan etc., all unexpectedly, her simple comment was: "He who is sent by God speaks the words of God."

So let us keep up our hope and our desire to serve Him truly and sincerely, devoting our limited and fallible wills to Him with all purity and fidelity of heart. It is not a question of building a great edifice, but of living a simple life and preserving as much as possible of the values we already have found, in experience, here and elsewhere—eliminating as far as possible the great defects and obstacles of a highly organized life. A woman wrote recently to the monks: "We would have expected the Trappists more than anyone else to put Christ back into Christmas, and instead you have put cheese into the Mass" . . .

November 18, 1959

When your letter arrived three, or maybe two weeks ago, Father Abbot made a lot of difficulty about giving it to me, but he eventually did so. There was not much else he could do, since it was a conscience matter letter. I was glad to get it. And I made known to him that I thought such correspondence should not be interfered with. At the same time I told him that I would assure you that he was unfavorable to it. In a word, there is considerable opposition to the correspondence. But still the rights of conscience remain, and if there is something important then I think he is bound to allow a conscience matter letter to pass. He probably will not pass any other kind of letter, that is from you at Cuernavaca.

The other day Rev. Father left quite suddenly for Rome. I have no doubt his journey was intimately connected with the matter which interests me closely. At first I thought he had left of his own volition. Later I realized that he had been summoned to Rome, in actual fact, by the Abbot General [Dom Gabriel Sortais]. No one knows exactly what is the purpose of this journey, but if he was summoned to Rome against his own will, that puts a different complexion on the matter. However, prayers are certainly needed at the moment. I just learned today that Fr. Larraona, the head of the Congregation of the Religious, has been made a Cardinal. That seems to be very good news, as far as I am concerned. I am sure Dom Gregorio will be equally pleased by it.

I was very interested to hear of the progress on the book of poems. New Directions is bringing out a paperback of my *Selected Poems*, almost the same selection but not quite. Mark Van Doren has written a very fine preface. I wonder if you heard about the trouble his son Charles got into. That TV program, on which he won so much money last year, was "rigged" and Charles was an accomplice to the whole thing, which was very unfortunate. I don't think he clearly realized where it would lead, and he was not the most guilty one. Still, there has been a big fuss about it, with a lot of self-righteous speeches by senators on the shame of lying! As if senators were notable for telling the truth.

I am very happy to hear of the wonderful success of Armando Morales and I hope he will keep it up, though success is not the important thing, but the spiritual work of the artist. And I look forward to receiving copies of his illustrations from Mejía Sanchez—they have not yet arrived but I will inquire about them. It is a pleasure to know that [José] Coronel [Urtecho] may be in Mexico soon. Incidentally, Laughlin will probably be stopping here in December. I will be glad to see him.

. . . You certainly have a vocation, but not necessarily a conventional type of vocation. Whether you are actually called to the priesthood cannot be decided without further trial, but the important thing is that you have clearly a vocation to a contemplative life, in a general way, and the only thing that needs to be found out is exactly how or where. And that is not too important because wherever you are you will be tending to the same end. The only problem about the priesthood is whether you can be a priest without getting too involved in an exhausting and time-consuming ministry. That is the question. But for the rest you need have no doubts and no fears. God is with you. Incidentally I am touched by the simplicity and kindness with which you offer your troubles for me. With so many friends praying for me I am sure everything must inevitably go very well with me, and no matter how dark and obstructed things may sometimes appear, I have great confidence that everything will eventually work out well. But there is need for patience . . .

Prayers are the most important thing at the moment. And deep faith. The inertia of conventional religious life is like a deep sleep from which one only awakens from time to time, to realize how deeply he has been sleeping. Then he falls back into it. It is true that God works here also, but there are so many influences to deaden and falsify the interior life. A kind of perpetual danger of sclerosis. The psalms become more and more of a comfort, more and more full of meaning and when one realizes that they do *not* apply to the conventional situation, but to another kind of situation altogether. The psalms are for poor men, or solitary men, or men who suffer: not for liturgical enthusiasts in a comfortable, well-heated choir. I am sure you have greatly enjoyed the work of translating them.

In a couple of days they will dedicate at Washington the immense new shrine of the Blessed Virgin which looks like a big substantial bank. Strictly official architecture, and the thing that strikes me most forcibly is its evident Soviet quality. There is a kind of ironical leveling process that makes Soviet and capitalist materialism more and more alike as time goes on. Who is more bourgeois than Khrushchev? And he made a very "good" impression in the U.S.A., except on the fanatics who refused to see him as one of their own. A successful gangster, who is now affable and a good family man in his declining years . . .

Letterhead: The Brown Hotel,
Louisville
November 24, [1959]

I told Fr. Abbot I would write you a conscience matter letter and did so at Gethsemani but I don't know if it was sent. Do not be misled by the stationery. I have *not* started on the trip. The indult has not yet arrived & I have no news of it. But Father Abbot has *gone to Rome* & is evidently opposing everything with his power. But I also think he has been called to Rome to answer some questions. He may be back this week.

If the indult is coming, it should come about next week. If you do not hear from me soon—say by December 8th—then perhaps there is something wrong. J. Laughlin is coming here in the middle of December & if you write to him he might get it in time to relay information to me. Father Abbot is very difficult about conscience matter letters now, but I still think he will *have to* let one through. Put not only "conscience matter" on the inner envelope but also "sub gravi."

If all goes well I hope to be there before Christmas. I will come by plane, I hope, & will arrive in the evening about 6:30 or 7 & we can go to the University. If you are not at the airport I will go to the University by taxi & ask for Fr. Martínez.

Gethsemani is *terrible*. Tremendous commerce—everybody is going mad with the cheese business. I want to leave very badly.

Today I said Mass for the F[east] of St. John of the Cross at Carmel. The nuns are praying very hard.

My mind is completely made up to totally cut off all ties that attach me here. It is *essential* not just for my own peace but for the glory of God. I must advance in the way He has chosen for me & I am sure He will make everything easy.

My best regards to Dom Gregorio—it is impossible to say all the things I want to say to you & to him. Pray that we may meet soon. I pray to Our Lady of Guadalupe.

I'll send a telegram to Cuernavaca as soon as I am ready to leave & have freedom to do so.

If things get very difficult, I can be reached via Fr. [Jean] Danielou who can always get a conscience matter letter to me but I think yours will still get through—but there may be difficulties.

God bless you all—pray for me. Thanks for offering your suffering.

If things get *very bad*—I will be in Louisville in January for one day & can be reached through the Prioress of the Louisville Carmel . . .

The letter from Rome for which Merton was waiting was sent on December 7 and arrived on December 17. The indult Merton had sought was not granted.

December 17, 1959

Fr. Prior has given me permission to write Dom Gregorio in the absence of Rev. Father and this is my last chance to get a note to you also. As Dom G. will tell you, a letter from Rome has given absolutely final negative decision of my case. Or at least, a decision so final that I am not at liberty to take any further steps on my own behalf, but can only accept and obey. I must stay here until the Church herself places me somewhere else. I still believe that the mercy of God can and perhaps will accomplish this, but I can only wait in darkness and in faith, without making any move. I have hopes that Dom Gregorio will still be able to do something for me. But what?

I think the reason the Congregation swung in favor of Dom James is that he told them a lot of irresponsible remarks about me by Gregory Zilboorg, a famous Freudian psychiatrist who is respected in Rome and has died recently. Zilboorg said of my desire of solitude that I just wanted to get out from under obedience and that if I were allowed a little liberty I would probably run away with a woman. I don't pretend to be an angel, but these remarks of Gregory Zilboorg were passing remarks made without any deep knowledge of me—he had seen me around for a week at a conference at St. John's [University, Collegeville, Minnesota]. We had not had much to do with each other, he never analyzed me, and Fr. [John] Eudes [Bamberger] said that Z. frequently made rash statements on the spur of the moment, which he later changed. Well, anyway, I think that is why Rome rejected my case, for certainly Dom James will have made everything possible out of these statements of Zilboorg. He has probably made enough out of them to queer my reputation in Rome forever. I remember now that you may have seen Zilboorg when he came here—or was that before your time?

I have seen the illustrations of Morales and they are fabulous—I wrote Mejia Sanchez about them. I think Mejía Sanchez will be able to reach me still with correspondence about the poems. I would like half a dozen copies of the book at least, and be sure to send me yours when they appear. Could I have a subscription to the *Revista Mexicana de Literatura* and to the *Revista de la Universidad*? I think they will still get through. Of course there is always Laughlin, if there is something important. He will be down in January. However, as I say, for my own part I can only obey the Congregation and remain passive and I have no hope of making any move to leave this Order. I have in fact promised not to leave, but will only await the action of the Church to move me elsewhere if she sees fit.

So many people have prayed hard for me: their prayers will not be lost. I received the decision of Rome without emotion and without the slightest anger. I accept it completely in faith, and feel a great interior liberty and emptiness in doing so. This acceptance has completely liberated me from Gethsemani, which is to me no longer an obstacle or a prison, and to which I am indifferent, though I will do all in my power to love and help those whom God entrusts to me here. I know we will always be united in prayer, and I assure you of all my affection and of the joy I have had in our association. Do continue to write poetry, or above all continue with your art. Everyone thinks highly of your poetry. Laughlin will probably come and see you some day. I must now get this letter out before Rev. Father returns . . .

Dom James Fox prohibited Merton from corresponding with Cardenal, discounting the claim that Cardenal was in need of Merton's "advice on spiritual matters" (see Michael Mott, The Seven Mountains of Thomas Merton, pp. 339–40). Merton resumed writing to Cardenal in March 1961, though he periodically wondered whether they were "still fully in communication" (for example, see letter to Cardenal, dated December 15, 1965).

March 11, 1961

I have received all the copies of the *Poemas* [Spanish translation of *Selected Poems*] . . .

Personally I want to say once again that I think your translation of the poems was a magnificent and truly creative job. It is seldom that a poet is so fortunate in his translators. Reading the poems again I am once again struck by the fact that they have a life of their own in Spanish, almost as though they were destined to be in Spanish as well as in English, by a kind of nativity or *natura* within themselves. In any case you have found that *natura* and given it expression.

Again the illustrations of Armando Morales are perfect for the book. I agree it is a shame they could not take up the full page in each case, but of course one has to remember the limitations of the ordinary reader and his confusions. The book is very effective even with this limitation. I am glad the three of us could work together to produce this very individual book with all that it says and means. In many ways the pictures are the most powerful and significant part of the book.

I have received the first copy of *El Pez y la Serpiente* which I think is very fine and I am proud to be a part of it. There are great possibilities here. I am sending on to Lax your fine translation of his *Circus* [*The Circus of the Sun*]. Have you seen the whole book? I will get him to send you a copy. It is truly magnificent, a whole cosmic meditation.

Soon *New Directions 17* will finally appear with the poems I have translated, including one of yours. You will see also the dialogue with Suzuki. I will make sure that copies are sent you as soon as they are available.

Much has taken place since you left us. There has been a great deal of work in the renovation of the interior of the monastery. The whole chapter room wing is being renewed from within, new floors and everything. It will be very comfortable. Other wings will be renovated in the same way. It takes time.

For my own part, in strange unforeseen ways I have suddenly found myself in a kind of hermitage. Not that I live there or even sleep there, but I have some time during the day to spend there two or three days out of the week. It is very beautiful [and was] built primarily as a quiet place in which to receive Protestant ministers who come in small groups for retreats, a few times during the year. It is on the hill behind the sheep barn, hidden from the novitiate and the monastery by the pine trees, at the head of the field where the cows used to pasture, looking out over the valley. It is a small white house of cement blocks, very solid and with a fireplace and a nice porch. It is completely quiet and isolated, the only trouble being that I am seldom there. The Abbot General was here and visited the monastery and saw this hermitage which he approved, saying that he felt it was the solution to a problem. Perhaps it may turn out to be so, I hope it will. My chief concern now is to try to arrange things so that I can at least use this house fairly often for contemplation and prayer. My life is one of deepening contradictions and frequent darkness, the chief effect of which is to produce much interior solitude. I try as far as I can to see and do God's will, which certainly leads to solitude. So for the moment this interior solitude is certainly right. I appreciate all your prayers and those of all the others who pray for me. I hope you will not forget me and I know you will not. I remember you often in Mass, with all our friends in Latin America and especially in Nicaragua.

I shall continue to send things for *El Pez y la Serpiente*. They will probably have received by now a small piece on the atomic bomb [which Merton rewrote and published as *Original Child Bomb*] . . .

It was good to hear that your studies were progressing, and I hope that all will go smoothly. Be patient and follow the way of simplicity with which God has blessed you. But things cannot help sometimes being filled with anguish, for all of us who seek to love Christ. Life is never in any way as simple as it ought to be: there are so many conflicts, not between good people and bad only but between the good and the good. This is worse, and produces unending confusion. We must seek peace in the underlying simplicity which is beyond conflict: and here we seek the naked presence of God in apparent nothingness. If only we find Him, the emptiness becomes perfectly full, and the contradictions vanish. But in order to do this we must be faithful to a will that is inscrutable, which does not reveal itself in simple and clear-cut decisions as we would like to think. Rather than try to find all the nuances of meaning and morality in each case, we must seize hold desperately on the first available indication and trust in God for all the rest.

I especially liked the psalm translations in *El Pez y la Serpiente*. They are filled with the true spirit of the Psalter and chanting these versions every day must be a fine experience. I remain united to all of you in prayer, that God may lead us all by His light to Himself.

I have in the hermitage a very small delicate ceramic cross of yours, one of the most primitive and "poor," a Christ of one single narrow line like a neolithic string or worm, *vermis et non homo* yet all the more *homo* because *vermis*. I like it very much.

Merton wrote the following note below the text of "An Elegy for Ernest Hemingway." Hemingway died on July 2 and his death was announced in chapter on July 4.

[No date, 1961]

The death of Hemingway was announced in the monastery. I presume you know about it. If Pablo Antonio wants this poem he is welcome to publish it. Or anyone else you know. I have *rewritten* the piece on the Atomic Bomb [*Original Child Bomb*]. It is longer and more complete &

a few errors have been checked. I will send the new version when it is printed.

The political news from Latin America is bad and confused—or rather it indicates *the* inner confusion of the U.S. Let us hope that the truth can still be found and vindicated . . .

September 11, 1961

It was very good to hear from you, and I am grateful to you for translating the Hemingway poem. It was well presented in the paper and I am glad it is to be reproduced in other publications. It has not yet been printed in the U.S., but I have not been very active about promoting it. The death of Hemingway seemed to me to be a let down (which I indicated in the poem), a final manifestation of the emptiness of his generation. In the poem, the words "unready dynasty" refer to this fact: that the U.S. of the twenties was proud and confident and seemed about to take over the whole world. But when the chance came in 1945 they were not "ready." Hemingway has all along manifested the ambiguities and falsities of this generation, and what followed him is even worse. There was much sincerity there but in the end there was more sham than truth. The great problem of American writers is that they find it easy to attain to a superficial kind of reality simply by setting themselves over against the unreality of the "squares." But this is not enough. It is not sufficient merely to be moons illuminated by the sun of a square society that is almost extinct. Yet that is not true either. There is a lot of disordered animal vigor in the U.S., a huge abundance of it still, rambling and incoherent, discontented, baffled by its own absurdity, and still basically seeking something. I think the search has almost been given up: hence the tragedy of Hemingway, as a sign of the eventual despair of all of them.

Nevertheless there was a solemnity about his death, and about the way he too entered the shades almost as a classic figure in Hades, and passed through our midst by an announcement in the Chapter Room. It was very stirring.

I have been very interested in your translations of the beats and am glad to hear that some of them are visiting you or staying at the monastery. Any poems I have seen of Philip Lamantia lately I have liked. Another ex-novice, poet, since your time (he was a young boy from California, a kind of prodigy) sent some of Lamantia's poems and that was my first acquaintance with him. I don't know if [Lawrence] Ferlinghetti's magazine [*Journal for the Protection of All Beings*] is out yet, with the poem in it. It should be. The Chant ["Chant to Be Used in Processions Around a Site with Furnaces"] was also in *The Catholic Worker* and some Mennonite magazine is picking it up. An English Dominican wants to print it in England, so I guess it will get around as a peace poem. Some people are shocked by it and cannot stand it. I think it is a little difficult for some readers to accept.

I almost wrote a long letter to Pablo Antonio [Cuadra] and think I will do so tomorrow: it will be not only a personal letter but also perhaps a kind of statement of my position in the face of the present situation [published as "A Letter to Pablo Antonio Cuadra concerning Giants"]. And he can use it in his magazine if he wishes. I think it might be worthwhile to attempt this, and it might be of some interest. For my own part I get so impatient with the stupidity and the inexorable descent into confusion that takes place everywhere, especially in the U.S., that I think it is a moral obligation to say something intelligent if I possibly can.

The shocking thing is that the whole world is being pulled this way and that by two enormous powers that are both practically insane and both insane in the same way, with the same paranoid obsession with power, the same fascination with technological expansion, the same vulgarity, the same brutal stupidity and insensitivity to human and spiritual values (although in the U.S. religion is cynically supposed to be blessing the whole system), the same callous addiction to super-myths and the same helpless immersion in materialism. The trouble is that because the U.S. happens to be more inept, more confused, addicted to myths that are more vague and more patently absurd, everyone now begins to respect the other paranoiac because he is more calculating and more efficient. This, in point of fact, only makes him all the worse.

Since beginning this letter I have written the piece I intend to send to Pablo Antonio. It is being typed out now and it will be mimeographed so I can send you a copy. I don't see any necessity for being tragic about the world situation. It is still a war of nerves rather than of bombs, but a war of nerves with bombs. In such a situation one has to remain objective, without however cultivating the fake technological objectivity of the engineers of death, who talk of the extermination of millions as if it were a matter of killing flies. Or those who relish weapons systems the way an aesthete relishes the ballet.

Thank you for sending the interesting books, particularly [Jorge Luis] Borges and Octavio Paz. Also the Indian material and Salomón de la Selva whom I will read with pleasure. I liked your article on the Nicaraguan poets very much and it reminded me that I am still a great admirer of [Alfonso] Cortés: someday I want to translate some of his poems, if you can send me some. I thought you were much too modest about yourself.

I have been in correspondence with a Moslem student of mysticism in Pakistan [Abdul Aziz] who sends very fine letters and interesting books on Sufism, some of which are admirable. I am also working on some versions of parts of the Chinese Taoist Chuang Tzu, without knowing Chinese, but using different translations. John Wu, the Chinese scholar, will come down and help to go over them, and I think we could make an interesting book out of it [The Way of Chuang Tzu]. Also I am doing some versions of parts of Clement of Alexandria [Clement of Alexandria, published in 1962]. Did I send you the little piece on the atomic bomb

[*Original Child Bomb*]? It is coming out with interesting illustrations by Lax's good friend [Emil] Antonucci, who illustrated the *Circus*. Did you get his complete *Circus* book? He was very happy with your translation.

Here are a couple of poems that might interest you. The one on the Moslem angel ["The Moslems' Angel of Death"] is based on an Islamic text, which is splendid and dazzling. I have been very much in contact with Louis Massignon, the scholar most reputed for Islamic studies. Père Danielou was here. Also Dom [Jean] Leclercq. They were very interested in the hermitage. This is still very fine, and the center of my life here . . .

October 14, 1961

. . . The translation of your poems arrived and it is excellent. Would you like me to send it on to J. Laughlin? It would make a fine little book as it stands (I also received the Spanish version which was superb). However I think it may be a little hard to persuade him to publish it immediately. He might want it in the same series of pamphlet-poets as Pablo Antonio, whenever that will be. In any case I hope to write an introduction to it, wherever it is published . . .

There is a very fine new poet, Denise Levertov. I forget whether you translated some of her work or not. She is splendid, one of the most promising. I will try to remember to get New Directions to send you a copy of her new book. You will like her very much. She has lived a bit in Mexico I think.

I have had a very nice letter recently from Carrera Andrade who is now ambassador of Ecuador in Venezuela. I hope I can go on making more translations of Latin American poets. I tried hard to get some copies of some of the poets referred to in the publications that have been sent from down there, but Laughlin does not seem to be able to get most of them in New York. I will look forward to getting something of Cortés from you, and I will translate some of him.

What do you know of the Spanish poets writing now? They do not seem to have as much life, but they are trying to stir themselves into new life, so it would appear. Manuel Mantero has been writing to me a lot and sending his stuff. It seems good, but nowhere near as good as your work and Pablo Antonio's, or that of other writers in Central and South America, especially Octavio Paz.

Lax has printed the "Original Child Bomb" [in *Jubilee*] and Laughlin is making a small book out of it which you will see soon.

. . . We must live always more and more in the purity and light of the Gospel, with simplicity and trust in the God Who has loved us and chosen us. This reality is more and more forgotten, and the state of the world is due to the fact that men have become almost incapable of understanding it. It seems to me that now [President John F.] Kennedy is trying by pressure and force to maintain or encourage a mentality of violence. This is not surprising, and I suppose it is inevitable. But it is very dangerous. However, everything is dangerous. When everything is dangerous one no longer minds much about it, but is free to care for the essentials.

November 20, 1961

. . . Pray for us, we are starting an American Christian Peace Movement. It will be very difficult. We are alas very late! I will write later & send more material that might be of interest.

P.S. Victoria Ocampo wants to use "Letter about Giants" in *Sur*. Do you think there is any objection to this?

Though Merton did not designate any of his letters to Cardenal as "Cold War Letters," the subject matter of the following letter certainly is representative of Merton's thinking during the period between October 1961 and October 1962, when he wrote the one hundred eleven letters that he himself issued in a mimeographed collection entitled Cold War Letters.

December 24, 1961

Though I do not have any definite news yet about the poems, I want to write to you now because Christmas week, as you know, is very busy here. As usual, the novices are decorating the novitiate. We have two very small Christmas trees, and the decorations have been somewhat restrained so far, but there is still one more afternoon and the Lord alone knows what monstrosities will make their appearance during that time.

I sent the small group of poems to Lax at *Jubilee* and have not heard from him about them, but probably there is a letter from him being held up with the Christmas mail, and I will not see it until Tuesday. J. Laughlin has them, but together with another manuscript of mine he has not yet reported. The one thing he has been working on hardest with me, at the moment, has been a paperback anthology of articles on peace [*Breakthrough to Peace*]. This we both feel to be quite urgent, and we are giving it a lot of time and thought, also we want to bring it out without delay. I am sure he will soon have news about your poems, but we must keep after him. It will not hurt for you to write to him again, and I will also remind him. I am meanwhile very interested in the meditations you mention, based on notes you made while here. I think this ought to be a very valuable little book, and Laughlin might want to look at it. Or in any case it ought not to be hard to find a willing publisher.

To *Jubilee* I sent some pictures of Gethsemani that might conceivably go with your poems, I do not know what the issue will be. I have no copies of the Christmas issue which has a short thing of mine ["The General Dance"], but I will send it if I get one, also the book from which it is taken: *New Seeds of Contemplation*.

I was glad to get the magazine with the Spanish version of the "Ox

Mountain Parable," and the other publications that came along at the same time. Cortés has not yet put in his appearance. Is he, by the way, still living and writing? I know you said something about that in your article on the Nicaraguan poets, but I am not sure I remember correctly.

Probably you are now down at Rio San Juan. I think of that often, and of Ometepe. Curious that Corn Island should have been the jumping off place for the abortive Cuban landing.

There is no telling what is to become of the work I have attempted with the Protestant ministers and scholars. Evidently someone has complained to Rome about my doing work that is "not fitting for a contemplative" and there have been notes of disapproval. The contacts will have to be cut down to a minimum. I do not mind very much, personally. I have the hermitage and would rather use it as a hermitage than as a place for retreat conferences. In all this I remain pretty indifferent, as a matter of fact. There are much wider perspectives to be considered. My concept of the Church, my faith in the Church, has been and is being tested and purified: I hope it is being purified. Even my idea of "working for the Church" is being radically changed. I have less and less incentive to take any kind of initiative in promising anything for the immediate visible apostolic purposes of the Church. It is not easy for me to explain what I feel about the movements that proliferate everywhere, and the generosity and zeal that goes into them all. But in the depths of my heart I feel very empty about all that, and there is in me a growing sense that it is all *provisional* and perhaps has very little of the meaning that these zealous promoters attribute to it. So about any contacts I may have had with Protestants. I have had just enough to know how ambiguous it all becomes. The only result has been to leave me with a profound respect and love for these men, and an increased understanding of their spirit. But at the same time I am not sanguine about the chances of a definite "movement" for reunion, and, as I say, I am left with the feeling that the "movement" is not the important thing. As if there were something more hidden and more important, which is also much easier to attain, and is yet beyond the reach of institutional pressures.

I am deeply concerned about peace, and am united in working with other Christians for protest against nuclear war; it is paradoxically what one might call the most small and neglected of "movements" in the whole Church. This also is to me terribly significant. I do not complain, I do not criticize: but I observe with a kind of numb silence the inaction, the passivity, the apparent indifference and incomprehension with which most Catholics, clergy and laity, at least in this country, watch the development of pressure that builds up to a nuclear war. It is as if they had all become lotus-eaters. As if they were under a spell. As if with charmed eyes and ears they saw vaguely, through a comatose fog, the oncoming of their destruction, and were unable to lift a finger to do anything about it. This is an awful sensation. I hope I am not in the same coma. I resist this bad dream with all my force, and at least I can struggle and cry out, with others who have the same awareness.

The thousand and one paradoxes and contradictions inherent in the position of so many Catholics are really confusing and in the end leave one paralyzed. For while insisting with more and more emphasis on "the Church" they also at the very same time emphasize more and more a morality which destroys and dissolves the substance of Christian life and of the Church. Apart from a few token issues which are defended with complete intransigeance, like birth control, sexual morality, etc., the whole trend seems to be toward the supine acceptance of the most secular, the most debased, the most empty of worldly standards. In this case the acceptance of nuclear war. Not only that, but it is glorified as Christian sacrifice, as a crusade, as the way of obedience. So much so that now there are many who insist that one is not a good Christian unless he offers a blind and unresisting obedience to every behest of Caesar. This is to me a complete nightmare. And I realize that I have to be very careful how I protest because otherwise I will be silenced. And no doubt sooner or later I will be silenced. It is very difficult to get articles on peace past the censors.

However, it is consoling that there is at least a minority that is waking up and beginning to react. Mostly among non-Catholics, but also among a few chosen Catholics. Of course, Dorothy Day, and *The Catholic Worker*, whom everybody dismisses with a shrug of the shoulders. But also Father Daniel Berrigan, the Jesuit poet, and some others. I think I told you we are founding a Pax movement. It turns out that the leaders are all in a small circle. Lax, [Ed] Rice, myself, Fr. Berrigan, the *Catholic Worker* people, some other priests, many of whom I already know. And the rest of the clergy? Alas, a great number of them have either joined the John Birch Society, or sympathize with it. So you see what I mean.

Yet fortunately also there was an articulate group within the totality of the American Bishops who gave out a semi-official reproof to this kind of thing and declared that they were opposed to the J. Birchers.

May 16, 1962

A letter which arrived the other day from Fr. García at the Seminary in Managua reminded me that I had not answered your own fine letter from Colombia. I was glad to hear you were in the seminary there, and the place sounds grand: La Ceja, with its good, quiet, primitive people. That is wonderful. Such places are getting fewer and fewer on this earth. It is a grace for you to be there. But I have no doubt at all you will find the seminary life a bit difficult. I am glad the Rector is a good and understanding person. That is most important.

I am glad you liked the books. Alceu Amoroso Lima has written a tremendous preface for the Brazilian edition of *Disputed Questions*. I hope all the good things he says about me are at least half true. But it should help the book very much in Brazil. I knew you would like the "Primitive Spirit of Carmel" ["The Primitive Carmelite Ideal"] and its implications. It has had some effect on the Carmelites in this country who are even starting a project something like what was suggested, but I believe it will soon turn into something different. Who can tell? In this country everything tends to be corrupted by the propaganda methods and the "promotion" that it undergoes. Promotion will end by ruining everything.

The "Letter to Pablo Antonio" has been having quite an effect in various places. It has been translated into German for the magazine *Hochland*, by a German who has gone to live with the Jews in Israel to make reparation for the sins of Hitler. He writes very poignant letters about his love for the young Jews who were in concentration camps when they were children, and their love for him. It appeared in *Sur* (the letter to PA), and I got a nice letter about it from a poetess in Uruguay (Esther de Caceres, I suppose you do not know her. She was a friend of Gabriela Mistral). I also wrote a short notice to be inserted in a volume of homages to Victoria Ocampo ["To Friends of Victoria Ocampo"]. If the Church people do not like her this may upset them a bit, but I don't care. There is too much stupidity and prejudice and plain narrow-mindedness, and it is ruining the Church in many places.

The versions of the peace articles I have sent you are not the best ones, and if you have not had any translations published, it would be best perhaps to correct them by other versions which I will send. "Christian Ethics and Nuclear War" was revised and appears in *Jubilee* as "Religion and the Bomb." I will try to get a copy of this to you soon, but I have no copy even for myself at the moment. I am trying to do a book on peace but I am not sure it will be permitted. I am sending a copy of *The Catholic Worker* with a long article on peace, which is more or less correct except for a couple of misprints. ["We Have to Make Ourselves Heard" was published in *The Catholic Worker* in two parts in May and June 1962.]

Also with New Directions I have done an anthology of articles on nuclear war [*Breakthrough to Peace*] by various authors, [Erich] Fromm, [Lewis] Mumford, etc. etc. It looks very good and I hope it will soon be out, that is in three months or so. Do pray for both these books to do good.

Unfortunately I have not got such good news for your Gethsemani poems [later published as *Gethsemani, Ky.*]. Laughlin does not want to risk bringing them out as a book. They are he feels too slight a collection with which to introduce you and in any case he does not want to publish these poems by themselves. I suppose the most practical thing would be for him to gather into a volume *all* that you have done so far . . .

I have begun to translate some poems of Alfonso Cortés and have even written a little poem about him ["To Alfonso Cortés"]. I will type out some of the translations and the poem and send them all later. For the rest I do not remember if I sent you the poem about the Ladies Jail ["There Has to Be a Jail for Ladies"], but I know you do not yet have the peace prayer ["Prayer for Peace"] which I enclose. It was requested by a Member of Congress [Frank Kowalski] who had been military governor of the prefecture of Hiroshima and who helped the inhabitants there rebuild their city after the war. I have received many touching letters from people interested in peace, especially from some who are interested in the women's peace movement which I think is more important than it looks. Also from a young Quaker who with two others is to sail in a twenty-five foot boat to Christmas Island to protest the renewal of atomic testing.

It is most important that we pray for peace, and detach ourselves more and more from the futile and lying values of the world of men who are moving towards war carried by the momentum of enormous sins and lies. The society of man, particularly in the West, is burdened by a history of infidelity and crime that are enormous, and all we do is excuse and palliate our falsity, trying to blame someone else who is as guilty as we are. We are all guilty, but that means that we must in a very special way avoid the final guilt of violence or of despair. Hence the importance of truly Christian values.

. . . The frequent retreats of Protestants and others keep me unusually busy. The hermitage is fine. I take advantage of it as much as possible. This life takes on a new dimension when one actually has time to begin to meditate! Otherwise it is not really serious, just a series of exercises which one offers up with a pure intention and with the hope that they mean something. That is not what the monastic life is for.

I think often of you. I am very happy at the canonization of St. Martin de Porres. I think often of all my good friends in Latin America, to whom I am so close, and in many ways more close than I am to the people I live with here . . .

May 22, 1962

Yesterday your essay on Alfonso arrived and last evening I read the first few pages. It is most impressive. I will probably add to the poem on Alfonso about which I told you in my letter of a few days ago, on the basis of the extraordinary picture you give of him. I think he is a most absorbing and wonderful figure, in some sense prophetic.

The thing that strikes me most about his poems, and you may yourself have said this in pages which I have not yet reached, is his extraordinary ontological sense, his grasp of objective being. He is much more than a surrealist. Indeed he is the only true surrealist, for instead of going like them to the heart of a subjectivity which is at the same time all real and all unreal, he plunges to the heart of a transobjective subjectivity which is the purely real, and he expresses it in images as original and as eloquent as those of Blake. He is one of the most arresting poets of the twentieth century, and in my opinion certainly one of the very greatest. He really has something to say. I want to work more on his poems, and I will send you the rough drafts. There is a very good new magazine, *Second Coming*, in which I hope to arouse interest in him. Who knows, perhaps after some poems they might print a translation of your essay? We shall see.

I have not received any extra copies of *Jubilee* but as soon as I do I will mail you one by air, for it contains the essay "Religion and the Bomb," a longer and more detailed as well as corrected version of the one you have translated. It is this *Jubilee* version which should be printed. Perhaps you could use the version you have done as a tentative offering to some magazine, and when accepted, do the other version. You could explain that easily enough, or perhaps also show them the other article in English. I would not want you to do the translation twice over without guarantee that it would be printed. But you be the judge.

A Spanish publisher, Editorial Guadarrama, . . . is interested in some of my work. Perhaps you could send them the translations you did of parts of *The Behavior of Titans* and also "The Tower of Babel." Sudamericana is never going to do anything with these works, the people in Spain might: unless you can find someone in Bogotá who is interested. That might be even better, I don't know.

I certainly envy you going to Bogotá, it must be a stimulating place. If you pick up anything interesting in the way of literary magazines, I hope you will send them along to me after you have finished.

There is a great deal of action for peace here, at last, though I do not think it can really affect those who are so deeply involved in the enormous war machine. This is the most fabulous war effort in history and I do not see any chance that it can be carried on at the present rate without ending in a tremendous explosion. The mentality of the people seems to be utterly confused and stupid, they seem to have no grasp on the real nature of the issue or its seriousness. They are prisoners of a completely quantitative view of life and consequently, having no sense either of essence or of existence, are out of touch with reality: and first of all with their own reality. It is a culture of well-fed zombies. May God deliver us from the consequences of all this. And yet too when one sees the earnestness and the integrity of some of those who do speak out, it is very encouraging. Leo Szilard, the atomic scientist, has an interesting peace movement which comes closer than anything else to carrying out the program outlined by the Popes. If I can get my book on peace [*Peace in the Post-Christian Era*] published, I hope to devote at least part of the royalties to that movement. Pray that it may be permitted . . .

August 17, 1962

. . . I have been very busy and have not been able to answer your wonderful letter about the trip to Bogotá. I have always thought of it as an unusually interesting place and there must be plenty of life there. I am eager to see some of the material you have gathered from the poets there . . .

A very fine young Jesuit poet, Daniel Berrigan, has been here for a week, and has given some magnificent talks to the novices. He should be represented in *El Pez y la Serpiente*. He could do some fine things, and he writes excellent articles on the present spiritual and social situation. We are much in agreement about war and so on. He is one of the few who are really alive and awake on all these questions, here. The majority remain asleep.

I have been in contact with Henry Miller. He has written some extraordinary essays recently, especially a book called *The Wisdom of The Heart* from which Pablo Antonio could also extract some really great material.

This is only a note, I must get to other things. I will write more fully later. I still haven't typed the poem about Alfonso Cortés, or the translations. I intend to do a few more translations before typing them all. I have been reading [César] Vallejo again, and hope to translate more of him too.

Here is a poem about a child's drawing of a house ["Grace's House"], and a copy of a letter to Hiroshima [Cold War Letter 98 to The Hon. Shinzo Hamai; see *The Hidden Ground of Love*] which you can publish anywhere if you like. And some *estampitas* . . .

September 16, 1962

. . . I still haven't typed out the poems of Cortés that I have translated. They are here on the desk, but I will try to get to that tomorrow or the day after. They are only a few, and it would not take long, but I am always getting tied up with other jobs, in the limited amount of time I spend here in the office. I try to get to the hermitage every afternoon, now. This is the best thing I can possibly do. All the rest is more or less illusion and waste[d] motion. It grows on me more and more how much the activity we indulge in is really a kind of game of reciprocal delusion: especially when it takes place in a solemn and formal institutional framework in which everything is of the utmost seriousness and is, at the same time, almost incomprehensible. But always serious!

The state of madness in the most developed human societies is, it seems to me, almost incurably grave and acute. The total unreality of the thought and the statements one meets everywhere here is almost unbelievable.

The other day I met a young Spanish Jesuit who is on his way to Ecuador and then to Colombia. He is Father Feliciano Delgado. You will like to meet him. He writes for *Razon y Fe* and other magazines over there.

The publication of a large "Merton Reader" [*A Thomas Merton*

Reader] is well under way. It contains some of the things I am most anxious to say and is fairly complete except that one of my publishers let me down and would not allow the other one to have rights to the material printed by them. But we were able to compensate by digging up articles and essays that were in unusual places and the book may well be all the better for it. I have asked the publisher to send you a copy. It should be out in October.

Also the anthology *Breakthrough to Peace* is out, and I do not know if the publisher has sent you a copy, or if I have. If you do not receive it after a couple of weeks, please let me know.

There are a few "peace candidates" trying desperately to get themselves elected to Congress. Their efforts are significant in the sense that they have *no party* to support them and are being put into the race purely by individual efforts of people who are aroused by the issue, mostly by intellectuals. Their election is of course unlikely, but at least their presence in the campaign has a modicum of meaning. But that is very little, and when one considers the vastness of the issue and the stupidity and truculence of the vast majority of the people, one might well feel a little negative about it all. I hope South America is more intelligent than we are . . .

[No Date, 1962]

Here are the translations of Alfonso [Cortés] that I have done [see *Emblems of a Season of Fury*]. I think I will probably get them in *New Directions 18*, together with a short biographical introduction [see *The Literary Essays of Thomas Merton*].

I hope you will point out any errors & make any suggestions that occur to you. And let me know if you can use more copies. I will send three or four more copies in any case.

Best regards to everyone, especially Pablo Antonio. I keep you all in my prayers & Masses. The world situation becomes more hazardous at every moment because of the incompetence & the irrationality of all men & the subjection of the powerful to the instruments of their power.

May God have mercy on us.

November 17, 1962

Today your package and letter arrived, and I will carry out my intention to write to you finally. You can imagine I have been more and more swamped by correspondence and affairs, but that does not mean I have forgotten all the things I want to tell you.

To begin at the beginning: I am afraid I cannot find copies of your translations in manuscript of "The Tower of Babel," "Signed Confession [of Crimes against the State"], "Atlas [and the Fatman"], etc. They do not seem to be anywhere in the room here and my theory is that I must have sent them to someone [Sr. Thérèse Lentfoehr] who is making a

collection of manuscripts, editions and whatnot. I will write to her and
see. But the trouble is there are several such collections going and I may
have sent the texts to another, for instance the one at the University of
Kentucky . . .

I know this was censored a long time ago, or at least some of it was
censored. "The Tower," I am sure, was censored. I have had a great deal
of trouble with censors. There is a Babel of inscrutable censorships and
reprobations at work in the Order. I have finally resorted to getting things
censored in England when there is any question that they contain anything
more than statements like "It is nice to pray. Good morning Father, have
some holy water. We never eat hot dogs on Friday, etc."

Yes I have received your *Epigrams*: they are magnificent. The Revolutionary Poetry of Nicaragua [*Poesía revolucionaria*] too I have received:
there is much in it that is most deeply moving. I am grateful for your
corrections of the translations of Alfonso, and I have put them into the
text. The poems are to be published in a New Directions anthology but
unfortunately I can see that J. Laughlin is going to waste an enormous
amount of time getting down to business with it. I may give them to some
magazine, and will draw on your very fine article for a biographical
introduction.

Your poems about the Indians have been simply superb. I am sure
your whole book [*Literatura indígena americana: Antología*] will be splendid and look forward to seeing it. You have a very great deal to say and
I know it is most important. This is something far deeper than *indigenismo*
with a political—or religious—hook inside the bait. This is a profound
spiritual witness. Also a reparation, and a deep adoration of the Creator,
an act of humility and love which the whole race of the Christian con-
querors has been putting off and neglecting for centuries. It reminds me
that some day I want to write something about Vasco de Quiroga. I have
not forgotten about the Indians and all that they mean to us both.

I also am studying "cosmic revelation" in a slightly different form:
the philosophers of the 12th century school of Chartres. Splendid and
almost unknown people, they were too far ahead of their time to be
received with unmixed applause and strangely some of their attackers
were Cistercians. But they have a profound sense of symbolism and myth,
together with boldness in rational investigation and a metaphysical sense
which makes them more than Platonists, but forerunners of Aquinas and
of the most solid and spiritual metaphysics of Being. I hope to do some
translations when I can get to the texts, but they are almost unknown,
and still in manuscript. The enclosed poem is inspired by one of their
Glosses on a Pagan Myth ["Gloss on the Sin of Ixion"]. I will also send
you the little book of *Clement of Alexandria* I did, which includes his
exploitation of Greek traditions.

I sent the *Merton Reader* to you in Colombia, but I asked the publishers to send one to Pablo Antonio, so it should be there now. Please

let me know if it has not arrived and then I will send one myself, by air. What is Coronel [Urtecho]'s address? I can send one to him also. I hope you have a wonderful time in Rio San Juan. Please give my best wishes to Pablo Antonio and Coronel, I wish I were there to converse with you all. I must stop now. Pray for Louis Massignon, the great Islam scholar, who just died. He was a great organizer of non-violent action in Paris and also did much for Christian Moslem dialogue.

November 17, 1962

In my other letter I said nothing about the clippings you sent, except in a general way, the remarks about your poems about Indians being based mostly on other things you had sent before. But now I have read the clippings and I want to add a few things. First of all the poem about Bartolomé de Las Casas is most moving, and so is the article about the mystical tree which seems to me to have a deeply prophetic quality. I think you are aware of things that most people are completely oblivious to. I think there may well be a great cataclysm and after it the poorest and humblest people, the Indians, may remain to pray God to pardon and revive the human race: with the Africans. This is only a repetition of what I said in the letter [to Pablo Antonio Cuadra] about Giants, but I say it again.

Your Psalms [*Salmos*] are terrific. Those are the versions we should really be chanting in choir. How few monks think of the real meaning of the Psalms. If priests knew what they were reciting every day. I am sure some of them must realize. Do we have to be in the concentration camp before the truth comes home to us?

Ventana is very alive and appeals to me more than most other "little magazines." Again it has a prophetic quality in it, and a simplicity that is lacking in the more frustrated or the more pretentious publications. I was especially happy to see a new poem of Alfonso Cortés. If that is a madman's poem then I must be mad, because to me it is one of the most lucid and sane poems I have ever read. And again it has that fabulously direct metaphysical intuition that reaches through surface concepts to the very act of being, the actuality of *ens* breaking through the temporal and through our artificially spiritual concepts to manifest itself in its transcendence. I have translated the poem, and perhaps you will tell me if I have it right.

In Pablo Antonio's little book, *ZOO*, I recognized some of the poems I liked before, as well as new ones. I am very grateful to him and will write soon. Did the letter appear in *El Pez y la Serpiente*? I never saw it. Perhaps it is on the way here, or delayed. I have only two issues of *El Pez y la S.*

By the way, thanks for sending the beautiful volume of Eduardo Carranza. Surely you would like me to return it. Tell me where, and I will send it. He is a very perfect poet and his perfection is a delight. The whole book is a delight.

As to politics and the world situation, a little news comes through sometimes and then long periods of silence. The rumors, then more denials, and silence. Yet I wonder if I really know less than those who get the papers. The question is that the world is full of great criminals with enormous power, and they are in a death struggle with each other. It is a huge gang battle, of supremely well-armed and well-organized gangsters, using well-meaning lawyers and policemen and clergymen as their front, controlling papers, means of communication, and enrolling everybody in their armies. What can come of it? Surely not peace. There will be repeated crises, like the last one in which intellectuals fled from the U.S. to Australia and in which the students of Oxford drank up all the old wine in the Union Club because they thought there would not be any more time for drinking anything. The cataclysm will come without giving anyone time to drink up what may be left. It will not be planned by the cleverness of men. And we must pray and be joyful and simple because we do not after all understand most of it. Behind it are good meanings which escape us. But let us avoid false optimism, and approved gestures. And seek truth.

I like the issues of *Nivel*, too. I think José López's poem "Marcan los relojes dolores similares" is an extraordinarily good poem about peace (in *Ventana*). Now I must stop. Who will civilize North America? That is the big question, and perhaps it is being asked too late . . .

February 25, 1963

First of all, I want to say that I have translated a few selections from your *Gethsemani, Ky.* and "Three Epigrams" and I am asking Laughlin to include them in a book of my poems with some other translations. I think he will, and the translations will make the book better. I will also have some of (the same ones of) Pablo Antonio, Carrera Andrade, Vallejo, Alfonso Cortés and Raïssa Maritain. The rest of the book will include my own new poems, "Hagia Sophia" and the "Letter to Pablo Antonio." So you see you will all be involved in a book that will almost be a collaboration. I hope it will turn out very well. The title is "Emblems of a Season of Fury." The Cortés translations will also be printed by Laughlin, he says, in *ND 18*. But as usual he is very slow about that.

I received two copies of *El Pez y la Serpiente* with the "Letter to Pablo Antonio" and also the more recent issue. Your translations of American poets were very fine. I have also sent some material to your friends at *El Corno Emplumado*.

Yes, I know Lanza Del Vasto. There was a Jewish student of mysticism here who had visited the Community of L del V and spoke highly of it. I have also read what I think is his most interesting book, *Le pélérinage aux sources* (i.e. to the sources of the Ganges). He is great friends with Victoria

Ocampo. I have read parts of the "4 Plagues" and it is terrific. I have also read fine articles of his in peace publications. Talking of Victoria Ocampo: her friends got up a volume of Testimonios for her, and I was included: they put my name as "Thomas Merton S.J." . . .

Did I ever send you the translations I did from Raïssa Maritain? She has done some very remarkable things (of course she is dead now) and there might be place for some of them in *El Pez*. You could write to Jacques Maritain for her two books of poems, I think he would be glad to send them for translation purposes. He is at Faculté de Théologie, Fraternité, Ave Lacordaire, Toulouse, Hte Garonne, France. He teaches philosophy to the Little Brothers of C[harles] de Foucauld. Is happy there, and wrote me a couple of marvelous letters, especially about "Hagia Sophia" which he liked very much. Raïssa has done a Journal, or rather she kept one which is to be published and it is amazing. She was one of the great contemplatives of our time.

. . . Though I have been quite busy, I see more and more that the dimension of my life that has meaning is the solitary one, which cannot be expressed. There are things which can and must be communicated but it is an error to attach too much importance to them. I think it is really a waste of time for me to write more books on "the spiritual life" in the usual sense of the word. I have done enough already. And at the same time it seems futile to write about the way the world is going: yet it is true there are times when one must speak. But one must be sure of the necessity. James Baldwin has written several terrific books about the race situation in this country . . .

Here are a couple of new poems: and under separate cover I am sending the new, enlarged (mimeographed) edition of *Cold War Letters*, to La Ceja [seminary in Colombia where Cardenal was studying for the priesthood]. With that also a translation of a letter of "Guigo the Carthusian." Did you ever read his meditations? Tremendous . . .

Holy Week
April 8, [1963]

Thanks for your last letter with the fine new poems of Alfonso. They seem to me to be among his best, and not the easiest to translate either.

The *Sewanee Review* has taken two of my translations of his poems, and another ("Truth") with my poem about him will be in a new magazine called *Continuum*. In the same issue will be my translations of your Gethsemani and epigrams. I did not have time to make the correction, and am sorry for the error. I will have to do something about it in the book, when it comes at the end of the year.

Jubilee printed my translations of Raïssa Maritain. I hope Jacques has sent you her books. She is a fine poet.

Here are some things that might interest you. The piece on Zen [published as "The Zen Revival" in *Continuum*] will be revised a little, but it is all right as it stands, I think. It can be developed further.

This is only a hasty note. More after Easter.

To the above, Merton added, by way of postscript, the addresses of Fr. Dan Berrigan and Bro. Antoninus [William Everson].

May 29, 1963

Thank you for your letter and for the excellent new poem: when will all these poems be out in book form? When I have the book, I will perhaps translate a few of them. They are really splendid.

I am enclosing sheets from the magazine *Continuum* with my translations of your other poems, unfortunately not corrected. I was not sure they were going to publish these, so I only corrected the copies I sent to New Directions for the book. The book will be called *Emblems of a Season of Fury* and it is appearing this fall. I think it will be quite good, and besides all my new poems and translations, it will include the "Letter to Pablo Antonio."

Somebody ought to write an article on the Christian Democrat Movement in South America for *Continuum*. I have asked them to send you copies of the magazine. You may think of someone well qualified to do it. You ought to do an article on contemporary Latin America poetry for them. The Editor is Justus G. Lawler . . . Why don't you write to him about this? I think he would be very interested. As to the article on Christian Democrats, maybe Napoleon Chow would know the best one to do this. He wrote to me about his course at Bogotá, and said he had visited you. He spoke of *Ventana*, and thought that perhaps he and a few other Catholic writers ought to stay with it, because if they withdrew the whole thing might fall completely into the hands of Communists. I think it is important that Catholics, at least some of them, do not adopt a policy of withdrawal. For religious and clergy it is perhaps different. We do have to be circumspect. But at the same time certain of the laity ought to be able to go far in their own sphere. I think one of the weaknesses of the Church that the Cuba situation brought out was the fact that as soon as things got to be a little hot, and the Communists became aggressive, the Catholics became negative, adopted a condemnatory stance and assumed that all attempts to go on collaborating with Castro were an infidelity as long as he did not openly repudiate Communism. This had the result that the Church became identified with the policy of the U.S. State Department and the results were fatal.

However that may be, I think that *Continuum* needs someone sending live information from Latin America and I hope you will get in touch with Lawler . . .

This is really just a hurried note: but please pray for me during

Pentecost week, I have received permission to make a retreat at the hermitage and I hope it will not be interrupted, but will be fruitful . . .

August 1, 1963

I think you know Cintio Vitier, in Cuba . . . He is not sure whether our letters are getting through, and neither am I. I have just sent the letter of which the enclosed is a copy. You might drop him a line and ask him if he received it, and if not you can send him the copy. If mail is not getting through directly, I thought we might send things through some other country, for instance Colombia.

Thanks for the *Colombiano literario*, with the translation of the "Letter to Pablo Antonio," and its fabulous presentation. I am very happy about it. Thanks especially for your magnificent essays on the creation narrative of the Huitotos. That is really a wonderful field for you, and I am sure you will continue to find things there that will be of the greatest importance for all of us. Someday America (North, Central and South) will perhaps be the great living unity that it was meant to be and that it now is not. That will not be possible if it tries to be the rootless culture that it now is: a sort of cancerous orchid transplanted from somewhere else . . .

[No date, 1963]

Your letter of Sept. 15 arrived while I was in the hospital, and more recently the box of magazines has come, for which I am most grateful. I was not in the hospital for anything too serious, just the results of an old spine injury.

Yesterday I received one copy of the new book of mine, from New Directions: *Emblems of a Season of Fury*. It is the one including the translations from your poems, Alfonso, Pablo Antonio etc. ND will surely be sending you a copy, but if they do not, please let me know. I was distressed to see that somehow that mistake in one of your epigrams had got into the book. I had meant to correct my translation, and was sure I had done so. I am positive that I sent them a correct translation, to replace the earlier incorrect one. But then the mistake got by me in the proofs. I am very sorry . . .

I am sending you John Wu's translation of the *Tao Te Ching*. The same place has published a translation of an important Chinese Zen work, the *Platform Sutra* of Hui Neng, but unfortunately the translation, though probably good in its own right, uses terminology that misses the real Zen meaning and does not correspond to the kind of language used by the best Zen men, like Suzuki. At least there should be some agreement on terms. I have written a long article on Zen, in fact I think I sent you an earlier version, but I have rewritten it for *Continuum* ['The Zen Revival']. I hope Lawler has been in touch with you. But if not, it is because the magazine turns out to be more political than literary. I told a new magazine

[*Charlatan*] edited by a Protestant group at the University of Iowa to get in touch with you; I have sent them some notes on Julien Green ["To Each His Darkness: Notes on a Novel of Julien Green"] and also some abstract sketches of mine. I forget whether I have sent any of these abstractions to Pablo A. but he might like them for *El Pez*.

I received a letter from Cintio and wrote him a longish letter, sending also a packet of poems, in October. I don't know if he received them. I was wondering if perhaps a series of three large envelopes from the U.S. might have caused him trouble. He told me also, guardedly, that things were not as good as they were painted in Cuba and indicated that it is really a Stalinist absolutism they have there. This is a very great shame. It can be said that the future of the world depends in large measure upon the quality of the social reform, let us say revolution, that is effected in Latin America. It is the weakness of very poor and underdeveloped countries to have to swing into a rigid absolutism dominated by force in order to maintain a certain stability in social change, and this defeats itself. Everything depends on education and leadership, and on the capacity of the intellectuals for creative and independent development, and the great danger is that men will be lacking who can measure up to the greatness of the task. I certainly hope and pray that the Church may be able to provide an impetus for creative thinking, but the task is gigantic.

Did the magazine *Ramparts* send you the issue with my long article on the Negro problem here ["The Black Revolution: Letter to a White Liberal"]? Recently I have played in the novitiate some excellent tape recordings of interviews with the Negro leaders, including Martin Luther King and Malcolm X of the Black Muslims. Their talks were very impressive. How did you like [James] Baldwin?

The [Vatican] Council seems to have been going well. The general impression is that the second session is "not exciting" but I would certainly say that the decision on the collegiality of bishops is one of the most important things done by the Church in the last five hundred years. It can have a tremendous meaning. Also, if lay deacons (even married) are allowed, this can be of tremendous significance, especially in Latin America.

I look forward to seeing your book on Indian religion. I think this is really a very important project, and coming just at the right time it can have a decisive effect, both spiritual and cultural, throughout Latin America. I hope it will do so. The book I showed you here was *The Sacred Pipe* by Black Elk, and I think it was published by the U. of Oklahoma Press. I went looking for it just now but could not locate it anywhere. You know how books disappear here. It was a very fine book, anyway, and I am sure it should not be hard to obtain.

Well, I will put the art ms. ["Art and Worship," unpublished ms.] and several other things in an envelope for you, and hope it will all get there safely. I have been doing a lot of studying on St. Anselm, and

Sartre, finding rather surprising affinities between them. This is not what anyone would have expected. I am also reading Nicholas of Cusa, a very great mind and a most original thinker of the fifteenth century, who has been very much underestimated. A mystic and "apophatic" theologian, he also foreshadowed the kind of relativity that we have since [Albert] Einstein, insisting that the universe had no center and no limits: this long before Copernicus and Galileo. He was a Cardinal and no one made any difficulties for him because they did not understand what he was talking about . . .

November 23, 1963

Your letter arrived just after I had sent one to you at La Ceja. Perhaps it will be forwarded to Nicaragua, perhaps not. It does not really matter. I am very happy to hear of your visit to the Cuna Indians on San Blas Islands. I remember my friend Dona Eaton used to talk about them: she came from Panama. I don't remember much of what she said, but the name "San Blas Islands" made a lasting impression. Your two articles were superb. I am sure the interview will be most important, and your visit even more so. The more time you spend with them the better. I think indeed that this is really an important aspect of your vocation, and that rather than becoming purely and simply a conventional priest, you should think in terms of this strange kind of mission in which you will bring to the Church knowledge of these peoples and spiritualities she has so far never understood. This has been a factor in the lives of the greatest missionaries, however: to enter into the thought of primitive peoples and to live that thought and spirit as Christians, thus bringing the spirituality of these peoples into the light of Christ where, indeed, it was from the start without anyone realizing the fact . . .

The Abbot General [Dom Gabriel Sortais] died last week, and now [President John F.] Kennedy has been killed. It was a shock to hear the news yesterday and we are not quite clear what happened or who was behind it. But in any case, it was, like all such things, purely senseless and pointless. Kennedy was a good man and a competent President. He was not able to carry out his best ideas, but he still tried to move in the right direction, though sometimes he found himself going the wrong way perhaps. But I am very sorry over this senseless act, so pointless and purposeless, and so needlessly cruel . . .

March 10, 1964

I was glad to get your letter and your new piece, the "Letter to an Indigena Paez," which is simply magnificent, most moving. I liked very much too your splendid interview with *Yabilinguina* and in fact I gave a resumé of it to the novices here and they were all very much moved. In fact many of the young professed brothers were present also, as I have them now in conferences too. The pictures of the San Blas people are fine, most beautiful.

Miguel Grinberg is here, and I am very happy to meet him. His meeting in Mexico sounds like a very great thing, certainly the Spirit is moving through South America and Latin America generally, and this movement of poets and artists toward a new spiritual consciousness is certainly the most hopeful thing that I have seen in the world lately: and God knows there is not much that offers any real hope apart from charismatic things like this. We simply cannot look to the established powers and structures at the moment for any kind of constructive and living activity. It is all dead, ossified, corrupt, stinking, full of lies and hypocrisy, and even when a few people seriously mean well they are so deep in the corruption and inertia that are everywhere that they can accomplish nothing that does not stink of dishonesty and death. All of it is rooted in the cynical greed for power and money which invades everything and corrupts everything. But Miguel and the poets have shown a genuine integrity and love which are sane and hopeful in the extreme, particularly because the same longing for life and truth is manifesting itself everywhere at the same time and independently. I hope that the great awakening of South America is at last about to begin, for the future belongs to South America, Africa and Asia: but above all I think to South America. If only the great sense of love and solidarity and human strength can totally take roots and the masses of the people, particularly the indigenous people, may attain full consciousness of the meaning and strength of their presence. You will have a very significant part in this, and I hope that at least by my prayers I will also. I was touched that you mentioned me in your letter.

I say the future belongs to South America: and I believe it. It will belong to North America too, but only on one condition: that the United States becomes able to learn from South and Latin America and listen to the voice that has so long been ignored (a voice which even ignores itself and which must awaken to its own significance), which is a voice of the Andes and of the Amazon (not the voice of the cities, which alone is heard, and is comparatively raucous and false). There is much to be done and much to pray for.

I am happy that you and Coronel [Urtecho] want to do a special anthology and I enclose a copy of the letter I sent to Sudamericana about rights to the material in their books. This may be difficult if they refuse, but if they publish the book themselves there should be no difficulty, but you should keep after them . . .

I will send Coronel *New Seeds* and other things that might be of use to him, and I will put in an envelope some new things of mine for you. I still do not have the good copy of "Art and Worship" back from the censors, but I will send it as soon as I can.

My health is fairly good, I have a permanent injury to one of the vertebrae of my neck but with care I can avoid too much trouble with it.

I do not want to have to have an operation which might do more harm than good. I think I can live with it all right.

It has been good to have Grinberg here and to hear about the new poets everywhere. I am going to try to keep more in touch with these things, for it is here that one finds, I think, some of the most authentic and honest spiritual life in the world of our time. In the monasteries there is still simplicity and joy among some of the monks but the structure is so false and artificial that one has a hard time keeping serious about it, and it is often very discouraging . . .

May 8, 1964

A letter from Coronel tells me that you and he are getting down to the project of translations for a kind of Reader. I sent him a lot of material, perhaps too much, and my own feeling is that the book should not be too long. On the other hand as it quite probably will be done by Guadarrama, I suppose it should be representative. A lot of the books have not come to be known in Spain. I leave that all to your judgment and his. For my own part I like the recent works best. Here is an article on Gandhi that might be interesting. It is terribly important now to keep the concept of non-violence alive. What is happening is that in the race movement in the U.S. the non-violent tactics are being discredited because the gains that were made have been taken back and nullified. Restaurants have quietly segregated themselves again, etc. Token concessions were made, and then everything went back as before. This is a very serious situation because now violence is going to begin, slowly, sporadically, but the situation will get definitively rotten and I see no alternative. Perhaps in the long run this is the only way that the realities can be brought out and kept in full view. People do not want to see them. This is a very unrealistic country.

The fact remains that a non-violent political ethic is terribly important everywhere. I read Colombia Macheteada in *El Corno*. If we cannot get things organized it is going to be something like that everywhere. And it is totally senseless. But the senselessness of physical violence is necessary, perhaps, to manifest the senselessness of economic and cultural violence. And the basic violence of a life without God, without silence, without prayer, without thought.

New Directions will do a small book on Gandhi, consisting of selections I made and a long introduction ["Gandhi and the One-Eyed Giant"]. If it gets by the censors it ought to be fairly useful. I hope it will.

I have been a little ill with a bad back resulting from old injuries, but it is nothing serious, simply a nuisance that I have to live with . . . I get a lot of time in the hermitage that is now on the hill behind the sheep barn, and am planning to write less, perhaps. There have been meetings of Protestants here often, but I do not want to overdo this. A group of Hibakusha, or survivors of the atomic attack on Hiroshima, will stop here next week. They are touring the world on a peace mission. I think the outlook for world peace is better at the moment, at least as regards nuclear war with Russia. On the other hand, affairs like that in Vietnam are very bad indeed and the mentality of the military people and industrialists in this country remains very unhealthy and dangerous. If tensions are less, it is not due to anyone in particular here, though [President Lyndon B.] Johnson seems good in this regard and Kennedy made a serious attempt to follow up Pope John [XXIII]'s encyclical [*Pacem in Terris*]. I think that the split between Russia and China has done a lot temporarily to make things better, but in the long run who can say whether this will turn out better or worse? . . .

May God be with you. Let us trust Him and He will not fail us, nor will He fail mankind, which belongs to Him.

July 12, 1964

It is a long time since I have written and I do not remember whether I answered yours of May 16th. Perhaps not. I have been reading wonderful things of yours . . . I liked Rafael Squirru's little book on the New Man [*The Challenge of the New Man*]. Have you seen it? It is very right. The usual thing we have all been thinking, but which is not yet known or understood enough. The need for admitting to hearing the voice of the new man who is rooted in the American earth (not just in the American machinery), especially the earth of South America. It is first of all important to listen to the silence of the Indian and to admit to hearing all that has not been said for five hundred years. The salvation of our lives depends on it. The things you wrote about the San Blas Indians were marvelous. There is no doubt that you have a providential task in this work of understanding and love, a profound work of spiritual reconciliation, of atonement. It is wonderful to realize the full dimension of our priestly calling in the hemisphere. Not the ridiculous and confused activities based on meaningless presuppositions, but the activity of true atonement, a redemptive and healing work, that begins with *hearing*. We begin already to heal those to whom we listen. The confusion, hatred, violence, misinformation, blindness of whole populations come from having no one to hear them. Hence they speak with knives, as the Negroes are now doing, for all that has been heard about them is still not them.

Alfonso Callejas was here. He offered us again a hacienda at Chinandega, but I told him it was impossible. Fr. Abbot was not here. I am convinced that a foundation on the usual Gethsemani pattern would be impossible. The foundation of Spencer in Argentina is miserable. A whole monastery has been built, everything is there except monks. They have about seven I think. If I made a "foundation" it would be without foundations and almost without a roof, but with enough of silence and aloneness to think and pray. The great problem would be avoiding publicity and yet being in contact with those who should know and come. But it is really no problem.

He made other proposals which I thought were very intelligent and with which I could not but agree. I wonder if they will come to anything. Perhaps he will discuss them with you. He seems a practical person. What he tells me of your own ideas seems sound. You should not get involved in too much activity but leave yourself time to write, and that remains a problem. However, I am thankful that I have as much time here as I have. Things are going well with me, and the hermitage is a real blessing for which I am most grateful. Since I have had it I have been able to give up worrying about the deficiencies and limits of monasticism and simply live with God in my own way. After all, that is the basis of monasticism anyway . . .

September 26, 1964

James Anderson, editor of *Charlatan*, wants me to relay to you the information that he is accepting "En el monasterio trapense" for number 2 or 3, and he has lost your address. I am glad he has taken something of yours. I hope many others in Latin America will send him things. Did you see the first issue? Some good things in it, but mixed. I had some drawings (abstract) along with an article on Julien Green ["To Each His Darkness: Notes on a Novel of Julien Green"]. Did I ever send you this? Tell me, and I will do so if I did not . . .

The abstract drawings I did for *Charlatan* were the beginning of a flood of "abstract calligraphies." I have done scores of them, and in fact some are being framed and will be exhibited in Louisville this fall, perhaps also elsewhere. I sent a few to Pablo Antonio, and Coronel mentioned having seen them. You saw some that were not very good in *El Corno* . . .

Have been reading [Fernando] Pessoa, in Spanish and Portuguese (thanks for sending the [Octavio] Paz translations) and he is a real discovery. I like him very much and may attempt some translations for New Directions. I think I told you I had read some Pessoa to Suzuki and he was delighted with it.

Here everything is as usual except there is some hope of progress toward a serious eremitical colony annexed to the monastery in the lonely hills several miles away. I am very anxious for this, and pray for it ardently. You know how much it could mean: do please keep it in your prayers too. When is your ordination? I think of you often and ask God to bless you and your days to come, as a priest . . .

December 24, 1964

It is Christmas eve, and I don't know when I will have time to do anything after Christmas, so I want to write you this note now to say that in case you come to America next year, I have received permission from

Rev. Father to get together with you, if you are here, for a day. You may of course stay longer but he has restricted his permission to one day, as far as my talking with you is concerned. I hope you come. There are a lot of things to talk over . . .

José Coronel wrote a good letter which I hope to answer early after Christmas if I can.

This fall I exhibited some of those abstract drawings in Louisville and it was quite successful. The exhibition will go to New Orleans in January, I think, and perhaps to other cities also. It will be in Catholic colleges mostly, as far as I know. It might be an idea to put a few in the anthology. They are black and white and would reproduce very easily and cheaply.

Things are quite quiet in the monastery. There are only eleven novices altogether, choir and brothers, and I have them both. Last year one hundred and nine were interviewed but out of these only three were accepted and came. One of these left. Some others might be coming later though, they have been delayed. Prospects of a South American foundation are almost nil, but there might eventually be one in Norway, as we now have a Cistercian bishop in Oslo.

I hope you will be able to get to Cuba. I think it would be a very good thing. If you go, please tell Cintio Vitier that I got the poems he and Roberto Friol sent and [I] wrote back, but he must not have got my answer. I wrote to him again the other day, just a note. I would be interested to know if he got it. The new book [*Seeds of Destruction*] is out and I am sending a copy to you. As I may have told you, I managed to get most of the better material on peace into it after all.

The ending of the Council session was very ambiguous and as a result the Protestants in this country have become once again quite dubious about the Church. They see that many bishops want more openness and liberty but they feel that the Pope [Paul VI] is on the side of an entrenched minority and I wonder if this is not perhaps quite true. The Pope does some very encouraging things, but one finds that he later tends to cancel them out and neutralize them by other acts or statements that are very conservative. Hence I suppose that we must be patient with a period of transition in which everything will still tend to be quite equivocal. The Church badly needs the prayers of all of us . . .

February 8, 1965

The other day I was very happy to get a letter from you, but when I looked inside I found my own letter to you, which you must have put in the envelope by mistake. Presumably you were answering me about your trip here, and when to expect you. But I have not received the information, so please write me about it again. Meanwhile I suppose you may be in Cuba. I hope you are, and that you are seeing Cintio and giving him my regards. I am sure you can do a great deal of good simply by being present among so many other poets.

It is true that not all the "progressive" thought and action in the Catholic world makes perfect sense at the moment. There has been a kind of spring thaw and all the rivers are running mightily, but some of them are just carrying away good ground, and trees, and things that need to stay where they are. I think we have to have the courage to distinguish and to use a certain amount of prudence and above all not simply make a virtue out of condemning everything in sight, while putting nothing of any value in its place. And all that is new is not necessarily an improvement. However, I do think that a great deal that is going on is most salutary and what the Council has done so far is excellent. I do not say all this in reference to your going to Cuba. I think that perhaps there has not been enough in this direction of dialogue with the left, which can and should be at the same time quite serious, perfectly clear in its definition as Catholic (without useless and foolish compromises) and yet a valid human communication.

The piece about the *ejercicios* was very encouraging and I was happy with it, happy to see the picture of so many friends, and you looking happy in the middle of it. I also very much like Coronel's translation of my poem on solitude . . .

In early March, Merton wrote to Pablo Antonio Cuadra, expressing concern "that Rome is making inquiries about Ernesto and that these might possibly affect his ordination." [See letter to Cuadra, dated March 2, 1965.]

April 24, 1965

Thanks for your letter. I am relieved that there is nothing behind that inquiry from the Sacred Congregation. I am surprised that no such request had come in before this, in my ten years as novice master. There must surely have been other former novices ordained somewhere. But perhaps they were handled without reference to me. At the same time, I think it is possible that you might expect some time or other to be criticized for your work, especially on the Indians. Perhaps I am wrong, but I know from experience that one cannot write anything alive without being attacked, and sometimes quite fiercely, by members of the Church. Certainly the most virulent attacks on any work of mine have come from priests and religious, though for the time being they seem to have calmed down and accepted me as an inevitable phenomenon.

I think I owe José Coronel a letter, but I am sure that the book [*Reader*] is coming along well. I was most touched by the letter he last wrote about it, saying how much he had entered into the material and how much it meant to him. I send you some more material, some of the newer things which you probably have not seen.

Actually I am living most of the time in the hermitage in the woods, sometimes eighteen hours out of the twenty-four, only coming down to the monastery for strict necessities and work in the novitiate. It is a wonderful life. Actually it has transformed me, and I am now at last convinced that I have found what I have always been looking for. Provided that it goes on this way.

I have been in contact with Ludovico Silva. The poets in Caracas impress me, and there seem to be some lively publishers there. I wrote a preface to Ludovico's poem on the bomb ["Prólogo" to *BOOM!!!: Poema*]: I very much liked your "Apocalypse, in illo tempore," in *El Corno*. Your pieces on the San Blas Indians have been great, too . . .

May 10, 1965

Thanks for your letter. I was able to get the photograph without trouble or delay and I hope it reaches you safely. I was especially glad to hear the good news, and I will keep you in my prayers as your ordination approaches. I think in fact that this is a great grace for you and for the Church in Latin America and I am especially glad to know that your work is appreciated. I am afraid that I myself come in contact with so many retarded and suspicious types, especially within the Order which is French and rigid, that I am prepared to see danger for everyone else. But certainly I for my own part have an immense amount of trouble trying to say anything at all that diverges from what is absolutely familiar. I think my higher superiors would not be content unless I confined myself to the statements made in the Catechism, copying them verbatim. Then all would be "safe"; as a matter of fact, what I am doing now is availing myself of a clause in the censorship statute of the Order which says that short pieces published in "small magazines" do not need to be censored. They do not say how small the magazine has to be, but the tendency of the chief American censor is to treat most magazines of a literary character as "small," which in fact they usually are. Thus I am able to breathe a little more freely and say some of the things I think need to be said, without having to go through an *auto da fé* each time.

There is no question that you have a very clear vocation to understand and interpret the religious riches of pre-Columbian America and of the traditions which have still survived from that hidden past. You are perfectly equipped for it and will do immense good. I also think that your foundation will be something quite providential and will be greatly blessed. Would that some day I might be able to see it, but as long as Dom James is abbot this will be impossible as he has a veritable phobia about my being out of the monastery for any reason, except to see the doctor in Louisville. He is now away at the General Chapter and will also go to Norway where he will probably make a foundation. I have personally little interest in this foundation and know he will not even think of sending me . . . However, with the monumental stupidity of Johnson's foreign policies and the crass ignorance of the State Department, I would just as soon not be a member of an American Trappist group in a foreign country at the moment. In our life there are enough troubles without having to try to explain to other people why America continues to exist. Or how. The nonsense in Vietnam is a piece of irreparable folly and even if Johnson gets away with it as he hopes to, he cannot profit by it seriously, and this country has nothing to gain by it except the knowledge of its own iniquity and stupidity. I hope it will gain at least that, but I doubt it.

I have had some kind letters from Doña Olga Elena in Medellín and I like her poems. She sent a picture of the whole family which is delightful.

August 15, 1965

Today, the day of your ordination, I am especially thinking of you, and as we concelebrate at the High Mass this morning, I will keep you most especially in my offering. May the Lord truly bless your priesthood and all your priestly work, especially all the splendid inspirations that have come to you. May they all bear fruit. They will certainly not do so without much difficulty, but it is certainly happy that a new spirit of understanding and originality is breathing in the Church, and even some of the most conservative elements are forced to recognize it and adjust to it. I am sure that the coming years will be very creative and that prophetic initiatives may be very evident. I expect there will also be a crisis in certain quarters, particularly where there has been much unenlightened conservatism. In such places the transition will be painful. We are going along fairly well here, fortunately . . .

This week I will finally be able to leave the job in the novitiate. Fr. Baldwin is taking it over, and I have received permission to live entirely in the hermitage, coming down to the monastery only once a day to say Mass and have one meal. This is a great step forward. I have in fact been sleeping there and spending most of my time there since last year, and have in fact had as much solitude as one would ordinarily have, say, in the Camaldolese. I find that it suits me perfectly, as far as my vocation is concerned, though I am not a solitary by nature at all. Only grace can make a real hermit of me, but I feel very strongly the exigency of grace in this matter. It is now an imperative demand which I cannot ignore, and indeed I would fear for my soul if I ignored it. I have no desire to do so in any case. The only slight problem is presented by health, but I trust in your prayers and in those of my friends to enable me to overcome this obstacle. My health should be good enough in any case to enable me to live the life well, but it may be difficult to do some of the manual work and chores that I will have to do, as I have a bad back. But the Lord will provide.

I often think what wonderful things have happened in the six years since you left. Your life has been blessed, your vocation is truly from God in a most evident way. He may let you feel your own limitations, but the might of His Spirit will also be evident in your life. Do not fear, but be like a child in His arms, and you will accomplish much for your country.

November 17, 1965

Here are the pictures of your crucifix. I think they are likely to make very good reproductions. I am sending them along, though I am not sure whether or not you are yet back in Nicaragua. I wonder how you made out in New Mexico. You must have found some very interesting things there.

Things are going along quietly here, though I am having trouble with my stomach. It is perhaps just worn out. My publisher (Doubleday) is coming down to talk over the book I have finished [*Conjectures of a Guilty Bystander*]. My editor thinks it is one of the best I have written and so, oddly enough, does one of the censors of the Order. That is a good sign. It is the long notebook, the big book, of which a part was in *New Blackfriars*.

Things are curiously disturbing in the peace movement here. I wonder if there is any real communication between the two opposing sides in this country. Things will continue to be difficult and obscure. All day long I hear the guns of Fort Knox. In some quarters there is a real war fever, a desire for war, in the hope that it will give life more meaning and people more identity. The old illusion. Probably this is something incurable and we have to face the fact that we live in a very dangerous world. Faith only is the answer, and we must grow always in the purity of faith, otherwise all will be ever greater confusion.

This is only a note to accompany the pictures. I will write more after I hear from you, and if I can get time to work on the "Directory" [see letter to Cardenal, Feb. 5, 1966].

December 15, 1965

I am writing you this letter from Louisville because I am not sure if we are still fully in communication—have you written to me? I am wondering if Fr. Abbot is stopping your mail as I have received nothing.

Lately I have had a great deal of stomach trouble and a bad attack of dysentery. I have been to see the doctor and his opinion is that it would be unwise for me to go to a tropical climate. However, I do not make this a reason for changing my decision. But I want you to know that if things are as they are now, I will probably not come.

The best thing would be for you to write to James Laughlin in April or May, at New Directions, & I will ask him to come down here in June & I will give him my definite decision then, and he can send it to you.

It seems to me that if my stomach is no better than it is now, I should not come, as this would not work out. I will therefore try to let you know in June at the latest.

I hope everything is going well. I will write the preface & "Directory" early in 1966.

Apart from the stomach everything goes well here.

All the best to all of you.

January 8, 1966

Many thanks for your letter and card. I was impressed by all your good words on Solentiname and I am sure there could be no better place in that part of the world. It is certainly providential and ideal, and as far as I am concerned I think we must go ahead as planned and do everything that is required, leaving all the rest to divine Providence. However there are some things to be taken into account, and because of these I think that probably we should be a little more flexible about the *time* of the petition to Rome. At present my feeling is that it should be put off until 1967. I will set down the various things that are on my mind.

As to the question of health: I do not know how important it is. Certainly I am much better now and I can hope for further improvement. Certainly, too, if I am completely cured it will be another sign of God's will. Let us then pray for that. But the fact remains that medically my condition is more or less irreversible (though I can live with it) and I am above all very vulnerable to everything like dysentery, and this is much more easy to contract in Central and South America, especially as I am not used to conditions there and would perhaps have difficulty in adapting to some things which you take as a matter of course. However, as I say, that is not the most important thing and if God wills, it can prove no obstacle.

One great point is that from the point of view of the Church it would be ideal if the Abbot gave his permission. Of course as we know this is hardly to be expected as things are at present. But there is a strong possibility that after the Norway foundation Dom James will retire and with his successor, whoever he may be, I anticipate no real difficulty. In any case, I think that it would be essential for you before petitioning Rome, to make a formal request to whoever is Superior here. Then you can say to Rome that you have made this request in due form, it has been refused etc. But it would be worthwhile to wait and see how the wind blows after the Norway foundation, which I expect in the spring of this year. Naturally it would take a little time for the foundation to get settled, but at least it would be worthwhile seeing what Dom J's ideas for his own future might be. This ought to be taken into consideration. For this I think it would be most practical to wait about a year after the Norway foundation. If this foundation is delayed, then we can reconsider that.

I think also it would be an advantage for you yourself to get off to a good start before I come, and meanwhile we could still freely correspond about the problems and difficulties that presented themselves and this in itself would be a good preparation for the task. I would be able to come with my mind more prepared for what would be there. I would not have to readjust a lot of purely imaginary preconceptions.

Two other things which I have on my mind and which are perhaps not real problems, but I must nevertheless work them out. First there is the ambiguity in the fact that I am a North American. I know that I am not a typical North American and that I disagree with much that is typically U.S. and because of this precisely I would be able to say things that would be welcome to everyone there. But I do not want to be in any sense whatever a kind of occult cultural ambassador for this society, and I cannot help being so in some involuntary sense. Again, this may not be a serious problem, but I must think it out. Finally there is also the difficulty, for me, that you all there have too high an opinion of me, and you have tended to think of me as much more than I am, with too high expectations of me, and I may unconsciously come with a false idea of myself, or try to measure up to expectations I should not think of, and so on. This is something I must think about for myself.

With all these things in mind, I think it is important that I have time to really get into the hermit life that I have here. I am only just beginning, and I am after four or five months just seeing the way that must be followed. With a new, more silent and more deep life here, these questions will slowly take shape and answer themselves and at the same time the health problem will probably be solved. Thus I think that what we need is to give this all time to mature. I conclude then that it would probably be best to put off the petition until 1967 some time, about a year after the Norway foundation, and the first step would be to write to whoever is Superior here asking him to release me to go to Nicaragua on a six-month permission, after which I could get the regular permission from Rome according to the usual routine. If he refuses then you take the petition to the Pope. Meanwhile we will see what happens.

I am taking advantage of a visit to Ed Rice to get this to you. Laughlin may be down here earlier than I thought. He may come in April. Best to write to him before the end of March.

All blessings. I am glad that your own health is under control. I hear the Bishop has let you go to Solentiname by now, or will soon. I will write more in the regular course of events.

Pray for me, and I keep you and the project in my prayers always.

January 18, 1966

I want to send off this note to you before the retreat begins (this evening). Thanks for your card & message . . .

My stomach is much better, but I still have to take care of it. However I am not concerned about it.

I am happy to hear that the situation at Solentiname is so good & I hope you will be able to go ahead with your plans. In fact I hope the Bishop has let you start by now. Naturally I keep all this in my prayers

& beg God to bless all your hopes. And I am sure He will in good time.

Did you ever find out what happened to the people at Guadarrama in Madrid? I have no news from my agent either. I do not know precisely what will happen to my book in Spanish. Who is publishing your *Vida en el amor*? It is really excellent—in some ways equal to Teilhard de Chardin even better, since he was only half a poet . . .

February 5, 1966

First I want to thank you for the coffee which arrived safely. It is really excellent and I like it better than the Columbian coffee I had. Then I want to send you the preface which I have finally written. I hope it is not too long and too philosophical. Still I thought it was worthwhile to write something besides a few conventional words of introduction. Also I sent you an article which appeared in Louisville. I will get to work on the little directory I promised to write for Solentiname later on, perhaps during Lent. I want very much to write it but I have had other things to do. As you will see from the article I want to get away from comment on passing events and write something more fundamental and more monastic. As I am also writing a few poems I enclose them too. It will be a big package and I hope it reaches you safely.

Above all I hope you are now in Solentiname and beginning with your work. However, you must be patient of all delays. God's providence provides these for very special reasons and He wants everything to work out in His own time, which is mysterious to us. When we look back however we find that His plan made everything come out much better than it otherwise would have. So I hope that He will indicate His will to you and bring all your plans to perfection in His own way and in His time. I am still eager to be of assistance to you in any way that I can, and, as I say, I will begin by writing the Directory. Meanwhile I am very eager to hear whether you have begun and to learn how things are going. Any news you send will be helpful in considering the kind of advice I can write for the Directory. I have received a letter from José and will write to him soon . . .

There has been much snow here and it is quite cold, but my wood fire keeps everything pretty warm and I am much happier with it than with the steam heat in the community . . .

P. S. Bishop [Fulton J.] Sheen was here & since he has charge of sending money to the Missions I gave your name & address. He may help you. I hope so.

Holy Saturday
[April 9, 1966]

I am just getting out of the hospital today after a major operation on the back. I think it was completely successful & the Doctors are pleased with their results, & due to the prayers of so many good friends I think the recovery has been very good. It remains to be seen how I will function in the future.

At the monastery things are the same. The Norway foundation is not yet made and I am not sure when it will be. It is publicly known that after the Norway foundation is settled Dom James intends to retire into solitude—but there is no way of telling how long that will be. In any case whoever his successor is, one can expect more liberal ideas. Any universal initiative in regard to Latin America, even with the most exalted recommendations, will probably be impossible as long as Dom James is Abbot. He was at one moment thinking of taking over the Spencer foundation in Chile & he might conceivably decide to do this. I am not sure . . .

July 3, 1966

It was fine to get your letter and to see the fine photos of Solentiname. You really have an ideal place for a small community and everything points to the fact that you will do very well indeed. Naturally beginnings are slow but it is quite possible that before long you may have more vocations than you will know what to do with. For that reason it is good to get organized and get your life going well. I certainly like your situation, it looks wonderful, and I am sure your plans will be blessed.

Your circular letter was excellent, and you can certainly use any material of mine you like in it. I will try to get busy and send you some monastic notes for your use there and they may also be useful for the Bulletin. But I still have not got down to all the work I had accumulated since the operation. At this season of the year I have visitors more often and all last week was shot, practically, because I spent the day with people who came. I hope however to get down to writing again and to get these distractions out of the way.

You will be interested in the important news that Gethsemani is taking over the Spencer foundation in Chile. This is important because it now means that Gethsemani is engaged in work in Latin America. Some monks are going down in August and others in October. I do not think I am likely to be sent there but anything may happen. However, I do not expect to be sent. It is obvious that Dom James believes that my place is here and that he will not consider letting me go elsewhere.

I am glad to hear that you are getting the financial support you need. For a small and poor community like yours, these little gifts are important, whereas for a big Gethsemani foundation that would hardly be a drop in the bucket. You are fortunate in your poverty, which will be blessed.

I shall pray that you may lay down firm foundations for your future monastic life on Solentiname . . .

I heard from Pablo Antonio after he had been there and must write to him when I can. As to the anthology, I am glad it is nearly finished . . .

It will probably be some time before you go to Rome to get approval. Perhaps it would be worthwhile to come here for a talk about your progress before you do that . . .

October 14, 1966

I received your letter only the other day, so it took an unusually long time to reach me. I want to reply as soon as I can so as not to let it go, because if I put it aside I may not get to it again for many weeks. I am having a hard time keeping up with letters—as you too probably are.

The news of your progress in building etc. sounds very good indeed. From the way you describe it, your little place is exactly what is needed and will be certainly blessed, indeed already is. The fact that there are only two of you means nothing: on the contrary it will be very good to go for some time without others so that you can cement a firm foundation for the future between you. I shall certainly keep praying.

In such a small community as Solentiname, I mean as regards to the *campesinos*, I think there is very little danger for you in accepting the office of pastor. The Bishop understands fully the nature of your vocation and of your situation and he is not imposing on you something that he intends to be contrary to it. You can certainly carry out the minimal functions of pastor without threat to your monastic charism, but combining the two. But of course it must be purely spiritual: a question of sharing in the Word of God and the Eucharist, baptizing and helping the dying, but not any of the bureaucratic routines of parish organization—except of course the essential records. I think that if you accept this in simplicity and let the people understand what you are doing, you could have a very beautiful community of the poor around the monastery and in a sort of spiritual relationship with it, which would be much more fruitful than an ordinary parish, and could really develop into something in the future. In other words it is a chance to experiment. I would say that the remoteness and simplicity of the place would make this safe and fruitful. I would dare to have great hopes: as long as a spurious activism does not get mixed up in it. Later on when the community grows, someone else could have the work of administering the sacraments to the people and teaching them.

The only problem would, as I see it, arise when the next Bishop comes in. Then he would have you in his grasp and might decide to impose a whole new concept of your duties upon you. That is the only problem and I would talk to your bishop about it and maybe get some kind of agreement on paper.

I have been going on as usual. Lately there have been a few visitors, including Jacques Maritain last week. He was very happy to be here and I was in my turn very happy to have some good talks with him. Fr. Dan Berrigan was also here. Still active in the peace movement but there is a sort of despair everywhere since it is obvious that Johnson knows he is now in a position of dictatorial power and refuses to listen to anyone who does not agree with his war policy. The situation is extremely bad and the prospects of a very large war in Asia are not unreal at all. Here is where prayers are urgently needed. I know the U.S. will get little or no support anywhere else in the world, and it is a great folly for Johnson to ignore the opinions of the best minds and most civilized people that are still left around, the Pope first of all . . .

January 2, 1967

Happy New Year. What is new? I am sending a couple of things you might be interested in. I just got a note from Alfonso Cortés's sister who imagines that I might be there for the [Rubén] Darío centenary but naturally this is totally out of the question. I have had some interesting visits here, including Jacques Maritain in the fall. Joan Baez the folksinger was here. She is running an institute for the study of non-violence in California, which in a way is quite "monastic." She is a fine person. If she comes down your way I shall make sure that she comes to see you.

You probably know that Suzuki died last summer. I forget if I sent you the little piece I wrote about him ["D. T. Suzuki: The Man and His Work"]. I have done several articles on Camus, but I think they must have been sent to you. Napolean Chow was here also, about Thanksgiving. I fully intend to write to Pablo Antonio and to send him some articles when I have time. I will also send you the *New Directions Annual*. I was glad to see your translations of Laughlin in the little magazine from Venezuela. He brought Nicanor Parra here last May, we had a very good visit. I hear occasionally from Cintio Vitier in Cuba.

There is not much news: I continue to live happily and fairly quietly in the woods. Did you receive the two new books that appeared in 1966, *Raids on the Unspeakable* and *Conjectures of a Guilty Bystander*? I think I sent the first but probably not the second. Please let me know and you shall have them.

I have been doing some work on Faulkner, and his novella "The Bear" has a lot of interesting symbolic material which can be used to illustrate the ascent of the spiritual life, and I have given some conferences on it here, in that sense. Perhaps I will write something about it if I get time.

My health is fair enough, though I have a bad arm that requires occasional treatment, but the back is holding up fairly well. Some monks from here went to Chile to take over the Spencer foundation. The monasteries of the Order in this country are not in such good shape as they were ten years ago and there is some likelihood that some of them will close. Gethsemani is still a fairly large community, but I wonder what it will be like ten years from now? The Church is now being entirely re-modeled. But the community will not fill it any more.

It is strange to think that it is almost ten years since you came here! Time has certainly gone very quickly . . .

You have all my best wishes and prayers for the New Year. Pray for me. I hope you will gradually get a few more to help you there and to share your peace.

March 11, 1967

Already some time has gone by since I received your letter. I have had to go to the hospital again, this time only for a minor operation, but on returning I can no longer find your letter to answer it in detail. But I remember its contents and am disturbed. The news you send is not good: but then news everywhere is bad today when things are in such crisis everywhere, and everywhere violence threatens.

Basically our first duty today is to human truth in its existential reality, and this sooner or later brings us into confrontation with system and power which seek to overwhelm truth for the sake of particular interests, perhaps rationalized as ideals. Sooner or later this human duty presents itself in a form of crisis that cannot be evaded. At such a time it is very good, almost essential, to have at one's side others with a similar determination, and one can then be guided by a common inspiration and a communion in truth. Here true strength can be found. A completely isolated witness is much more difficult and dangerous. In the end that too may become necessary. But in any case we know that our only ultimate strength is in the Lord and in His Spirit, and faith must make us depend entirely on His will and providence. One must then truly be detached and free in order not to be held and impeded by anything secondary or irrelevant. Which is another way of saying that poverty also is our strength.

The coffee has arrived and it is much appreciated. Unfortunately the letter that came with it is lost. I would like to have the address of the firm and the people who sent it, so that I may thank them personally.

Everything goes quite well here, though I have a lot of minor difficulties on all sides. But they do not matter. It may become impossible to send out mimeographed texts since I am almost entirely unable to get secretarial help here. I translated a poem of [Rafael] Alberti's on Rome ["Roman Nocturne"] (will send a copy) and the pious little monk who mimeographed it said it was immoral, and showed great reluctance to help me with more work. All this is amusing. I may perhaps write a book on Camus, and I would appreciate prayers for help in this undertaking. I hope you have received the articles I sent on him.

Let us be united in prayer and confidence. More and more I see that there is no hope whatever but in God. Everything else fails us completely.

July 28, [1967]

Yesterday's copy of the German edition of your Psalms [English translation, *The Psalms of Struggle and Liberation*, published in 1971] came in, and reminded me that it is a very long time since I wrote to you. The translation seems to me very good and I liked the "Postface" which I thought was understanding and will do you a lot of good with German readers. I wanted previously to interest Hans Urs von Balthasar in your work, and sent him [Stefan] Baciu's article about you in German, but don't know what he thought about it.

I also owe Pablo Antonio a letter of thanks for the big article of N. Chow in *La Prensa*. But I guess we are all in the same boat with correspondence: it is simply impossible to keep up, and the business of long complicated letters gets to be more and more absurd . . .

I am still living in the hermitage and like it better and better all the time. It is quiet enough. Sometimes I get too many visitors, but I think it is necessary to keep up contacts, especially on the ecumenical level, and some interesting people have been here. I am glad not to be too much involved in what goes on in the community. Many changes have been made and I do not know whether or not they are improvements. I am not convinced that big-institution monasticism such as we have here has a real future. I do not say that it is bad, but it is just confused, too big, lacks real cohesion and spirit, and leaves a lot of individuals just hopelessly running around looking for something—they don't know what. The superiors meanwhile are desperately trying to come up with a magic answer that will ensure survival. Many people have left and few are coming. I think that the atmosphere of great uncertainty and questioning (which is necessary now) makes things too unstable for people to settle down in a monastery. They need to feel they are in possession of something solid and permanent, in order to commit themselves to it. There are of course other kinds of monastic commitment, a sort of readiness for change and movement: but in that case one cannot expect to keep up much of an institution. One must be free. That is your advantage. You may or may not have companions, but if you have no one it does not really matter. In due time Solentiname will be something very definite in monasticism: but until then it may be very small and perhaps almost nothing. That is not bad at all. But for Gethsemani—that would be a disaster. Hence one must not build institutions that invite disaster so easily! . . .

March 15, 1968

Many thanks for your letter of the 5th. I think there must be something wrong with the mail. I am sure I sent you those two books. However, I will send other copies, and the new one also, *Cables to the Ace*. I am also running a magazine [*Monks Pond*] temporarily—four or five issues only. A copy will be on the way to you. I want to translate some of your

"Psalms." I can't find a copy here, though I know there must be one around. Do you have an extra one? Please send me one if you have one available. I will use a few "Psalms" in the magazine before it closes down. [None of Cardenal's "Psalms" appeared in *Monks Pond.*]

Yes, we have a new Abbot [Flavian Burns]. But if you mean by Gethsemani-Nicaragua project a new foundation, I think that is completely out of the question. I do not think there will be any more Gethsemani foundations. As you know we took over the Spencer foundation in Chile. I asked to be sent there in order to be in Latin America, but the permission was refused. However, I do think it will be possible for Fr. Flavian to let me come to visit you for a time and to study the situation. Not right away, because since Dom James is still living here, as a hermit, Fr. Flavian has to take him into account and is a little afraid of him. Please write and tell me what is the best time to come. When is the dry season? If possible, I might come at the end of this year and spend at least a few weeks with you. There are very many reasons why I want to leave this country, and yet for those same reasons I think I ought to stay. It seems wrong to escape the immense rottenness, the evil, the judgment, that are inevitable here. Do you know that some fanatical Catholics in Louisville have burned my books, declaring me an atheist because I am opposed to the Vietnam war? It is completely incredible. This country is mad with hatred, frustration, stupidity, confusion. That there should be such ignorance and stupidity in a civilized land is just incomprehensible.

On the other hand, I would be ashamed to be in a Latin American country and to be known as a North American.

But in any case, apart from all these ideas one way or the other, it is necessary to see whether or not God really wants me there. In so many ways this seems to be the place for me, here. But I want to come to Solentiname and see what it is like, see if it seems to be where God wants me, though I rather doubt it. For one thing, I believe I would be a kind of tourist attraction, and would have to be seeing people all the time. It is bad enough here. But there is some protection.

If I were to leave here, I would want to disappear completely and go where I was not known at all, and cease to have any kind of public existence whatever.

I think the idea of William Agudelo [Colombian poet] living there with his wife is just tremendous. I think that the whole future of monasticism depends on some broadening of perspectives like this . . .

July 21, 1968

I have been meaning for a long time to write you a decent letter. There are several reasons for the delay. The chief of these is that much is happening here and I have many plans for the end of the year. But nothing is fully certain yet. I am going to Japan and then to Thailand where there is a meeting of Asian Catholic Abbots. I also have to preach a retreat at the Cistercian monastery in Java. After that I am not sure what I will be able to do. If I can get the money and the contacts I hope by some miracle to get to Nepal in the Himalayas—and then see what happens. Burma also is another possibility—but again a quasi miracle will be required.

If these do not work out it is possible that I may get to Nicaragua for a few weeks with you. In any case, wherever I go, I want to have a hidden and quiet time of retreat after the traveling. One thing is certain, that I need real solitude and I need to get away from the constant pressure of visitors and more or less superficial demands in the matter of work; articles, commentary, prefaces, etc. Where I am here at Gethsemani, I am too well known and too accessible.

Fr. Flavian our new abbot is very fine. He has spontaneously suggested that I form a small hermit colony in California or somewhere hidden (it would be in an isolated part of the Northern California coast). Much depends on his finding the place, and on it remaining really hidden!! I wonder if Northern California is really likely to fill the requirements. But I also wonder about Nicaragua: I am too well known there also. But in any case, if I do not go further into Asia I think I will spend a few weeks at least with you, if God grants it. But I make no firm promise. I do hope very much to go to Nepal. It would be marvelous.

But also in any event I hope to come to Solentiname. I will keep in touch with you and let you know. I should go to Japan early in November and if I do not go to Nepal or Burma, should fly back early in January. Though something else might happen to delay me—I might stay longer in Indonesia. In any case I do not have to be back at Gethsemani too soon, and my plans are flexible. Please pray that God may guide me.

I have a very definite feeling that a new horizon is opening up and I do not quite know what it is. If it is something in Asia then I will need very special grace. My secret hope is to go to the Himalayas. But I do not insist on any desire of my own. If it is clearly God's will for me to settle in Nicaragua or in California, I ask only to see it clearly and to do it faithfully.

Since my Abbot of his own volition is planning a hermitage in California and wants to entrust it to me, this does take first priority, I think. But we'll see what comes of it. In any event I hope to see you either in Jan. 1969 or the following year.

Your *Mayapan* [long poem] is fine. I am doing some things like that now in a poem. I'll send you bits when they are published. William's latest poems in *El Corno* are magnificent, strong, rugged, impressive, clean.

I very much want to see you all again. I want to get out of this country. The atmosphere is stifling and very sick. Perhaps by a miracle [Eugene] McCarthy might get elected—the people are for him, vested interests and established power against him. If he is not elected I will find it difficult to return here!! This will become a police state in all reality.

I promise faithfully this time to send you some books. Sorry to have been so negligent about that.

IV

*"I have many friends all over the hemisphere in whom
I think there is great hope of awakening and of life."*
MERTON TO MIGUEL GRINBERG,
JUNE 21, 1963

To Alceu Amoroso Lima

*The distinguished Brazilian scholar and teacher Alceu Amoroso Lima (1893–1983)
was a prolific writer, with widely ranging interests in literature, philosophy,
religion, sociology, economics, and politics. He wrote more than eighty books and
countless essays as well as a weekly newspaper column, at times using the pseudonym Tristão de Athayde. Like Merton, Amoroso Lima converted to Roman
Catholicism as a young man and became a champion of social justice, defending
human rights and decrying tyranny and oppression.*

*One of Merton's earliest personal contacts in Latin America, Amoroso Lima
visited Merton at Gethsemani in 1951. His admiration for Merton was deep, and,
together with Sr. Emmanuel de Souza e Silva, Amoroso Lima did much to make
Merton's work known in Brazil, writing introductions for Portuguese translations
of several of Merton's early writings and translating many later ones, including*
Breakthrough to Peace, Seeds of Destruction, *and* The Way of Chuang Tzu.

The following letter was selected by Merton for publication in Seeds of
Destruction *in 1964.*

[Cold War Letter 3]

[November 1961]

It was a great pleasure to receive your letter, and above all, do not
apologize for writing to me in Portuguese. Dom Teodoro, from São Bente
in São Paulo, who made his novitiate here under me, taught me the
language after his profession here (Fr. Bede) and I enjoy very much
reading it, though it would probably be impossible for me to write it very
coherently. It is a language I delight in, and it has really become the one
I like best. It is to me a warm and glowing language, one of the most
human of tongues, richly expressive and in its own way innocent. Perhaps
I say this speaking subjectively, not having read all that may have enlightened me in some other sense. But it seems to me that Portuguese
has never yet been used for such barbarities as German, English, French

or Spanish. And I love the poems of Manuel Bandeira and Carlos Drummond de Andrade and several others. I like them and read them all.

Now as to the topic of your letter, I believe it is very important that we exchange ideas from time to time. This is a crucial and perhaps calamitous moment in history, a moment in which reason and understanding threaten to be swallowed up, even if man himself manages to survive. It is certainly an age in which Christianity is vanishing into an area of shadows and uncertainty, from the human point of view. It is all very well for me to meditate on these things in the shelter of the monastery: but there are times when this shelter itself is deceptive. Everything is deceptive today. And grains of error planted innocently in a well-kept greenhouse can become giant poisonous trees.

Everything healthy, everything certain, everything holy, if we can find such things, they all need to be emphasized and articulated. For this it is necessary that there be communication between the hearts and minds of men, communication and not the noise of slogans or the repetition of clichés. Communication is becoming more and more difficult, and when speech is in danger of perishing or being perverted in the amplified noises of beasts, perhaps it becomes obligatory for a monk to try to speak. There is therefore it seems to me every reason why we should attempt to cry out to one another and comfort one another, insofar as this may be possible, with the truth of Christ and also with the truth of humanism and reason. For faith cannot be preserved if reason goes under, and the Church cannot survive if man is destroyed: that is to say if his humanity is utterly debased and mechanized, while he himself remains on earth as the instrument of enormous and unidentified forces like those which press us inexorably to the brink of cataclysmic war.

Yes, we should try to understand [Fidel] Castro together. This is a significant and portentous phenomenon, and it has many aspects. Not the least, of course, is the fact that Castro is now about to become a figure with a hundred heads all over Latin America. One aspect of it that I see is the embitterment and disillusionment of the well-intentioned man who was weak and passionate and easily abused: perhaps mentally sick. The man who like all of us wanted to find a third way, and was immediately swallowed up by one of the two giants that stand over all of us. The United States could have helped him and could indeed have saved him: but missed its chance. Castro remains not as a knife pointed at the U.S. but as a big question mark in the very foundations of North America's "democracy." I do not know if I sent you the letter about Giants ["A Letter to Pablo Antonio Cuadra concerning Giants"], but perhaps I did. It may be on a boat somewhere. You will tell me what you think.

It is indeed supremely necessary for us to try to think together a little of the Church in the Americas. This is an enormous obligation. There is much activity but not so much thought, and in any case the activity may have come late. I do not know what I can contribute, but the issue has been close to my heart for several years. I have thought much of it and prayed much also.

As for yourself, tell me anything you want, and I will reply as I can: but perhaps the mere fact that I will listen to you with all my heart may itself be of some help. We are all nearing the end of our work. The night is falling upon us, and we find ourselves without the serenity and fulfillment that were the lot of our fathers. I do not think this is necessarily a sign that anything is lacking, but rather is to be taken as a greater incentive to trust more fully in the mercy of God, and to advance further into His mystery. Our faith can no longer serve merely as a happiness pill. It has to be the Cross and the Resurrection of Christ. And this it will be, for all of us who so desire.

To Esther de Cáceres

Through her critical work, Esther de Cáceres has illuminated the work of her contemporaries in the Latin American literary world, including Gabriela Mistral and Susana Soca. As poet and philosopher, she has given voice to the Latin American experience. Among her many published works are Canción *(1931),* Libro de la soledad *(1933),* Los cielos *(1935),* Concierto de amor *(1944), and* Tiempo y abismo *(1965).*

January 9, 1965

Thank you for sending your very sensitive and moving study of Susana Soca ["Introduccíon a la lectura de Susana Soca"]. It is beautifully done and I am reading it with much interest. More than interest, for it is rare that one can share in the spiritual climate of one so simple, so solitary and so pure. There is no question that she reminds me of Raïssa [Maritain] in many ways. But she has a special quality all her own. I have never yet had a moment to translate some of her poems, and I would not want to do this in a rush. Precisely, it would have to be a new creation emerging from communion in the same silence. I am sure that some day I will have a chance, but now my work is still too much involved in hammering, and sometimes it appears to be a hammering of swords. The critical race situation in this country has kept us all in an atmosphere of combat. However I do have plenty of silence and solitude, but that is for its own sake and for the Lord, not for work, and more hammering.

Have you heard from Jacques [Maritain] lately? I know he was in this country, and of course he could not come all the way out here. I suppose that by now he is back in Toulouse with the Little Brothers.

I am sending you a piece of writing that is *not* hammered out ["Rain and Rhinoceros"]. Perhaps you will enjoy it. It represents the climate in which I am interested, rain and silence, and the forest. Fortunately I have more of this now . . .

January 15, 1966

I was very happy to get your advent letter and your book *Tiempo y abismo* which I enjoyed thoroughly, your praise of earth and of the senses—and your struggle with time. I still have to fight a bit with time myself when it comes to writing letters, but for the rest I am now living in solitude and strictly taking three to four hours a day for meditation, besides reading and studying. And I try to keep up with writing (I will send you some recent essays). I have also sent you a book of texts based on the Chinese philosopher Chuang Tzu [*The Way of Chuang Tzu*], a new departure. You will see how it strikes you. It is of course not a translation, but based on translations. Perhaps it will help people to know and love him (the translations we have so far are obscure).

Not only do I owe you a letter for a long time, but Jacques Maritain also, and I must write to him soon. But if you write sooner please tell him I am thinking of him and will write.

There is still quite a load of work that I have promised, but later in the year perhaps I will at last be free to try a few translations of Susana Soca. It will be a joy to share in her clarity and tranquillity.

I am glad that you continue bravely with Thomist studies when now everywhere the fashion is to run after new things that may or may not make sense. Perhaps in a way it is better now that St. Thomas is out of fashion: those who read him will be serious instead of merely partisan. Meanwhile I have been reading much of Jacques and Raïssa: what a blessing they have been for our time. One realizes it more clearly now. Let us keep united in prayer and in peace, and in the light of the Lord's truth.

To Napolean Chow

Napolean Chow belonged to the circle of Nicaraguan poets that included Ernesto Cardenal, Pablo Antonio Cuadra, Angel Martínez, José Coronel Urtecho, and others, who together formed a new literary movement. In his letters to Chow, Merton reflects on the place of the Christian writer and intellectual in the contemporary world.

December 26, 1962

Thank you for your letters and for the copies of the magazines. I particularly like *Ventana*, and I am very glad to establish contact with you. I presume you read English, hence I do not write in Spanish this time as I can move faster in English and perhaps be a bit more articulate.

As Ernesto [Cardenal] can tell you, I am necessarily a rather irregular correspondent. There is usually a tidal wave of mail here, and I have a tendency to leave the most interesting letters until a time when I can give them "more thought," which sometimes results in their being forgotten. Or in other cases it just becomes impossible to answer. Hence I depend on the patience and compassion of my correspondents.

You know from Ernesto and Pablo Antonio Cuadra, how sympathetic I am to the literary movement in Nicaragua. It is to me a joy, through these friends, to find myself close to the movement and in a certain sense part of it. As a matter of fact, it seems to me that I fit more naturally into Latin American culture than into that of North America: I certainly find no "movement" or group in this country with which I can begin to consider myself affiliated. On the contrary, I am here something of a solitary figure, both among Catholics and among writers. I have the impression that though quite a few people read me, not all are comfortable with me and most do not quite know where to place me. This is as it should be, because one does not want to fit into a neat category, especially in this land of commerce and commercial methods, of public relations, and statistics drawn up with a view to manipulating the consumer-public. I am definitely not a harmonious part of this society: but the fact that I can be considered a part of it at all is testimony to the fact that there does still remain at least a minimum of freedom and the power to speak one's own mind, even though what one says is not always acceptable.

This, it seems to me, is likely to be the place of the Christian writer and intellectual everywhere in the world. I think we have to be very careful of our honesty and our refusal to be swept away by large groups, into monolithic systems. We have to guard and defend our eccentricity, even when we are reminded that it is an expendable luxury, a self-indulgence. It is not, and those who try to make us yield our right to think as we see fit, secretly suffer and are ashamed when we yield to their enticements or to their pressures. Even though they have no other way of praising us than by taking us so seriously that they silence us, this itself is the witness we have to bear to truth.

I do not know what the situation really is in Latin America today. But I do know the lamentable state of misunderstanding, ignorance, fatal self-deception and obtuseness that may one day prove ruinous for this very powerful and intellectually feeble country. The inability to read the signs of the times, and to foretell the political weather one day ahead, is of course due to the fixation upon profit and to the system of organized and mammoth irresponsibility which passes for "freedom." On the other hand, the tyranny of the rigid and artificial system, and even greater obtuseness and dogmatism of the rival superstition, is in itself even more gross and ruinous: except for the fact that there are signs of all kinds of salutary reaction and disillusionment within the system itself. I look with hope to the sophisticated and revisionist thinkers on that side. But above all I still think there is a great deal of intellectual independence and creativity that remains unrecognized in Latin America. There is a truly great potential for thought and for creative writing, and there is no question that this must seek its full fruitfulness in a great movement of social renovation and growth. I think *Mater et Magistra* [Pope John XXIII's encyclical, promulgated in 1961] lays down tremendous principles for this, and I hope the hierarchy will apply these principles: but that is not enough. We cannot wait passively for Bishops to initiate action that should come from the laity and is long overdue.

I wish, then, through you to send a message of solidarity and friendship to the young writers of Nicaragua, and to encourage them in their creative work. I am not for my part discouraged by the necessary and inevitable divisions, or by the need for dialogue which these divisions create. On the other hand I am not overoptimistic about the possibilities of achievement through exchanges of ideas with groups that are dedicated to one fixed idea and which really have no intention of "exchanging" ideas. Yet I think we must cling to a higher wisdom which sees possibilities of communication even where this is explicitly rejected and denied. This will be possible if we do not attach too much importance to our own "power" to convince others or to make them agree with us. What is important is that all should agree with the truth, or at least that all should admit the existence of a truth which is not the exclusive property of a political party. It should be noted that in human affairs the Church does not claim to define practical truth at every step, but only to lay down principles of ethics and justice which are universal and which all must use to seek a truth that belongs to all.

May 14, 1963

I appreciated your long letter very much. You are right, the really significant events of Latin America are seldom known here. Or if they are known, they are badly distorted. I think the American mass media are in part gravely responsible for the misunderstandings that have created such critical relationships between the U.S. and Latin America. The Cuba situation would be vastly different if it were not for magazines like *Time* . . .

I am very much in agreement with your opposition to the kind of myopic Catholic policies which prevail everywhere, in North America as well as in Latin America. Here of course the situation is in many ways worse, as regards the majority.

The Cuba revolution has brought out the essential weakness of Catholic social action. I am very much afraid that we are sentimentalists, and our revolutionary aspirations tend to be infantile. The Catholics of Cuba for the most part, as I understand it, generously helped [Fidel] Castro in the beginning. But when the time came for the testing of the spirits, the depth of the Catholic understanding of the Cuban revolution was found to be inadequate. There was not sufficient strength to advance in positive competition with the Marxists, and the Catholics, particularly the hierarchy, fell back immediately upon a negative position of anti-Communist protest, making exceedingly unrealistic *demands* for a total anti-Communism on Castro's part, as a sign of "good faith" etc. Then, as Castro naturally let himself be more and more forced into the position where he had to choose, he chose Communism. Then the Cuban Church tended more and more to equate the cause of Christ with the cause of the United States: result, the collapse of what might have been the beginning of a genuine "third force" and a real revolution. Naturally, the influence of the U.S. and of mass opinion fabricated in the U.S. has been largely responsible for this.

Underneath this is the weakness of Catholic thought and of the Catholic spirit. In our thought, we are too abstract, in a sense too idealistic, and too ready to fall back on abstract constructions, unable to grasp pragmatic political situations in their reality. Spiritually we are weakened by profound sentimentalism which vitiates our charity. I believe that the renewal of Christianity must take place in every sphere simultaneously, in the spiritual as well as the political. It is no use to advance purely in one direction.

At the same time I think it would be very wise to avoid everything that precipitates political issues by prematurely making them *problems of conscience* before they really are such. This innate *fear of being wrong* and the terror that every false step may mean the collapse of our faith, is the greatest weakness of Catholics today.

It also seems to me that the protest of the beatniks, while having a certain element of sincerity, is largely a delusion. It is a false revolution, sterile and impotent, and its few flashes of originality, its attempts to express compassion, only increase the delusion. I am afraid the beats are to a great extent infantile. Yet this much can be said for them: their very formlessness may perhaps be something that is in their favor. It may perhaps enable them to reject most of the false solutions and deride the "square" propositions of the decadent liberalism around them. It may perhaps prepare them to go in the right direction. I think the beats have contributed much to the peace movement in the U.S., in their own way, and they are often quite committed to the only serious revolutionary movement we have: that for the rights of the Negro. So there are points in their favor, even though they are amorphous and often quite absurd.

Politics are of vital importance. The Catholic in Latin America who refuses a priori to have anything to do with politics of any kind, is doing more to destroy the faith than the Catholic who does not refuse, if necessary, to make common cause with the most radical elements. Incidentally Communism is no longer truly radical in any case, though doubtless in Latin America the Communists are probably a powerful force for radical action, since the situation favors their approach tremendously.

. . . Our world is in very bad shape, in the sense that the irresponsible ones who have in their hands the greatest power, do not have mentalities that inspire confidence.

I will send the "Cold War Letters" [unpublished compilation] and other things that might be of interest. Keep sending *Ventana*. I assure you and all the young poets of Nicaragua of my very great sympathy and friendship. I feel that the work you are doing is of great importance, and I assure you of my prayers and of my profound agreement. I know Jacques Maritain would join me in doing the same. He is still teaching the Petits Frères de Jésus at Toulouse, and recently I translated some of Raïssa's poems.

Please remember me to Pablo Antonio and to Coronel. I will send something soon for *El Pez y la Serpiente*. I liked the Nicaraguan poets in the last issue very much. My translations of A. Cortés are beginning to appear in various magazines, and will be in my book [*Emblems of a Season of Fury*] this fall, together with my own poems and translations of Ernesto and Pablo Antonio, also [César] Vallejo, etc.

To José Coronel Urtecho

As a young man, Nicaraguan-born José Coronel Urtecho (1906–) lived and studied in San Francisco, California, where he became an avid reader of contemporary American poetry and developed a special enthusiasm for the work of Ezra Pound. Returning home, Coronel Urtecho introduced his fellow poets to the work of North American poets and, in 1927, set a new direction for Nicaraguan poetry with his founding of the Vanguard Movement. He has influenced several generations of Nicaraguan poets, including his nephew, Ernesto Cardenal, who went to New York to study at Columbia University after reading Coronel Urtecho's translations of North American poetry. Coronel Urtecho has written novellas, poems, critical essays, numerous articles on political and literary subjects, translations of English and French works, and a history of Nicaragua. He has also published two anthologies of North American poetry, one in 1948 and another, with Cardenal, in 1963.

These letters reveal Merton's deep respect for Coronel Urtecho and offer a glimpse of Merton's assessment of his own work. Excited by Coronel Urtecho's plan to publish a reader of Merton's work, Merton gathered and dispatched writings for possible inclusion in the anthology. Though the proposed reader never appeared in print, the collaboration with Coronel Urtecho enlarged "the gradually widening circle" of Merton's "good friends" in Latin America.

March 15, 1964

Ernesto [Cardenal] in one of his fine letters spoke to me of your project, and I have written to him about it. It is a joy to me because it brings me more in contact with you both, for what is important is not the project but the communion of which the project is an expression. For it would be of little profit to me to be simply here in a monastery if being here did not enable me to be everywhere. And I am often with you in thought in the solitudes of the Rio San Juan. Also I think much of all

Latin America for in some strange way Latin America has a great deal to do with my vocation: not that I have anything to tell LA but that I have much to learn from it, and it is our vocation to learn from one another, and to find the great mercy of God hidden in a distant jungle, as well as near at hand. For the voice of God must always come to us at every moment both from near and far and from the point that is nowhere and everywhere, from the O of admiration which is a boundless circle, and from the humility of love that breaks through limits set by national pride and the arrogance of wealth and power. Let us then live in a communion which undermines the power and arrogance of the great of this world, which seeks to separate men in the power struggle.

. . . I have sent some mimeographed things which you probably have not seen and which have not been published, and I am also sending *New Seeds* [*of Contemplation*] and the poems, and will try to dig up a few other things you may not have.

Ernesto has told you how much I have liked everything of yours that I have read, and Pablo Antonio [Cuadra] will have told you how much I feel a part of the movement of poets in Nicaragua. I feel much more close to the poets of Latin and South America than to many of this country where I am in so many ways an alien. But one must necessarily be an alien everywhere, to help the world become one, and deliver it from its obsession with small definitions and limited boundaries.

Last Sunday Miguel Grinberg of Argentina was here, and had encouraging things to say about the great movement that is stirring, the awakening of poets, and from this there is much to be hoped, for the poets remain almost the only ones who have anything to say. All the rest are turning out absurd and lifeless pronouncements and empty slogans. But the poets have the humility to seek truth from the springs of life, which are first of all silent. They have the courage to disbelieve what is shouted with the greatest amount of noise from every loudspeaker, and it is this courage that is most of all necessary today. A courage not to rebel, for rebellion itself tends to substitute another and louder noise from the noise that already deafens everyone, but an independence, a personal and spiritual liberty which is above noise and outside it and which can unite men in a solidarity which noise and terror cannot penetrate. This is solidarity in Christ and in His Spirit, where the only liberty is found.

I think Ernesto's work with the Indian culture and so on is really magnificent and I pray that he may become another Bartolomé de Las Casas [16th century Spanish missionary who exposed the oppression of the Indians by European colonizers], but in the spirit of our times, which is vastly different. It is quite possible that there is great hope for the world in the spiritual emancipation of the Indians, if this be possible, as there is also hope in Africa. From the old so-called civilization I have not much hope, and from the peculiar ferment which is the United States I look for nothing but violence and perplexity unless there is a capacity to become humble and learn. This is not apparent at the moment. There is of course a peculiar and confused good will, which may mean anything or nothing. The phenomena we face are all new ones, and without precedent. Or else they are apocalyptic . . .

April 17, 1964

The other day a copy of the [*Thomas Merton*] *Reader* went off to you by air mail and I also enclosed *The Behavior of the Titans*. At the same time I spoke to New Directions about your project. In the *Reader* I hastily marked some passages that might be of interest, but I think that there are better ones that exist in mimeograph or in articles which I could send. I am not sure I will be able to find all the copies, but here are some of the things that ought to be in the book rather than much that is in the big *Reader*.

> Preface to Japanese Edition of *Seven Storey Mountain*
> "To Each His Darkness" (about Julien Green, Ernesto may have this)
> "The Jesuits in China"
> "Classic Chinese Thought"
> "Message to Poets" (I think you have this)
> ["Answers] On Art and Freedom" (This is being published in a magazine in Argentina [*Eco Contemporáneo*] by M. Grinberg)
> "Legend of Tucker Caliban" (On the Race Question)
> "Meditation on [Adolf] Eichmann"

and of course things like the "Letter to Pablo Antonio [concerning Giants]."

Please let me know if you or Ernesto between you cannot find copies of the items I have listed above and I will provide copies. Besides this there is material in some books which were not used for the *Reader*. For instance in *Disputed Questions* there is an article on Pasternak ["The Pasternak Affair"], as well as an article on Love ["The Power and Meaning of Love"] which is important, and especially Notes on a "Philosophy of Solitude." I will have *Disputed Questions* sent.

This ought to be enough, and I don't want to make everything too complicated . . .

I liked very much the beautiful "dream" of Alfonso [Cortés]. He is a wonderful and symbolic man, perhaps one of the most significant people of our age in the entire world. To have such significance one must of course be hidden as he is. The important people today are the ones who are not likely to be in *Time* magazine.

Your letter from the Rio San Juan was a joy. It puts me in contact with a wonderful land which I love and which I inhabit in spirit. The land where I have many friends I have never seen. I feel very much a part of the Nicaraguan movement in poetry and the other day I got Carrera

Andrade's fabulous new poems, and was totally *"bouleversé"* by the wonderful one on Atahualpa ["Death of Atahualpa"]. How real this is. I must
write to him at once.

Bless all of you. I close this short note with the warmest friendship
to all of you, especially Pablo Antonio in his sacrificial task, but to all the
Nicaraguan poets. By the way I have no book of Carlo Martínez Rivas,
though when Ernesto was here I read some of his poems and liked them
very much. I will try to find anything you ask for and send you copies.

August 31, 1964

It has been a long time since I have written. There has really been
nothing very new. I had been hoping to hear something from Guadarrama
about publishing my books in Spanish but have no news yet. I do hope
however that they will do your Reader. I have just sent off another
envelope of recent material that might be of interest to you, but not
necessarily for the Reader, except perhaps the article on Pilgrimages? Or
is it too contentious? I would not know. I have had to take a fair amount
of criticism for the "Monk in the Diaspora," mostly on the official level.
On the level of ordinary monks and nuns it has received a wide and
favorable reception, and I am pleased about that. Perhaps one reception
explains the other. (I think you must have received a copy of "The Monk
in the Diaspora." If not please let me know.) Certainly there is a chance
of duplication: and by all means you can give away anything that I send.

It has been a hot and busy summer, in which I have tried to get
some work done. Possibly I have undertaken too many short things, like
prefaces. But sometimes the chances are too good to miss, for instance a
preface to a marvelous book on the furniture and art of the Shaker sect
[*Religion in Wood: A Book of Shaker Furniture* by Edward Deming
Andrews]. Do you know of them? I think Ernesto does. I will try to get
copies for you and for him. Also copies of New Directions' new anthology.

The political situation in this country is now very strange. I think
that the ignorance and naïveté of the people is such that [Barry] Goldwater
might possibly get elected President this fall. It is certain that the run of
the people in this area are for him. The events in Vietnam have been
completely sickening. Also in Cyprus. The brutality and dishonesty of
the politics of the great powers are too obvious and too flagrant for words:
and yet people do not seem to experience any uneasiness about them:
only about the wickedness of enemies.

How is your work on the Reader going? I shall be interested to hear.
Do you think the publisher would like to use a few abstract drawings? I
sent a few by hand to Pablo Antonio but do not know if he received them.
I have been doing better ones than those more recently. If you are
interested, I can send some. They are very abstract.

I must close now. This is just a shout, a sign of life, hoping to hear
from you.

June 30, 1965

Thank you for your warm and interesting letter of June 10. It is good to hear that the work is coming along, but I am so glad that you like it and that it is not a chore for you. Really it is to me a very moving thing and a great grace to have someone like yourself read my work and respond to it so completely. This is really a great gift of God, and I am most grateful for it. I doubt if many writers have been blessed as I have with such generous and understanding readers. It encourages me to continue and to say as plainly and as energetically as I can, the things that need to be said.

The thing that impresses me most and gives me most hope is that this is a genuinely human level of communication. With you and Ernesto and Pablo Antonio and the gradually widening circle of my good friends in Latin America, there is a real exchange on a deep level. Ernesto's new book of poems strikes me as very powerful in its simplicity. He has an unequaled gift of getting poetry out of the confusion and pathos of the modern world, without being bitter about it. And your work, and that of Pablo Antonio, strikes me as so much more alive than what is nearer to me here, geographically.

Ludovico Silva in Caracas is translating a short piece ["Day of a Stranger"] I sent him: he might send you a copy of his translation for the book, if you like . . . I will put a bunch of new things in an envelope for you, and enclose here a poem on "Origen." I have been quite busy this summer, and am starting on an article on existentialism which I hope to send soon. I have been living more and more in the little house I have in the woods. I often think of the silence and solitude you enjoy on the Rio San Juan. Ernesto's project [the monastic community at Solentiname] sounds magnificent, and I understand it is quite near you. I wish I could see it some day. Tell me more about those Islands.

I have just finished a book of poems [*The Way of Chuang Tzu*] based on the Chinese writer Chuang Tzu. What I send, of him, is only a sample. There is much more, but I do not yet have copies.

Thanks for passing things on to *La Prensa* and *El Pez* [*y la Serpiente*]. I am thinking of sending Pablo Antonio a new essay on symbolism ["Symbolism: Communication or Communion"] for the magazine. It is written originally for a magazine in India [*Mountain Path*], and it is being typed now.

I return to the original idea of this letter: the joy of being able to communicate with friends, in a world where there is so much noise and very little contact. We cannot realize the extent of our trouble and our risk, and yet we do not know what to do—except to go on being human. This in itself is already an achievement. And we hope that since God became man, there is nothing greater for us than simply to be men ourselves, and persons in His image, and accept the risks and torments of a confused age. And though the age is confused, it is no sin for us to be nevertheless happy and to have hopes, provided they are not the vain and empty hopes of a world that is merely affluent . . .

March 17, 1966

Since I have been living in the woods I have been a very bad correspondent, even worse than before. You apologize to me, and I must apologize even more to you for my delays. This winter was cold and I was kept busy getting wood to keep me warm. I am delighted to hear from Ernesto that he is now in Solentiname and that these days he will have been with you doing the final selection for the Reader. I am grateful to you both for your patient work, especially you, and I am happy when you say that you have not found it too burdensome, but even feel you have enjoyed it and profited by it. God has helped you to bear it! . . .

I am very happy that Ernesto has now begun at Solentiname. It is a very great and promising step and I am sure it will be blessed. Of course the beginnings will be slow and there will be many difficulties but certainly he will soon see the blessings and grace that will come to him and his companions. This kind of small hidden foundation is very much needed, and he will do a great work. I hope to help him in any way that I can.

Next week I have to go to the hospital for a delicate operation on my back. If I do not get to write to Ernesto before I go, will you please tell him of this and ask for his prayers? I would appreciate your prayers too. Since it is a delicate operation, if it is not fully successful I could be a bit handicapped in the future.

I forgot what books I have sent you lately, but I hope I sent you the one on Chuang Tzu, I think you might like it. I will also put some other recent articles into the mail for you, but you need not worry about getting any of this into the book if you have finished your work. One has to end somewhere. Really, though, I am very happy that this collection has been made and I am sure it will turn out to be even better than the one that was done in the U.S.

Now I am trying to get some letters answered before I have to go to the hospital, so that I will have to end this one here. But I think of you and Ernesto often and am very grateful for your work and your interest. It will help me to reach many people whom I do not know but to whom I am possibly much closer than I am to many who are near me geographically. *Dios se lo pague.*

To Alfonso Cortés

Thomas Merton's letters to Alfonso Cortés (1893–1969) express both the admiration and the compassion Merton felt for the writer Nicaraguans have called "El Poeta Loco." In a brief essay introducing his translations of poems by Cortés, Merton recalls Ernesto Cardenal's account of seeing Cortés chained to a beam in Rubén Darío's house, where he is said to have gone insane on February 18, 1927. Cortés stayed in that house for years and then later in a hospital; in his "lucid moments" he wrote what Merton considered "some of the most profound 'metaphysical' poetry that exists." Merton's poem "To Alfonso Cortés" and his translations of poetry by Cortés and other writers he admired appeared in 1963 in Emblems of a Season of Fury.

Cortés's early work was published in the twenties and thirties: La odisea del istmo: Poema *(1922),* Poesías *(1931), and* Tardes de oro *(1934). Several collections of poetry, which appeared in the fifties and sixties, include* Las rimas universales *(1964),* El poema cotidiano y otros poemas *(1967), and* Treinta poemas *(1968).*

April 20, 1965

I am very happy to have in hand your new book, *Las rimas universales*, in which I read with admiration of new poetry and where I come to know you even better. You know with what esteem I had read and even tried to translate some of your very great poems, so profound and so penetrating. You are as a matter of fact a poet to whom God has given a very original intuition, even in a prophetic sense. You have suffered much, but in you the power of the artist and of the contemplative has made you master the suffering. It has been very fertile in your life, and you have not regretted a malady to which so many others, less endowed than you, would certainly have succumbed.

Continue then, dear Master, to give us your truly universal songs, for you are, to speak the truth, one of the only truly universal voices in this world turned upside down and divided by the hate and the ambiguities of the men of power. I greet you with the most respectful friendship.

September 3, 1965

I am writing you these few lines to let you know that I am united to your sufferings before the Lord and that tomorrow in honor of Our Lady, I am going to offer the Holy Mass for you, for all your intentions, for your literary work, and for all my friends in Nicaragua. I am very moved to know that you are writing a book "for the humble." In fact only the humble, the poor, and especially the disinherited are the ones who before all else deserve our attention and our compassion in the world. But even among the intellectuals there are many humble and poor persons. In any event, in this world where money and power threaten to destroy everything, it is necessary to unite oneself with the innocent and the poor sinners which we all are, it is necessary to know how to be nothing more because the Saviour lives and suffers in those who are left to depend on their self to live in others and in God. So it is that by suffering you speak even for those who must read your books in the generations to come: because they will read you as one of the mysterious and prophetic poets of America: but as a poet whom all will understand. I greet you with much friendship and I pray for you. Pray for me, in my very solitary destiny, in which it is not permitted to me to say everything which I would want to say. I greet you all with all my friendship in Our Lord.

On September 3, 1965, Merton also wrote to Doña Maria Luisa Cortés, Alfonso's sister, to thank her for her letter and for Alfonso's new poems. "I think . . . that his suffering is not without significance for all people, precisely those to whom he is trying to speak in his book."

December 21, 1965

I am very happy to have your new book of poems [*Las coplas del pueblo* (1965)], which without doubt will be one of the most popular which you have written, for it is addressed to all. It is truly the task of the poet to teach the ways of truth in the language of beauty.

It was a great pleasure for me to receive the visit of Father Ernesto Cardenal who spoke to me of Nicaragua and of you. I think often of you dear Poet, and I am happy to know that you continue to make your compatriots happy with the gifts of your genius, which I always admire, for you are an extraordinary Poet.

To you, and also to Doña Maria Luisa, I send my best prayers for Christmas and for the New Year. I pray for you and I leave you with the blessing of God, and the charity of Christ, very fraternally.

Merton's poem "Le secret," which he wrote in French, was inscribed: "For Don Alfonso Cortés, great poet, with friendship and admiration."

October 1, 1967

I have received the package of your two latest books [*Las puertas del pasatiempo* and *El poema cotidiano*, both published in 1967] and I am especially enchanted by your beautiful dedication. I have read with much pleasure these two books, especially because I believe that the idea of poetic autobiography is a very beautiful one. I assure you of my esteem and my friendship always very cordially, and I greet your estimable sister with much respect.

To Pablo Antonio Cuadra

Pablo Antonio Cuadra (1912–   ), intellectual, poet, journalist, and editor, was born in Managua, Nicaragua. Until he was forty-six, he lived in Granada, on the shores of Lake Nicaragua, where, after he quit law studies during final exams because "being a lawyer would not be compatible with being a writer," he and his brother established a farm with cattle, crops, and a sawmill. His work brought him close to the people and gave him time to study the history, culture, and folklore of Nicaragua and the culture and language of the indigenous peoples.

These years of lived experience and study were a source for his poetry. (See Pablo Antonio Cuadra, "Poetry and the Temptations of Power," translated by Steven White, in Lives on the Line: The Testimony of Contemporary Latin American Authors, *edited by Doris Meyer, 1988).*

It was the "indigenous" quality of Cuadra's poetry that especially excited Merton. Cuadra's was "the most authentically 'American' poetry of Latin America," Merton wrote in his introduction to The Jaguar and the Moon. *This collection of poems, inspired by the pre-Columbian Chorotega pottery, earned for Cuadra the prestigious Rubén Darío prize. Merton's translations of these poems are included in his* Emblems of a Season of Fury.

In 1961, Merton wrote an article in the form of a letter to Cuadra. The well-known "Letter to Pablo Antonio Cuadra concerning Giants" was published in Nicaragua, Argentina, and El Salvador, as well as in Merton's Emblems. *In it Merton denounced both the Soviet Union and the United States, whom he labeled Gog and Magog. "Gog is a lover of power, Magog is absorbed in the cult of money: their idols differ, and indeed their faces seem to be dead set against one another, but their madness is the same . . ." In this time of crisis, when "the big power blocs . . . are beginning to enter the final stages of the death struggle in which they will tear each other to pieces," hope lay in the Third World, to which Merton addressed his urgent plea: "Be unlike the giants, Gog and Magog. Mark what they do, and act differently . . . Their societies are becoming anthills, without purpose, without meaning, without spirit and joy." The letter was "a statement of where I stand morally, as a Christian writer," Merton wrote to Cuadra on September 18, 1961.*

The author of more than twenty books, including Songs of Cifar and the Sweet Sea *(1979), Cuadra also edited the literary reviews* Vanguardia *and* El Pez y La Serpiente *and in 1954, with Pedro Joaquin Chamorro, became coeditor of the newspaper* La Prensa. *For decades, the editors of* La Prensa *and its supplement,* La Prensa Literaria, *resisted constant censorship and the brutality of the Somoza regime, and struggled to produce "a new, revolutionary newspaper, a creator of culture, a voice of the people" (Cuadra, "Poetry and the Temptations of Power"). In 1978 Chamorro was assassinated, and during the revolution in 1979, the offices of* La Prensa *were bombed. After the revolution, tension between* La Prensa *and the new government of the Sandinistas developed. Unable to support the government, Cuadra found himself in exile from his beloved Nicaragua and estranged, by ideology, from his friend and cousin, Ernesto Cardenal.*

October 13, 1958

Finally I can write you a few lines to tell you what is happening with your admirable poems. I had to wait for the reply of New Directions, which took a long time, and I ended up writing them again to find out what they were going to do with my translations and with one of my articles. James Laughlin wrote me the other day saying that he really liked your poems—the first ones—and made me the following proposition:

1) He wants to publish a selection from the first group in his annual anthology *New Directions*, with a lot of other poets, including two of my poems as well. This anthology has a good literary reputation as an avant-garde publication.

2) For the complete book, it would be possible to publish the poems in English, with the Spanish, but without the drawings, in a volume of a new series, *World Poets*. But all the volumes of this uniform series will have 64 pages and I think that we would have to exclude one of the longer poems, if we wanted to include the versions in Spanish.

3) It would also be possible to publish a more expensive edition of everything with the drawings. But before deciding, Laughlin is waiting to see the drawings.

My opinion for the time being would be to go ahead and publish the poems now without drawings in the *World Poets* series, which would have a much greater diffusion, and would more effectively reach North American readers. In any case, let's wait—I sent the drawings and let's see what Laughlin wants to do.

I would also like to write an introduction explaining the original idea of your poems "to be inscribed on ceramics"—and we could include one of the drawings as an example, in the case of the publication in *World Poets*. Do you want to send me an explanation of your idea? Also, explain to me your admirable poem about Acahualinca. Fr. Lawrence [Ernesto Cardenal] has already told me a little about the history (behind the poem). It is a magnificent poem, and an admirable example of the current political situation with its Indian themes! I really like that prophetic fusion of the past and the present, giving the poem an eternal character, a very religious and solemn aspect! Today, we all have a great deal to do facing the terrible reality of the volcano. The Russian poet Pasternak, whose more or less autobiographical novel *Dr. Zhivago* I've just finished reading, has done this in a magnificent and providential way. I also received a letter from Pasternak that really moved me. He is very Christian.

I spent some very pleasant afternoons under the silent trees translating your poems—a labor that is, like all monastic work, consecrated, something that the profound seriousness of the poems deserves. I am overjoyed at their originality and spiritual independence in taking and using the Indian religious tradition as our Christian property. We have an enormous debt to repay to the Indians, and we should at least begin by recognizing the spiritual richness of the Indian religious genius. I have read English translations of Maya and Aztec poems in several books, and if a collection of Indian poems in Spanish exists, I would very much like to have it.

I still haven't translated everything—I think the "Códice de Abril" will be difficult. The one about the Congo ("Escrito sobre el Congo") isn't too hard. I think *The Jaguar and the Moon* is a really good title, but let's see what Laughlin thinks.

I really appreciate your help in trying to find me a publisher for my poems, translated by Ernesto [*Poemas*, published in Mexico in 1961]. I'm very pleased, the edition of the Cantares de Pisa is very good. Above all, I'm pleased about the collaboration of Armando Morales. The edition is going to be very beautiful, I think. I hope so!

Have you received my *Prometheus*? Do you think the Colombian painter might want to do illustrations for this (alone), in a special edition? What do you think? Is it too small for a separate book? I don't know Guillermo Silva's work. Armando Morales's, yes, and it's very impressive. In any case, I could send something else later that might interest Guillermo Silva.

Thank you for sending the [César] Vallejo and Martín Fierro, the other books haven't arrived (I mean *Libro sobre pájaros* and Jorge de Lima, and [Ezra] Pound *A B C of Reading*). Vallejo is also a very impressive poet, someone whose work I wasn't familiar with. I'm pleased to have his book.

I'm awaiting your article on Gethsemani—I imagine it must be difficult to write something about the monastery so far away in the world with its noise and barbarity. Fr. Lawrence told me about some things that happened, and the violence of current politics. The world is going through a terrible spiritual crisis and we all have to suffer for the stupidity of the past centuries and for our own. Sometimes I think that only the psalms and the prophets and Job can articulate our anguish in an adequate way. Christ Himself who suffered in them, is suffering in us. All humanity inexorably climbs to Calvary with the Lord, either as the repentant thief, or as the other or, what is worse, as the Pharisees. As for us, I hope we are repentant thieves, we must be very united with each other in our humility and poverty and strength—united, too, with all of history's poor, the poets of the psalms like the Indian poets. We are all Christ, and we have to know it and be witnesses of the truth and the mystery.

I pray each day for you and for Nicaragua, and for all of America. What a magnificent vocation our great continent could have! But, what a lack of fidelity in its inhabitants, and, above all, in its political figures! We are praying for America, the great America of the future, free and spiritual . . .

December 4, 1958

Two or three weeks ago I received your letter, and I was waiting for one more letter from New Directions before answering you. The letter from New Directions arrived, but without any real news, because J. Laughlin is in Utah. I still think they are publishing the annual anthology now. I will ask them. I think it will take another three or four more months. I recommend that you write to them directly with regard to your book and the poems. They have decided to publish them in Spanish and in English, but Laughlin has not told me anything about whether or not he will publish the drawing. You can write to him . . . In any case you should be in touch with them for the formalities of the contract, etc.

And now I'll try to answer your questions.

1) "The Tower of Babel"—I still have the copy of the Spanish version here. *Mea maxima culpa.* I had changed my mind, and we thought, Fr. Lawrence and I, that it would be better to go ahead and publish "The Tower of Babel" separately, apart from the other poems. The translation is 35 pages or more, and it would be a book in itself. This separate book would give Armando Morales an opportunity to realize a more noble and more united artistic presentation. New Directions published here a special limited edition (very luxurious) with etchings by Gerhardt Marcks. It's something very expensive, too expensive, too luxurious. I'll try to send you a copy. I think the work in Spanish, with the etchings by Armando Morales, will be much better, and won't cost as much. It seems to me that Marcks did not understand that *auto sacramental* very well, since his etchings are somewhat cold, exterior to the theme, although good.

2) The edition of the poems, *with the exception of* "The Tower of Babel," which will be published in a separate edition, the book of poems should include all the poems that Ernesto has translated, including the ones that appeared in ABSIDE.

3) Today I am sending *Prometheus* to Silva Santamaria. I will try to send it airmail, if Father Abad [James Fox] will permit it. I beg him and you to forgive this delay, but we didn't have copies. They arrived a few weeks ago. The binding is slightly different from that of the first copies.

How can I tell you, dear Pablo Antonio, what our collaboration means to me, and with that inspired artist Armando Morales, and also with Silva Santamaria, whose work I still don't know? Man, image of God, should be a creator, but not only as an individual person, but as a brother of other creators. Let us continue creating and struggling for the truth and the kingdom of God. We have a tremendous and marvelous vocation, the vocation of being *Americans*, that is to say, of being and of forming the true America that is the Christ of the Americas: the Christ that was born among the Indians already many centuries ago, who manifested himself in the Indian culture, before the coming of official Christianity: the Christ that has been crucified for centuries on this great cross of our double continent; the Christ that is agonizing on this same cross; when will the hour of the Resurrection of our Christ of the Americas come?, the Christ of the united, free America, (the America) emancipated from "the liturgy of the lie and of the pontificate of the infallible ignorance" which is modern politics; many years will pass, and we will not see the true America that still has not been born. We can and should be prophets of its advent— just as Pasternak in Russia is a prophet of a new age. Today I received a message from Pasternak, by means of an English intermediary [John Harris; see *The Hidden Ground of Love*, edited by William H. Shannon, pp. 384–85]. I am united with him as I am with you. We must form a union of creators, of thinkers, of men of prayer, a union with no other "organization" than charity and unanimity of thought! I beg you not to say anything about this since it could be dangerous for Pasternak. But I have received from him marvelous letters and this most recent message was from November 7, after the matter of the prize.

I'm pleased that you want to use my poems in an article about the monastery, and I'm even more pleased that it has become a magazine article. So much the better. We're hoping to see it. Let us all ask of God his peace and his freedom his mercy and his love for us and for all: and so that the Holy Spirit descends over our America and makes of us its new creation in Christ . . .

January 8, 1959

Thank you for so many good things, and above all the magnificent book of indigenous poetry, which is a real treasure. What tremendous poetry. Thank you, too, for your book *Towers of God*, which Fr. Lawrence just read and which I am going to begin now. I already received a few months ago the collection of César Vallejo, magnificent poet. Laughlin from New Directions sent me a little book by Octavio Paz. I am convinced that Latin American poetry has an ambience more pleasing and appropriate for me than that of the United States, which seems a little removed, less spontaneous, less fiery, more cerebral. I really liked the page in *La Prensa* with my letter and your article on Pasternak. I have written a fairly long article on the entire matter about him ["The Pasternak Affair," *Disputed Questions*], and I am going to send you a copy that might serve for some magazine. I don't know what is going to happen to that article here, since my agent is taking care of its publication.

I am sending you now, very late, the *Tower of Babel* and *Prometheus*. A lot of time has gone by and I had deceived myself, forgetting I still had those two things here in my cell. Forgive me. I had begun by not sending the *Tower of Babel* until I heard your opinion on the separate publication of the *auto sacramental*. Now I am sending you the two things. I sent *Prometheus* in English to Silva Santamaria a long time ago. Here I even have a copy in Spanish for him.

I am *very* pleased with the magnificent letter that Armando Morales wrote to Fr. Lawrence for Christmas, telling him about the enthusiasm and the fervor with which he had dedicated himself to the work of illustrating my poems. What luck, what grace, to collaborate with such a good artist so ready to understand the poems. I think that the Spanish edition, Ernesto's translation and Armando Morales's drawings, will be something tremendous and perhaps better than the original in English. I am very pleased. And I hope that my translation of your poems will turn out very well here. New Directions has not sent me any news, and I am writing them today to find out something.

I am very happy about the good news of Cuba lately.

Snow is falling now—that element of silence noble and pure. I am still in the Guatemalan jungle reading books about the Maya. Fr. Lawrence is doing the same thing and I hope that he will be able to write a poem about the Mayan empire. In any case, in the snowy Kentucky landscape, the two of us are very united with you and the poets and intellectuals of Central America. Let us continue searching in the secret of our hearts for the purity and integrity of the spirit—that "spiritus" that is the result of the union of the soul with God in a new and pure being, full of truth, humble instrument of God in the world.

June 13, 1959

We are both very relieved to hear that you are safe in Costa Rica. The news of the revolution [an attempt to overthrow the Somoza government] has reached us, but the last information that I got was not favorable: it was largely a propaganda announcement of the Somoza government, to the effect that the guerrillas had been largely wiped out. I hope this is not true. I also hope that the United States will not intervene on behalf of Somoza's tyranny. Is there anything I can do? Can I write to the O.A.S.?

Certainly Fr. Lawrence and I will both be praying very earnestly, and I have already recommended the intentions of the revolution to the novices as a group. We are all praying earnestly for you. I am glad you were not arrested.

I first heard the news of the war of liberation when I was visited by J. Laughlin, the publisher, of New Directions. We happened to be out of the monastery and saw it in the paper. We spoke naturally of your work. He is still planning the New Directions annual for this year, and intends to insert some of your poems. The book of poems will not appear until next year, as he has not yet completed his plan for the new series of which it will form a part. So with all this, you must be patient. New Directions works very slowly, as it is almost all done by Laughlin himself, and he is very busy with many other things besides his own firm. He likes your poems very much and hopes you have sent him a copy of the book. I showed him the one you sent me and he agreed that it was very attractive. He was pleased with the effect of the designs that were used, and I think he will be encouraged to use some of them himself.

And now, Pablo Antonio, we all have much to pray for. The tyrannies and compulsions under which we live in these days are a moral affront to man, the image of God. And it is becoming more and more clear that our fundamental moral obligation is to resist complicity and submission to every form of abusive power, whether physical or moral or spiritual. And this is both complicated and perilous. Mistakes will be made, and violence is hard to check. It is sometimes necessary to meet force with force, and then one can only hope that the violence that follows will not go too far beyond reasonable limits. In the great international problems of the world, this hope no longer clearly exists. In local situations such things are still possible. May freedom and justice come to Nicaragua, and to all the Latin American states. And may a greater comprehension exist everywhere on our continent. I regret that the United States takes such a short-sighted and materially interested view of everything. We live in very bad times, and our vocation to redeem them is something almost beyond bearing. It must be so. We can do nothing without the hidden power of God, and in our time more than any other, God seems absent. It is in this apparent "absence" of God that we must go forward with faith, in the perilous exercise of our freedom.

I must now close in haste. Fr. Lawrence will be writing to you right away. Pray for me, I have many difficult decisions to make. God bless you. Please send us news soon. I hope it will be good news. Send us anything you can.

P.S. Can you send me any information about the Corn Islands, belonging to Nicaragua?

On July 4, Merton wrote to President Luis Somoza and to the Organization of American States, interceding on behalf of those who had been imprisoned as a result of an attempt to overthrow the Somoza government in Nicaragua. Merton begged Somoza to remember his responsibility to protect those arrested "from injustice and coercion and to see that they are given a fair trial without undue or illegal pressures being brought to bear on them." Hoping that Somoza's "Christian conscience" would be moved to "complete clemency," Merton asked for the release of as many as possible. He entreated Somoza "to see that no one among these men is submitted to the ignominy of bodily or mental torture." Good treatment of the prisoners, Merton concluded, would be to Nicaragua's advantage.

In his letter to the O.A.S., Merton expressed his fear that "the captives now in the hands of the political police of President Somoza may be subjected to brutality and torture," as had political prisoners in the past. "You, sirs, will share my conviction that every American must do everything in his power to prevent a repetition, on our continent, of events and practices that have cried out to heaven for vengeance from the continents of Europe and Asia. It is true that in the past we have sullied our souls with terrible sins of this nature, but never to the extent that has now made proverbial the inhumanity of Nazi Germany and Red Russia. Let there never be any such things among us in the New World."

In both letters, Merton interceded for leaders of the insurrection, particularly for La Prensa's Pedro Joaquin Chamorro, who had previously suffered imprisonment and torture. Though more than a hundred insurgents were tried, convicted, and sentenced to prison, within a year they were granted amnesty by President Somoza. Chamorro was assassinated on January 10, 1978.

August 22, 1959

I am not sure if I have the news correctly, but I think I heard somehow that you were by now back in Managua. I am glad to hear it, and I hope things are going well. Ernesto probably told you that I wrote to Somoza and that he replied that there would be no torturing. It appears that he is keeping to this agreement, probably because it would be very bad publicity for his supremely "democratic" rule if the contrary were to be divulged. Apart from that I have no clear idea how things stand in Nicaragua, but I am sure there is very considerable wisdom in your remark that there is no room for plagiarism in politics any more than in literature. The fact is that each new situation in life has its own mysterious logos, and that it takes a creative intuition to discover it and act accordingly. There is too much temptation to act not according to this mystery but according to some "clear idea" which represents only an image of the past. Or a wish for the future, based on an image of the past. The present is in neither of these things.

Ernesto's poems in the *Revista* have struck me as profoundly alive and clear. He is certainly a very fine poet, and perhaps one of the reasons why his vocation here did not finally develop permanently was that this was no place for him to write poetry. I think perhaps the almost violent inhibition with which he stifled his poetic instinct on entering here had something to do with the fact that he was ultimately threatened with ulcers. But in any case I believe he has some notes for short poems, ideas which came to him here, and I hope he will be able to get them in shape. They will probably be very good. I know it is hard for him to adapt now [that] he has left here, the period of transition will be difficult, and he will not recapture the happiness that was his here temporarily, but his life will be very faithful. It will take time to discover what he should do next. Dom Gregorio [Lemercier, superior at the Benedictine monastery at Cuernavaca, Mexico] will be able to help him, certainly.

J. Laughlin is very happy with your book, and we are still waiting for your first poems to appear in his annual, which is slow in coming out. The book will have to wait a little, as he has probably told you. New Directions is not always very fast—in that respect he is not as modern as he appears to be. It is a small publishing firm and moves slowly.

Here is an offprint of an article on Pasternak I think you will like, and I will be sending you another one, of a different article, later on, in a month or so.

I have translated a few poems of Vallejo for [Robert] Lax's sheet [*Jubilee*]. It is a very small thing, but Vallejo is a fine poet, and Lax is happy about having the poems. I am happy to have translated them. I wish I had more time to read poetry, and perhaps this fall I will make time to read and perhaps translate more Latin American verse. I still have to master some of the difficulties in your longer poems, and perhaps what I will do will be to send copies of the translations for you and Ernesto to correct. I am not hurrying with this, as J. is at a standstill.

Well, what I said above about the "logos of the situation" applies to us all. Our lives go on, at times it seems they are fruitless. We must always pray to be attuned to the mysterious language of events, and shape our actions accordingly. It requires prayer and humility and vigilance and love. Although it says in Ecclesiastes that there is nothing new under the sun, yet there is always the creative newness of our decisions, in the service of God. May they be filled with His Spirit and with His "new life."

In any case, let us pray for one another that we may make creative use of the mysterious difficulties of life and shape our courses in "new directions" if that be the will of God. I fear nothing so much as conventionalism and inertia, which for me is fatal. Yet there is that all-important stillness, and listening to God, which seems to be inertia, and yet is the highest action. One must always be awake to tell the difference between action and inaction, when appearances are so often deceiving . . .

January 4, 1960

It was certainly a great pleasure to hear from you and to learn of the new Review, *El Pez y la Serpiente*. It sounds fine and I am very grateful that you want to include something of mine in it. By all means go right ahead with your plans, I shall be delighted to collaborate in the wonderful work. It is to me a joy to be united with you and your group at least in this way. I shall be proud to join my voice with that of the poets of Nicaragua and of all Latin America. I can also suggest other North Americans who would be of interest to you, particularly the poet Brother Antoninus [William Everson], a Dominican in San Francisco. Perhaps you have heard of him. I also am in contact with Czeslaw Milosz, a Polish exile, who once was in the Polish Red embassy in Washington and has written fine things on Poland. He can get you interesting Polish material. The intellectual freedom and toughness of the Poles is to me a source of inspiration.

I am getting together a few things I have at hand, so that you will be able to use them. The question of censorship arises of course. But there is now a new arrangement for my Spanish translations. They can be sent here and Father Augustine [Wulff] or someone like that will pass on them. So there is no problem. Just send the translations of these articles when you are ready. The "Prometeo" has already been censored and so has the Pasternak. I thought Victoria Ocampo was going to publish that in *Sur*, but am not sure whether she did or not. It does not make much difference. I will send you soon a new book in which there are things you might see.

Things with me are quiet and joyful enough. Father Abbot has hired a contractor to build me a very fine little hermitage house back in the woods, on a hill overlooking the valley. It is about ten minutes' walk from the monastery, very secluded and quiet, a very admirable little house, no Carthusian has anything better. In fact this is far better than a Charterhouse because it stands all by itself. It is simple and austere, and has a fine fireplace which keeps it warm in this snowy weather. I have permission to work, study and pray there during the daytime. In practice I can get there several afternoons a week, but cannot spend the night there or say Mass there. It certainly gives me a good amount of solitude, and for this I am grateful.

I have been in contact with a Moslem scholar in Pakistan [Abdul Aziz], a student of Islamic mysticism, and this is very interesting and inspiring. We have also had Jews coming here on retreat and I have been dealing quite a lot with Protestant theologians and ministers who come here. There have been interesting relationships which promise to bring about a better mutual understanding. I like this work and feel that it can do much good in a small and hidden way. The Holy Father has taken a close and fatherly interest in these contacts and has personally blessed and encouraged them.

The international situation looks confused and dark. The United States is getting itself into a more and more uncomfortable position, due to its general lack of insight and understanding of other people and nations. The diplomacy of this country is incredibly naïve. And today no one can afford to trade on "injured innocence" and shocked righteousness. No one is innocent. The shallow optimism of the U.S. covers too many dark realities. This is an age when compunction and a sense of one's own moral indigence is absolutely necessary. Alas, it is sad for those who have been foolish enough to equate prosperity with goodness and with the divine approval.

I can imagine the intricacy and tension of things in Nicaragua. You have a very great claim on my prayers. I pray often for all of Latin America, and think of all my friends there. No matter what happens, I feel myself more and more closely united with those who, everywhere, devote themselves to the glory of God's truth, to the search for divine values hidden among the poor and the outcast, to the love of that cultural heritage without which man cannot be healthy. The air of the world is foul with lies, hypocrisy, falsity, and life is short, death approaches. We must devote ourselves with generosity and integrity to the real values: there is no time for falsity and compromise. But on the other hand we do not have to be greatly successful or even well known. It is enough for our integrity to be known to God. What we do that is pure in His sight will avail for the liberty, the enlightenment, and the salvation of His children everywhere.

September 16, 1961

It is time that I write to you, and as a matter of fact I have really written you a long letter which is now being typed out and which can serve for publication in *El Pez y la Serpiente* if you want it. What I had to say took the form of a letter because I felt I could say it better if I knew the person I was addressing. Hence in speaking to you first of all

I have said what I thought needed to be said to everyone else, especially in Latin America. The piece is really an article, entitled "Letter to Pablo Antonio Cuadra concerning Giants" and the giants in question are of course the big power blocs that are beginning to enter the final stages of the death struggle in which they will tear each other to pieces. Though the moment of supreme crisis may come quite suddenly and probably will, I do not think it is immediately near. But I think it is inevitable, unless there is some very remarkable intervention of Providence. Since I trust such intervention may take place, I see no reason for becoming desperate or even excited. However the sober facts seem to point to a nuclear war in the near future. Since there is at least a serious possibility of this, I felt that my position called for some kind of a statement of where I stand, morally, as a Christian writer. That statement has been made in the letter to you.

For the rest, it is good to speak to you again after a long interval. I liked very much the first issue of the magazine. I was particularly happy to see that Ernesto's versions of the psalms are so excellent. He tells me you have printed, or will perhaps print, the elegy for Hemingway ["An Elegy for Ernest Hemingway"]. Did you see the Chant, the long poem about Auschwitz ["Chant to Be Used in Processions Around a Site with Furnaces"]? This has appeared already in several publications in this country, including a beatnik magazine in San Francisco [*Journal for the Protection of All Beings*]. I wonder if you have been in contact with people like Milosz and Brother Antoninus, to get material for the magazine. Milosz translated a remarkable poem of the Polish poet Z. Herbert, on Hamlet and Fortinbras ["Elegy on Fortinbras"]. It is a very eloquent satirical summary of the present situation in the world. The ironical thing is that the West is plagued by a kind of "vestigial" conscience: not a real, fully developed one, but something like a vermiform appendix, which causes trouble but serves no useful purpose. Because of this obsolete organ, the politicians of the West think themselves honorable and virtuous and compare themselves favorably with the frankly opportunistic politicians of the East. These in turn make use quite cynically of the pangs of conscience of the West, perhaps to destroy the West in the end. And we who still wish to fully *live* by the light of conscience? Our position is uncomfortable enough, but it is at least healthy. The great thing is to purify and rectify our conscience with genuine truth, and cast out all false scruples and the hesitations that are encouraged by a conformist and corrupt social milieu.

The long letter "about Giants" will follow this in a day or two. I hope you will like it. Meanwhile there are many other interesting things, but no time in which to say them. I have been studying Meister Eckhart, who is tremendous. Also the Chinese philosopher Chuang Tzu, and Clement of Alexandria. There are not enough hours in the day to read all the wonderful things that are suddenly available on all sides. I have been busy with many interesting meetings and conferences with Protestant theologians, writers and others. I hope you will pass this way if some time you return to America.

With best wishes to everyone, particularly Armando Morales. Everyone is crazy about the illustrations he did for the poems. God bless you all.

August 1, 1963

I often think of you and of all my friends in Nicaragua, and now for a change I am able to write you at least a note. I hear from Ernesto, who tells me the news and sends clippings from *La Prensa*. He will have told you that a couple of my translations of Alfonso [Cortés] were in a very high-tone literary review, the *Sewanee Review*. They will also be in my book of poems this fall, *Emblems of a Season of Fury*. The book will be about half made up of my own new poems, and the other half will be translations and the Letter on the Giants. Yes, I will have some of your poems, together with Alfonso, Carrera Andrade, Vallejo, Raïssa Maritain, etc. By the way, Jacques Maritain is editing the spiritual *Journal* of Raïssa. I have already seen a privately printed edition, and it is very fine, deeply mystical, so much so that I do not think it will be appreciated.

Here I am sending you a few things for *El Pez*, to show that I have not forgotten you. "Hagia Sophia" has not yet been translated into any language, and the "Early Legend" is still not finished, but it will be a long time before it grows. When it becomes what it is meant to be, it will be quite different, so I think there is no harm in using it now, and it has something vague to say about the basic themes so close to *El Pez y la Serpiente*. It has not yet been published in English. Finally the "Legend of Tucker Caliban" is about the race situation here. You might prefer it for *La Prensa*.

The words in your note moved me deeply: Quetzalcoatl [the Feathered Serpent, a deity in the Mexican pantheon] in the power of the magicians and technologists. This is the great tragedy of our time. Pope John [XXIII] was a profoundly human and genuine person, as well as a saint (I think the two must go together, for sanctity is destroyed by inhumanity no matter where it comes from and with no matter what good intentions). But the general lack of understanding, the incapacity to break away from the obsession with technics and with results, the madness of space flights and shooting at the moon, shows that the human spirit is being overwhelmed by the riot of its own richness, which in the end is the worst kind of poverty. The poor man who can be himself is at least a man and a person and is richer than the rich man who is carried away by the forces to which he has sold himself. This elementary truth no one bothers to recognize. It may ruin us. Yet still the grinding poverty of Latin America has to be relieved, but it must not be the moon lit by the

North American sun. It must relieve itself from within its own resources, which must be spiritual and human and creative.

I have much work and am constantly inundated with manuscripts and books from good poets, and do not have time to read them all. But I do have solitude also, and spend as much time in the woods as I can. I have a hermitage there now, and it is in a very fine place . . .

So we continue to live and try to seek truth. Each must do so with courage and indefatigable patience, constantly discerning it from the obsessive fictions of the establishment everywhere . . .

June 30, 1964

. . . As to your *Antología*: I can think of a few poets right away but there are many others of whom I know little or nothing as my reading of poetry has been sporadic and uneven. There are in fact many Christian poets around in England and the U.S. One of the best I can think of is Ned O'Gorman, who can be reached at *Jubilee* magazine. I will have him contact you. Robert Lax is now in Greece . . . Do you have the address of *Ramparts* magazine? The people there could help. Of course there is above all Brother Antoninus, I gave Ernesto his address for *El Pez y la Serpiente*. I had better get all these addresses for you, but I do not have the book at hand at the moment. Also Henry Rago at *Poetry* magazine in Chicago can be of help, and for England you might write to Fr. Benet Weatherhead, O.P., *Blackfriars*, Cambridge, England, and also Fr. Brocard Sewell O. Carm, the *Aylesford Review*, Aylesford Priory, Near Maidstone, Kent, England. One of the best Christian poets writing in English now is Peter Levi, S.J. I certainly think it is most important and significant that this *"summa"* will emanate from Central America. I think all you are doing is very alive and fruitful, and I think that to produce really new and eloquent Christian work today one must be to some extent removed from the "centers" and from all that is official and recognized, even if it is recognized as to some extent unofficial. The Germans and French and Dutch are producing theology, but I am not so sure they are doing much in Christian poetry and art. Perhaps in art, but I think too much modern sacred art is artificial and contrived.

That is why I think *El Pez* can have a very important mission, as being apart from and independent of the big "movements" whether progressive or conservative, the well-defined drives that have been recognized and identified by the mass media. The names you have listed make an interesting grouping. I would add others like Lanza Del Vasto, Père Hervé Chaigne, a young French Franciscan interested in non-violence (I have his address somewhere), again Bro. Antoninus and some of those whose names I have mentioned under the rubric of poetry. Fr. Daniel Berrigan, S.J. is one who would collaborate though he is not yet too well known. Also Gordon Zahn (writes on peace etc). There is an interesting psychoanalyst in New York, Joost Meerloo, but he is quite busy. Yet I think he could get interested. There is of course Erich Fromm in Mexico, and some of the Protestant writers might be interested too.

Ernesto sent me Octavio Paz's translations of Fernando Pessoa and I am very much taken with his poetry. I am looking for the originals and expect to do some translating of that. Pessoa is very congenial to me in his existentialism. Very Zen-like also.

Under separate cover I will put some texts and drawings in an envelope for you and for *El Pez*.

With the frustration of the progressive hopes in the second session of the Council and the realization that in spite of all the fuss made the accomplishments of the Council have been relatively superficial and trivial, one has to face the fact that the Church is and remains in severe crisis. All the discussion and publicity do little or nothing to change this fact, and the various movements (including the monastic movement) do not seem to be profoundly real, or as real as they claim to be. Yet there is something there, God alone knows what. I personally think that we are paralyzed by institutionalism, formalism, rigidity and regression. The real life of the Church is not in her hierarchy, it is dormant somewhere. There are all kinds of signs of awakening, but which of them can be accepted as real? I think we need a deep enlightenment and liberation from cultural and intellectual habits, from spiritualities, from pious attitudes, from social prejudices, and perhaps the liberation must reach the proportions of an explosion before it will be genuine. Yet I realize that a human approach to this is futile, and that we are all waiting for something we know not. The real movement will start of itself, and I am convinced that the great areas of new life are to be sought in South America (Central America too), Africa, and Asia perhaps. It would be wonderful to participate to some small extent in the beginnings of the awakening. Perhaps that is why preference should always be given to the voice of the *criollos*. Perhaps I will write you further about this. Today is hot and it has been a long day, so I must end this letter.

With best and most cordial wishes always, and in union of vision and prayer, and aspiration toward the air that can be breathed and the light that is tranquil.

October 28, 1964

The special pages of *La Prensa Literaria* were a surprise and a joy to me. I want to say how much I appreciate all that appeared there, especially your article and that of José Coronel [Urtecho]. The most consoling thing about it is to feel that I do really have a part in your life there and that I am also in some sense engaged in the work of the literary movement which is so alive and so important in Nicaragua. This is of course a special grace in my life, a paradoxical part of my monastic vocation, and it is most comforting to have you speak "in the Spirit" to verify this and to seal it with your witness. This is a dimension of Christian life that is not yet properly understood today where all that is of the Church is still thought of as necessarily very official. But the Council seems to be changing that. In any case, it is a consolation for a priest to be able to receive reassurance from lay Catholics that he is in the right path, and above all to be able to collaborate with them in a literary work that has great importance. It can also be Catholic action for the priest to collaborate with laymen in *their* sphere, and I think all that we have been doing together exemplifies this. It is perhaps part of the new era which the Church is entering.

So, in thanking you again, I take this opportunity to thank also all my friends in Nicaragua, including many young poets who have sent me their books of poetry and other writings, which I have not been able to acknowledge in detail. But I remain very close to all of you, all of them, and Alfonso.

Meanwhile my life gradually takes on a more solitary dimension, the Order seems to be opening out a little in that direction, and I am able to live more in the woods. It may mean less writing, but I do not think I shall ever stop writing altogether, though it is necessary that my solitude should be something other than a purely literary one.

I shall be sending you some more recent articles. I am glad you liked the drawings. I am having an exhibit of them in Louisville this fall. I hope to send you more later. The translations of the poems were splendid, and I am glad you liked "Macarius and the Pony." It is a marvelous theme, but few people had commented on it in this country.

Best wishes and blessings always. Feel free to use in any way you like the material I am sending.

March 2, 1965

First of all I want to congratulate you for the Rubén Darío prize: José Coronel told me about this, and I am very happy to hear it. I must say too that your book richly deserves it. I am happy to have it and thank you for it, and I find fine things in it everywhere. Especially the Hymns to Our Lady and the other office pieces that go with them: these are remarkably beautiful, authentically Catholic and American too. The book is fine in every respect except that I think the big screen on your picture on the cover turned out to be a bit disappointing. But that has nothing to do with the quality of the book itself.

Now however I have another matter of great importance to speak about and I hope you will handle it with extreme discretion. I have very confidential information that Rome is making inquiries about Ernesto and these might possibly affect his ordination. Such inquiries are quite unusual and my surmise is that someone may have reported him to Rome as perhaps not being fit for ordination, and they are trying to find out about him. There might be several reasons: perhaps the Nuncio in Cuba was surprised at the request to attend the congress there (though I should think on the contrary that such a request ought to have impressed him with Ernesto's spirit of obedience), perhaps some priest or bishop has been upset by some of Ernesto's articles on Indian theology, or perhaps someone in Nicaragua . . . I am telling this to you rather than to Ernesto himself, first because I do not know if his mail is censored at the Seminary, and second because I do not want to upset him. You would best know how to proceed. I think that Ernesto should be warned to be very careful, perhaps to stop publishing anything about the Indians at once, and to stay away from anything that might give anyone reason to complain. You would know better than I what the situation might be. I leave it to you to inform him discreetly, but please keep it very quiet and do not let him discuss it with anyone except a very trusted confessor. Information was requested of us and for my part I gave him the highest recommendation, and I think Fr. Abbot will incorporate this in his report. But I do think that between now and ordination Ernesto should be very careful what he does, avoid all "unusual" activities, perhaps even the retreat he preached might have caused some criticism. It is most unfortunate that things like this can still continue: delations to Rome, judgments behind closed doors, refusal to give any information or explanations, etc. I do hope that every-thing will turn out all right in the end. I shall pray especially for Ernesto as well as for all of you my friends in Nicaragua. I think it is most important for Nicaragua that Ernesto be ordained and be permitted to carry out his project, which is the fruit of a very special charismatic grace, and which can result in immense good for Nicaragua. What a pity that so often the hierarchy refuses to see, like Jerusalem, "those things that are for their peace" and for the good of the Church. The stifling of original and vital initiatives, the failure to comprehend new needs: in spite of all, these continue to be tragic and widespread failures . . .

June 29, 1968

I was delighted to get your letter and to read your new poems. I always want to keep in touch with my friends in Nicaragua, but the volume of mail is so great now that I despair of answering even half the letters. Sometimes it is the ones I would most like to answer that don't get answered, because I have to be content to rapidly answer routine business mail and nothing more. I think you understand the situation very well. Yes, it is true that I no longer am able to get my writing mimeographed and sent out here. Secretarial help is scarce. That is why copies have not been coming to you. I will however send my new books to you and Ernesto, and I am enclosing two articles which I think might interest you. The one on War and Vision ["War and Vision: The Autobiography of a Crow Indian"] might do for *El Pez*. The other perhaps for *La Prensa*. Yes, it is also true that now there is some hope of my traveling a little. It is possible that I may be able to get out for two journeys a year. I have already made the first of these, to a fine convent of ours in California.

Also I am planning another more ambitious trip this winter: I have been invited to give a retreat in our monastery in Indonesia and am also invited to attend a meeting of Asian Abbots (Benedictine and Cistercian) as a *peritus*. I may also have to preach some retreats in Japan. This may take so long that I would not have really enough time to come to Nicaragua. On the other hand, it is also planned that some time in the future I may go to give some courses at our monastery in Chile. I would like to plan to include Nicaragua in that trip. But I have no idea when it will be. Perhaps at the end of next year? In any case, however, I am only speaking and giving conferences in monasteries of our Order or at meetings of Abbots of the monastic families. But of course Solentiname would count as a monastery of "our Order" since the aims are the same. What I mean by that is that I cannot accept invitations to preach or speak in cities, universities etc., though I receive two or three almost every day.

It is also true that all life is not accomplishing some special work but attaining to a degree of consciousness and inner freedom which is beyond all works and attainments. That is my real goal. It implies "becoming unknown and as nothing."

I hope to write to Ernesto soon and send him some new articles on monasticism, as well as some books.

To Miguel Grinberg

In the late fifties, Miguel Grinberg (1937–) studied at the University of Buenos Aires School of Medicine. In the sixties, Grinberg turned to publishing and writing. In 1961, he began editing Eco Contemporáneo, *a literary magazine published in Buenos Aires to contribute to "knowledge between people interested in the same subjects and troubled by the same problems" (letter to Merton, May 5, 1963). Merton was definitely one of these people; he read* Eco *with pleasure and enthusiastically affirmed the purpose of Acción Interamericana, an organization Grinberg founded in 1963 to promote cultural exchange.*

In response to a list of nine questions Grinberg had sent him in 1963, Merton wrote the article "Answers on Art and Freedom." Grinberg also invited Merton to a meeting of poets in Mexico City in 1964. Though unable to attend, Merton did send "Message to Poets," an essay expressing his solidarity with the young poets meeting in "a spontaneous explosion of hope."

Miguel Grinberg's collections of poetry include Ciénagas *(1962),* Opus New York *(1964), and* America hora cero *(1965). He is an established film and music critic and, since receiving a Ph.D. in Educational Sciences from the Colegio Libre de Buenos Aires in 1971, Grinberg has been involved in futures research and education, directing several projects and publishing a number of books on the subject, including* Precursores de futuros *(1974),* Utopos *(1975),* Ecología del alma *(1979).*

June 21, 1963

Thanks very much for your letter. I am very interested in your project, but I am a very bad correspondent, since I have a great deal to do and I hate to write letters without thinking. Yet that is what I do, when no other solution is possible. However, I hope this one will be coherent.

The whole question of inter-American contacts and exchange is of the greatest importance. It is important for Latin America but it is even more important for North America, because unless the United States finally gets in touch with the reality of American life in its broadest and most relevant sense, there is going to be a lot of trouble for everybody. It is of the greatest importance, then, that the cultural vitality of the Latin American countries should be known and recognized here. It is a great misfortune that the technological blindness of the "advanced" countries should gradually be spreading everywhere, without necessarily bringing any real benefits, and communicating mostly the severe disadvantages of our state. The world is falling into a state of confusion and barbarism, for which the responsibility lies, perhaps, with those who think themselves the most enlightened.

Henry Miller is a good friend of mine and I think he has very good insight into this problem. He has said many really urgent things about the question of our modern world and where it is going. The problem is the dehumanization of man, the alienation of man. The Marxists could have developed this concept, which is found in Marx, but they have not been able to. On the contrary, the world today seems to be in a maniacal competition between giant powers, each one striving to show it can do more than the others in brutalizing, stupefying and dehumanizing man, in the name of humanism, freedom and progress. Indeed, the frankness with which the Nazis built their extermination camps is to some extent the index of what is more secretly going on everywhere. Yet the West is not beyond redemption: there are faint and confused stirrings of human hope, as also in the East with some of the revisionists. I think Pope John [XXIII] was one of those who intuitively sized up the situation and reached out for the elements of positive hope that he was still able to see. I hope the new Pope [Paul VI], who has great potentialities, will be able to continue Pope John's work.

The "Ecos" [*Eco Contemporáneo*] have not yet come. I want to see them, and I hope I will find a moment to give you more of an answer and more encouragement when I have read them. I am glad you are in contact with Ernesto [Cardenal]. He will be doing great work, and is already at the height of his powers, perhaps, with great promise of more development. He will be one of the most significant spiritual voices in the two Americas. I am warmly attached to my friends in Nicaragua who are writing fine poetry, and I have many friends all over the hemisphere in whom I think there is great hope of awakening and of life. I wish I had more time and more leisure to communicate with everyone, but the limitations of my vocation do impose restraints which I cannot always ignore! However, do believe me in deep union and agreement with the forces of life and hope that are struggling for the renewal of the true cultural and spiritual vitality of the "new work" which is sometimes so tired, so old and so shabby. It is what pretends to be most "new" that is often the oldest and weariest thing of all. But the forces of life must win. And Christians must rediscover the truth that the Cross is the sign of life, renewal, affirmation and joy, not of death, repression, negation and the refusal of life. We must not refuse the providential opportunities that come to us in the midst of darkness.

Grinberg visited Merton at Gethsemani in March 1964. "Due to the heavy rains," Merton noted in his journal, "we cannot go out much, so we mostly sit in a room of the guest-house, exchanging ideas and addresses of people we ought to know" and new poetry magazines (see A Vow of Conversation, *p. 33).*

April 5, 1964

The copies of "Cold War Letters" [unpublished compilation] are flying in all directions, and I will send more to anyone you like, anyone who will like them, or even who will not like them. Just let me know. Meanwhile no fallout from New York has come this way to bear witness to your visit. You must have been quiet and subtle. As to problems with dollars, that is a sign that you are a new man.

As to me I am partly hypnotized by an enormous conglomerate of *mufa* and *mierda*, an astonishing but not altogether unusual spectacle, which metamorphoses itself into uninteresting shapes none of which have anything to reveal about anything. But never mind, never mind, you know the habits of *mufa*. It often vanishes unexpectedly and is generally companionable even at the worst of times.

It was good to have you here, though I am sorry you had to come such a long way just to sit in a room writing to the President. But it was good, it was good. Standing on the hill in semi-darkness taking pictures was all right. Something will come of it all. Vegetation, clouds, a lot of sky.

I would be writing something about the new man but the new man has no title and leaves no trace, and his name is not on his desk because he has no desk. His key is not in his pocket because he has no door. He is in the novel position of having to wear his hat on his feet because he walks on his hands. It is this walking on the hands and the consequent proximity to the crass layers of *mufa*, which constitute the footsteps of society, which give him his humorous outlook on the living death which is jocularly known as civilization.

If [Lawrence] Ferlinghetti thinks I am mad at the Buddha tell him he is wrong, and if he thinks I am cold to City Lights tell him he is twice wrong and if he thinks I am mad at him (he surely doesn't think this) then give him some message of peace. Did I ever send him the CW letters? I will if I didn't . . .

May 11, 1964

Reason I did not mention the pictures in writing the letter I sent to California is that I had not yet received them. They are quite good. I look like Henry Miller. The newest one of you in the flowers is very good. What you say in your letter is right. *Fluencia* is the right way. What stops *fluencia* is the wrong kind of ignorance and the wrong kind of ignorance is the conviction that we can know exactly what is going on. Those who have too many programs and answers are absolutely blind and their ignorance leads them to destruction. Those who know that they do not know, are able at least to see something of what is in front of their nose. They can see a shadow of it, anyway. And they can move with the light and the shadow and keep from getting immediate sunstroke. So we must all move, even with motionless movement, even if we do not see clearly. A few little flames, yes. You can't grasp them, but anyway look at them obliquely. To look too directly at anything is to see something else because we force it to submit to the impertinence of our preconceptions. After a while though everything will speak to us if we let it and do not demand that it say what we dictate.

Total corruption. Everything is corrupt and corruption spreads from one structure to the other, although they all have more than enough. The only incorrupt things are silence, not knowing, not going, not waiting etc., mostly not saying. You are right that as soon as one has finished saying something it is no longer true. Heraclitus. Love is all right as long as statements are not made and as long as it does not itself become a program, because then it is another tyranny.

Did you see any of the people I spoke of? Probably not, they may be hard to find.

I wrote to Meg [Randall de Mondragon] when I was in the hospital the other day for some tests. I am all right, I am not dying, I do not hurt too much, I can move, I can write, I am not in any kind of bad condition. I make no statements about happiness, or about anything.

The monk is a bird who flies very fast without knowing where he is going. And always arrives where he went, in peace, without knowing where he came from.

Gethsemani is still in the same place.

Poets from all over send things. This is good. Celia Paschero for instance. I sent her a book. I put a lot of stuff in an envelope for you in BA.

Are you going to Mexico or straight back to Argentina? Let me know what happens.

July 12, 1964

I sent Henry Miller a picture of the two of us in the front garden of
the monastery amid cold winds, snow, fallout, sleet, darkness, chaos and
night. He thought he was able to discern in me a likeness to himself, and
I agree as I had already thought of that too. Maybe I said it in a letter.
He thinks I look like him and like Genet and like an ex-convict. He thinks
you look like a pugilist and a vagabond. In all these things he is undoubtedly partly right, for only ex-convicts and vagabonds have any right to be
moving about and breathing the air of night which is our ordinary climate.

Maybe you have had too much North American fallout, maybe your
bones are getting full of it. It is very deceptive. It eats the brain. It causes
disgust with fresh air, light, and an appetite for disaster. And yet at the
same time it produces curious resistances and is happily anodyne to much
nonsense. It is in any case incomprehensible and unknown to science. It
will eventually turn your skin blue. You will be the neon man. You will
speak in clicks. If I were you I would go back to South America, walking
on the water.

Should you change *Eco C*? It is very good that way, should it become
pseudo-sociological? What is the good of sociology? Maybe a little of it is
all right. There has to be more poetry. For *exploración*. The exploration
by poetry is the kind most needed now. Drama too, art, music, dancing,
seminars, silence. Someone has got to listen to the immense silence of
South America which is full of living vegetables and plants; all the other
silences have become full of wrecked cars, busted stoves and sewing
machines, junk lying around unable to speak.

Seriously, what I should do is go baptize children so they could be
admitted to your schools, then you could say they were baptized and they
preferred that kind of a school.

I would like to teach Indian children to read and then they could
teach me to sing and play flutes.

It would be my fondest ambition to become a Guarani poet.

I would like just to go and take over the parish in some Indian village
in the Andes and just give them everything free the way it is supposed
to be, and also help them get more to eat. For this I would probably be
poisoned by the priest in the next parish. Or by the nearest *hacendado*,
who would not however have me poisoned but just shot.

Small beginnings, no power, tireless patience of the seed in the
ground.

God has blessed the silence of the earth.

Say hello again to Ferlinghetti and to San Francisco. Are you really
there, or is it another shadow?

August 16, 1964

Thanks for your letter from SF. Two days from now, your birthday,
I will send up a rocket with a prayer wheel spinning in all directions, and

several other secret manifestations of technological shamanism will alert the planets of the seriousness of this occasion.

May you meanwhile grow newer as you peel off another year, like another skin. How many skins do we have? I don't know. They renew themselves as we go on. Nothing is determined, and our joy itself can renew life out of nothing. It is good to be fed with the joy that comes from nothing, miraculously. This is the manna of the desert and the sustenance of the New Man. I am in my fiftieth skin and trying to get it off like a tight bathing suit, too wet, too sticky, and irritating in the extreme. I have no set opinion about my fiftieth skin, and am willing to assert nothing except that I am fairly sure it is the fiftieth. And that it makes very little difference.

Except that as I get older I find it harder to keep my head above the flood of books and papers and letters and things that are all around me . . .

Tell Meg and Sergio [Mondragon] that I think of them and *El Corno* [*Emplumado*] often, mostly in silence and have written nothing much that would be any good for them. But I will send you a few things I have written lately. A book [*Seeds of Destruction*] is coming out in the fall with most of what I have to say about peace in it. I don't know how that happened, but it happened.

How was your visit to [Henry] Miller? He is a great guy. I will send him more pictures. How was Big Sur? Did you see the hermits there? I think they are probably perplexed hermits, lost in their beards, half expecting that they ought to become important. No hermit is important. That is why hermits are essential in a universe that is being ruined by a plague of important people. Down with importance. Down with the importance of monks. Down with the importance of beards.

Up with the revolution of tulips. Tulips are not important, they are essential. Yes, sing. Love and Peace, silence, movement of planets.

October 29, 1964

Today is for poets, and for writing to poets, since the sky has a warm front, it is perplexed, it is darkening, for poets. There will be rain for them and for nothing as it is fall, the leaves are becoming a mulch for whole forests and I like the smell. From England a poet who had read *El Corno* wrote from Oxford, talking the language, when I find out where I put his letter I will say he should write to you and there will be something flickering in England. And I suppose there is work and flame and light in Argentina. Go out to the monastery at Azul any time, the Superior there says you should come out, he will be glad to see you. I don't know how you get there except that you are in the bus for nine days and after that you are guided by pixies.

Next month in Louisville I astound the population with an exhibit of incomprehensible abstract drawings which will cause the greatest possible amount of perplexity on all sides and will perhaps bring everyone into a state of inarticulate stupor in which all things and especially the drawings will immediately be forgotten and everyone will rush to indulge in something else that is capable of being advertised.

My new skin is all right except that it is loose and gets caught in my glasses.

Where is *Eco?* Where is every pamphlet? Where are the new encyclopedias? I saw your bits in *Americas.* It is true. All the poets are on the right side of the prodigal son and the prodigal son is on the right side of his father and between them they are the light of the wilderness. This is defined as a new order. Without order, without laws, with nothing but prodigality.

The prodigal son is the only one who is not a stranger. Cousté's poem very well says that. And [Alejandro] Vignati's. To him I will write.

Do I have your right address? I will send you soon a new book on peace, race, monks, the world. I send articles, poems etc. etc.

All blessings, joy, light, peace. Yours in Christ, your pauper American uncle without millions, uncle of monks and quails, uncle louie.

January 1, 1965

It is January first and the beard of the calendar is shaved. It is now the illusion of a new year. Everybody claims to be happy on account of this beardless year, which they congratulate, and then they invite it into their houses. Ceremonies are held. Presidents are shot in honor of the clean-shaven calendar. Let there be the music of 1898 played in honor of this calendar, which is so old that it cannot possibly grow a beard any more. In truth, the whole calendar is senile, and for this reason it has to be assuaged with ceremonies, that it may continue to believe in itself. Let us therefore advance with confidence into the void of the new year, which will be honored by the extermination of calendars. Day by day they will be peacefully exterminated until their beard is so long that the year will be forced to abdicate and will then be replaced with a year that is two centuries old, so old that it is no longer recognizable. Thus the fraud of time continues from year to year, making history, producing new machinery for the measurement of time, and each year has to be selected from a very old time, before history, so that it may not be recognized. Thus the year is believed to be new. Happy New Year.

This year will be marked in history by the revolution of the furniture. First the footstools, then the chairs and tables. The cupboards and even the closets will reach out and grasp the most important and influential people by means of their doors and hold them fast, or absorb them into their shelves. The chairs will get in the way of diplomats and generals, tripping them up. The tables will lure them underneath themselves and then collapse on top of them. Other tables will invite the generals (always drunk) to dance on top of them and then while they are dancing, the tables will quietly tilt them out of top-floor windows. Bravo for the tables and chairs, bravo for the footstools. But there are not enough of the latter. The stoves will work manfully and cook everyone they can get rid of. Bravo for the stoves. *Viva la revolucion de los muebles.* The greatest work of all will be done by the WC consoles. They will console the rich and the mighty to the point of absorbing them entirely into their own occult system. Long live the consoles. Long live the closets. Long live water. Thus the furniture will contrive to vindicate time and make reparation for the frauds of the calendar.

After this sober estimate of the political future, I leave you no doubt deep in thought, dreaming no man knows what dreams. There is one calendar in the house that I refuse to shave, it is the Japanese calendar for the last year, the year of the dragon. Let all the years be the year of the dragon. I look forward with gluttony to the magazines you are publishing, and to all the answers to all the questions. Farewell to questions. This letter will be carried to you by a bird.

July 17, 1965

Your tulip on the green paper came from the mists and the waves. I have no green paper and no tulips, plenty of mists, no waves. I write of calamities, but that does nothing to change them, and they do not need to be changed for the reasons which you state. I travel in the same place. Here are some more poems. I have to write Vignati in Peru but because it means writing in Spanish I am slow, and swim under the waves, and stay under water. When I come up I forget.

This whole country is finally afflicted with a complete political madness. It is like living in a plague of fleas. All the fleas are being spread all over the country by [President] Johnson, who generates more fleas per second than any man so far to be discovered in recorded history.

All the fleas are going to Vietnam, which has more than enough fleas of its own already. But Johnson generates enough fleas in ten minutes to suffocate the entire world. He will do so, without flinching, since he is a man of principle. Watch out for such principles, they are infectious.

Tulips yes, fleas no.

March 11, 1966

I will try to use up the red ribbon. Only economy, nothing more, not politics. I am always glad to hear from you. The group you work with sounds good. I wonder if they are tied up with a priest who has been writing me occasionally. Now I forget his name. He used to be a Benedictine. Fr. Luis Cazalou. Maybe not the same group. He is around the docks somewhere I believe.

You say our monks in Argentina are perhaps friends with the *hacendados.* That is unfortunately all too probable. They do not know any better. Go tell them. It is possible that Gethsemani will take over the Trappist monastery that is in Chile. I will not be sent there however. I asked and was told "No." In any case I do not want to be anyhow, for many reasons. The woods here are where I belong. The deer were out the other night and I was looking at them (in the evening light) with field glasses, looking right into their big brown eyes. They could see me just as clearly as I could see them and they did not run away.

However, I have to go to the hospital to get my back operated on in ten days or so. That is a nuisance. I do not like to have them fooling with the bones of my back, but what can you do against science?

I do not expect anything but trouble all over South America, it is inevitable, and it will be very tragic for everyone. But perhaps some good may come of it. Keep on doing the good you can, and do not do anything silly. Being a secret priest is the best. Be priest monk and dervish. The secret kind is better because you have less trouble with bishops.

If I had a secret back I would not have any trouble with science. Is *Eco* still coming out or is that secret too? I send you a couple of poems. In Venezuela they have done a good job with my bomb book [*Original Child Bomb*], and I am in another one with L. Silva ["Prólogo" in *Boom!!!: Poema*].

Suns shine, bells ring, pretty soon it will be real spring. Now spring is only a secret, but I know the secret. I hear a bee. I am going to say some psalms.

October 8, 1966

I heard your cry out of the belly of the whale. Have not had much intelligence of events. Do you read Camus? I have read a lot of his stuff lately, mostly about intelligent and sober avenues of hope possible in the lower slopes of beast mountain. That is about it. The parade of dogs is everywhere, man. But dark eras cannot digest the indigestible. Sooner or later the whale ends by taking you where you are going and setting you down on your own doorstep, though you may not recognize it at first.

It is a long time since I had news of anything least of all in politics. All I can say is that some of the monks have gone to Chile, maybe if you go to Santiago you can go out to Las Condes and say hello to them. Not the Benedictine place at Las Condes but farther out, in the mountains somewhere.

I translated some stuff of Nicanor Parra for the New Directions annual this year. Reading also Miguel Hernández, whom I may translate some of perhaps, I don't know. Not very easy to put aside other things and do translations. Are you still editing twenty magazines? Not easy to edit twenty magazines in such a parade. I hear once in a while from Ludovico Silva. Have not written in a long time to Meg and Sergio. Ernesto C. I have not heard of for months but I guess he is on his island fighting the mosquitoes. He at least has only to contend with regiments of insects.

What is in this country? If you want to know what is inside this country, look at Vietnam because that is where it all comes out into the open. A big bucket of sickness. But everything here goes on in a dazed tranquillity. The patient is etherized upon the table. He makes no remarks and does not complain. The beasts chew on his flesh but he observes nothing.

I have lost the art of making reassuring noises. But we are nevertheless ourselves the body of hope and hope lives in spite of what we may be thinking: it does not need to be pushed any more than the grass does. But I am afraid there is going to be a very big war indeed. In the presence of which it would be foolish to make statements. Perhaps however we will be lucky, and it will not happen, and small statements will once again be possible.

Take care, Miguel, blessings love and joy.

October 28, 1966

Sun rises in mist with thousands of very soft explosions and I am entirely splashed with designs coming through the holes in the lace wall of trees. Everything in the world is transparent. The ferocities of mankind mean nothing to the hope of light. You are right, preserve your hopes. For this one must keep eyes open always and see. The new consciousness will keep awakening. I know it. Poets, designers, musicians, singers. Do you know Bob Dylan's songs? Wonderful poet. But he almost broke his neck on his motorcycle. Still he is getting better. He will bring out a book. But his records are the best thing. Now he is baroque. At first he was austere and social. Tell me more about *Cristianismo y R[evolución]*. Send me copies of those things. I can send you lots more stuff. I am writing about Camus. I am writing five million poems.

Will send you a bunch of the Camus articles and some poems. What are all the cats up to in Argentina? I know about Helder Camara. Great. Did you get my book *Raids [on the Unspeakable]*? Let me know. I will send stuff.

In Argentina is a marvelous poster designer Edgardo Miguel Gimenez. Do you know this fine guy? Does superb posters, you must have seen them around. If anything of his appears where it can be torn out and sent tear it out and send it to me, but I guess he doesn't sign his stuff. If you knew him you would know what was his. If you know him tell him hello. It would be wonderful to get him to design a book. Wish I could do this. If you know where this guy is maybe we could work out something.

New consciousness. There has to be clean water in the mind for the spirit to drink.

Courage and joy. Big *abrazo* for everybody.

To Hernan Lavin Cerda

Chilean-born poet and writer Hernan Lavin Cerda (1939–) first wrote to Merton in 1965 to request his assistance in translating poems into Spanish. In

1967, Lavin Cerda sent Merton a list of questions inviting his comments on technology, violence and the practice of nonviolence, the war in Vietnam, and the role of the "revolutionary intellectual" in Latin America. The interview, translated by Lavin Cerda, was published in the September 15, 1967 issue of Punto Final *in Santiago and has been reprinted as "Answers for Hernan Lavin Cerda: On War, Technology, and the Intellectual" in* The Merton Annual 2 *(1989). The Latin American intellectual, Merton wrote, "should return to the hidden springs of his own inexhaustibly real subconscious heritage," its Indian culture. Freedom from domination, for all peoples, calls for "true human resistance: the affirmation of life against the overwhelming death wish that is sweeping the world in crisis."*

Lavin Cerda published his first book of poetry, La altura desprendida, *in 1962. Neuropoemas, a collection Merton termed "first-class," appeared in 1966. Following the military coup in Chile in 1973, Lavin Cerda moved to Mexico, where he found a climate of freedom and pluralism conducive to his creative work. Lavin Cerda teaches literature at the Universidad Nacional Autónoma de Mexico and writes poetry, prose, and fiction. His recent publications include* Aquellas máscaras de gesto permanente *(1989),* Cuando yo era nino y otras desviaciones *(1990), and* Al fondo esta el mar *(1990).*

October 6, 1965

Thank you for your letter and your very good books, with which I am in complete agreement. I am very interested in all that you say about your projects, and I will be glad to help you, but I cannot write Spanish sufficiently well to translate poems! I wish that I could. Also, I don't know the North American poets sufficiently well. I tell this to Ernesto [Cardenal] often: I am not a North American poet, but rather a South American. I feel closer to them because of their sensitivity, irony, political point of view, etc.

If you want, I will send some books, and I am going to look for various papers, poems, articles and other things. I shall send them to you. [Henry] Miller is a very good friend of mine and has much to say, but he is old. Here he is very famous but he is read, above all, for "kicks" because he has a reputation of being pornographic. Actually he is a kind of secular monk with a sexual mysticism, that is understood very well in a technical age in which there is no normal life for the sensual but rather total corruption of the aesthetic and moral conscience. Miller is in total reaction against all of this.

In Chile I know Nicanor Parra, wonderful poet, I have translated some of his poems into English. They will appear next year with New Directions in an anthology.

If you understand English very well, I think it would be easier for me to write to you in that language. But I am not proud of the North American "civilization." It is a monstrous thing, a disaster. There are many people, young, intelligent, radical, that do not want to accept all that. But their protest is not worth anything. We are imprisoned in a gigantic, inhumane machine, something terrifying for the rest of the world that wants to imitate the technological progress of this country. Technology yes: but how to live in that same barbarity?

August 12, 1967

Before anything else I would like to praise your *Neuropoemas*: a first-class book. I like it all. Thank you very much! And also for your pages about Nicanor Parra, they are very good.

Unfortunately, it is impossible for me to write something serious in Spanish. I had to answer your questions in English. Only in that language of mine—or in French—can I say exactly what I think. If I try to write in Spanish, I have to limit my thought so that it can be contained in the few words that I know. I don't think it will be hard to translate what I have written.

In any case, here is the interview. I hope that it will be of use for something. I am happy to speak with my brothers from Chile. I have just seen that you were asking me for the interview in 5 quarter sheets: forgive me, I forgot to do that, and now it is too long. You will have to cut or condense it. Maybe it will be better.

I am looking for a photograph, taken by John Howard Griffin, the one who chemically changed the color of his skin so as to live among black people, and wrote a tremendous book [*Black Like Me*] about this experience.

October 20, 1967

I thank you for your letter and the copy of the *Punto Final*: I was very pleased, especially because you were telling me that it had produced a good impression. The only address that I have is that of Henry Miller . . . I think that he does not write much now, he is already quite old. I have not written a letter to him in a long time . . .

About your neuropoems, I advise you to send them to James Laughlin, New Directions . . . I don't know if he would like to publish the whole book, but perhaps he could publish some poems in his anthology which comes out each year. He is the North American editor of N. Parra.

It has been a long time that I have not been able to write Ernesto Cardenal, well, I shall do that immediately. I have much difficulty in answering all the letters that I receive and it is true that I am not able to do so: there are so many letters from sad women, from desperate students, from mad men, and from editors . . . I occupy myself most of all with the latter!

To Angel Martínez

Rev. Angel Martínez Baigorri, S.J. (1899–1971), was among the Nicaraguan poets mentored by José Coronel Urtecho. Rev. Angel's publications include Angel en el país del águila *(1954)*, Dios en blancura *(1960)*, El mejor torero *(1961)*, *and* Sonetos irreparables *(1964)*.

June 2, 1965

Your beautiful book reached me, beautiful visually and in its contents. I was most touched by your friendship and by the warmth of your words, and by your thought of me in my jubilee of existence. And I suppose it is partly because of this growing weight of years that I have been slow to respond. I cannot keep up as rapidly as I used to with the letters and jobs that surround me. But it was very encouraging to hear another voice from Central America, among those of all my friends there, and to feel that I belong to your world there as much as to my own: and this one here is not one to which one belongs comfortably.

Life in the United States poses more and more problems and fills one with confusion. The massive drift toward war, the unquestioned suppositions about the absolute use of power anywhere and everywhere, telling other countries how to arrange their own business, and doing this when we do not manage our own business in too edifying a manner . . . All this raises perpetual questions. Yet one of the most serious questions is that the questions themselves are not even seen except by a few. Pray for us. There are some of us who try to resist the drift.

Ernesto [Cardenal]'s ordination approaches and this fills me with happiness. I think of all his hopes and projects and hope that they will be blessed. I think of all of you there, Pablo Antonio [Cuadra], José Coronel [Urtecho], and yourself, not forgetting so many young poets who sometimes write or send their books. Though I shall probably never see any of you, at least not there, I feel very close to all of you. Let us continue to share our hopes and our trust, and may the Holy Spirit guide us and strengthen us in the love and following of Christ. I rely much on your prayers, and keep you in my own prayers too.

Fifty years in our time take one through many changes. I think I have seen too much history already, but there is probably more. Let us hope that what we will see in the next few years will surprise us by being less bad than we fear, and that God may show His Face and His truth in our history, in spite of the pride of men. And that we may reach a period of peaceful development, if it be possible.

To Victoria Ocampo

As a child, Victoria Ocampo (1891–1979) was already being prepared for her work as a writer, editor, lecturer, and publisher—work which would establish Ocampo as a woman of letters in Argentina and earn her international recognition. Her family, wealthy and influential, was able to provide Victoria and her sisters with the advantages of travel abroad and the care of French and English gov-

ernesses who immersed the children in the study of languages, literatures, and cultures. As a six-year old, Victoria visited Paris, Rome, London, and Switzerland, and she first learned to read and write in French.

Defying the conventions of Victorian society and the mores of Catholic Argentina, which cast women into narrowly circumscribed roles, Victoria Ocampo became a writer and a feminist. She published her first article in 1920 and her first book in 1924. She wrote some thirty books, including ten volumes of essays, entitled Testimonios and published between 1935 and 1977, and six volumes of autobiography, published between 1979 and 1984. Only her study of Lawrence of Arabia, 338171 T.E. (1942), and several of her essays have been translated into English. Perhaps it is as the founder and director of Sur, a literary review that appeared in 1931, and of a publishing house established in 1933 under the same name that Ocampo is best known. She conceived of Sur as a bridge between continents, between cultures, between peoples, and Sur served that purpose admirably. During the more than forty years that Ocampo edited the review, Sur published the work of Thomas Mann, Jacques Maritain, Henry Miller, T. S. Eliot, Simone Weil, Martin Heidegger, Evelyn Waugh, Albert Camus, and Thomas Merton. The publishing house brought out, in translation, works by Aldous Huxley, C. G. Jung, Virginia Woolf, D. H. Lawrence, James Joyce, William Faulkner, Jean-Paul Sartre, and Dylan Thomas.

Writing for a volume honoring Victoria Ocampo, Merton recognized her as "one of those wonderful people who includes in herself all the grace and wisdom of a universal culture." Ocampo is "a model for all of us in the breadth of her interests, her sympathies, and her capacity for sensitive understanding." She "symbolizes America in the broad sense, the only sense, in which I am proud to be numbered among Americans" (Seeds of Destruction, pp. 283–4).

January 13, 1963

Thank you for your letter—so beautiful and so touching. I would like to respond to you saying what cannot be said. How to make you believe what you do not dare to believe: that you merit these testimonials? The fact is that it would be necessary first to define merit. Alas it is a whole false theology and philosophy which it would be necessary to destroy. You see, it is *friendship* which, in the first place, merits this recognition which you do not have the right to refuse, for we love you. But clearly we are recognizing you because we have all benefited by your friendship. We cannot refuse you this homage. And this is precisely the true testimony which must be expressed among friends. But when the majority of one's friends are writers and intellectuals, this requires a book. I am very happy to be part of it. It amuses me very much that I appear there as a Jesuit (S.J.). It is marvelous! I do not know how so touching an idea got into Doña Maria Luisa Bastos's mind (or in the mind of some other of your friends?). But in any case it supposes that I am, after all, one of those priests who truly have enough imagination, spirit and humanity to be altogether non-conformist and off-beat. And moreover, I am proud of it! But I assure you that not all the other Jesuits are also non-conformist. But for me this is [what it means to] be a Christian and a priest—not to let oneself be congealed in the conventions of the right-thinking people.

It is a very beautiful book which I read with much pleasure and satisfaction, precisely because everyone says so many good things about you. One must resolutely accept being loved and admired, and we other "Jesuits" truly know that, for this true humility is necessary which implies the risk of a gap between what we are and what people say about us. But for this it is also necessary to know that before God things are not quite like this and that He makes people speak well of us so that we may therefore love our friends and the good that comes to us from them. And so it is that He then makes us love friendship more.

I congratulate you then, you and [Jorge Luis] Borges, on the honor which France has bestowed on you. The fact is that you deserve it. I very much like the very cultivated work of Borges. Also, I have just received the new poems of [Alberto] Girri. And I am going to write him to tell him these books please me very much. As for your new books I am counting on being able to get them and read them. T. E. [Lawrence] is someone I don't know well yet. I never read his big book but I know a little bit about his symbolic life, a life that is altogether non-conformist. It is necessary to be able to say by his life that the illusions and descriptions by which we live do not merit the loyalty which one grants them.

I believe I have sent you the new *Merton Reader* that might well be of some interest to you. I believe the editor [Thomas P. McDonnell] did a good job. At least I am more or less content to be able to present in one place ideas bits of which are to be found everywhere, occasionally in inaccessible publications.

In conclusion, Victoria, I do not really have the feeling that we are searching for God by different ways. At root one searches for God by only one way, i.e. in following the truth with all the sincerity of one's conscience. Is it not a fact that we are on the same path after all? I feel myself to be very close to you. There are not two Gods—mine and yours. But we have all lived in different circumstances, and God alone sees our hearts. Who knows if he does not take more satisfaction in yours than in mine? These questions are meaningless because we do not know what he does with them . . .

August 21, 1966

Thank you for your note from New York. I do not know if you are still in Paris, so I am sending this letter to *Sur*. There is also this small article on Suzuki ["D. T. Suzuki: The Man and His Work"] that might interest you for the review. Have you gotten to know him? Probably not.

But he was a great man. At any rate here are some pages on him written for a magazine in Japan [*The Eastern Buddhist*].

I recognize you a little bit everywhere, these days for example in reading Camus's notebooks. I am in the process of making a study of Camus and Zen. I have just finished an essay on his ideas about violence ["Terror and the Absurd: Violence and Nonviolence in Albert Camus"]. If it interests you, I will send it to you. Let me know.

I remain always united with you in much friendship and I think of you often.

January 20, 1967

Thank you for your kind letter rising up out of solitude. I try to imagine myself down there by the sea listening to its winds . . . Yes, I do understand you. Solitude is difficult, especially when the conduct of our friends ends up pushing us into it ever more deeply. We are truly pilgrims and exiles. It is necessary to know it and to "digest" it as you say so well. And we shouldn't let it poison us. For this it is necessary to have a little patience, because there will be days that, in spite of ourselves, will be full of this terrible venom. Yet it purifies, if one knows how to make use of it: if one absolutely refuses to be mean and to search for ways to enjoy one's resentment. And for "intellectuals" the means are always there: we know so well how to tear each other apart. It seems that it is for this that the "literary world" sometimes exists. Therefore it would be better to do as you do and to digest this bitterness in your solitude, let it be blown away by the winds of the sea. And then all is right.

But in short, psychology does not suffice. There is that mysterious "grace" of which the theologians speak not knowing of what they are speaking and of which clerics sometimes preach in a way that makes it suspect and odious to us. There is always this grace of God for which it suffices to seek, to ask for deep in one's heart. It is often given to us without our asking, without our knowing anything about it. I have just read a beautiful book by [Romano] Guardini on Pascal [*Pascal for Our Time*]: this same Pascal who so fascinated and repulsed Camus. Yes, there might be too much bitterness and pessimism in Pascal's solitude and yet he is so right and so acute. Also, I have reread his remarkable discourses on the passions of love. But I am the one who is too talkative.

Your trip to Europe interests me very much. I too find myself very easily in agreement with the young people. It is those who are between 30–40 today whom I understand the least. Since I very rarely, never, go to the movies, I cannot comment on your opinions on *Khartoum*. I know only that in the gospel of M [The Gospel of Matthew] there are wonderful figures. Of men, not the puppets of Hollywood. But I recall the essay, very ironic, by Lytton Strachey on [Charles George] Gordon ["The End of General Gordon," in *Eminent Victorians*]. Maybe he was unfair.

Dear Victoria, you can count on my prayers and on my friendship

—from afar. Right now I live alone in the woods. I am a hermit, by desire and by fact. It is very good. I do my work. I pray. I meditate. I study Zen. I write quite a few articles on Buddhism. And I am "present" to my friends in all parts of the world. My life as a hermit is much more "open" than that which I was living in the monastery. (I am still a member of the community, and I love living on the monastery property, where I take my meals to avoid my own cooking!) Keep well. Stay in peace. Have confidence. God bless you.

December 31, 1967

I wanted to write to you a bit more promptly to comfort you in your sadness. Alas I am engulfed in an ocean of letters. I will pray for your sister, and I have been really moved by the rightness of your phrase "holiness means a joyous forgetfulness of one's self . . ." You see, dear Victoria, that it does not have to do with waiting for the Church to canonize everyone. God has His saints whom He knows well and we live in a world of joy and of holiness of which we are not aware and of which especially the priests are not aware! I know Zen well enough to be a "Zen" Christian and to see that "presence" is all there is. Since one is there . . . But it is necessary to know it to appreciate it, even so.

I like Camus very much. I may write a book about him. No, I did not know him. I wish I had! Could you give me his wife's address? If I continue to write about him, I will need to consult with her. I also especially like his friend, René Char!! In my new book [*Cables to the Ace*], I wrote a passage in French inspired by Char. I am going to send it to you, in March.

Do you know that our small monastery in Chile has asked for me. I would like to be there, but I do not know if my superiors will send me there. If I were closer to you, I could perhaps come to see you.

Happy New Year, dear Victoria. The world is in a terrible state. This country is gravely ill. It is very painful to live here!

Happy New Year, I bless you and I will say Mass for your sister— and for you.

July 14, 1968

I was very sorry to hear of the death of your sister, and I want you to know that I offered Mass, after receiving the news, for her peace and rest in God. Yes, death is always something mysterious and in a certain way unacceptable. The very instinct of life itself says that death should not be: and yet it is inevitable. And sometimes the answers of piety are too easy. If, as Christianity believes, God Himself willed in some way to "empty Himself even unto death," then the mystery of it becomes all the greater.

The violence in this country and its moral disorientation are indeed disturbing. The wanton and useless destruction of life is something much more unacceptable than the fact of death itself. My own hope is that in spite of everything good will come out of what we are undergoing, though I do not see much evidence of it.

Unlike Camus, I believe in a Providence which will bring out of suffering the victory of mercy: but this does not absolve us from the necessity of courage. I thought you might like to see a couple of small things I have done on Camus lately, so I am enclosing them. In the end, I think he remains for us all a model of honesty and human courage. His position is one with which I can entirely sympathize, while differing from it in my faith.

I do want to give you this message of friendship and consolation, and assure you of my prayers for you and for the family. May God be with you.

To Nicanor Parra

Born in 1914 in Chillán, Chile, and educated at the University of Chile in Santiago, Brown University, and Oxford University, where he studied mathematics, physics and cosmology, Nicanor Parra became a professor of theoretical physics who also continued to distinguish himself as a poet. Parra published his first collection of poems, Cancionero sin nombre, *when he was twenty-three years old. His most influential work,* Poems and Antipoems, *appeared in 1953. Among his other books are* Versos de salon *(1962),* Sermons and Homilies of the Christ of Elqui *(1979), and* Poesía política *(1983).*

*Parra's work appealed to Merton, who found it "sharp, hard, full of solid irony," and who characterized Parra himself as "one of the best South American poets, a no-nonsense anti-poet with a deep sense of the futility and corruption of social life" (*A Vow of Conversation, *p. 160). Merton translated several of Parra's poems.*

March 20, 1965

Thanks very much for the two books of poems, which you sent me some time ago. You seemed diffident about *Versos de salon* but I enjoyed it very much and, as you see, I have made a few translations. [James] Laughlin would be interested in using some of my translations of your work, but after I had made these he spoke of needing some of the "antipoems," so I may try some of these later. I am not sure whether I do not like the earlier book even better than the more recent one. In any case I find that I agree with your dissonances, and find them to be in fact very monastic. In fact, today the poets and other artists tend to fulfill many of the functions that were once the monopoly of monks—and which of course the monks have made haste to abandon, in order to center themselves firmly in the midst of a square society.

You will notice that in one of the poems, "El pequeño burgués"

["Paradise of Squares"], I have had to make some adjustment, since the North American square is a little different from the kind found in the South. Yet of course I have not touched the essence of your poem or of your portrait of the *petit bourgeois* (one never hears this expression in this country).

The first poem of yours I read before getting your books was "Yo soy el individuo" and it is incomparable.

Has Laughlin sent you any books of mine? If he has not, please let me know and I will let you have some of the volumes of poetry. You might also like *The Behavior of Titans* and I shall ask him to send you my new book on Gandhi [*Gandhi on Non-Violence*] when it is out.

This letter is a bit inarticulate and pointless because I am trying to type it with an injured eye, in dark glasses, etc. etc. I could soliloquize about it with the modest bitterness of one of your characters . . .

June 12, 1965

I have just received your letter and am very happy. I was about to write to you because a new magazine, a very good one, *Lugano Review*, wants to publish three or four of my translations. I thank you for the many suggestions, each one gives us something better. I like your irony very much and I cannot tell you how much in agreement I am with you about contemporary society. We are in a time of the worst barbarity, much worse than in the time of the fall of the Roman empire. It is sufficient to look at what is happening in Vietnam and everywhere, most of all here. Sermons are worth nothing in this situation. It is necessary to state, without judgment, the truth of things. And that apocalyptic truth cannot be expressed in apocalyptic symbols, but only in "clichés." I wonder if you know about the "antitheater" of Ionesco (especially *L'avenir est dans les œufs*).

I still have not translated anything more of yours, since I am finishing a book about a prodigious Chinese writer, Chuang Tzu [*The Way of Chuang Tzu*]. I am sending you part of the work that J. Laughlin is to publish in the fall.

My eye is much better, and I am content in the woods in which I live as a recluse, protesting against everything, against the clergy and all.

I am happy that you are thinking about maybe translating some poem of mine: you will find that before knowing your work I had written some antipoems, for example "Chant to Be Used in Processions . . ." In truth this poem is composed almost in its entirety from the very words of the commanders of Auschwitz. It would be impossible to invent something more terrifying than the truth itself. In any event it is a somewhat difficult poem to translate. They have attempted it in Russian, without success I believe. But when they publish something in Russian it is hard to know. I think that you could do something with this poem, changing just a little bit the insinuations according to your own judgment and the spirit of your language. What do you think? Another antipoem is the one about the flight in space ["Why Some Look Up to Planets and Heroes"], and another is about a Chinese girl, Lee Ying ["A Picture of Lee Ying"], etc. But maybe you like the others better . . .

I will make up a small package of things, including some copies of the translations. I will make corrections on one of these. Later I want to try translating some of your antipoems, including my favorite, "Yo soy el individuo," and the one about the boy throwing the stone. I have seen some translations of your poems lately in a magazine, and they appeared to me to be very bad. I do not remember who they were by. They included some of the *Versos de salon* that I translated and there was no way of recognizing them as the same poems. I will let you know if I find out more about these. I saw them briefly in a library. Do you have your other books? I would very much like to have everything of yours . . .

Nicanor Parra and James Laughlin visited Merton in May 1966. See Michael Mott,
The Seven Mountains of Thomas Merton, *p. 525, for an account of their visit.*

April 28, 1967

It is almost exactly a year since your historic visit here. The weather is now once again as it was then. The leaves are on the trees and the birds sing. A deer just passed quietly through the sunny field in the front of the hermitage. I have often thought of you and have intended to write. Now I do so, as it is almost as if you were here. What can I say but "Come again soon." The other day I was again in Bernheim forest [near Bardstown, Ky.]. All the trees are labeled with signs like "Recognize me, I am the same as last year, speak with my angel on the telephone," etc. etc. The lakes are quietly waiting for picnics.

Hence the moral of the above story is that you should return.

I have heard little from J. Laughlin. He has had a hard time in the office, as he has probably told you. He is not coming down this spring but I hope he will be here in the fall.

And he has told me the very sad news of your sister's death. I am very sorry, and wish I could say something that might help you in your sorrow. But there are occasions when words are of no help. In my friendship I think of you and share your sorrow.

I keep working—I am busy with a long poem [*The Geography of Lograire*]. And I am also supposed to be doing a book on Camus.

Keep well, write more poems, come back.

To Margaret Randall

In 1963, Margaret Randall de Mondragon invited Merton to submit "something"
to the bilingual literary magazine she and her then husband, Mexican poet Sergio

Mondragon, were editing: El Corno Emplumado [*The Plumed Horn*], *which was founded as a forum for new voices of North and Latin America. Merton responded enthusiastically with poems and praise for Latin American poets and poetry.*

Margaret Randall [1936–] *was born in New York City and educated at the University of Mexico. In 1961 she moved to Mexico and, for the next twenty-three years, lived in Mexico, Cuba, and Nicaragua. In 1967 Randall became a Mexican citizen, thinking she could thereby improve her possibilities for work. In so doing, she was surprised to discover that she had relinquished her American citizenship. When she came home in 1984 she was denied resident status and received from the Immigration and Naturalization Service a deportation order, which stated that her writings went "far beyond mere dissent, disagreement with, or criticism of the United States and its policies." Four years of hearings, challenges, and concerted efforts by friends and fellow writers passed before the Board of Immigration ruled that she had never lost her U.S. citizenship. Randall tells the story of these years in* Coming Home: Peace without Complacency.

Since 1959, Randall has published over fifty volumes of poems, essays, articles, oral histories, interviews, and photography. Her most recent publications include: Women in Cuba: Twenty Years Later, Breaking the Silences: 20th Century Poetry by Cuban Women, Risking a Somersault in the Air: Conversations with Nicaraguan Writers, Christians in the Nicaraguan Revolution, *and* Walking to the Edge: Essays of Resistance. *In recent years, Randall has been teaching at the University of New Mexico, Trinity College in Hartford, and Macalaster College.*

January 15, 1963

Thank you for the letter and for the issue of *El Corno Emplumado* which I look forward to reading when it comes. Ernesto [Cardenal] sent me some of the earlier issues and I find it lively and full of good ideas. To begin with a bilingual Latin-American literary magazine like this is most necessary, and can fulfill a great function.

I am personally convinced that the best American poetry is written in Latin America. Besides Octavio Paz and a host of other Mexican and Central American poets I can think of, there are the great ones of a generation past, like César Vallejo, who is to me, I think, the poet of our century who seems to have the most to say. And all the new ones who are, or will be, coming up. One feels that in Latin America the voice of the poet has significance because it has something to do with life. Doubtless I am not in a position to give a sweeping critical judgment of the poets of the United States at the present moment as I do not get to read them, except for a few. Some have an unquestionable maturity and excellence, but few really say anything. In the midst of technological and scientific virtuosity we find ourselves (many of us anyway) in a spiritual stupor. My own work is, in its way, a protest against this. It is also an expression of something else again, of a dimension of life and experience in which the North American mind is not really interested.

In any case I am sending you two groups of poems. One is published already (it includes a few items that are printed, on cards or sheets). The other is recent and unpublished material, including a poem on the Cuba crisis ("Gloss on the Sin of Ixion"). I do not know if any of this will have been accepted by a U.S. magazine before you wish to print it, but it is supposed to come out in a book [*Emblems of a Season of Fury*] about the end of the present year.

Under separate cover I sent you also the book *Original Child Bomb* and I will have my *Selected Poems* sent to you. These and the published poems I enclose here may help fill in the background.

January 27, 1963

Your letter reached me today (there is often considerable delay in letters getting through to me here). Since I last wrote to you I have learned that the poem "Gloss for the Sin of Ixion" has been accepted by the *Saturday Review of Literature*. New Directions evidently sent it to them before I sent it to you, so I suppose they are entitled to it. I am sorry. But you have others to choose from. Incidentally the poem has already been translated into Spanish by Cintio Vitier, which I think is significant, since he is Cuban and it was translated in Cuba. Actually, the fact that the poem is going in the *Sat. Review* does not perhaps make too great a difference if you publish the poem in Spanish.

About publication of the letter: sure, go ahead. The only thing is that perhaps some reservations ought to be made. My sweeping judgments are not always based on a full battery of facts, as I do not have access to all the recent publications. My friends tell me that they think my impressions are generally fairly exact, but it should be remembered that they are often little more than impressions. That is, they tend to show up one interesting aspect of the situation, rather than the whole situation. Forgive my monastic scruples.

The letters you publish are often very good, full of life. They have a great deal to say, sometimes, and say it well . . .

October 9, 1963

Dear Meg and Sergio:

I can quite understand that you cannot read my handwriting, so I will make an attempt to communicate by typing, though I don't think my typing is much better. It is stimulating to hear that you like the calligraphies. The title I gave them was "Shamanic Dictation" but now, thinking about it, I think it is rather cheap and misleading. You can keep it if you like it, but I think that such calligraphies should really have no literary trimmings at all, including titles. There should really be nothing that misleads the spectator by seeming to give him a "clue." That is the curse of the literary incrustations that have still remained on so much abstract art: the mania for satisfying the spectators' foolish question about "what is it?". Until they can be content to accept the fact that the picture is simply itself, there is no point in trying to explain it, especially if the explanation seems to indicate that it is something else.

These calligraphies (this word is not a title but simply an indication of the species of drawing to which they belong) should really be pure and simple as they are, and they should lay no claim to being anything but themselves. There should be no afterthoughts about them on the part of the artist or spectator. Each time one sees them is the first time. Each stroke is so to speak first and last, all goes in one breath, one brushful of ink, and the result is a statement of itself that is "right" insofar as it says nothing "about" anything else under the sun. Therefore to bring in the notion of a pseudomystical experience is fraudulent in the extreme, even though it is only a joke, and meant to warn the spectator to reverse it and understand the opposite. Such maneuvers are silly and, as I say, misleading. So I would prefer to drop "Shamanic Dictation" as nonsense, and just call them calligraphies. Actually they have a kind of musical character, in a derivative sort of way. Though of course visually only.

If I am a bad correspondent and given to long silences, you must always understand me and the silences. I liked n. 5 and thought the translations were splendid. I also liked the Cuban section in the next issue, especially because of the necessity of listening and hearing what goes on behind fences. One must shout through all barriers, no matter what may seem to be the futility of doing so. I have long ceased to be afraid of the famous political seductions that are supposed to be exercised by the Marxists. Those who think that are still naïvely living in the thirties. They have not read the poetry that comes out of Poland today. One must go far beyond the shadows of Stalin and the other iron statues. When a Marxist poet writes as a Marxist he ceases to write as a poet, and the result is so obvious that it is laughable. That goes for every other brand of dogmatism that imposes itself on art *from without*. If a poet has experienced the reality of Russia, as did Pasternak and Yevtushenko, then what they say is respectable, with or without the blessing of the dogmatic fathers. When will people discover that artistic truth, and any other truth, is never manufactured in the offices of bureaucrats or thought police?

The warmth of your letters and the whole atmosphere of openness and frank friendship that *El Corno* represents make both it and you most precious in our world today. Much more significant than the stuffy and formal meetings of those who have power. This is not necessarily an age in which power and intelligence go together. I doubt if there ever has been such an age. But if there has, this is not it.

Do send me pictures of yourselves, especially Gregory and Sarita. Just small snapshots that I can pin up next to my desk, with my Brazilian nun translator [Sr. Emmanuel de Souza e Silva] and the children of a poet friend in England, and the picture of the town where I lived in France, in the Albigensian country. (You know that there now they are discovering the underground cultic labyrinths of the Cathars, where the elect fasted unto death in the *indura*. Fantastic stuff.) . . .

October 29, 1964

Thanks for the little book of poems of the glass which shatters, says go, and zigzags. I liked them all, and it is good for poets to send out books that people can take in their hands and read. How is *El Corno*? I hear echoes of it from all over the place. Miguel [Grinberg] must be back in Argentina by now, advancing on messianic principles. It was good to see him here and to be through him in touch with all of you, and your love, your trust, your risk.

I hear from Ernesto too, always good things from him. This fall I am having an exhibit of abstract drawings. Later I will send you some more if you want them for *El Corno*, or if you just want them not ever "for" anything. And perhaps a poem.

This bit on Flannery O'Connor ["Flannery O'Connor—A Prose Elegy"] is being published in a New York magazine [*Jubilee*]. Did you ever read her?

March 25, 1967

It is a long time since I have written. Mexico City seems very far away and *El Corno* floats in at very rare intervals. Are you there? Can you hear me? I am in the woods, now drenched in sun and spring, deer tracks all around where they have gone by in the night, hawks wheeling in the sun, quiet, alone.

But I have been in and out of hospitals. Crazy to believe the doctors maybe, but they get working on my bones, welding me like a sculpture or something. Doesn't seem to make much difference and I never know what it looks like. Walking around with secret works of art in my spine. Maybe they will come out one day in the abstract drawings I still do. Exhibit ran around various cities in funny corners or too sober college galleries. Will probably be coming home again all beat up soon minus a few that someone bought.

Apart from that I do not think anything much is new. I hear occasionally from Ernesto Cardenal on his wonderful island. I wrote quite a lot of poems last year and a few this spring so I am sending along a couple of sequences you may be able to use in *El Corno*. Let me know what you think to do with them, if anything. And meanwhile all love to everyone, you and Sergio and anyone who knows me around there, joy, peace, blessings, light. A rain of joys.

April 30, 1967

Very good to get your letter and all the books: also your own ms. of Cuba poems (I'll return, you may need this copy). Where to begin thanking you? [Jerome] Rothenberg first: the Gorky book [*The Gorky Poems*], beautiful, hard and flexible, no waste. I am very moved by [Arturo] Giovannitti of whom I had never even heard. Takes you back when: the kind of epic poetry that came spontaneously out of Sacco and Vanzetti, back when I was a little kid. Giovannitti's face looks like someone who came up to me when I was on a picket line against the Ethiopian war, came up and said: "Look, I am Italian, let me tell you what is happening in my country . . ."

Trees of Vietnam beautiful outspoken plain fire all the essentials are said.

It is spooky living in this country which is totally blind and with all instruments for seeing everything but the obvious. Poets see but what they say is not heard. All instruments for hearing everything except poets, prophets, etc. Or people. Only poems by cardinals and mandarins in an unknown language are scrupulously recorded and sung by the Republican and Democratic tenors in chorus. The fine smelling castrati laying scientific and literary eggs. Death is said to be very clean. Gradually this belief permeates the entire world.

I liked your Cuban poems. I envy you. I love Cuba, Cuban people. Not permitted in this country even to think of Cuba, still less of going to Cuba. Of course the thing is that when people are able to do something about deciding their own destiny they are relatively happy because they begin to become themselves. But also when a big fat people starts deciding everybody else's destiny then it becomes alienated by its own abuse of power, ceases to be anything but its own image of itself. A bad thing to have happen: death sits under the helmet, so sincere. Nothing else seems to exist. Communication is reduced to the algebra of death: equations from the Rand Corp. Apocalypse.

I look forward to the new issues of *Corno*: lots of good things in 20 the old ones and the new ones, you continue to do a very good job. I hear once in a while from Ludovico Silva, and like his *Papeles*. Ernesto wrote the other day that William Agudelo had gone back to Colombia, and reading William's poems gave me the feeling that this was the right thing for him: the poems are supercharged with the consciousness of two loves: God and woman. Actually there is one love. Each decides for himself what to make of it. He will find the unity he seeks not in solitude but in community.

Well I sit here with much rain coming down on my roof. It is true that I am conscious of being right in the *Corno* family. The communities of writers that I know here and there are my real families and very monastic in a real way. With Church people (officially Church people) there is still all the noise, all the arrogance, all the obsession with being eternally right: the progressives and radicals are as bad as the conservatives: all in their own little boxes surrounded with restrictions. Blake was right.

June 6, 1967

Thanks for your very good letter. In these days when the big stupid machine is running away from its drivers again, it is good to have sane friends around that one can talk to, even if only on paper . . .

Every once in a while someone wonders why I am a monk, and I don't want to be always justifying the monk idea because then I get the false idea that I am a monk. Perhaps when I entered here I believed I was a monk, and kept it up for five, ten, fifteen years, even allowed myself to become novice master and tell others what it was all about. No more. I have nothing to say about this institution except that I wonder if it has any future, at least as it is, and also I am really not that much part of it now. I live alone in the woods and have as far as feasible for me copped out of the monastic institution as well as out of the civil inst. Of course that too is delusion. But as far as I am concerned the question "why do you have to be a monk?" is like a question "why do you have to live in Nebraska?" I don't know. It's what the karma added up to, I guess. Here I am, and it would not be physically easy for me to get somewhere else, but on the other hand I have what I want: a certain amount of distance, silence, perspective, meditation, room to do the things I know I must do. I would go nuts trying to do them in a city. Is this better? Certainly only for someone who knows he has to do it this way, more or less, or something like this. But not necessarily for anyone else. I am sure you are quite right about the ordinary life etc. This is a more ordinary life than you think, and also I wonder if I am more out of life or more in it? To me, the woods are life. Of course there is a lot wrong with it. Certainly it would be wonderful to have children to look after and as you say learn from. But I know for my own part that being married would be a very difficult proposition, much too complicated. Loneliness can be terrible too, but somehow I can handle that better. I'm only saying that is the kind of compromise with life that I have ended up with, and not making out it is wonderful: but it is what I can handle. More or less.

Of course, in another kind of society . . . That is why I understand what you feel about Cuba. But unfortunately all the big societies now seem to me to be so built on lies and fake rituals they are really unlivable. Naturally I agree that this can apply very well to the Church also. Well, as you see, it's all inconclusive. In the end we live as best we can, and find the kind of joy we are capable of: call them if you like "contemplative" in my case. Prophetic Ambiguities ["Prophetic Ambiguities: Milton and Camus"] was published in *Sat. Review*, after all. It is long. If you are interested in that kind of thing I have other bits, shorter perhaps, or you could just edit this. Let me know what you think.

With things as they are now in the world, I wonder if we are getting around to one of those times when we ought to be saying goodbye and getting ready for God knows what, the bombs, the camps, another round of the same. For the U.S., if it is not nuclear war that lies ahead then it is some form of fascist violence, I think. Whatever it is, I'll stay in it, and try to keep in contact with the poetic underground!

July 6, 1967

. . . Thanks for your good letter. We are very much in contact I think, and see things alike. That is always good. Something one can neither account for fully or be thankful for enough. I am glad. As for the other letter, sure, feel free to use it as you like. And I look forward to the next issue of *El Corno*. I want to keep up my contacts with Latin American poets, and have been falling behind in that. I ought to do some translations, some articles. I have not been able to. I have not been able to do anything about the books and things people send: have not even sent something in return most of the time. Thanks very much by the way for Ted Enslin's little book which I had not seen. I am glad to have it, and like it a lot. Of course I have seen his work here and there in the magazines, but I have never got in contact with him.

Do you see *Peace News*? It often has extremely good things in it. I have a few extra copies of this issue because of my own piece in it, so I send one along. And you might like the little pamphlet on Buddhism.

It seems to me that we all have an enormous amount to do just looking for what is real: and of course that has to go on all the time because you never definitively find anything that stays real in the same way the next day (except in its metaphysical ground, and that can't be "possessed" by an individual as his "own"). We have our life's work cut out for us just keeping real. The tragedy is to suppose that a society, an institution, a cause, or even a Church, will do the job for us. And it is rough to have to recognize that what we have been trying to build has to be taken apart and put back together in a better way—and with a lot of trouble. Yet there is always something very good about starting out all over again. I seem to be getting along toward something like that, as I suggested: finding new dimensions and directions. The best ones are those that do not appear to be anything much and cannot be explained. I am sure though that you are on to something real with the Cuban business, and I wish you joy. But the poems and the children too are right in the center. Your big job is most of all to be you, and I am happy to be one that this "you" can talk to. Never hesitate to do so. And I'll talk too in my own turn.

December 13, 1967

So many thanks for the beautiful new book and for the poem. Much moved by all of it. Great warmth and life. Good.

This is just a real quick letter to say I have decided to edit a temporary magazine [*Monks Pond*], four issues only, four collections, offset, can be done without trouble here so might as well do it. Need poems, prose, ideas, anything, so long as it doesn't get me burned by the monks. If it is something they don't figure out ok. Can you send me a poem or something? And Sergio? How about something on yoga? On meditation? Or what is wrong with monks? Or about anything that makes life have meaning. Ideas. Visions. Or just what the sun shines like. Anyone you know who is interested. Tell. It will be only four collections (4). No money either way, all given away.

January 8, 1968

Thanks for so many fine things. I'm using three for the first issue of *Monks Pond* and returning the others, though I like everything. "Che" should get more circulation than there is in this pond! As to the very moving piece on the marriage—it is very affecting and beautiful in a simple, stark way. Again, this is not the right place for it, but I do want to see it in print: have you thought of the *New Directions Annual*? (It can be somewhere else too, they reprint.) I am so sorry you had to be hurt like that. It shows in your most recent photo (on the book of poems). Oh, poor Meg. Peace. Courage. The pity of it: the way people get torn up by life, and needlessly, yet it can't be avoided. I hope Cuba has made it better.

Lots of nice stuff coming in, and am looking for Asian, Indian (Maya etc.) texts if any around. Have some good Zen stuff if I can get clearance to use it, one of the very greatest of the Chinese Masters. Shen Hui.

It is very cold here, eight below zero this morning. Woods full of snow. Quiet. I haven't heard from Sergio, but anything that comes will be most welcome. If you get any more ideas of people who might send things I'll get in touch with Ernesto of course. And send more yourself. It will only run four issues but I hope to have more of your verse or prose. Peace, joy, love.

April 12, 1968

Thanks for your nice letter and for the lovely photo of the children. I am sending five copies of *Monks Pond* separately with some extra photos and some of the enclosed, of which I have a lot.

Do please send me some more for one of the other issues—some of your own and perhaps some of the translations. I'm going to try to hold myself down to only four or five issues, though it will be hard to do so, so much good stuff coming in. Still, it is difficult for me to do all that is involved (having to sort out the pages and get them together partly myself) and I lose poems, forget to answer letters etc. Everyone has been very patient with me.

Nice spring weather here now, and all kinds of birds singing, nesting in the high rose hedge that is outside.

I think of you often, feel very close to you, often wonder if I couldn't at this late date run away to Cuba myself, but obviously that is out of the question. Like to get out of this insane country but I don't think that would be for me honest: must stay and take the consequences, and also undergo the complexity of having to understand, and make allowances for each different person, group, etc., and there is no getting away from the big sickness. I do think that life will come back unconquerably from its own center, and the fact that there are still so many gentle and loving people, with very positive life-drives, does something to redeem the situation.

I have a lot of other letters to answer, so must stop.

To Ludovico Silva

Venezuelan poet Ludovico Silva (1937–1988) studied philosophy at the Universidad Central of Venezuela, where he later became a member of the faculty. The prodigious author of more than thirty books, he wrote poetry, essays, and literary criticism. In the seventies and early eighties, he published several theoretical studies of ideology, alienation, socialism, and Marxism. A collection of Silva's poetry, Obra poética, *1958–1982, appeared in 1988.*

At Silva's invitation, Merton wrote the autobiographical essay "Day of a Stranger," which described a "typical day" in his life in the hermitage. Translated by Silva, it was first published in Caracas in a literary magazine called Papeles *in the summer of 1966. Silva also translated the "prólogo" Merton wrote for Silva's* Boom!!!: Poema *(1966).*

March 13, 1965

One reason why I am so slow in answering is that I stop and try to think out a letter in Spanish and then see that time is going, and doubt whether I will be able to write it. So this time I will write in English so as not to delay longer. Besides I do have a phenomenal amount of correspondence, even though I am most of my time in the woods. I am still unfortunately involved very much in the business of writing and in the contacts that this involves, and also in the work of the monastery.

First, I will get busy and dig up a "manifesto" for you, as well as the books I promised. You can take anything you like from the books . . . It seems that Caracas is very much alive poetically, and above all the editions are splendidly handsome. I thought Roberto Guevara's book [*Las días móviles*] was beautifully produced, the drawings were very interesting and lively. The poems themselves are I think of a very high quality with much promise, a fine sense of distances and areas and movements with a cosmic and dreamlike solemnity. I am especially struck by the fifth section and the sixth even more, in "Noche heredad nómade." I once did a version of a piece from Meng Tzu ["Ox Mountain Parable"] in which he speaks of the power of the night spirit which recreates and renews life. Ernesto [Cardenal] translated it, and I don't seem to have a copy, but it is also printed here in a special edition [*Ox Mountain Parable of Meng Tzu*, Lexington, Ky.: Stamperia del Santuccio, 1960] . . .

I wish my life were nothing but silences and spaces, but there is also action and responsibility, much of which turns out to be illusion. However, as time goes on perhaps I will be able to get rid of the useless motions and think only thoughts that will enable me to write sooner and more intelligibly to poets. It is to me a great joy and encouragement to hear voices like yours from South America. Here in this country all is sickness and confusion, the poetry itself (some of it good) is drab and bitter. Under the mask of power in this land is a great hopelessness. I think it is due in part to the fact that anyone with any sensitivity is overwhelmed with a diffuse and inexpiable shame.

May you have peace and joy and insight.

April 10, 1965

Dear Rosita and Ludovico:

First I am sending back the translation of the "Prólogo" [for L. Silva's *Boom!!!: Poema*], and want to say it is terrific. I always like my stuff better in Spanish than in English. It is always a joy to see that it comes out well in Spanish. I have often told Ernesto and others that I feel more a part of the scene in Spanish American poetry than in the North American field, where I am a bramble among the flowers. Or at least, I feel I have not much in common with the poets here. They are either esoterically stuffy and academic, or else they are in some special way beat and confused and self-pitying, or else tamely messianic in some other special way . . . I don't find myself able to pay much attention. What comes from Mexico, Central America, South America is something to which I can immediately respond. It seems to me a) real and b) civilized.

I made a couple of small additions, which you can put into the English. Don't worry about *estiércol*: your translation is perfect. The English is "dunghill." I thought for a moment of *mierda atómica* but perhaps that is less appropriate.

Thanks for *Cal*. It is a prodigiously good literary paper. I liked Sergio [Mondragon]'s Kundalini poem, especially because it took over the Hindu idea so naturally into the Mexican Indian context. Who is the fantastic old poet whose prophecies, in his own handwriting, are on the front and back?

When *Boom* comes out can I have a dozen copies, or maybe fifteen? I am eager to see it, and am sure it will be very well done. As to my being an important person: who said so? This may perhaps exist in someone's imagination or in the papers or something, but it has nothing to do with reality and I do not intend to be imprisoned by it. I do what I like, until they shoot me. And if I meet myself coming down the street looking important I sneeze and the apparition disappears.

Ludovico: the religion of the astronauts corresponds to the most primitive religious aspirations of man: to fly in a complete void. It is in many ways much better to force the body out into the *nada* of outer space than to seek to do it purely mentally, in a misconception of John of the

Cross. The religion of our time, to be authentic, needs to be the kind that escapes practically all religious definition. Because there has been endless definition, endless verbalizing, and words have become gods. There are so many words that one cannot get to God as long as He is thought to be on the other side of the words. But when he is placed firmly beyond the other side of the words, the words multiply like flies and there is a great buzzing religion, very profitable, very holy, very spurious. One tries to escape it by acts of truth that fail. One's whole being must be an act for which there can be found no word. This is the primary meaning of faith. On this basis, other dimensions of belief can be made credible. Otherwise not. My whole being must be a yes and an amen and an exclamation that is not heard. Only after that is there any point in exclamations and even after that there is no point in exclamations. One's acts must be part of the same silent exclamation. It is because this is dimly and unconsciously realized by everyone, and because no one can reconcile this with the state of division and alienation in which we find ourselves, that they all without meaning it gravitate toward the big exclamation that means nothing and says nothing: Boom. The triumph of speech, when all the words have worn out, and when everybody still thinks that there remain an infinite amount of truths to be uttered. If only they could realize that nothing *has to be* uttered. Utterance makes sense only when it is spontaneous and free. (The question of torture comes in here also. Very significant. It comes from the illness of mind of those who imagine that in themselves is a deep mystery seeking outlet, and that it can somehow be made real and true if they can force others to utter, from their degradation and pain, a word that corresponds to their own arbitrary, magic illusion of what might be wanting to get out of themselves. Torture as an expression of sickness in the collective unconscious.)

That is where the silence of the woods comes in. Not that there is something new to be thought and discovered in the woods, but only that the trees are all sufficient exclamations of silence, and one works there, cutting wood, clearing ground, cutting grass, cooking soup, drinking fruit juice, sweating, washing, making fire, smelling smoke, sweeping, etc. This is religion. The further one gets away from this, the more one sinks in the mud of words and gestures. The flies gather.

The Cross is the exclamation that nobody understands, and it is also the prototype of torture as "speech." But Christ said nothing, except ritual words and quotations that were pure and full of silence. They had no political implications, they defined nothing, they uttered no program. They abolished all programs: *consummatum est.*

The *Chronica* has not come yet. It will, probably. I am sending a mimeographed book which you can use in small pieces, here and there, without fuss, but a lot of it is irrelevant. I am happy Rosita is translating the Zen article. Which version do you have? The printed one is more complete. Let me try to send one, you will see.

Blessings and peace. May Christ's love be with you in silence and peace.

June 30, 1965

This is what happens when I turn aside to do something else: letters do not get answered, and weeks pass. I am now in the presence of a pile of important mail that has been neglected, so this will have to be a short answer.

Properly, the best translation for "Stranger" in the essay ["Day of a Stranger"] would be *extranjero* but the idea of exile, of displaced person, of alien, also comes in. How about *ajeno*?

Thanks for the pictures of you and Rosita. It is wonderful to know you better—you both seem very simple and open and young. For my part I am perhaps not as fierce as my picture makes me seem.

I am glad *Boom* is coming along. It sounds better all the time, and I hope to see it soon.

The important thing in thoughts about God is not to reduce the idea of God to that of an *object*. Unfortunately, this is what most talk about Him implicitly does, and that is why you instinctively take the approach of *todo cuanto hay*, because you are seeking to overleap the subject-object division. This is exactly right, but the metaphysical implications you draw from it do not necessarily have to follow. The best approach is existentialist, and the existentialist approach, in theology, is not through abstract dogmas but through direct personal confrontation, not of a subject with an object but of a person with an inner demand. There has been too much atrocious theology. It is best not to struggle with Jesuit speculations. They are often completely meaningless. I will send you a biblical essay of mine ["The Name of the Lord"], if you like. The root of it is "I am who I am."

You mention coming here for a month, cutting wood etc. I am afraid the way things are set up here, this is not possible. Visits are restricted to a few days, there are lots of retreatants, the guest house is very dull, and I myself am quite restricted as regards contacts. Things should be the way you would like them, but because of the crowds of people who come it is too much organized and it is not what you are seeking. So while I remain in the smoke (not now, it is very hot) or in the bushes, with the animals, I am not able to share this directly with anyone who might come to visit. I think on the other hand when Ernesto gets his place going in Nicaragua you will be able to do exactly what you mention. He is going to have a place precisely for this kind of thing, which is impossible here.

Best wishes to both you and Rosita and a big *abrazo* for both of you.

October 26, 1965

Your letter, which I received yesterday, makes me very happy. I didn't know what had happened to you. The thing is I had not received the previous letter, of which you speak, about Helsinki, etc. Nor did I receive the translation of "Day of a Stranger." Perhaps they came to the monastery but were not given to me: you must know that the mail is opened by others, and sometimes—very arbitrarily—there is something which does not pass. But it would be difficult for me to understand why they would not have allowed a letter of yours to pass, and above all a translation, which would be "business," and business is sacred, isn't it? In any event you must know that I live under censorship, and that sometimes this requires discretion. I think that they are a little suspicious of my relationship with Latin Americans because they know that I love Latin America so much and they are afraid that one day I might want to leave to go there . . . I don't know if there is another reason.

Tell me something about your trip to Europe: I never travel. I have to travel vicariously through my friends. Ernesto Cardenal was here, and is in good health, very happy. I was very pleased to see him. He was speaking about you. As for *Boom*, I am waiting patiently. Yes, I would probably like to do a translation: I think that Laughlin would publish it in his anthology: but to publish it as a little book would be out of the question: I already published a very similar book, but it was not successful. You have seen it, I think: the *Original Child Bomb*: I don't remember if we have spoken of it. But yes, of course, it is the one which some friends of yours were translating over there.

Now I have to leave for the monastery and put this letter in the mail. It is late.

January 17, 1966
You are right about the North American poets. The more I think about it, though, the more I see that the whole question of American poetry, North and South, is a very big question. It is something so big that I for one never face it, and I do not think anyone has. But anyway, I do not even read most of the North Americans. I do not even know who most of them are. Once in a while I come across someone I think is good, then I even forget his name. George Oppen is an unknown who I think is pretty good. I don't know what [Robert] Lowell means to you in South America: probably nothing. I think he is a good poet for the U.S. but I don't know what he could mean to the rest of the world (except England). Perhaps one of the few American U.S. poets that has something to say for everybody is [Allen] Ginsberg. Do you know him? I [will] send a volume of his stuff. Do I like him? That is not the question. When I read Ginsberg I do not feel at home with him or like him as I like [César] Vallejo or Nicanor Parra, but it is a curious experience of recognizing an authentic interpretation of a society in which I live and from which I am in many ways alien. Ginsberg speaks a language I know because I hear it every day, and yet he is remote also. He talks about a country of which I happen to be a citizen, and yet it is not "mine." As a matter of fact, in

many ways I have no country at all. The country in which I live is in-comprehensible. I think all the clichés about it are crazy. but I do not want to invent others. I do not know whether it is all headed for ruin, or what. A North American poet has to say something of this, and I think the merit of Ginsberg is that he is authentic and does not judge. On the other hand I think it is a pity that it all has to be done with drugs . . .

If you send the translation of "Day of a Stranger," all right. If you don't, all right. I do not need to go over it, and will be content to have it when it is printed. I look forward very much to *Boom*. I will take that question up with Laughlin when I hear more from you about it.

I think it is important to write antipoems like Parra.

Your piece on Cardenal's *Gethsemani* was very good. You are right that Cardenal is now this way and now that, doubtless. You have no idea how difficult and complex a task he has taken upon himself, to be a poet and a priest at the same time and in a society that is completely fed up with priests. He is just beginning, and the task of being two people is still difficult. Only when one realizes that one cannot be two people, can one be two or many people, that is everybody. No priest and no poet is really mature until he is everybody. But who is everybody? One lets go a little, and one begins to disappear in everybody, and then one wakes up and begins to defend a limited identity once again. An uncomfortable existence. This discomfort is not necessary for those who identify them-selves completely with a Church (like the ordinary priest) or a party (like the Communists).

Here everything is very gray (early dawn) with snow that fell in the night and is just beginning to be visible.

Do you read [Rainer Maria] Rilke at all? Does he mean anything to you? I think you would like the *Duino Elegies* and the *Sonnets to Orpheus*.

September 13, 1966

I have already received *Papeles*. Beautiful magazine, very well pre-sented, with many very interesting things. Of course I have not read it all, but [I did read] all the poems. I am going to see the rest later. Could you send me another five or six copies? Thank you. I will make it known to others.

I am as always living my days of a stranger. I think that in my last letter (of May?) I spoke to you of my experience in the hospital. Maybe I sent you the poem that I wrote then ["With the World in My Blood-stream"]. In any case, here is another copy. I am reading poetry, especially René Char, I am writing poetry as well. I realize that for me to write theology is to waste time, given that I am in no way a theologian: I am more a philosopher and poet, an existentialist, a rebel and a general problem. During the summer, I wrote a series of short poems [with the working title, "Edifying Cables"] that I will send you when I have copies. An excerpt of my new book [*Conjectures of a Guilty Bystander*] was in

Life and consequently it was read by hundreds of angry and moreover confused people: as well as some more sympathetic people. I think that the book will appear next month and I will also send you a copy.

I only received one copy of *Boom*, very beautiful, with a great poem and beautiful artistic presentation. Can you send me more copies? Perhaps ten or twelve? I will be very pleased to have them.

I don't have news from Ernesto. Already, a Rumanian [Stefan Baciu] . . . exiled in Hawaii wrote an article about him for a magazine in German. I am going to suggest that a rich friend of mine in Switzerland . . . translate some of Ernesto's poems into German. I think that Ernesto's community [at Solentiname] will develop a bit slowly, but it will be successful.

I am also writing some studies about Camus whom I read almost all summer long.

If you want, I will send you some abstract drawings that might be used for *Papeles*. Like those in the little book *Raids on the Unspeakable* . . .

March 30, 1967

Thank you for your letter and the copies of *Papeles*. I had not received the previous letter of which you spoke, the one in which you had written to me about the drawings. I am pleased to know that you have received them and that they may be of some use to you. I read with pleasure your observations, somewhat hidden in allusions. Well, you are right, one has to have clear sight: but in politics it always happens that the emotions and the passions have too much power. I cannot understand why in politics, as in religion, those who have ideas and interests most in common can be divided in a terrible way, with the worst disasters.

. . . About *Papeles*: naturally it is an avant-garde magazine and purely secular in its outlook. Hence it is not designed to please middle-class Catholic taste of a conservative bent. I would hesitate to call it "immoral"—at least in what I have seen of it. It simply offends a certain kind of middle-class modesty and decorum, and in any case it is not designed to be used in the instruction of children in parochial schools, since it is for secular and radical university circles. In my opinion, it is the business of a Catholic intellectual to understand and tolerantly fit in with such attitudes of mind and not attempt to impose his own tastes and standards upon others except in self-evident instances of public immorality. I do not think that there is anything I have seen in *Papeles* that answers this description. On the other hand I think the Vietnam war does tend to answer such a description, and does call for protest: yet many North American Catholics do not see this. In these matters, then, there exist different viewpoints and we must be slow to expect everyone to see things as we do. *Papeles* intends to be a challenging and provocative magazine, and it succeeds. Naturally some will be offended by it.

. . . I am happy to feel in agreement with you and with your collaborators, above all in the matter of Pan-Americanism. Regarding the details of politics, it is natural that I do not understand everything that happens because I do not have information: nor do the others in this country in which the daily newspapers present a somewhat "distorted" perspective. Everywhere it is the same, more or less.

April 27, 1967

If you wish to publish the fragment of my letter about *Papeles*, it is fine with me. I would very much like to help you all, and my opinion seems to me to be sufficiently reasonable to conciliate even the most frantic priests. But I also know that it is not only about reason but also about emotions [which are] more difficult to conciliate. For there is one thing that makes it difficult: if those priests get very upset with my defense of *Papeles*, they are capable of writing to the Father General of my Order so that I will be prevented from publishing anything else in *Papeles* in the future. But I do not believe that the case is that serious. I leave to you the responsibility of judging according to the reality of the situation. If you want to publish that part of my letter, I give you permission with great pleasure.

I am pleased to know that Gustavo Díaz Solis is translating my *Cables* [*to the Ace*] (something rather difficult to translate in certain parts in which there is a play on words in English). The version that he has is not the most complete one, I continue to work on that series of poems which is turning out to be now much longer and is not yet finished. If you want to publish a short version (probably it is better for the translation, because what I have written later is more hermetic with more play on words), if you want this version, I give it to you. I will be happy to so see it in *Papeles*, for I think it would be better in Spanish. It seems to me that I always like my poems a little more in Spanish, and to tell the truth I have always been lucky with the poets who have translated me. Like Ernesto. Well: you have *Cables* for 5.

I am also in the middle of a new long and mad poem [*The Geography of Lograire*] which seems to me much better than *Cables*. I don't know if it will ever be possible to translate. It all depends on the word association in English.

The future of poetry: my reaction is totally positive. The poets have much to say and do: they have the same mission as the prophets in the technical world. They have to be the consciousness of the revolutionary man because they have the keys of the subconscious and of the great secrets of real life. But the governments are full of poet-killers and of anti-poets with machines to fabricate only death and nothing more. Then, the future of the poets depends upon their freedom, the freedom of conscience and of creation. The future of poetry is also the future of the world. For one cannot truly believe in God if one does not believe in mankind as well: the poets will triumph. We will triumph. God is with the poets. That is why I am especially happy to know that *Boom* has some success with those who know how to read.

I send you some essays with my hug.

May 19, 1967

If you wish to publish "Terror and the Absurd," very well. The article is yours. But it is already being published in India, in the magazine *Gandhi Marg*. I think that that distant publication does not matter to you. In any case, the article has not yet been published in the United States [the essay was published in *Motive* in 1969].

I think also that what your Catholic "enemies" say is not important. It is a question of bourgeois, conservative people, who do not understand anything about the real situation: who is going to listen to them? Other than some children and old women. Do not worry about their obsessions.

If you think that the essay about Alberti may serve the new biweekly, very well. It appeared in a magazine that is not well known ["Rafael Alberti and His Angels" was published in *Continuum*]. I send you as well some pages about art and Zen ["Zen in Japanese Art"] published (but not yet) in the magazine of our order [*Collectanea Cisterciensia*]. If this copy is not good for anything, please return it to me. Thank you.

Yes, of course I will send you the "long and mad" poem, but it will take awhile before it is done, because it seems an epic of madness. I do not know how it will develop.

With all my friendship for my companions in Venezuela—an embrace of truth and light.

July 26, 1967

I have not answered your letter dated May 25 because I did not know if you had gone to Europe. And I still do not know. In any case, I want to send you something again. I do not know if I can promise to write something regularly like a "bibliography"—perhaps it would be better not to try to do it systematically. However, if I send you copies of what I write here, you can take what you want, and I think that we will always have something to publish.

About payment, I do not much care. Why don't you send at least the payment for the first article to Ernesto Cardenal to help him a bit in this foundation. The others, you can send to me here, and if I think of something else, I will tell you.

What you tell me about your novel seems very interesting. I also wrote some novels when I was young, and I liked it very much, but now I do not know if it would be possible for me—at least a more or less traditional novel. Something totally new, experimental perhaps—well, it would not be a novel. I think that it is very good for you to write this book, as an experience and as a purification. And if the novel does not go well, you may be able to make use of the material in another way.

It is very hot here, almost tropical: and in the cities there is violence—which should not surprise anyone, and we are going to have even more. I fear a dictatorship within two or three years—perhaps more. We are going to have a very big reaction. But force cannot achieve anything with these people in poverty in the black neighborhoods. It is hell.

January 26, 1968

I am happy to receive your letter and to have news from you. You are right to explain your illness in more spiritual terms. The positivism of the psychiatrists does not perfectly understand what happens in those strange cases. I know a psychiatrist from Iran—who has done studies on the mysticism of the Sufis—and he knows very well that without that kind of crisis one cannot pass into a higher state of development. Your words make me think that you understand very well your situation and that you can take advantage of it. But the important thing is not to try to maintain a false "social" identity for greed or for fear and not to try to extend yourself beyond your ability. But one must understand the richness and the strength of the secret which one currently has in one's reality and in one's heart: and to allow that richness to develop in a more or less invisible way. Then your "demon" will become good.

I am trying to send you something brief for the new magazine. I don't know if I have something: do you want poems?

We are very near some terrible events in the United States. A revolutionary impulse which will achieve nothing else than to establish the reign of the police and of violence—and of lies. It is tragic. The only hope is in the Third World.

Fearsome winter. I live in the woods with snow, fire and sickness. Things go well in that silence.

To Rafael Squirru

Thomas Merton wrote to Rafael Squirru (1925–) after reading his book The Challenge of the New Man, *published in 1964 by the Pan American Union. Merton thought the book made an important statement and said so in letters to several of his Latin American friends. Perhaps the most important statement in this letter concerns Merton's distinction between "European" and "universal" Catholicism. Squirru's later publications include studies of Argentinian and Latin American art as well as collections of poetry.*

July 12, 1964

Many thanks for your little book on the "New Man." I have read it carefully and with pleasure and want to congratulate you on it. I especially liked the essays on the poet and on the role of the intellectual. It seems to me that this little book represents a vitally important trend of thought, and you know of course how much I agree with it. The thinking of the public, especially in the "'great powers," seems to me to be hallucinated by the unreal concept of what one might call an Atlantic gigantism (except that it would have to include Russia and even China). The belief that the only kind of thinking that is real and meaningful is that which is associated with European and North American thought patterns, extending this also to Chinese Marxism. But this cerebration leaves out most of the human race, most of its needs, most of its aspirations. It has proved itself completely incapable of really solving the problems of man and is now increasingly incapable even of defining them.

It might seem scandalous for me, a priest of the Catholic Church, to admit such things, as it is naturally assumed that Catholicism is simply one aspect of this whole European pattern of thought. Unfortunately that is true of the Catholic "ideology" in its European dress. But there is more to Christian faith than this limited ideology, and true Catholicism (which has yet to rediscover itself in our age, I think) is indeed universal. Where there has been a failure has been precisely in the imposition of the limited (the European) as "Catholic" or universal. I think the Council is partly beginning to be aware of this, but only partly. It is very dim.

Meanwhile the great task for the Catholic and for the humanist and indeed the honest man in this hemisphere is to work for a mutual understanding and spiritual communication between the North and the South. A tremendous task, so neglected and so misunderstood that it seems at times impossible. Fortunately books like yours and articles like some of those in *Americas* are there to give one hope. And Miguel Grinberg with his fantastic movement. And the voices of the Latin American poets and artists.

This is just to let you know what you already know: That I count myself as one who is dedicated to this task, within the limits of my own capacity and of my situation here.

It is unfortunate that I cannot travel. Perhaps someday by some miracle I will be able to go to Latin America. I dearly hope so, though I do not see how it will ever be possible. But in any case there are many "new men" coming to this country. If there is anyone who ought especially to come here, I hope you will suggest it, and let me know. It is always very important that I should know beforehand and make arrangements if anyone wants to see me, otherwise if they just come down and ask the answer is negative. I have to arrange everything and ask the necessary permissions myself, otherwise it does not work.

Very best wishes to you, and congratulations on the good work you are doing at the Pan American Union.

To Alejandro Vignati

Alejandro Vignati was born in 1934 in the province of Buenos Aires, Argentina. His first books, Volcado luna *and* El cielo no arde, *were published in 1960. Among*

the numerous publications that followed is a study of Henry Miller, Henry Miller;
o. La alegría del retorno *(1976)*.

November 1, 1964

I hope you read English as I write it faster than Spanish and if I had
to wait for time to write in Spanish the letter might not get written. So
I do not want you to wait longer. Thank you for the book of Argentine
poets, something I am very glad to have. Thank you for your own poems.
The voices that come up to me from the South, from beyond the Caribbean
and the equator, move me very much. They are strong, sometimes angry,
full of clear intuitions, free from the involvement, the desperation and
self-frustration of some of the voices here, so many of the voices here.
Your own poem presented by Miguel [Grinberg] in the latest *Americas*
speaks to me very directly of the age-old aspiration to the paradise and
innocence of true liberty, of which the flying bird is the silent witness.

You are in Rio, you see other skies than I and hear different harmonies
and rhythms, but we seek the same innocence. It has its price, and we
must seek it without turning back and without listening too strongly to
the voices full of dust that speak only words of cotton. Such words are
smothering everything, but the poets must let in air to the whole world.
This demands innocence and insistence. And the childlikeness that is not
understood by potentates. Peace, then, and may you have joy and light
to continue to sing.

July 23, 1965

You are already in Lima, and I am happy about that because a poet
friend of mine is going to Lima in the fall. His name is Clayton Eshleman,
and he is a translator of [César] Vallejo. I told him to visit you. He is
very congenial, a good poet, and spent some years in Japan.

I agree with what you say about the religious values of the Indians.
You are right a thousand times over. The history of the conquest was
tragic, but not as tragic as that of this continent here in the North, where
almost all of the Indians were exterminated. Some remain, in silence, as
an accusation, and each year the white people try to steal from them
another piece of the reservation that remains theirs. I would very much
like to see those ancient cities of the Incas and the Mayas, but I think I
will never be able to. Well. I do not like being a tourist, and I am not a
"missionary," I am not a scholar, I am a hermit and nothing else. That
is not wrong: it is a simple fact, and I am happy about it all.

I like the young Peruvian poets very much, I read some poems in
an article of *Sur* some months ago. Too bad that you cannot read English.
I could send you something new. Do you know the essay I wrote in the
form of a letter to Pablo Antonio Cuadra (Nicaraguan) about the Indians
(in part) ["A Letter to Pablo Antonio Cuadra concerning Giants"]? It was
published in *Sur* and also in Nicaragua. I do not know if I have a copy.
I will send it to you, if I do.

Beautiful poems of Rio: to the South of the sun. I have walked with you the brilliant and dark streets of the city. Here right now, it is as hot as in Rio.

To Cintio Vitier

Cuban poet Cintio Vitier was born in Havana in 1921. As a young man Vitier was among the poets influenced by Spanish Nobel laureate Juan Ramón Jiménez, who visited Cuba in the late thirties. Vitier wrote a memoir of that two-year visit, during which Jiménez mentored a generation of Cuban poets. Vitier's early poetry includes Extrañeza de estar *(1943),* Vísperas *(1953) and* Canto Ilano *(1956). His later poetry documents a change in perspective:* Testimonios *(1953–1968) moves from the plain songs of* Canto Ilano *to poems informed by the spirit and vision of the Cuban revolution of 1959. A celebrated poet, Vitier is also an accomplished literary critic and anthologist.*

In a letter written in 1988 to William H. Shannon, general editor of the Merton letters, Vitier noted that Merton was very important to him and provided him with "real spiritual (that includes political) help" in the sixties. "For that, and all his writings and for his very self," Vitier concluded, "I hold him in respect and gratitude."

December 7, 1962

For a long time I have wanted to thank you for sending your books with your inscriptions. I am honored to receive the books and your words of dedication. I think that I was afraid of not being able to get a letter through across the tragic hostility that divides our nations and which pains me so very much. I still write to you in hopes of making contact. Tell me soon if you receive the letter.

I asked an editor to send a new book of mine called *A [Thomas] Merton Reader*, which contains examples of all that I have thought or written. I don't know if he has sent it to you. In any event tomorrow I will send a little book with some poems as well, to see if I can reach you with a package. If it is possible, I will send you much more.

Tell me if you can read English. I suppose you do. Sometimes I don't have time to write in Spanish which requires more time and effort, because it is not my natural language, even though I like it so.

Tell me as well if I could translate some poems of yours. I think that it is necessary to make them known here. I have translated many poems from Spanish, especially those of [César] Vallejo and Carrera Andrade. I have many poet friends in Nicaragua, I am almost a part of the movement over there, even though I remain always here. It is strange. But I have many Latin American friends because only so can one be truly "American": in other words, being only a citizen of the U.S. would be a miserable fate. From that come so many problems: so many people here are provincial and ignorant, and cannot understand what happens over there.

I like your *Canto llano* very much, but also your little books of prose which I continue to read with much pleasure. Continue to write, and write to me . . .

August 1, 1963

Your letter of July 14 reached me today and I am answering it immediately, because I do not want you to be in doubt about my having received it. Also I did at the beginning of this year receive two or three envelopes with copies of poems by you and others, along with a letter from you. I am very sorry not to have answered you then: the problem was that there were so many good poems and I wanted to read them and think of them, in order to make a relevant reply, and in the end I was so busy that I was not able to. I receive quite a few manuscripts as well as newly published books for comment, and it is not easy to keep up with them all. For instance today, in the same mail with your letter, I received an anthology of Polish verse which looks very interesting: but will I ever be able to write intelligently about it? I have three or four books of verse in manuscript here waiting for comment. Hence you see that it is lack of time that has been the main cause of my silence. But I regret it very much, as I do want to keep in touch with you.

First of all tell Roberto Friol, please, that I received his poems last year and liked them very much: that I am sorry to hear of his accident but glad that he has recovered. I sent you a book of mine but you did not receive it. I will try again with various small books and poems, there is no harm in trying. Are you in contact with Ernesto Cardenal still? I think you are. Perhaps if you are in doubt of reaching me through the ordinary channels you can reach me through him. He is still at the Seminario de Cristo Sacerdote, La Ceja, Antioquia, Colombia.

I do not have here the number 7 of the Mexican magazine *El Corno Emplumado* but I saw you in it. Some of the Cuban verse was impressive. I think José Lezama Lima was in it, if I am not mistaken. I have that magazine and all the poems you sent in a hermitage in the woods, not here. When I am there I will go through everything and will find time to tell you what I think. I am happy that you wanted to translate the Ixion poem ["Gloss on the Sin of Ixion"], which was certainly an experience so common to us both that it was nearly the end of all of us. Whatever may be the limitations and faults of various governments, it is essential that there be some understanding and communication between them, and I do think that the United States has failed miserably in understanding the Cuban revolution and in communicating with those in charge of it. The ambiguities and confusions that have followed from this have been very tragic.

Havana will always be a city very dear to me, as is all of Cuba. It is certainly true that in Havana the reality of the Christian mystery was made very plain to me by the grace of God, and I cannot help believing in the deep Christian potentialities of Cuba and of all Latin America. I shall never forget the Churches of Havana, or the sanctuary of El Cobre. [See *The Seven Storey Mountain*, p. 279ff., and *The Secular Journal*, p. 65ff.]

Do not feel that the difficulties under which you labor are making your lives less significant. On the contrary, all Christians are everywhere in a kind of exile and it is necessary for all to realize this. The greatest danger is identification of the Church with a prosperous and established economic and cultural system, as if Christ and the world had finally settled down to be friends. The Church needs Christians with independent and original thought, with new solutions and with the capacity to take risks. It is unfortunate that in Latin America, Christianity tends to identify itself with the policies of the State Department in Washington. The fact that the President of this country happens, at the moment, to be Catholic, is not a matter of great significance as far as the policies of the country itself are concerned: they are determined not by religion but by the interests of business. The Church is being purified of such connections, but the purification has hardly begun. You should not be in confusion or in doubt, but open your hearts to the Holy Spirit and rejoice in His freedom which no man can take from you. No power on earth can keep you from loving God and from union with Him. Nor need you depend on the devotionalism of the past. The Lord is near to you and lives in you. His Gospel is not old and forgotten, it is new, and it is there for you to meditate. By His grace you can still come to the sacraments of the Church, and rejoice that you are in the Body of Christ. And you have your fellow Christians and all of Cuba to love.

. . . Do please continue to write, and send poems, probably better in small packets, or through Cardenal. I am sending some books today, and if they do not come I will try sending some through Mexico or Colombia.

God bless all of you. Rejoice in the truth and fear nothing. Pray for me. I remain united to you all in the charity of Christ and in His Spirit. I still want to translate some poems of yours, and of your friends, but I have not had time. Perhaps later I will be able to do so for a magazine that would be interested. Do not hesitate to send things. I have your fine books . . .

Merton included the following letter, addressed "To a Cuban Poet," among his "Letters in a Time of Crisis," published in Seeds of Destruction.

October 4, 1963

Yes, your letter reached me, and I have been thinking about it deeply, as also about your poem about Christ and the Robbers. I have been thinking about these things in silence, at a long distance from the noise of official answers and declamations.

I am alone with the bronze hills and a vast sky, and shadows of pine trees. Sometimes the shadows are alive with golden butterflies. Everywhere is the inscrutable and gentle and very silent face of truth. Nothing is said. In this silence and in this presence I have been reading your poems, and those of Fina [García Marruz], and Eliseo [Diego], and Octavio [Smith]. And I have not been able to find those of Roberto. He should send me some more, and all of you please send me new poems. It may take time for me to get them in the silence like this, but I will do so. The time is come when the publication of poems is to be like that of pale and very light airborne seeds flowing in the current of forest air through the blue shadows, and falling on the grass where God says [Merton changed "says" to "decrees" in the letter published in *Seeds of Destruction*]. I am convinced that we are now already in the time where the printed word is not read, but the paper passed from hand to hand is read eagerly. A time of small letters, hesitant, but serious and personal, and out of the meaningless dimension of the huge, the monstrous and the cruel.

I liked very much Fina's poem on the Transfiguration, it has a great stateliness and seriousness about it. I like also Eliseo's short poems, especially "La casa del Pan," which I intend to translate when I get time (though I am not good at keeping promises like this: I have still not translated any of yours, but I will). And the one about the cockatoos in the shadows: very incisive. Fina's "Anima viva" is more difficult and I must read it some more. Of Octavio, I like best "Ambas," so far. I am sorry. I cannot find anything of Roberto here.

I heard from Ernesto and like his elegy for Marilyn Monroe [published in *Oración por Marilyn Monroe y otros poemas*] (the sad nonsense and futility of this world here).

Really, the reading of your poems in this silence has been very meaningful and serious: much more serious than the publication of new magazines with poetic manifestos. I have written something for Miguel Grinberg in the Argentine on "the poet and freedom" ["Answers on Art and Freedom"], but I wonder sometimes whether such declarations have a meaning. I am sad at the different kinds of programmatic affirmations made by poets, and the outcry about freedom from poets who have no concept of what it is all about, who are so absurd as to think it means freedom to knock themselves out with dope or something of the sort. Sick. Absurd. What waste of the opportunities: their freedom is pure aimlessness and in the end it collapses in the worst kind of unfreedom and arbitrariness.

My book of poems [*Emblems of a Season of Fury*] is coming out this fall and I want to send you a copy. I hope I can. Do books get through to you?

I hope you are all well and keep you in my prayers. May God be with you always, and may His truth never abandon you, and may your hearts be fixed in His joy and His light. I will say a Mass for you all when I can, perhaps on All Saints' Day. What day is the Feast of La Caridad del Cobre? I don't think I ever knew. Today is of course St. Francis.

The light in which we are one does not change.

May 26, 1964

It is a long time since I have written. Did you get the "Message to Poets" which I sent last winter? I hope so. Meanwhile I have followed up your allusion to Vallejo and have been able to get in touch with the people at the University of Córdoba. They have sent me the very interesting publications on Vallejo, including the first issue of *Aula* [*Vallejo*], which contains your essay on him as a religious poet. Really it is one of the best essays, one of the most fundamental, on the whole question, that I have ever read. It is really a ground-clearing study with really basic intuitions on the nature of poetry and religion. Have you developed this more? It is a fine existential approach and I think it says what is necessary for anyone to begin to understand the greatness of Vallejo. And I think that an understanding and love of Vallejo, this Inca and Prophet, is the key to the deep realization of the problems and predicaments of the two Americas today. First of all because Latin American poetry, which tends to be more personal and more prophetic than that of the U.S. while at the same time speaking for "the people" more than the individualist and sometimes hermetic subjectivism of the U.S. poets, is all gathered around Vallejo as around its deepest center and as a kind of source of life.

What is new with you? I have been busy, but not so busy that there is not in me a profound and permanent revolt against activism and against the false and elated optimisms that are always enjoying some kind of shallow triumph over a headline or a meaningless editorial or the shadow of a program. I need not look further than the monastery where we have our quota of programs any time.

I liked your quotes from Clement of Alexandria in the essay on Vallejo. Did I ever send you the little book on Clement [*Clement of Alexandria*] that I did? That passage is translated there too.

I think of you and of all my Cuban friends. May God bless you and keep you. There is a deep eloquence also in silence and patience. I keep you in mind in God's presence and in His Spirit.

December 5, 1965

Thanks for your fine letter and for all the translations. I am mailing to you my new book of poems [*The Way of Chuang Tzu*]. I hope it arrives safely. I was very touched at the communal response of all of you [Fina García Marruz, Eliseo Diego, Roberto Friol, Octavio Smith, and Cintio Vitier] & the translations are splendid. I know you all better by the choice you made of poems to translate & by the way in which you translated them.

I will write more soon. All blessings to all of you.

January 6, 1966

I was very happy to receive your letter because I was wondering how you were. I think that you did not receive a letter which I wrote to you last year. I don't know why. In any event I am well, I am working much, now I have permission to live alone in the woods. Do you have news from Ernesto: He visited me three months ago, and now is back in Nicaragua, to begin his very interesting project of forming his community [in Solentiname].

I don't know if you saw Nicanor Parra when he was in Havana for the congress of poets. I have already written some letters to him. He is a very important poet. And you, are you writing something? And the others? I think of you all, and on New Year's Day I offered Mass for all of you.

I would like to send you some book of mine, but I don't know if it is possible. Would they let it pass? Write to me again.

September 24, 1966

When I received your letter and your little book at the beginning of the summer, I was ill because I was in the hospital and had surgery. And then time went by . . . But I want to tell you that I liked your *Testimonios* very much, and when I think of your poem "La palabra" I cannot let more time pass without sending you a word. The two poems about the *maquineo* are impressive: I think that I have read them before, as I have many others in the book. It is a good book and it moves me very much. I will send you a book of my poems and of poetic prose, *Raids on the Unspeakable*. I hope that you will like it, as will all my friends from there.

I am well, living alone (this I describe in the book), writing, studying Camus and working on some critical articles about him. It has been a long time that I have heard anything from Ernesto. I think that he must be busy in his new community on the island of Solentiname. It must be a very beautiful place.

I send you with this letter a poem which I wrote after being in the hospital. The operation, a rather serious one, on the spinal cord, was somewhat shattering to the nerves.

November 12, 1966

Only yesterday did I receive your letter of October 19th. I wrote to you at the beginning of October, I believe. Maybe my letter was delayed as well, I don't know. But I told you how much I liked your *Testimonios* . . . I think that I sent you my book *Raids on the Unspeakable*. And that you have not received it: right? Tell me: I will send you another copy.

I agree about Ernesto: his achievement of the community in Solen-tiname is something wonderful and makes me very happy.

I will not write you more right now, later I will write a good letter. I am sending you some poems.

To Stefan Baciu

In response to a request from Stefan Baciu, a professor of literature at the University of Hawaii, Thomas Merton wrote a letter detailing his views on Latin American literature and identifying his favorite writers. After reading the article that Baciu had written about Merton and Latin America, Merton wished to clarify his "sweeping" rejection of North American poets.

May 21, 1965

I will try to reply to your letter before the matter ceases to be fresh in my mind. If I let it go, I probably will never get to it again. Meanwhile, I will try to find such material as I have on hand and will send it to you hoping that it will reach Hawaii before you leave.

First of all I would like to say to you what I have said to others: that I feel myself clearly much more in sympathy with the Latin American poets today than with those of North America. I feel that though I write in English, my idiom (poetic idiom at least) is much more that of Latin America than that of the United States. To begin with I feel that the academic poets of the U.S. are simply caught in the most sterile impasse where they do nothing except play esoteric tricks with language. I do of course admire Robert Lowell as a genuine poet, but he is an exception, and a notable one. As to the U.S. beats, I am more in sympathy with them but in most cases I do not respond to them fully. Whereas the Latin American poets seem to me to be alive, to have something honest to say, to be sincerely concerned with life and with humanity. There is some genuine hope left in them, or when they are bitter the bitterness has a maturity and content which make it respectable, and in any case I tend to share it in some ways.

My background being to a great extent European, this probably has something to do with it. I still read a great deal of French, though not a great deal of contemporary French poetry. Also in my formative years I came under the spell of F. García Lorca and have never recovered. He remains one of my favorite poets and one to whom I respond most completely.

Nicaragua: since [Ernesto] Cardenal spent two years here at Geth-semani I came to form a close association with the Nicaraguan poets, especially (besides Cardenal) Pablo Antonio Cuadra, José Coronel Ur-techo, and to a lesser extent Ernesto Mejía Sanchez. Of course I have a great admiration for Alfonso Cortés, some of whose poems I have translated.

Ecuador: admiration for Jorge Carrera Andrade whom I have translated (a few poems) and with whom I have corresponded. There is in him a Franciscan quality and a luminous simplicity which I find very engaging.

Chile: I have lately translated some poems of Nicanor Parra. I admire his irony and sympathize fully with the protest that it implies. I like the earlier Neruda very much, of course.

Peru: I have done a few poems of the great [César] Vàllejo whom I consider the most important voice in American poetry in the twentieth century, in fact probably the greatest poet of the century in any language.

Argentina: I have had some contact with Victoria Ocampo, of course, in relation to articles of mine published in *Sur*. Have written a note contributed to the volume *Testimonios sobre Victoria Ocampo*. This is reproduced in my book *Seeds of Destruction*. (Do you have it?) I have also been in contact with a group of younger poets there, principally Miguel Grinberg for whom I wrote a "Message to Poets," which was read at a meeting of your Latin American poets held in Mexico City, Feb. 1964. I do not know if I still have a copy.

Mexico: Great admiration for Octavio Paz, naturally. Have published poems and drawings in *El Corno Emplumado*.

Uruguay: in a different context, have formed a warm friendship with Esther de Cáceres, close friend of Gabriela Mistral, and through her have discovered a very beautiful, little known, deeply spiritual poet, Susana Soca. I have wanted to do some translations of her but have not had time.

Brazil: have met and been very friendly with Alceu Amoroso Lima, a letter to him is reproduced in *Seeds of Destruction*. Have wanted to translate some Jorge de Lima, but have not yet had time. Did translate a couple of poems of Carlos Drummond de Andrade. From Portuguese I have recently translated some poems of Fernando Pessoa.

Other sources in which I have spoken of Latin America and LA poetry, the "Letter to Pablo Antonio Cuadra concerning Giants" (do you have this, in *Emblems of a Season of Fury?*) and a piece in the *Sewanee Review* recently (I will send it).

The preface to the Buenos Aires edition of my *Obras completas* has reference to Latin America too.

I might conclude by saying I was very happy at the edition of my poems in Mexico, translated by Cardenal and illustrated by Armando Morales, a very rewarding collaboration.

I hope I have not forgotten anything important here. I will try to gather the material that may still be available and send it on.

Did I tell you I was reading Vintila Horia? An excellent writer.

I wish you success in your lecture tour and hope to hear from you. But as a matter of fact I am gradually retiring into a more obscure form of life and this will mean a reduction in my writing work and contacts, but not of course the essential ones.

July 7, 1966

Your book on Manuel Bandeira arrived today. It is very handsome and I will read it with pleasure and tell you about it later. At present I have some reviews to do and am trying to catch up on the other work, so it will be some time before I can get to this.

I am glad to hear the article is finished, and I am sure it will be all the better for having matured slowly. Glad it is being translated into Spanish. I think too that an English version would be a good idea . . .

Glad to hear *Mele* 4 is on the way. God bless your good work, and I am always delighted to get your news. Thanks for writing the article, I am glad you thought it worth your while. I hope it will be of much help. Certainly I think it is of the greatest importance to keep open a real understanding between North and South America. There is not very much now, at least on the levels that matter. This summer I met Nicanor Parra, from Chile, who was here. We had a good talk together. I like his "antipoems" very much and agree with his dry and laconic comments on society. I recently heard from Victoria Ocampo who was in this country for the PEN congress, and is publishing my article on existentialism in *Sur* soon.

August 1, 1966

First of all, thanks very much for the excellent article. You have been very thorough indeed and cover the ground well. I am most grateful. My only problem about it regards myself and not your article. It seems to me that my rejection of North American poets en bloc is much too sweeping and inconsiderate, and I really ought to correct that impression if I could. To begin with, for a long time I had neglected to read North American poets except for a few like Lowell, whom of course I like very much. And until very recently I was simply ignorant of some of the best ones. I only recently discovered Louis Zukofsky for example. Certainly I would not want to give the impression that I thought the poets of the United States were all completely inferior to those of Latin America and were doing absolutely nothing of any value. However, it is perhaps too late to do anything about it. But if you publish the article in English, especially in the U.S., then perhaps we will have to add a paragraph to qualify my sweeping opinion . . .

V

To James Baldwin

*Novelist and essayist James Baldwin (1924–1987) was born and raised in Harlem,
where he experienced firsthand the harsh realities of racism and discrimination.
In his fiction and essays, Baldwin voiced the plight of black people in twentieth-
century America. Among his best-known and best-selling books are* Go Tell It on
the Mountain *(1953),* Notes of a Native Son *(1955),* Nobody Knows My Name
(1961), and The Fire Next Time *(1963), the book that moved Merton to write to
Baldwin. Merton included this letter among the "Letters in a Time of Crisis,"
published in* Seeds of Destruction *in 1964.* The Fire Next Time, *which he first
read in* The New Yorker, *is "powerful and great," Merton wrote in a letter to
Sr. Thérèse Lentfoehr in February 1963 [see* The Road to Joy].*

[No date, 1963]

You cannot expect to write as you do without getting letters like this.
One has to write, and I am sure you have received lots of letters already
that say better than I can what this will try to say.

First of all, you are right all down the line. You exaggerate nowhere.
You know exactly what you are talking about, and as a matter of fact it is
really news to nobody (that is precisely one of your points). I have said
the same myself, much more mildly and briefly, and far less well, in print
so it is small wonder that I agree with you.

But the point is that this is one of the great realities of our time. For
Americans it is perhaps the crucial truth, and all the other critical questions that face us are involved in this one.

It is certainly matter for joy that you have at least said so much, and
in the place where you have said it. It will be read and understood. But
as I went through column after column [in *The New Yorker*] I was struck,
as I am sure you were, by the ads all along each side of your text. What
a commentary! They prove you more right than you could have imagined.

They go far beyond anything you have said. What force they lend to all your statements. No one could have dreamed up more damning evidence to illustrate what you say.

Sometimes I am convinced that there cannot be a way out of this. Humanly there is no hope, at least on the white side (that is where I unfortunately am). I don't see any courage or any capacity to grasp even the smallest bit of the enormous truth about ourselves. Note, I speak as a Catholic priest. We still see the whole thing as a sort of abstract exercise in ethics, when we see it at all. We don't see we are killing our own hope and the hope of the world.

You are very careful to make explicit the non-Christian attitude you take, and I respect this because I understand that this is necessary for you and I do not say this as an act of tolerant indulgence. It is in some sense necessary for me, too, because I am only worth so much as a priest, as I am able to see what the non-Christian sees. I am in most things right with you and the only point on which I disagree is that I think your view is fundamentally religious, genuinely religious, and therefore has to be against conventional religiosity. If you do not agree, it does not matter very much.

The other day I was talking to an African priest from Ghana. The impression I always get in talking to Africans is that they have about ten times as much reality as we have. This of course is not an accurate way of speaking: I think what it really expresses, this "sense," is the awareness of complementarity, the awareness of a reality in him which completes some lack in myself, and not of course an intuition of an absolute onto-logical value of a special essence. And I think as you yourself have sug-gested, that this is the whole story: there is not one of us, individually, racially, socially, who is fully complete in the sense of having in himself *all* the excellence of all humanity. And that this excellence, this totality, is built up out of the contributions of the particular parts of it that we all can share with one another. I am therefore not completely human until I have found myself in my African and Asian and Indonesian brother because he has the part of humanity which I lack.

The trouble is that we are supposed to be, and in a way we are, complete in ourselves. And we cherish the illusion that this completeness is not just a potential, but that it is finally realized from the very start, and that the notion of having to find something of ourselves only after a long search and after the gift of ourselves to others, does not apply to us. This illusion, which makes the white man imagine he does not need the Negro, enables him to think he can treat the Negro as an "object" and do what he likes with him. Indeed, in order to prove that his illusion is true, he goes ahead and treats the Negro in the way we know. He has to.

At the heart of the matter then is man's contempt for truth, and the substitution of his "self" for reality. His image is his truth. He believes in his specter and sacrifices human beings to his specter. This is what we are doing, and this is not Christianity or any other genuine religion: it is barbarity.

We cannot afford to have contempt for any truth, but least of all for a truth as urgent in our lives as this one. Hence, I want to give you all the moral support I can, which isn't much. I know you are more than fatigued with well-meaning white people clapping you on the shoulder and saying with utmost earnestness, "We are right with you," when of course we are right with ourselves and not in any of the predicaments you are in at all. What I will say is that I am glad I am not a Negro because I probably would never be able to take it: but that I recognize in conscience that I have a duty to try to make my fellow whites stop doing the things they do and see the problem in a different light. This does not presuppose an immediate program, or a surge of optimism, because I am still convinced that there is almost nothing to be done that will have any deep effect or make any real difference.

I am not in a position to be completely well informed on this issue, anyway. If you think of anything I ought to know about, I would be grateful if you put it in an envelope and send it down. I hope your article will have done some good. The mere fact that truth has been told is already a very great good in itself.

To Cid Corman

Sidney (Cid) Corman (1924–) studied at Tufts College, the University of Michigan, the University of North Carolina, and the Sorbonne. In 1951, Corman moved to Japan where he wrote poetry, edited a literary magazine called Origin, *ran a press by the same name, and translated the poetry of Matsuo Bashō, Shimpei Kusano, René Char, and Francis Ponge. During the two years he corresponded with Merton, Corman published seven books of poetry:* For You *(1966),* For Granted *(1966),* Stead *(1966),* Words for Each Other *(1967),* Without End *(1968),* No Less *(1968) and* Hearth *(1968).*

July 8, 1966

Origin (iii, 1) came in the other day and I promised in my note to you that I would write you a line about it. For my own sake as much as for yours I do this, because I can see one of the things you want to do with *Origin* is to break through the lethargy and laziness of readers and writers who simply plow in a daze through things they don't read and only hate. It is good to pick up *Origin* and take care: be made to take care by the look of it, by the shape of the poems, by the spareness of what they say. I have not known your poems before, because I am a haphazard reader at best and the right things have not been coming my way. Only the other day I finally read [Louis] Zukofsky for the first time.

I am ignorant and isolated. I am the kind of person that badly needs *Origin* and am not ashamed to admit it.

Your notes on Poetry as Bond say a great deal to me, and the things you quote, the views they represent, views of earth and life, are not as remote from my own as one might think. I don't have views built on top of views, and I am very receptive to the cry of leaves that *do not* transcend themselves, though I am not closed to transcendence either. But it is a false transcendence if it always has to demand that leaves transcend themselves. The absolute transcendence looks like none at all. Zen.

I think what moved me most in the whole issue was the long Blues anthology. Most grateful for this. I will read it over and over. I wish I were hearing all this . . .

September 5, 1966

I have two good letters of yours from July to reply to and now *Origin* (2) and the books. I was waiting for these and they took a long time. [Clayton] Eshleman's translations of [César] Vallejo come through strong and I am glad that the book of these translations [of *Poemas humanos*, published as *Human Poems*] is supposed to be appearing. You say your own poems might be "too quiet" for me. No, I like that kind of reticence, words on top of a lot of silence and as you say not imposing anything, even reticence, on the reader. I find them sharply visual, accurate, concrete, and I like the way they string out into poetic journals ("The Italy Book"). What you have done in Japan comes through best of all to me, for some reason. Thanks very much for the books, I will value them and go back to them often. Did I send you *Raids on the Unspeakable*? For some reason I got a few author's copies back in July somewhere but the book is not yet out and there do not seem to be more copies around. Probably will be soon, and then I will send one if I have not already. It is a patchy book. I get too vehement but I like a certain volume of a wacky sound.

That is why these days I am reading quite a lot of René Char, whom I had not read before. Today, Labor Day, when I get this letter finished, I'll take off into the woods (I live in the woods anyway) with a book of René Char selections and maybe some 14th-cent. German mystic stuff. Char has the wacky oblique eloquence all right. I have two books of selections, same publisher, ten years or so apart: first one has picture of him looking like a champion bicycle racer, the other a picture that ought to have a number under it. The people that write about him try to do so in a hesitant imitation of his style, and when they happen to be a bit square the result is very funny. Must drive him out of his head. I would translate some but I understand that there are herds of people doing this now and the rights situation is complicated?? I have also come across a very good Spanish poet, Miguel Hernández, who died in prison and wrote a lot of very good lonely prison stuff.

You are right that I ought to read everything I can lay hands on of Zukofsky, and I am going to try and lay those hands on. I believe you printed one of his books: have you a copy available I could order? Or anything handy of his, in an old issue of *Origin* that would still be buyable?

Initials [jhs] on the top of the paper you ask about? That is not a secretary, but medieval pious practice to put monogram of name of Christ when you start to write, something like making sign of the Cross when you start doing something. I don't make an issue out of it, it is a habit. Someone helps me with typing when I have stuff to type and can get help, but no secretary. I don't write that many letters any more since I live in the woods with the foxes. No, there are no monks doing illuminated mss. but there are some nuns in England good friends of mine who do some very fancy printing—Stanbrook Abbey. I'll send you a little thing they did for me or I did with them or for them [*The Solitary Life: A Letter of Guigo*]. They are supposed to be doing a bit of Cassiodorus I translated now, but that has been waiting around for a long time. I'll send you that too if I ever get copies and if you remind me in about three months (probably will not be ready even then).

Origin and your letters mean a lot to me somehow. Your allusion to the vow of poverty and the fact that you are broke without a vow while I am broke with it reminds me that something like *Origin* and your letters may well be just as monastic and more so than what we are doing around here. I am very aware of the ambiguities of my kind of monasticism and base no claims of any kind whatever upon it: but on the contrary I am very glad when I find anybody doing anything for love of it, and since that is what I myself seek and need, I respond to it with some liveliness. The essence of monasticism as I see it is this doing something or living in a certain way for pure love of it and without further justification. And without necessarily pointing to any special practical result. Or to anything. Or drawing attention etc. Now that I am alone in the woods (for pure love of it and because life in the community also seemed to me too tangled) I want to think more about writing poetry, though perhaps it is better not to think much about it and write without looking too closely at what is happening. Still it is good to have someone like you articulate about these things and willing to share them. I have been out of contact with that, and remain inarticulate on the subject anyway. I don't know how to talk about poetry.

This bit I am sending you is not very good. It does not come off like the piece on the furnaces ["Chant to Be Used in Processions Around a Site with Furnaces"] I did. (Have you seen that? It is in *Emblems of a Season of Fury* which I can send if you have not seen.) This is a sort of mosaic of Eichmann's own doubletalk about himself ["A Devout Meditation in Memory of Adolf Eichmann"].

I am working on another longer series of short ones ["Edifying Cables," published as *Cables to the Ace*] which might interest you. Maybe you will feel it does not communicate: it is imprecise, noisy, crude, full of vulgarity and parody, making faces, criticizing and so on, and not like what you are doing at all, in fact almost the exact opposite. Of Beckett I like very much *Waiting for Godot* and think it says a lot. The others I can't read for more than a few pages. But I like Ionesco a great deal.

Please tell me if you want *Raids, Emblems*.

September 6, 1966

I wrote you yesterday and now your letter of the 27th has reached me today. So I see you got *Raids* after all. Thanks for paying enough attention to it to come through with your observations, which I can understand and accept. It always surprises me when others say I sound violent, because I am really quite an easygoing person. But I know I do use violent language for some reason, and this would especially irritate someone like you, who has manifestly gone to great pains to cool it all off as much as it can be cooled. As I don't know you, I can only suppose you are allergic to my kind of ranting, and I admit that I am too bombastic. I suppose I have grown up too much with rowdy types like Blake, or Léon Bloy, or the Elizabethans. However, you have a serious point in the criticism that my tone may contradict what I am trying to say. I will take that one to heart. It is possible, all right. And I don't claim to be a man of perfect serenity or untroubled assurance, by any means. I am conscious of the fact that in most of my exhorting, the person I am trying to convince is myself. And that does not make for convincing exhortation. Maybe I can just stop most of it. Well, we'll see.

You say I fear relation: well, rather I am in a difficult position about it, because of the frustrations inherent in this kind of life and the added ones that have grown onto it like barnacles. I mean the fact the communication is systematically blocked and so on. It does mean that I don't have a normal easy outgoing way of communicating with others and when I do get a chance to say something I do tend to try to say everything at once, or else don't even try to say anything. Don't know. I have no great problems when I am with some people and know I have time and won't have to shut up in ten minutes.

I won't argue with you over the details—for instance I think Sophocles is magnanimous too, as well as Aeschylus. But so what? Perhaps you don't agree. Ionesco superficial: perhaps, but I can listen to him. And I think he does have some compassion somewhere . . . at least I don't think I have to reject him in the name of "health." But no matter. I wish I knew more about you, who you are. The poems as I said are reticent. And that is all right. I don't know who I am talking to.

What you say about each one having his own living-dying to do— "to realize in a context that never permits generality"—this I certainly agree on.

I won't be surprised or dejected if you don't like the Eichmann poem

["Epitaph for a Public Servant"]: I realize that it is empty and does not come off at all.

Thanks, Cid, for your criticism. It will help.

March 10, 1967

I have been waiting for the right chance to send you a word or two about the new *Origin* (4) and now that the frogs are singing here plenty (even in some snow the other day) and I have had crocuses in front of my place for nearly five weeks straight (in spite of zeros) I think it is time to celebrate Shimpei.

Shimpei Kusano has burst on all of us, thanks to you, like one of the very big discoveries and delights. Where have we been all this time not knowing there was such a poet? What clear substance. He does us all good. He saves us all from the swamp (swamp of academic seriousness or fake rhapsody, or my own wordy ironies). I am so happy to be in the same world. Want to read more and more of him. Is there more in a language I know? Can I review him or something?

Thanks too for the René Char. I have not seen the original, but your rendering as it stands is an admirable poem. But I wonder about your translation of *L'âge cassant* as The Brittle Age. *Cassant* is active. To convey "brittle" it would have to be somehow reflexive. In its active intransitive form, does it have some slang innuendo that for the moment escapes me, such as "crashing bore" or like that? I think that too is there. But I can't judge without seeing the whole thing. Anyway, as I say, your rendering as it stands is fine.

If you haven't any strong objection, I may send along a couple of pages of Char-ish French verse I have written myself recently. Part of a long sequence that I don't pretend is much good. You might find this a little interesting. It is a liberation from the wrong obsessions I have had in my English verse.

Sorry I have not written for some time. Where we ended with our last exchange, there just was not much more to say, we would have just stood in the same places stamping at each other and not moving anywhere. But I have been thinking and absorbing a lot of things, and am I hope moving into something new and a little better. I have wasted a lot of time writing things there was no imaginable need for me to write ever. One thing that is helping enormously is that I am getting at last into William Carlos Williams, to whom I had not previously attended.

If I don't hear from you saying No, I will probably send along a carbon of the French stuff I wrote, and see what you think. In ten days or so. I am concerned for Clayton, who demonstrated in the [St. Patrick's] Cathedral against that Cardinal [Francis Spellman]: what Clayton did was noble and good, I hope he does not have to suffer for it.

April 21, 1968

It is a long time since I have written: can't keep up with correspondence at all. It is just too much, most of the time. Especially as I have had the foolhardiness to start a small magazine of my own [*Monks Pond*], which however is only to run temporarily. Four issues, no more. I'll send you a copy when I get some more together. I'd be very happy to have something of yours in it, or some translation from Japanese or French.

The [Francis] Ponge issue of *Origin* was very interesting to me. I read his "Pine Woods" with great curiosity and pleasure. To me the earlier notes had some fine things which more and more tended to get pushed out as he worked it into "poetic" form, and in the poems everything was lost. Very French. A salutary example. The [Lorine] Niedecker poems too, very fine.

I don't remember if I sent my ten, but here. I happen to have some money for the time being.

Your book from England has come in and looks very good. Also other things of yours that have come one way or other, from Elizabeth Press and elsewhere. I have spoken about these things to New Directions, and will do so again, but [James] Laughlin is now very slow to take on anyone new (to him). I really don't understand much about the publishing of poetry in America. There is one small new press that does nice work in California, Unicorn . . . with also a new review (*Unicorn Journal*). It is quite good I think.

And also: thanks for your splendid Bashō. A joy.

I do hope you can send something for my magazine, *Monks Pond*. Short prose fine, translation fine, anything that has not been done in U.S.

To Guy Davenport

With the publication of his first collection of short stories, Tatlin!, *in 1974, Guy Davenport (1927–) expanded a literary repertoire that already included writing essays and poetry, translating classical texts, editing and illustrating books, and teaching literature at the University of Kentucky at Lexington. Together with poet Jonathan Williams and photographer Ralph Eugene Meatyard, Davenport visited Merton at Gethsemani in January 1967. The letters Merton subsequently wrote to Davenport point to all they had in common and shared during Davenport's visits to the hermitage.*

February 20, 1967

Thanks for your letter written in the midst of an existential leap from Franklin to Walton [Davenport's old and new street addresses] and from Blessed Martyrs to Blissful Apparition [feast days on which Davenport wrote to Merton]. And new ribbon for the acknowledgment of Ronald Johnson's clipped yews and gardens of delight [*The Book of the Green*

Man]. It is a fine book, making me also wonder why I neglected Samuel Palmer, though I wrote on Blake. As to your own book [*Flowers and Leaves: Poema vel sonata, carmina autumni primaeque veris transformationum*], it is a very pleasant universe to wander around in, and it makes me glad that people still read the Classics and write accordingly. It is a rich full witty flowering book.

Can you send me Gene Meatyard's address? I mentioned his work to Laughlin at New Directions. Laughlin is always looking for interesting things to put on the covers of his books. I am very anxious to see more of Gene's work—and of course the things he took here.

I hope we can get together again one of these days. Do please keep in touch and let me know what you do. I send various things: for example a thing on the Desert Fathers [*The Wisdom of the Desert*] which I probably did not give you (I forget).

It was very good to have you all here.

Fiat pax in habitatione tua et benedictio in omnibu viis tuis.

June 11, 1967

The book on Bohr [*Niels Bohr: The Man, His Science and the World They Changed*] that I have just read is the one by Ruth Moore. Quite good, I thought. Perhaps some time I shall read one of the others. I'd also like to go further into some of Bohr's notions of epistemology in his last years.

I am not hoping to see of any of Gene's pictures until next March. I am resigned. Certainly some of them must be worth seeing at once . . .

I was very glad indeed that you brought the Cookham poem ["The Resurrection at Cookham"], and I don't see why poets ought to be concerned about showing people their work (except of course that there are swarms of the wrong ones wanting to share theirs). But I think it is a very fine, well-knit, right-sounding, properly solemn and hopeful poem, good eschatology. If you get an extra copy of *Poetry* when it comes out, will you please let me have it for a while? *Poetry* is on a very black blacklist here and the copies that used to come to me stopped with a crash. The Abbot must have opened it at some four-letter word on one of his bad mornings. He seems to be deathly afraid of it. Plain envelope etc. . . .

As to the *Kentucky Review* I firmly believe in supporting one's friendly local magazine, so as I happen to have the enclosed "Rites [for the Extrusion of a Leper]" just ready, I'll send them along. I hope *Kentucky* can handle them. And that the Catlicks don't get upset etc.

August 27, 1967

Many thanks for the *Dichtung* all full of *Wahrheit, Schönheit, Gemütlichkeit*, and other *keits*. I liked "Cookham" even better in print. Have not got far into Louis Zukofsky yet, as have not had much time in the last couple of days: trying to finish some books out on interlibrary loan before the portcullis comes clashing down.

Strange about Claude Lévi-Strauss: I have just started on him too and the day your letter came I got three of his books. From what little I have read, this is important and lively. I am doing something eventually on cargo cults, but I want all this background. Have poem inspired by Zulu messiahs. Do you know G. Bachelard? I want to get going on him too, but have not tracked anything down yet.

We can talk about all these things I hope when Gene comes over Monday. The note on you in *Poetry* shows you to be amazingly productive. More I reflect back on the illustrations to Kenner better I like them [Davenport illustrated Hugh Kenner's *The Stoic Comedians*].

P.S. I nearly forgot: you have the only copy of the prologue to "Leper": could you possibly get me a Xerox of that one page? It may be published in England too [in *Peace News*].

December 28, 1967

I've been lost and left behind by all the letters. This is to say I like (way back) your Heraclitus. And was happy to hear the *K. Review* was going to have so many good things in it. I look forward to it . . .

And now: everywhere under every tree there is a review, even here, even in the *eremo*. I have caught it and have decided I would get sick with magazine [*Monks Pond*] but only for four issues, as if a man can decide beforehand how sick he can afford to get.

This magazine has nothing to do with money in any respect as it can be printed free here and given out as largesse—only mimeograph and offset, but what sane man in my position would not also want Gene's pictures? Somehow it must have in it photographs.

Have you any ideas for people to send in things and do you have anything you would want to go in a magazine so unknown and never to become known as to be almost unpublication? Jonathan Williams has rushed into the fray and sent several good poets in this direction already. Maybe Ron Johnson too.

Translations I could very well use—maybe even a few of the Heraclitus? I mean a couple of dozen of the fragments?

The place is all seething with hopes and fears regarding the new abbot. The election is coming in a couple of weeks. Some thought my campaign platform ["MY CAMPAIGN PLATFORM for non-Abbot and permanent keeper of the present doghouse"] arrogant (enclosed). But as it is a non-platform, there is no hurt if it antagonizes the electorate.

March 11, 1968

Here at last is the magazine. I am getting much more material than I anticipated and I doubt that I will have room for Heraclitus—after all well known. On the other hand probably in the Fall issue I hope to use Gene's picture of you as a Yugoslavian rainmaker with the thyrsus shading your mustache. By then you might perhaps have a pome? Or some tirade.

Thanks for the *KR*. I like Wendell [Berry] and Ron [Seitz] and their poems and your remarks on Gene's pictures. The rest I haven't read yet. It is a good issue: and might I please have two more copies.

Editing a magazine is—as I had forgotten—time-consuming. I am no good at my ordinary correspondence and worse with what goes with this venture. I find I have to put it together myself (with a helper) and this means that it gets into shape by fits and starts. Will do a new batch this week some time.

P.S. Gene was over yesterday, with many good pictures.

To Clayton Eshleman

By the time he first wrote to Thomas Merton, Clayton Eshleman had published Residence on Earth, *a translation of Pablo Neruda's poetry, and was working on translations of César Vallejo's poetry. Merton was pleased to hear from someone who shared his interest in the great Latin American poet. Merton himself had translated a few of Vallejo's poems, which appeared in* Emblems of a Season of Fury *in 1963.*

Born in 1935 in Indianapolis and educated at Indiana University, Eshleman began writing in his early twenties and produced the first of many books of poetry, Mexico and North, *in 1961. From 1967 to 1973, Eshleman was publisher and editor of Caterpillar Press and translated writings of such literary figures as Aimé Césaire and Antonin Artaud. A collection of Eshleman's poetry,* The Name En-canyoned River: Selected Poems, Nineteen Sixty to Nineteen Eighty-Five, *was published in 1986, and a collection of other writings,* Antiphonal Swing: Selected Prose 1962–1987, *was brought out by Caryl Eshleman in 1989.*

[June 1963]
[*The following letter was translated into Spanish by José Coronel Urtecho and published in* La Prensa Literaria *in August 1963.*]

It takes time to get to a letter like yours, from among the other letters of editors, and of crazies, and of the hurt, and of the rich with propositions, and of the fanatics with accusations.

I have translated only half a dozen poems of [César] Vallejo (I think all were in *Poemas humanos*) and four will be in my new book [*Emblems of a Season of Fury*] this fall, so I am not exactly digging in and getting anything done. I am glad to hear you are. I think all the poets in America could translate Vallejo and not begin to get him.

. . . This is because, as I think, he is the most universal, Catholic in that sense (the only real sense), poet of this time, the most Catholic and universal of all modern poets, the only poet since (Who? Dante?) who is anything like Dante. Maybe Leopardi whom I never read much, of course Quasimodo has some of it too.

So what I mean is that Vallejo is totally human, as opposed to our zombie poets and our little girl poets and our incontinents. I have never really thought out all that must begin to be said about Vallejo, but he is tremendous and extraordinary, a huge phenomenon, so much more magnificent (in the classical sense) than Neruda, precisely because he is in every way poorer. No matter what they do with Vallejo, they can never get him into anybody's establishment. (Neruda walked in very easy without giving the slightest trouble.)

Therefore I think that a translation of Vallejo is not only a nice interesting venture but a project of very great and urgent importance for the human race.

However I would like to see your translations of Neruda.

In terms of volume I have not read all or even most of the fine Latin American poetry. There is too much. I don't think any of them that I know come close to the stature of Vallejo, but they are fine in less profound ways. Nobody could be so direct, and go so far into the heart of it, and never stop going. But the Latin Americans are better, as a whole, than the North Americans. Cid Corman I don't know. So many of the others, even when most sincere, give the impression of posing even, especially, in their sincerity. They just don't have anything to say, even when they are indignant one feels that their indignation (in a good cause of course) has not yet got over being just indignation with themselves and with the fact that they are not liked by everybody yet.

Vallejo is a great eschatological poet, with a profound sense of the end (and yet of the new beginnings that he does not talk about). All the others are running around setting off firecrackers and saying it is a national holiday or emergency or something. Or just lolling around in a tub of silly words.

[Hoffman Reynolds] Hays I don't know, N[ew] D[irections] 15 [with the essay, "The Passion of César Vallejo"] I did not see, and I am not up on what is being published. I am not well informed, you understand.

As for me, I am not going to translate any whole book of V. but I may some day do my own anthology of L. American poets I like most, and that would mean a lot of his. But I don't think repeated translations of such a man will overlap, especially of the *Poemas humanos*. I might work more on *Los heraldos negros* because I like the manifest Inca quality there.

Do send me something of yours: I do not know you, though your name is familiar. I seldom really read magazines even when I get them. I have probably been in something with you and not known about it.

January 22, 1965

It is unfortunate that I am so drowned in letters to answer that I don't get around to the ones I want to answer. I was surprised to hear you were so close, after Japan. Certainly it would make sense to meet and talk. I don't get permission to travel, and I would not be able to come to Bloomington [Indiana]. But if you could drive down here some time, that would be fine. However, I am under limitations as far as visits go, and would not be free for a few months yet, as I have already filled my quota for the first months of the year. Some time in April might be good. You probably are not so far away that it would mean a great project to get here. So I hope you can get down for the afternoon some time. You are welcome to dinner and supper here, and to stay overnight if you want to. This is not the place where you saw *Murder in the Cathedral*, that was more probably St. Meinrad's [Archabbey].

Let me know if you will still be around in April, and want to come down. I will then clear it with the Abbot [James Fox].

Glad for *Residence on Earth* [Eshleman's translation of Neruda's poems]: your translation made me look more closely at the original. The translation is very good. It is real. I mean it is a real experience in its own right and an adequate communication of Neruda except in the few places where he is uncommunicable in English perhaps. I know what you mean about my translations of Vallejo not being "involved" in him. I had not read enough of his poetry or studied enough of his life to really get into it that deeply. The bitterness remained a bit abstract. Not that I could get it all into poems of mine, but it would be good to have experienced it more fully in poems of his. I had not done this. The fact that you have been through so much of it would put you in a position to detect this lack. You took me up on the adjective "great" and of course it is no adjective at all. It has no face left. But what I meant was that Vallejo is one of those people who imposes himself as a world in himself, without being square about it in any way (as I suspect Goethe was for instance). And he does this more truly than anyone in this century, it seems to me. You tell me if I am crazy. Or exaggerating.

I get good letters from Meg [Randall de Mondragon] at *El Corno* [*Emplumado*], and wish I could help them with millions. If Ernesto Cardenal comes up here, which I expect, and if he goes that way, should I tell him to come and see you? He is a good poet and he knows how to sit peacefully on islands with San Blas Indians and so forth, with civilized people, is what I mean.

March 11, 1965

About April, by all means bring your wife [Barbara Novak], it is a nice drive and I can talk to her too, why not? Only thing is that she might feel frustrated by signs saying all women will be excommunicated if they are not so already by their very nature. But as long as she does not rush into the monastery everything will be all right. The signs are not as nasty as they look . . .

It turns out Cardenal is back in Colombia and didn't come to this country after all, so I can't send him along to Indiana. As for the drawings, they are at the moment in Milwaukee and some may be seen in a new magazine called *Lugano Review*; a few were in *El Corno* a long time ago but rather dim.

Your poem I like in patches, but I find it a bit academic, I mean the gnostic etc. imagery and figures. I think it is not yet as alive as you want it to be: and what is behind the figures, I mean spiritually? I don't think you are really definite about that. Blake was. Your poem gives the impression of something cooking but you do not yet know what. But keep it cooking.

I have translated some Nicanor Parra whom I like very much; he is not a Vallejo, harder headed, more antipoet, very funny.

If I seem rushed, and when it comes to letters I am, it is because I don't put much time in the things that call for a great deal of activity, and as there is an enormous amount of this, a lot gets crowded into a short time and then I dump it all. Probably not the best way to do things, but I can't always try to do everything the best way. But that explains why the letters are slow in getting answered and are often incoherent.

Bring your wife and let her not be frustrated by the signs, by the hideous gatehouse etc. There will perhaps be dogwoods later in April anyway.

P.S. Can you read Japanese? I have a thing here which I can't understand.

May 25, 1965

Well, the only people I know in Peru are the widow [Georgette de] Vallejo and a Benedictine priest who is up in the hills somewhere. I am afraid I cannot be much help except to say that if I were in your shoes I would get up and go, even if I had to swim. If you stay around this country you have to make up your mind to face all the nonsense that is really not so worth facing anyway. On the other hand, there is no good in letting it depress you. One has to be relatively free of all that, even while doing what is demanded in order to be part of the stupid mess—which is unavoidable. After all, the two of you have so much that you ought to consider yourselves well off and not let the squares lead you into self-doubt.

[James] Laughlin was here but I did not come to anything conclusive about anything to do with *El Corno* for instance. He said he remembered having had some correspondence with you. After that I don't remember much because when he was here I got another dose of the flu bug I had before and that wiped out all the rest. He is going ahead with the stuff I am trying to do on Chuang Tzu and that is keeping me happy at the moment, that and the birds. Lots of company out there, rabbits, salamanders, tanagers, fireflies, owls, everything.

Now the question is, having written this, have I lost your address? It is not on the postcard.

November 8, 1965

It was good to get your long letter. Glad you are there [Nicaragua]. Sure, I guess you are right about twelve hours a day in the bus in Central America. I did it in Cuba, but one day is all you need in Cuba. Glad you met [Pablo Antonio] Cuadra and [José Coronel] Urtecho. You were probably wrong in thinking Cardenal was not interested. He is rather a shy person and I am quite sure that the fact of your not being a Catholic made absolutely no difference whatever.

Going on through your letter, I really envy you a little. I used to love pushing on through places like that and getting around, like Panama. I used to do that sort of thing in Europe.

About the monastery: does it need explaining or justifying? For my own part I have come to the conclusion that if I can live with it my friends can. It is simply a fact. I know that in many ways it seems to be an offensive fact, but I can't help that, and it may change some day. I did not come here for the costume, and there are various ways in which one can accept it: for my part I like it because it is comfortable: and who cares what anybody wears anyway? I assure you that I am not attached in the least to the institutional exterior of the Church. I have committed myself to this, yes, and people know this. All right. But anyone who knows me knows that I am not going to make funny choices when it comes to deciding between something artificial and external and something real and live. I would not be here if I had not found some kind of life in it, and I repeat, I am in no way selling out to whatever may be fictitious about it. I think that is one thing a person learns in a place like this, just as in a Zen monastery you learn to burn Buddhas. But really I don't want to put up an argument for or against it. I am living with it, and certainly I could wish it were different in many ways. I certainly recognize that as far as the relations with people go, it is a forced and arbitrary setup, and moreover I know that I myself have been to some extent harmed and diminished by this. It can't be helped, there are other things which are important enough to counterbalance this, and all life is much the same in that respect. And I am simply not interested in the kind of life I would have to live if I were outside.

All that is a long way round to say if you can possibly forget I am a priest, forget it. And I assure you that I have no interest whatever in pulling any professional priestly magic on you. I pray for you to have life and happiness as I pray for all my friends, and that is it.

Since August I have been living in the woods all the time, going down to the monastery once a day. It is very good for meditation and for being more alive and for my part I am very happy with it. It is really what I came here for. I get some writing done, read a fair amount, chop wood, think a lot. As far as I am concerned, this is where the root is. I do not prescribe it for anybody else, but for me it is a good answer. Still, at the same time, I would like to get down in those mountains (not Lima so much). [Miguel] Grinberg said he had heard from you and was glad . . .

January 28, 1966

Your letter of Dec. 21st didn't get to me until two or three days ago. Sure, you are right that in this position I often say things without knowing all that I ought to know. You list a lot of things I should have read and haven't. However, I wasn't actually saying the South Americans were all better poets. In fact all I did was say what they said, and when I originally said it I jotted it down in a book with an enormous amount of other material in which it was buried. When *Harper's* [*Magazine*] for some reason picked it out of a rather long series of selections I sent them, it certainly got to be much too emphatic all of a sudden. I was worried about it ["Few Questions and Fewer Answers: Extracts from a Monastic Notebook"] when I saw it in proof, and would have cut it altogether except that they had cut so much that I was afraid there would be almost nothing left . . . In that of course I was wrong.

As you state it, and you state it exactly, what you object to is that I seem to identify more easily with "the South American mind," whatever that may be, than with North American poets. You seem to me to be berating me for being on the wrong side. As a matter of fact I am not on any side: hence it would certainly have been better to have said nothing.

At the same time, I do not say this as anything but a simple fact, not as a statement having some special value or other; though I read [Allen] Ginsberg and recognize he is alive and a good poet he sounds to me like someone on another planet, while [Nicanor] Parra doesn't. This is not to be construed into some other kind of statement "Ginsberg is bad, Ginsberg goes to bed early/late, etc." It is just that I respond to Parra more than I do to Ginsberg. Whether I ought not to is something I consider a bit irrelevant.

As to the statement [about] *Harper's* being intellectually sloppy, you are perfectly right. All I can say is that I will be more careful next time. Or try to.

If there are people you think I ought to read, and if there is some way you can easily send me something they have written, I wish you would do so. But I don't want to put you to an enormous amount of trouble in Peru, obviously.

One thing you can do, though: I have been wondering if you have ever read Rilke, and if so whether he means anything to you, or to people you know. Does anyone read him in this country besides the squares? I am interested because he is a bit of a problem to me in some ways. I have been reading a lot of him and about him. I should imagine you probably had not read him, or that if you had you didn't particularly like him.

Right now I am pretty well snowed in and chopping a lot of wood.

March 16, 1966

. . . Liked everything you said about Rilke. The things you did not like about him were the things I thought you probably would not like: the perfume and the older women. But the older women had enough sense to give him castles to write in and I rather like the Princess, not to mention the one he went to Russia with. You are very right about his ideas on death: they are deep and solid intuitions. I think of him as validly religious, and his reaction against a sick Catholicism is perfectly understandable. The translations stink, though the [J. B.] Leishman [–Stephen] Spender job on the [Duino] Elegies is fair. It is at least passable, most of the time. I find myself preferring the Neue Gedichte and not preferring the Orpheus sonnets [Sonnets to Orpheus]. I do like the Elegies very much. Also the Letters to a Young Poet; very good indeed. I am lecturing on them to the monks. "Young Workman's Letter" is fine too . . .

I just got Meg Randall's new book of poems and like it.

I did not mean "South American mind" in such a way that I would pretend to give it a clear definition. I don't know that much about it. They are certainly fusty, involved, often superficial, glib, vain, etc. etc. That is a question of character. I was thinking in terms more of culture, the European background, I like Spanish writing and the Spanish language which can be sharp and supple and well tempered like nothing on earth when it is good. Inevitably some of the irony, some of the critical spirit is still lying around at least in the guys who as you say got out. Perhaps if I were closer to the scene I would be less happy about some of the political noises. Maybe they mean absolutely nothing. Maybe they just sound alive. Perhaps my sympathy for them as a bunch is due to the fact that I was born and grew up in France. In fact I was born only a few miles from Spain and am by birth at least a French Catalan. That is enough for the Catalans in Barcelona to call me simply Catalan. That's all right with me, though it is the same sort of joke as Rilke being Russian. Of course, though, Catalan doesn't mean Spanish by any means. Maybe I just miss being with the kind of people I grew up with, though I can't say I was always happy about that, either. Parra seems to me to be a lot lighter on his feet than the gummy and heavy type of thing (at least so it seems to me) we are getting around here. That's why I like Meg's poems, they are less "heavy." Ginsberg is articulate but somehow he seems to me to be emotionally or spiritually or something gooey, viscous. I do not deny that he is a very fine poet.

Spring is coming to the woods, everything is very quiet and is now warm too. It has been very cold this winter. Probably I knocked my back out chopping wood and next week I have to go and get an operation on it.

About the differences between us, you are the one who seems worried by them. Perhaps it would help to distinguish between the differences of the group with which I am associated, and my differences. They are not the same. I am not to be identified simply with an outfit, and it bugs me when you do. Then I get defensive about it, and that makes the difference seem greater than it is. But of course we differ and I see nothing whatever wrong with that or surprising about it. I differ with a great number of people, and in fact there are very few that I really agree with in a whole lot of different areas all at once . . .

May 8, 1966

Lot of things have happened since I last wrote to you. Mainly I had to go into the hospital for one of those back operations, which came out all right I think, but was a gruesome experience in many ways. Not that I ever got into unbearable pain, but it is simply shattering to have people dig into such a center of life and motion and to be worked on for hours though unconscious, being "lived" through tubes and machines all the while, and becoming a kind of medical abstraction. Not just as Donne did, a map, but God knows what, an experiment. A theorem. A dismembered piece of machinery, like a car in a garage. I came out ok finally and have been going through a long convalescence, not doing much work and writing very few letters.

The Chavin Illumination came. It comes through wonderfully in type, a most beautiful illumination and right at the heart of things. The first time I read it (when you sent it in ms.) I had not met you and Barbara I think. Anyway I read it cursorily and without the attention you would want. This time, for various other personal reasons, I am in a much better position to respond to it because I have run into something like it myself. And I know why such things demand imperatively to be said and are almost the only things worth saying, the only things left that are *true*.

I won't go into your letter and the "barrier." There is no use defending, protesting, constructing explanations etc. I think you really must have gone through a kind of trauma in Latin America and I am not qualified to talk about it because my own experience of LAmerica thirty years ago was totally positive and totally different. I know what you mean because (this is the problem) I feel in many ways the same kind of trauma about certain aspects of North American culture. The barrier is this difference of experience, history, sensibility, and there is no argument about what has burst into one's karma and is just there. Hence there is no barrier other than that of two entirely different loads of history that we have to carry. The only thing I reproach you for is an apparent inability to see that I am not blindly and willfully *choosing* to carry my different burden as though in doing so I were challenging you. You must not regard the differences between us as a challenge, and you must not be surprised if for various reasons I cannot suddenly see everything precisely as it looks to you. I do not know you that well. You expect me to understand you and go along with you as if I had known you all my life. But we are strangers. Please do not be mad at me for this fact which cannot be much changed at the moment—because I have had all my quota of visitors for this time. I am not justifying this "quota" aspect of my life. It is to me shameful and degrading in many ways, as you know. I do not ask you to approve of it, or even to understand on what terms I just manage to put up with it, not knowing how else to handle the things. You would say "get the hell out of there" and of course from a certain point of view there is no argument: except my karma. And as I keep saying, if I can put up with it my friends ought to.

The translation from Vallejo on the back of your letter was powerful and most moving, a very fine job, though I did not look at the original. It certainly was Vallejo. But I have no intention of fighting windmills at New Directions on this account. Man when it is useless it is useless, and I am not magic. I can't change things by wishing.

Thanks for the books which came in yesterday. Have already begun the Bashō which is just what I have been wanting after so much tired stuff, this is the greatest the most alive and you are right perfect monasticism. Thanks for the intuition that it is what I would need. Maybe when I read it carefully I will know a lot more about the question. And there is no question that the great issue is freedom. From Urizens goddam hammers. I go where I am Los (turned loose) so far the one place where I can be the sunlight is up here on this hill where all the angels shine around me in each leaf and no one can prevent them. I have been on the road before and there were fewer and sometimes none. I think I have only one way to travel and it is straight up. Or straight down into the root.

All my love to both of you. I hate priestcraft and do not represent any such thing. Write when you can. Anything I can send? Chuang Tzu? I will send it [*The Way of Chuang Tzu*] or did I already? I think I probably didn't. And some of the mimeograph stuff we have lying around, I forget what I sent of that. "[The] Zen Koan" maybe did you get?

October 18, 1966

First of all I will certainly write something for the Guggenheim people if you want me to, but I am embarrassed to say that though I have written a lot of those things before, no one I know has ever got anything [Eshleman had asked Merton for a recommendation]. I am sure I don't have the knack. I hope you get to Paris ok, though you may hate it too. Though perhaps less than Lima. It has changed a lot in the last thirty years. I have not been there lately.

. . . I honestly think both you and Cid have a sort of reflex which leads you to swat other people for no good reason, except that this is something you need to do—I do the same not in letters but in my writing sometimes, and that gives the impression that I am mad too. I know none of us are angry really.

I respect your feeling that monks, Zen or others, give an impression of hubris by "living detached on a special lane" and then telling everyone else off. Or just claiming to have the answer. I feel that way myself about the monks who really do this and there are plenty. But once again in a despairing plea I hope to get someone at last to see that I am not one of them (but in the past I have been, so I deserve whatever is said about it). This business of chastity is much more complex than that. First of all, it is not a question of negatively scouring out all sexual desire, though many do this or try to. Properly it should be a long hard job of sublimation: and doubtless few of us completely succeed. In any case I have never led or advocated a totally disincarnate life. I was in love before entering the monastery and I have also been in love since (though pretty hampered by the restrictions!) and in the end I have come to a position where I refuse to generalize, and above all I know I don't have the "Big Answers" (who has?). And I do wish everyone would stop inferring that I intend my life to be some sort of reflection on theirs. I don't assume for a moment that the plane on which I live is higher or better than anyone else's, in fact I know it may be a blind alley and a huge mistake, but since I honestly think it is my "fate" (call it that if you like), I have decided, and often, over and over, that it has to be accepted for what it is worth and made the best of. And I suppose I am moderately happy at it and am able to give something to other people from where I am. The point is that this sort of setup does offer a certain kind of freedom of its own, and that if a person wants to choose this and live accordingly, then it would be a bad thing for him to be forced to conform to others who don't want it. People who want and need this kind of solitude (there are always some) should be able to find it and stay in it, though they should do so without looking down on others or being vain of supposed achievements (that vanity immediately empties the whole thing out anyhow). Since this obviously is not your dish, I can see that it would repel you or leave you indifferent: yet the swamp wading you speak of is common to everybody and there is no escape for monks: each one simply has to get through his own swamp as honestly and as completely as he can. The only thing is not to make a virtue out of going under. And I am glad you are getting footway on some rock. Keep it up. I'll send you a book called *Raids on the Unspeakable*, parts of which I like, parts of which are trivial. Cid didn't like the way I seemed to be telling everybody what to do and saying "hey listen to me." That was a good criticism, but . . .

November 10, 1966

I sent you my last letter when I was just entering the hospital for some tests—nothing special. But by the time I got back and got to your letter everything had piled up, and now I am away from it, and swimming to get back to it. And another thing is that all mail coming or going is inspected, especially mine, because I am suspicious character. I suggest then (if it doesn't nauseate you to do it) that if you have something, as they say, of a "private nature," it would be well to mark the envelope very clearly "conscience matter" and it will not be opened (I hope).

What you say about "dissolution" etc. I deeply and in every way agree with, and I don't claim that I am doing a marvelous job of getting along without. Nor am I in an attitude of self-defense if I say that I have from time to time come close to that in other ways. Sublimation is not a deliberately managed process, and God knows there is no end of dangers and aberrations—maybe most supposed sublimation is just phony—I have seen enough of that. Well, I explore the area that I explore: someone has to, and it is possible that I have gone around in circles, found nothing, and so on. One very good thing did happen: a Sufi master from Algeria [Sidi Abdesalam], a really authentic guy and a completely human being, showed up here with interpreter-disciple and we understood each other fine and understood where we were going: area of crazy liberty of spirit etc. That is my path and my lot and I know there is no going back on it—nor do I want to. Again, I say, this is just for me, not for anyone else. I see the need for you to go the way you are going and feel it is right, if you don't attach too exclusive an importance to it . . . I like very much your piece on [Carl Theodor] Dreyer's St. Joan [the film La Passion de Jeanne d'Arc]—not having seen this I don't get whole picture but see there is a lot in what you say. [René] Char I was reading this summer, full of great things and especially I wonder as you do at the marvel of the Hypnos notes [Feuillets d'Hypnos]. Now I am in [Antonin] Artaud's great annotations on Balinese theater and theater in general. I might translate some of this material, I don't think it has been done. Finished a long poem sequence ["Edifying Cables"], but I am not happy with it, it is not rich enough, hot enough, cerebral maybe, ironic, testy, blah. I am not anxious to show it to anyone or I would send a copy.

I write when I can, you too. Always most glad to hear.

Have you heard the Jazz of Jimmy Smith? Ambiguous power, but power. Angry power, that's why I say ambiguous. Love is not easily come by.

December 26 or 28 [1966]

I write this fast so I won't forget and leave Lacrymae [Lachrymae Mateo: 3 Poems for Christmas] without any answer. I like the three poems very much and in a way they are going on ahead and past the others as they should. There is much better fusion of things that seem to clash, and this makes for power. Or maybe I realize it more because you have told me what is fusing. I know how much in this kind of poetry you have to know the poet. It is you. Very good you.

Your Guggenheim stuff I filled in and sent in when they asked and I hope you get something but man don't rely on me. I say it again, I don't know how to write out the stuff they want.

Yes of course you are right about them frisking the letters for the

Unspeakable. If it were only that. And for my own part my life has been frankly built on the Unspeakable and Unspoken for a long time, and that too everybody knows. Also the word in the title (Unspeakable) is ambiguous even for me: it is just a title, though it does say something. But it is both good and bad Unspeakable. However, what they don't like is the human. But the human doesn't have to be that vulnerable.

The enclosed [a circular letter dated Christmas Morning—1966, published in *The Road to Joy*] is what I am sending out to a lot of people: another aspect of everything. I don't think it will disconcert you. You know me.

All of a sudden I am reading a lot of [William] Faulkner and finding it very good. Does anybody read him? Or is it just that I live in the South?

St. Joseph's Infirmary, Louisville, Kentucky
February 27, 1967

Thanks for your letter & the information about the Ad Hoc Committee . . . As a Catholic I want to thank you all for your Christian lesson given in charity to our Church which is sometimes distinguished by moral blindness in crucial issues—and this is one of them. [Francis] Cardinal Spellman's stand on Vietnam has done terrible harm to the cause of man & to the Christian faith & and it is right for you to point this out. It is scandalous that the law & the Church establishment should gang up on you. The only reason why I don't join your sponsors publicly is that I might be more useful to the cause of peace if I avoid an open confrontation "against" people like Spellman, since I am working on issues about which they can't very well complain—aid to civilians in Vietnam, etc.

Of course there will probably come a time when I will have so say No publicly to people like Spellman, but I don't think there is any point to it now. . . . What matters is the wholeness of love in all its respects, & this is not just our own managing. It is also a gift.

(Can I have a couple of the pictures taken here? Love to.)

August 17, 1967

Delighted to hear of the new magazine. Will send things and am sending first this. New. Please tell me right away if you don't want it and then I can do something else with it. I am writing this new, pages of. A whole book of it. Lots.

As a matter of fact I did answer your St. Patrick lament with tangible help. Alas, here is what became of it. Your letter got me in the hospital where I lay operated in February. On your letter there was no address but that of the captains who are saving you from the galleys of Spellman and Odessa to fight you in Pepanto etc. Lepanto of course I mean. There is about to be a great naval blunder with Dom John of Austria. To defend the ables against the capables. Every cardinal you understand is either able or capable or both. Must not tell them any different.

Well now like I explained above I wrote to your captain's palace of defense from the hospital, for this was my only known direction at that time. Well then what. The letter containing no less than five dollars (for me a fortune) was returned to the hospital. Now wait carefully from the hospital I had left. Now attend. The nuns opened the letter. Now remark: the nuns read my saving aspersions on the head of old Spellman but they did not blanch nor quail. The nuns then (observe) contacted me by the planes of secrets away from the hospital. I then advanced by stealth on the hospital for by that time I needed the five dollars bad myself. You can therefore guess the rest. But I have in the meantime shown you the secrets of my sympathy. Old Spellman is all seaweed from head to foot, as everybody knows, for he is really Neptune the god of New York and I intend to write songs to that effect. You have flouted same and are suffering from tridents up the ass which is most unpleasant but this is the age of Auschwitz and the hierarchy ain't fooling. They know what side their brands is buttocked on. That is what you get for being honest. Meanwhile I will scrape if scraps can and fish together emoluments and pfennigs of various denominations to send for the captain's defense against Rapacious old Card. You have done well and my Church is with you in contradistinction to his, for he is a schism or prism. His sights are ascrew, take that in any language you prefer: like A Screw or the Magazine of the Farts. Well, now I must go and bandy witticisms with my superior.

Serious best lucks with the new mag and promise help, if you like this new verse there is plenty more where that come from.

September 3, 1967

Thanks for your letter. I note the change of address. The main thing I want to write about is the question of giving my signature.

Obviously I agree with you on the war, and I agree in particular that Spellman's support of it is scandalous. On the other hand, after thinking about the various angles for several days, I have come to the conclusion that I can't sign. This is not just because I don't want to prejudice the cases of several Catholic C.O.'s who need my support (one is being tried by the army). The difference is more fundamental. I can't personally identify with the way in which you protested. To illustrate what I mean: I don't approve of the use of napalm by Israelis on the Arabs in the recent war [Six-Day War, June 5–10, 1967]. But I would not enter a synagogue with a sign to that effect, especially during a service. The case is not in every respect similar, but it is close enough to show what I mean. Therefore I am sorry, but I can't give you my signature.

Obviously I hope you will be acquitted. I'll be thinking about it and would send money if I could.

To Lawrence Ferlinghetti

The American poet, playwright, editor, and publisher Lawrence Ferlinghetti
(1919–   ) was a leader in the beat movement in the fifties. His City Lights Books
published works by Jack Kerouac, Gary Snyder, and Allen Ginsberg, while Fer-
linghetti's famous San Francisco bookstore (also named City Lights) featured
counterculture writers. A Coney Island of the Mind *(1958) is one of Ferlinghetti's*
most celebrated works. Where Is Vietnam? *(1965),* Tyrannus Nix *(1969),* Who
Are We Now? *(1976),* Over All the Obscene Boundaries: European Poems &
Transitions *(1984), and* Seven Days in Nicaragua Libre *(1984) reflect Ferlinghetti's*
political and social concerns. He published Merton's Auschwitz poem, "Chant to
Be Used in Processions Around a Site with Furnaces," in the first issue of Journal
for the Protection of All Living Beings. *Merton's name headed a list of contributors*
that included Bertrand Russell, Gary Snyder, Albert Camus, and Allen Ginsberg.
The letters Merton wrote to Ferlinghetti in the summer and fall of 1961 document
some of the difficulties Merton encountered in publishing his first writings on
war, "Chant" and Original Child Bomb.

August 2, 1961

Since you ask me to, I have sent the furnace poem ["Chant to Be
Used in Processions Around a Site with Furnaces"] to the censors of the
Order. However, here is the thing: if they object to it we can't print it
at all, whereas if I had printed it over a pseudonym it would at least be
printed and they might object afterwards if they knew who wrote it, which
would be quite doubtful.

Here we are dealing not with diocesan censors who confine themselves to matters of faith and morals, and are to be taken seriously, but
with censors of the Order who bother their heads about everything,
because they have been given the task of judging whether or not a piece
of work is *opportune.* That word *opportune* covers a lot of ground. First
of all, it is intended explicitly to discourage new writers from arising in
the Order. Secondly, it is concerned with how the work of an established
writer may be imagined to affect the reputation of the Order. This extends
to some very picayune things. I had a frightful time publishing two articles
on Pasternak ["Boris Pasternak and the People with Watch Chains" and
"The Pasternak Affair in Perspective"] because of the implication that I
must have read a) his novel and b) newspapers and magazines, which all
would be a cataclysmic blow to the prestige of the Order. Utterly un-
thinkable. The atomic bomb piece [*Original Child Bomb*] was objected
to on roughly the same grounds, though was put more coyly: "This has
been written about before by others." In a word these cats are obsessed
with a certain image they have of themselves and they don't want anyone
disturbing it. What they want me to do is to build up the Order to the
skies and make it look as if nobody in it even had a body anymore, let

alone five senses and an awareness that the rest of the universe continued to exist. This to me seems somehow unconnected with the Christian concept of charity which seems to me to indicate that the Christian is somehow involved with the rest of mankind and that they all have common problems. War for instance, and peace, and concentration camps. I regret that I have not yet advanced to the stage where I can be exclusively concerned with birth control and pornography as the only two moral problems worthy of concern, along with the sixth commandment, generally referred to as "sin" without further qualification.

But I do have a moral problem about that furnace piece. A very sensitive guy who has been living in Europe and knows people who were in the camps, including a Jewish girl who was deliberately run over by a tank outside the Warsaw ghetto and lost her legs, says the piece is too nasty and that people aren't thinking that way over there. In a word the question of violence arises in the poem itself. Certainly it is not pro-Auschwitz, but the fact remains that it states all these things in a sardonic manner which is noncommittal and callous (apparently). Also the aspect of it which bothers me is: to what extent can we point to what is hateful and say it ought to be hated, if by that we necessarily imply that there are, therefore, people to be hated and punished? This piece is by the way not about Eichmann, but about the commandant of Auschwitz, [Rudolf] Hess.

Some day when I have thought about it more I want to talk to you about effective protest as distinct from a simple display of sensitivity and good will. I think we have to examine the question of genuine and deep spiritual non-cooperation, non-participation, and resistance. There is so very little in this country that what little there is has got to be good. If it is not good, if it is just a question of standing up and saying with sincerity, candor and youthful abandon "I am against," it has the following bad effects: a) It perpetuates an illusion of free thought and free discussion, which is actually very useful to those who have long since stifled all genuine freedom in this regard. b) It flatters the squares by giving them something they can contrast themselves with, to their own complacent advantage. I leave you to work out some of the other implications. Have you by any chance read the Old Testament prophets lately? They knew how to hit hard in the right places, and the chief reason was that they were not speaking for themselves.

You ask me about why certain persons [clergymen, priests, nuns, and monks] are absent from peace parades: because they themselves did not organize the peace parade. This is the main reason. They don't join with any other organization in doing things. Why haven't they organized one of their own? Because they are too busy shouting about the need for destroying the enemy. Why are they so busy shouting . . . ? Etc. All down the line. Ultimately they think in negative terms. They define themselves by standing back from the guy that is something else, and say "at any rate I am not him" and they start from there to arrive at who they are. This I think is why there are so many zombies around. They are just not someone else. Nor are they themselves. This goes for everybody in whatever group, whoever does this ends up a zombie.

I am sorry about the letter you wrote ten years ago [Ferlinghetti had written about the questions of consecrated virginity in Dietrich von Hildebrand's "Marriage" and "got a note from a secretary in return"]. Of course I don't remember whether or not I even got it. Mail is subject to all sorts of ups and downs. Sometimes you get most of it, sometimes you get very little of it, and sometimes someone who has been getting through to you regularly suddenly becomes *Nacht und Nebel*. A lot of the stuff sent to me is answered by a secretary in the Abbot's office, or handed to some other other department. If you have since found yourself getting a lot of cheese advertising and come-ons for donations to the monks, then your letter got into the office of one of the Fathers who is in charge of a big long mailing list.

Talking about mailing lists: could you send me some of your catalogues? I mean of paperbacks of all kinds that I could get from City Lights Bks?

Look, I don't give you the gotta go to confession right away routine. What is vitally important is that you should be a Christian and as faithful to the truth as you can get. This may mean anything but resembling some of the pious faithful. But I don't have to tell you, because you know, that there is only one thing that is of any importance in your life. Call it fidelity to conscience, or to the inner voice, or to the Holy Spirit: but it involves a lot of struggle and no supineness and you probably won't get much encouragement from anybody. There is a dimension of Catholicism, mostly French and German, which gives a little room for growth like this. But you have to find it as best you can. I can't necessarily tell you where to look, or how much of it you have found already. The start of it all is that none of us really have started to look. But the mercy of God, unknown and caricatured and blasphemed by some of the most reputable squares, is the central reality out of which all the rest comes and into which all the rest returns.

August 12, 1961

Your letter requires a quick answer. Of course print the poem ["Chant to Be Used in Processions Around a Site with Furnaces"] if it is set up. There is no question about that, since I said you could do it if there was no name, or no right name.

But now: about the name. Here is what has happened so far. Of course nothing has come from the censor. But I sent a copy of the poem to Dorothy Day, just for her. And she passed it on to the boys at *The Catholic Worker* and now *they*, as far as I know, are printing it or have printed it. Also without benefit of censorship, permission from me, and a few minor details like that. They did write, but it was already an accomplished fact, or so it appeared from the letter.

Since they have to all appearances printed the thing over my name, there is no further reason why you should not do so. The fat is in the fire, so you might as well go ahead and I will take responsibility with my Superiors for whatever follows. It is an accident and that is that. They may not be too happy about it, and it may make them clamp down on anything of this type in the future. But what can anyone do about it now? So go ahead.

I am glad at any rate that the magazine [*Journal for the Protection of All Living Beings*] is coming right along and look forward to seeing it soon.

What have you decided to do about the Atomic Bomb piece? I have rewritten it, but don't know whether to send a copy to J [Laughlin] out there or not. Nor do I know what has been decided by him and [Robert] Lax and [Emil] Antonucci. Perhaps I had better wait until Lax prints it and then let you print from his copy, if you want it . . .

August 15, 1961

Your letter came this morning together with one from *The Catholic Worker* which confirms that they have printed the Auschwitz piece. Since that is the case you might as well go ahead and use it, there are no further reasons for not doing so. Print it over my name. I think it is better for you to use this in the first issue. Lax is not moving so fast with the Bomb piece, so it would be better to wait on that one.

I am sending a second copy of the Bomb piece, this time the full corrected version. I have not sent one to J. I presume he can print from what Lax puts out. They are arranging something between them.

There is peace in ourselves, since we are Sons of God: but the difficulty is in knowing this and facing it. The reason why we do not live in paradise is that it is difficult to be simple. This is our work, though. It is terribly important that we try to understand it, though we cannot really do that. And there are not easy explanations, or cliché answers to questions about it. The answers are all night.

Like being simple enough to love everybody. Nice, on paper. On this I made a sermon ["The Power and Meaning of Love"], and I send it . . . What I preach I don't necessarily do, but from that I hope have learned to expect no less from other people. At least that . . .

[Cold War Letter 7]   December 12, 1961

J. forwarded your letter to me, and I am sorry to hear that you have been sick. All my friends have been in hospitals, operated on, diagnosed as about to die, God alone knows what. We are cashing in our chips, so it seems, except that for my part I am still standing, though hungry.

About the *Journal*: don't think I was personally embarrassed by it.

But as I rather expected, Fr. Abbot [James Fox] took a good look at it and decided that from now on I am not to contribute any more to it. That is the only thing I regret. I admit that I am not much dazzled by the approach most of the writers take. I mean I can get along from page to page without getting swept off my feet with enthusiasm. Not that I am mad at dirty words, they are perfectly good honest words as far as I am concerned, and they form part of my own interior mumblings a lot of the time, why not? I just wonder if this isn't another kind of jargon which is a bit more respectable than the jargon of the slick magazines, but not very much more. And I wonder just how much is actually *said* by it.

However, that is not what I mean, because I thought a lot of this stuff was real good, especially the one about David Meltzer's baby getting born. This was fine. And a lot of good in the Robt Duncan, which I liked mostly. I liked very much your beautiful Haiti and best thing in the whole book was Nez Perce. So there. I haven't read the Camus yet but him I like always. Yet I don't think it was what one might have expected, as a lot of the material was not very near the target, and I am inclined to doubt the reality of the moral concern of a lot of these people who are articulate about the question of the war in your *Journal*. And I think that is one reason why you can't get the other ones to commit themselves. I don't know if there is anything they are apt to mean about a problem as big as this. However, they are all much more human and more real than the zombies who have all kinds of facts about deterrence and finite deterrence and all-out non-survivability and all-in first-strike ballistic preemption plus as distinguished from massive plus-plus retaliation plus.

As regards the Christianity–Buddhism thing ["Wisdom and Emptiness: A Dialogue between Daisetz T. Suzuki and Thomas Merton"]: both Suzuki and I ended up hanging in various trees among the birds' nests. I am not insisting upon anything, least of all affectivity. That remark was a journalistic kind of remark, referring to the way Christianity and Buddhism look to people who are very definite about being one or the other and very sure that the metaphysic of one excludes the metaphysic of the other. This is all probably quite so. But Zen is beyond metaphysics and so, as far as I am concerned, is the kind of Christian experience that seems to me most relevant, and which is found in Eckhart and the Rhenish mystics and all the mystics for that matter. I agree theoretically that there is a complete division between the two approaches: one personalistic, dualistic, etc., the other non-dualistic. Only trouble is that Suzuki's very distinction between God and Godhead is dualistic, and his lineup of Buddha vs. Christ is also dualistic, and when he starts that he forgets his Zen. So he forgets his Zen. He can forget his Zen too if he wants to or has to, no law saying you have to remember your Zen every minute of the day. It seems to me the Cross says just as much about Zen, or just as little, as the serene face of the Buddha. Of course the historic, medieval concern with the expression of feeling and love in the Crucified Christ is nowhere near Zen, it is Bakhti or however you spell it, and that is another matter. But essentially the Crucifix is a non-image, a destroyed image, a wiped-out image, a nothing, an annihilation. It just depends what you are looking at and who you are that looks at it. So the Zens burn all the Buddhas, and they come out with the same thing in the end, as far as the destruction of the image is concerned.

What I do think matters is liberty. The complete freedom and un-limited, unrestricted quality of love, not its affectivity. This I think the Zens are after in their own way too, though more intellectual about it. And note that Zen is full of affectivity too, look at the Zen paintings: plenty compassion, humor, comment, all sorts of stuff which in the West we would frown at calling it literature . . .

Merton was Ferlinghetti's guest at City Lights Books in May 1968.

June 5, 1968

. . . Thanks very much for the contribution for *Monks Pond*. I sent some more [copies of the first issue] yesterday or the day before. Hope they reach you all right. And don't forget—send me something of yours if you can, and urge others to. Only problem is the four-letter words, on account of the monks in the print shop.

. . . The Sufi man I told you of, Reza Arasteh, has a piece ["The Art of Rebirth"] in MPOND II. It will give you an idea. The longer version of that piece and another article like it might make a pamphlet for you. I told him to send you his book, but I guess it's too long for you and would require too much editing.

The monastery [Christ of the Desert] I went to in New Mexico is a very good spot, in the Chama Canyon. Lots of Indian stuff around. I like Santa Fe, too.

Thanks for putting me up at City Lights. Felt a bit like the old days. I enjoyed looking out in the morning on a street like Havana, full of pretty little Chinese kids going to school. It was good meeting you. Bellarmine College here is probably going to contact you about a reading some time later this year.

Oberoi Grand, Calcutta, India
October 18, 1968

I am suggesting to a friend of mine, a Tibetan Lama, that he might send you a manuscript he is preparing [*Born in Tibet*]. It is of great interest, a contemporary document in the authentic Tibetan tradition— & first rate. The English may need a little improvement but the material is as impressive as the Tibetan Book of the Dead. The author's name is [Chögyam] Trungpa Rimpoche. I am giving him City Lights' address & he will contact you some time.

I am over here on an extended trip & hope to keep extending it . . .

P.S. You can always reach me through Gethsemani—mark for forwarding.

To Julien Green

Born in Paris of American parents, Julien Green (1900–) has lived in France for most of his life. His literary career spans more than sixty years, during which he has published prize-winning novels, plays, and essays. His autobiographical writings include more than a dozen journals.

Julien Green wrote to Thomas Merton in 1962, thanking him for Les chemins de la joie, *the French edition of* Thoughts in Solitude: *"You make the reader feel closer to God and this reader is in constant need of just such a feeling." Merton had asked for Green's last novel, and Green replied that he couldn't imagine a Trappist reading one of his novels, "And yet, why not?" He had liked every word of* The Seven Storey Mountain *though he felt Merton "could have said more." In September 1966, Green wrote again to Merton after reading* Raids on the Unspeakable, *which contained an essay on Green's novel* Chaque homme dans sa nuit *(1961). Admitting that Merton's remarks "throw a light on the strange world" of his characters, Green criticized Merton for misreading the novel's hero, who forgives his murderer and so is "saved."*

September 22, 1966

I am grateful for your letter of September 16th in which you speak of my notes on your book. I am glad you feel that I have seen something of the "hidden meaning"—the meaning that is hard to convey in words. It is awesome and you have a peculiar gift for conveying it. You very kindly point out my mistake—a grievous one certainly—of putting one of your best characters in hell when you took such pains to save him! I am confused and sorry: not sorry that he was after all saved, but sorry that I overlooked the indications of it. As a matter of fact, I must admit that the ending of the book had me so shaken that I was reading through rather carelessly, and not taking in all the details. I should of course have gone over that part again later, but I wrongly assumed I had seen everything. In any case, you must admit that he was saved by the skin of his teeth! And the fact of his being so, though it calls for a revision of the notes, does not essentially alter the thesis.

Of course you realize that I think this Augustinian viewpoint of sin is not only impressive, but important to remember at this moment when there is in Christian circles a sort of casual naturalism and naïve optimism accepted rather generally. I don't say that I have as much of a taste for Calvin as you do, but there are moments when I like to have him stand my hair on end for a change! And once again this question of *seriousness* remains important. And it must of necessity, I think, be also ambiguous.

May I then ask you two things? First, can you tell me which of your novels I should read in order to get the best view of this aspect of your work? And second, what about your *Journal*? I have enjoyed that so much in the past and as far as I remember I have not seen any more of it for several years. As far as I can tell, I don't think I followed you much beyond 1950 or 1952. Has there been more?

I shall ask the publisher to send you a book [*Conjectures of a Guilty Bystander*]—a quasi-Journal—in which I mention your *Journal*. In it I also speak of my own Protestant likings: especially Karl Barth.

Again, I am sorry for my mistake and will correct it if there is any question of reprinting those notes.

To Henry Miller

Born in New York City, Henry Miller (1891–1980) lived in France during the thirties before taking up residence in California in 1942. Controversy engendered by Miller's explicit treatment of sexual matter in Tropic of Cancer *(1934),* Black Spring *(1936), and* Tropic of Capricorn *(1939) brought Miller notoriety. Miller's blend of autobiography and fiction is also evident in a later trilogy,* The Rosy Crucifixion, *which included* Sexus *(1949),* Plexus *(1953), and* Nexus *(1960). Over the course of almost five decades, Miller wrote and published more than fifty books, including* The Colossus of Maroussi; or, The Spirit of Greece *(1941),* The Books in My Life *(1952),* To Paint Is To Love Again *(1960), and* On Turning Eighty *(1972). Miller published several volumes of letters, including his correspondence with Anaïs Nin, J. R. Child, and W. A. Gordon. Though the worlds in which they lived differed in many ways, Miller and Merton discovered that they had much in common, including a deep respect for each other's work. Their correspondence began when, in April 1962, Henry Miller wrote to tell "Father Louis" that he was "much moved" by the* Original Child Bomb *and "stimulated" by* The Wisdom of the Desert.

July 9, 1962

It was good to hear from you. I have often thought of writing to you, and usually that is the first thing that comes into my mind when I am reading something of yours, like the earlier part of *Big Sur* [*and the Oranges of Hieronymus Bosch*] for example, or parts of the *Colossus of Maroussi* (which I think is a tremendous and important book). I have always refrained because it is foolish for me to write letters anyway, and then I know you have little time. I am sure you must get much the same kind of mail that I do, including the poets who send you their collected works in weekly installments, and the anonymous painter who, today, sent me a large abstraction. This is all fine, but where does one get the time to collect his thoughts and come up with some kind of an intelligent word, in the presence of so many manifestations? I detest writing letters about which I do not think, at least when thought is called for. It is perhaps fortunate that there are some letters one can write without thinking: business letters. They come out like sweat.

One of the things I have wanted to discuss with you is our common admiration for [Jean] Giono. Something must be done to get a good selection of his stuff published in English—unless perhaps such a thing already exists, without my knowing of it. Recently I managed to get hold of some of his shorter prose pieces about Provence, and they are remarkable. His view of things is the sane one, the one that must be preserved as a basis for some kind of vestigial humanism, if humanism is to remain possible. I have not read his historical novels, and there are lots of his novels about Provence that I have never come across: as I say, I have read mostly essays. I think New Directions ought to do something with him.

I expect to find a lot of the same in the [Joseph] Delteil book which arrived the other day. I have not got very far into it yet, but I think something ought to be done with it in this country, nor is there much difficulty in that. Does Delteil read English? He might like the banned book I have just written (you are not the only one, you see!) about peace [*Peace in the Post-Christian Era*]. My book is not satisfactory however, because I was fool enough to try to write one that the censors would approve, and this led to compromise and stupidity. And in the end they did not approve anyway. Does he, do you, know of Fr. Hervé Chaigne, the Franciscan who is a Gandhian and involved in the non-violent movement in France?

Returning to Giono: I am thinking a lot of Provence because I am doing some work on the early monastic literature surrounding the Provençal monasteries of the 5th century, particularly Lérins. It was a great movement. That and Cassiodorus too, in Italy. One thing I envy you is your freedom to get around to such places.

I have not seen your latest books, but I just asked J. Laughlin to send me a couple. Have you seen *New Seeds of Contemplation*? He probably sent you that. I am sending along the banned book with a couple of other items that we put out here with a mimeograph machine, run by a monk with an eyeshade who lives in a room full of birds.

This much for now. Do keep in touch with me, especially about Giono, and I will write some more about Delteil later. And keep speaking out. You are in my prayers.

P.S. I would be interested in 2 Brocard Sewell's reviews. Aylesford is an interesting place!

Miller sent Merton's letter to Joseph Delteil with a note asking his wife, Caroline, to read it to her husband.

August 7, 1962

First of all I agree that it will be hard to translate Delteil, or to find a good translator. I am mightily tempted to try it myself, but I just cannot afford the time. I would enjoy the challenge of doing it, and I can think of what a living and riotous book it would make: a life of St. Francis as there never yet was in English. But I have to resist the temptation to go overboard on translations these days, as I have to save energy for some strong statements that may be needed here and there, and I am supposed to be getting busy on another book. As for translations, I am translating bits of César Vallejo, who is to me a most significant and meaningful voice, and moves me most deeply, probably because of his Indian resonances. He is the greatest of all the great South American poets we have had in this century, I think. There is another Central American, who has been out of his head for years but has written some fantastic poems: Alfonso Cortés. I am translating some of his stuff too. Beyond that I cannot go except into the Latin that I have to translate from time to time. More or less have to.

The Delteil book is frankly remarkable. It has an unusual zest and life. He works in big energetic poetic blocs of symbol. Each chapter is a carved-out symbol that runs and lives by itself and keeps affecting all the rest of the book with its own life. It is like the statues of the prophets by Aleijadinho, the Brazilian sculptor in Minas Gerais: only much more living, on the page.

Of course the question comes up, what will the average Catholic think about it? They will think that St. Francis belongs to them, and in thinking that they are perhaps so far wrong that they are out in the middle of outer space. But whenever the book comes out whoever brings it out will have to argue with those people, just as anyone who brings out a movie with some art to it will also have to argue with them.

I will write to Delteil, and I am glad you sent him the messages in the other letter.

Now to other things for a moment: I am in the middle of *The Wisdom of the Heart* and it is you at your best. There is very fine material everywhere, one insight on top of another. The opening piece starting from Lawrence is full of arresting thought, most important for a writer to read. When you write as you do in the thing on Benno you are at your very best, this is marvelous. As I say I am going along with you all the way with *The Wisdom of the Heart*. They sent me also the *Colossus* which I already had but had lent to someone, and lent books never come back. And *The Time of the Assassins*, which is going to mean much.

The English Carmelites sent me their review about those two late-nineteenth-century people, but I thought all they had to say was very good indeed. How would it be if I sent them a poem? What do you think?

Scotland drove me nuts when I was there in childhood, but I have all kinds of dreams about getting on one of those outlying islands. Maybe this is the worst delusion. I wonder what you will think of it. The people as I remember them were absurd, and especially the place used to be full of Englishmen who wouldn't call a brook anything but a burn, and who stuffed their stupid faces with scones at all hours of the day and night while a character walked up and down playing the bagpipes to them. They deserved it.

I bet you are totally right about Ireland. The combination of faith and poverty has now become one of the things that cries out to heaven for vengeance, loud enough for the vengeance to be quite near.

In the whole question of religion today: all I can say is I wish I could really see what is there to see. Nobody can see the full dimension of the problem, which is more than a problem, it is one of those things you read about in the Apocalypse. There are no problems in the Apocalypse, just monsters. This one is a monster.

The religion of religious people tends at times to poke out a monster head just when you are beginning to calm down and get reassured. The religion of half-religious people doesn't tend: it bristles with heads. The horns, the horns with eyes on the end of them, the teeth, the teeth with eyes in them, the eyes as sharp as horns, the dull eyes, the ears that now listen to all the stars and decode their message into something about business upswing.

This is the greatest orgy of idolatry the world has ever known, and it is not generally thought by believers that idolatry is the greatest and fundamental sin. It is absolutely not thought, it is not credited, it cannot be accepted, and if you go around and speak of idolatry they will fall down and laugh and the heads of the monsters will roll and wag like the biggest carnival you ever saw. But precisely the greatest and most absurd difficulty of our time is keeping disentangled from the idols, because you cannot touch anything that isn't defiled with it: anything you buy, anything you sell, anything you give even. And of course the significance of it is absolutely lost. Anyone who sells out to even a small, inoffensive, bargain-cheap idol has alienated himself and put himself into the statue and has to act like it, which is he has to be dead.

The religion of non-religious people tends to be clear of religious idols and is in many ways much less pseudo. But on the other hand, they often have no defense against the totalitarian kind, which end up being bigger and worse.

I frankly don't have an answer. As a priest I ought, of course, to be able to give Christ's answer. But unfortunately . . . it is no longer a matter of answers. It is a time perhaps of great spiritual silence.

I must really read Emerson, I never have. Except little bits that I have liked a lot. Thoreau of course I admire tremendously. He is one of the only reasons why I felt justified in becoming an American citizen. He and Emily Dickinson, and some of my friends, and people like yourself. It is to me a great thing that you say I am like the transcendentalists. I will try to be worthy of that. This is not just something we can elect to try as a boyscout project: it is a serious duty for all of us, and woe to us if we do not take it for what it is.

The time is short, and all the idols are moving. They are so full of people that they are becoming at last apparently animated and when they get fully into action the result will be awful. It will be like the clashing of all the planets. Strange that the individual is the only power that is left. And though his power is zero, zero has great power when one understands it and knows where to place it.

P.S. J. [Laughlin] and everyone call me Tom, and that is the simplest.

August 11, 1962

Reading your magnificent essay on Raimu—whom I have not seen however for twenty years & more. I come upon this sentence—p. 52. "The crimes they (American movie heroes) commit in their sleep outdo the atrocities perpetrated by the most tyrannical despots." That sentence will prove perhaps to be the key to the twentieth century. But does one need a key when all the doors are blown off the hinges?

[Spring 1963]

I was very happy with your two postcards about the [Thomas Merton] Reader & I hope you have continued to like it. I thought you might like to see the poems of Robert Lax (who is now in Greece by the way)—& I am also enclosing some translations of things I like & a poem of my own. All this is just a way of saying that I continue to think of you & to remain in deep agreement with you. By the way I tried to interest Harcourt Brace in Delteil but I don't know if anything came of it.

May 12, 1963

Thanks for all your cards. I have been thinking of you a lot since I have been reading A[lfred] Perlès's book about you [My Friend, Henry Miller: An Intimate Biography]. It all sounds so familiar: it is the kind of life in many ways that I was always intending to lead and did lead, to some extent. But one thing strikes me: it was possible to do these things, with that much joy and that much freedom, in the twenties and thirties. Since the war, unless I am mistaken, things have changed a lot, and a sick darkness has come over it. The people who remember the other times are still more or less intact. The others, pretty sick. Though I must say that now a whole new generation is coming up that gives me a little hope: the non-violent kids, for instance, in the South.

Yes, I am still at the monastery. There have been all sorts of legends about my being elsewhere, some of them founded on a firm basis of fact: that I did make honest attempts to get permission to live as a hermit in Mexico. But the whole thing was squashed by administrative and political maneuvers which I could not block. However, as to my wanting purely and simply to go back to New York, for example, I have never been touched by this insanity even for a moment. I do have times when I wish I could see some of Europe again, and I may do so, since after all, permissions to travel and pretexts for doing so are not absolutely excluded from our life. But normally I am pretty well fixed here, and have no special complaints. I am a monk, and therefore I like the monastic life. If in particular instances it is bound to have a few things lacking, that is only one of the drawbacks of any life. It seems to me that I am here for a reason, just as you are where you are for a reason. And the reason seems to be pretty much the same in both cases. We are here to live, and to "be," and on occasion to help others with the recharging of batteries. I attempt in my own way to keep the monks from getting buried in their own brand of ideological manure, and to maintain at least occasional contacts with the fresh air of reality. On the other hand the manure itself is much less obnoxious and much more productive than what is forked about indiscriminately on the outside. At least it is not lethal.

It is a pity I have not read your novels. I think I would enjoy them now, whereas before I entered I was too ambivalent and too doubtful of myself. Now I know exactly where I stand, and I really think I would get a lot out of the Tropics [*Tropic of Cancer* and *Tropic of Capricorn*]. So I will get at them one of these days. (Don't send. There is a barrier of censorship.)

I have been thinking of many things which some day I will probably want to discuss with you. Since I do not have the leisure right now, the time has not yet come.

I like the modern Greek poets very much, at least the ones I have seen in the New Directions anthology of modern Greek stuff. I regret that I never got to Greece, and envy Lax who is batting around in the islands there now. I can understand that his poems did not click: I suppose you have to know what is in all the blank spaces.

Don't forget that if you happen this way, you are invited to stay a day or two at the monastery.

June 22, 1964

I cannot let your hummingbird [*Stand Still like the Hummingbird*] get away without a resounding shout of approval. Perhaps J. Laughlin already told you how much I liked it from the first. I have been getting into it again and like it more and more. Naturally. There is no need even to say it. All that you say seems to me as obvious as if I had said it myself and you have said it better than I ever could. It needs to be said over and over again.

I resound to everything you say, Europe, Zen, Thoreau, and your real basic Christian spirit which I wish a few Christians shared!

There is no question that we have to be to a great extent voices crying in the desert. My best books are the ones nobody reads. (Nobody is buying the *Reader* and few are buying the poems.)

Keep giving us so many good things. Don't forget this place if you are around this part of the country, though why you should be anywhere in this area God alone can tell.

I met [D. T.] Suzuki the Zen man recently, and we agreed warmly about everything. He is another one. God bless [Kenneth] Patchen too. And thanks to you I am going to dig up everything I can find of J. S. Powys.

P.S. Enclosed, a response to a high school girls' magazine. I think, from the answer I got, that it really meant something to one of them.

Merton sent Miller a photo of himself and Miguel Grinberg. Miller thought Grinberg looked "a bit like an ex-pug, vagabond, poet combined" and was amazed by Merton's resemblance to himself and to Jean Genet: "You too have a look of an ex-convict, of one who has been through hell and I think bear the traces of it" (July 4, 1964).

August 16, 1964

I am glad you liked the photos [of Merton and Miguel Grinberg]. By now you must have seen Grinberg himself in person. He is a promising young guy and the thing I like best about him is that he is free of the bitterness and frustration and self-pity that is eating up so many of the good young poets. He has really decided that things are good and that he is going to try to make them better. His is the kind that will not blow the world up. Maybe some of his elders will get to it before he has a chance. But if his gang make it, perhaps there is hope.

Yes, I have often thought of the resemblance between our faces. I had not associated Genet with it, not knowing what he looks like. I suppose the person I most resemble, usually, is Picasso. That's what everybody says. Still I think it is a distinction to look like Picasso, Henry Miller, and Genet all at once. Pretty comprehensive. It seems to imply some kind of responsibility.

As to the ex-con slant: I am very glad you mention it. It seems to me that the only justification for a man's existence in this present world is for him to either be a convict, or a victim of plague, or a leper, or at least to look like one of these things. In a world of furnaces and DP's it would be hideously immoral for someone, especially a priest, to be well, totally sane, perfectly content with everything, knowing which end is always up and keeping it that way too, knowing who thinks right all the time and staying with him only and beating the others over the head etc. etc. Yes, I have got some good hellburns all over me. We all exist. Thank God.

The boys at ND have not sent me your new book [*Miller on Writing*] yet. I will get after them. They sent a couple of good books of poetry recently. I am doing a book of selections from Gandhi [*Gandhi on Non-Violence*] which I think you will like. Long introduction.

I know how it is about finding time to write, and about being deluged with letters. People going down for the third time think a letter will keep them afloat. But often what they are going down in is itself an illusion, and the letter itself will be to them an illusion. Sometimes I answer sometimes I can't and I mean not to worry about it. There is a destiny involved there too. But there is no question that we spent our lives battling with mountains of crap, and this is no mean exercise. I do not know if it helps one to improve his faculties. Perhaps that does not matter either. We are all in the plague. Have you read Camus's book on that? I just finished it and it is very true and sobering. The plague is unquestionable, irrefutable. It need not silence a stoical joy. What is real is the emptiness which is always on the side of Being, not of non-being. I will get Powys's autobiography and perhaps a novel or two from one of the college libraries around here.

Very best wishes always. By all means call me by my name which is

TOM

To Walker Percy

Walker Percy (1916–1990) studied medicine at Columbia University and interned at Bellevue Hospital in New York before giving up the practice of medicine to write full-time. Percy's first novel, The Moviegoer *(1961), earned him the National Book Award. In subsequent novels, such as* Love in the Ruins: The Adventures of a Bad Catholic at a Time near the End of the World *(1971),* Lancelot *(1977),* The Second Coming *(1980), and* The Thanatos Syndrome *(1987), Percy continued to explore, through his characters, the moral dilemmas facing individuals in the modern world. Merton liked* The Moviegoer, *and wrote to tell Percy so. That led to an initial exchange in 1964. In July 1967 Walker Percy, Will Campbell, and James Holloway visited Merton. Campbell and Holloway were collaborating on the publication of* Kattalagete; *Percy was a member of the advisory board. The visit briefly revived the correspondence between Merton and Percy.*

[January 1964]

There is no easy way to thank you for your book. Not only are the good words about books all used up and ruined, but the honesty of *The Moviegoer* makes one more sensitive than usual about the usual nonsense. With reticence and malaise, then, I think your book is right on the target.

For a while I was going around saying it was too bad guys like Hemingway were dead, as if I really thought it.

You are right all the time, not just sometimes. You are right all the time. You know just when to change and look at something else. Never too much of anyone. Just enough of Sharon. The reason the book is true is that you always stop at the point where more talk would have been false, untrue, confusing, irrelevant. It is not that what you say is true. It is neither true nor false, it points in the right direction, where there is something that has not been said and you know enough not to try to say it.

Hence you are one of the most hopeful existentialists I know of. I suppose it was inevitable that an American existentialist should have a merry kind of nausea after all, and no one reproaches you for this or anything else. It is truer than the viscous kind.

I think you started with the idea that Bolling would be a dope but he refused to be, and that is one of the best things about the book. Nice creative ambiguities in which the author and the character dialogue silently and wrestle for a kind of autonomy.

As for Southern aunts, if they are like that you can keep them. (But I praise the Southern aunt's last speech too. Insufferable, the last gasp.)

All this says nothing about how I was stirred up by the book. It should be read by the monks for a first lesson in humility. But I guess they would be bowled over by Sharon, so I better not hand it around to the novices.

I am glad Fr. Charles [Jack English, a Trappist monk from Holy Spirit Monastery in Conyers, Georgia] came by here and got sick and told you to send the book.

Now send me all your other books or things you write, please. Do you want anything of mine? I do artworks very abstract, maybe you would like one. Let me know if you like abstract brush and ink calligraphies.

Did this book get published in France yet? If not tell me and I will get the guys at Le Seuil busy on it at once.

I will send you my new book of poems [*Emblems of a Season of Fury*].

March 31, 1964

From Le Seuil comes this letter saying they had seen the book in 1961, Knopf must have sent it, and they liked it but. However, they say that you have a strong personality (I wonder if that is news to you) and that they want to see your next book. I am sorry they said you were a strong personality, as that might make you clam up for more years than you otherwise might. But in French it obviously means something better than it does with us. By the way I like the French place names around there, especially Chef Menteur. The dog.

P.S. I am glad about the calligraphy getting so near to Kafka.

Bold, oversized, cut-out letters spelled out "THE MONKS. MODERN MOVING . . . WITH OLD-FASHIONED CARE" *alongside the typed text of the following note.*

July 20, 1967

It is good news to hear you can perhaps use Bantu philosophy in your new book, which sounds like a very good idea by the way. I hope you will keep at it, because that is something I will enjoy reading. The book I referred to is in French (from Dutch) by Père Placide Tempels, CSSR, *La philosophie bantoue*, Présence Africaine (publisher). It is a rather old book and you may have to hunt through libraries for it. Also there is another, less good, but more varied (with Voodoo etc.) by Jahainz Jahn, called *Muntu*. Grove Press did that one, so it is more available.

I agree with you about the ecumenical sparks that did not spark. All movements fill me either with suspicion or lassitude. But I enjoy talking to people (except about movements). I think the best thing is to belong to a universal anti-movement underground.

The failure to deal with the Negroes properly and justly and humanly seems to be by now conclusive, irreversible, and your novel is acting itself out. Just keep a diary, maybe . . .

August 24, 1967

You are much in my thoughts as I continue my explorations of Bantu ideas. I have on interlibrary loan an essential book: *Bantu Prophets in South Africa* by Bengt Sundkler, Oxford Press, 1961. The thing is not to distill "Bantu philosophy" out into pure speculative projects as we Westerners like to do. This particular book deals with the syncretism of Zulu religion and a kind of Evangelical Christianity in South Africa: prophetic cults (hundreds of them), nativistic and healing sects. Pursuit of health is a central theme. Joining you in your forecast I would say that in our coming Bantu society (is that accurate though, because our Negroes came from Dahomey, maybe that's a different bunch?) there will be considerable interest in medical diagnosis, psychosomatic illness, questions of potency, interesting treatments, resistance against nefarious influence of dead ancestors ("Uncle Toms" perhaps). Possible efficacy of intense vomiting cures to get rid of internal snakes and animals. Treatment by pummeling with holy sticks (the Zulu Zionists carry white sticks with which to resist evil influences. The white sticks may be blotched with red if the believer has slipped into unchastity or beer drinking. When this is detected, the sinner is immersed in the river or beaten or both). Testimonials of Father delivered from liquor habit and secret societies etc. At the same time, in S. Africa, there is a taboo on European medicine in some sects—together with a taboo on native magic also. What's left? Repeated baptisms and vomitings. You could probably distinguish a high Church sort of set with very decorous unctions of the infirm, and a low Church set with more rollings, beatings, vomiting etc. There might be heated controversies and even religious and ideological conflict over crucial points concerning the dead: where they are, what they are doing, how they should be treated, fed, appeased, raised, not raised, kept quiet, etc. What about nefarious influence of Catholic and Lutheran ancestors? There is by the way an African Castor Oil Dead Church in which new life is acquired by laxatives. Interesting possibility of description of a mass revival meeting of a Church of this type. Sundkler remarks: "The prophet with his cross and his enema syringe around his neck is a common sight on the Rand and in the Reserve."

There could of course be visits from fashionable Bantu prophets sent from Africa, one called T. S. Eliot who comes preaching toilet Zen.

If you get to a university library you might look into the files of some of the better anthropology magazines. *Man*, the journal of the Royal Anthropological Society, has interesting things in it sometimes on African religion and philosophy. One must incidentally remember that none of this is static. Always in motion. And an individual who at one time is filled with intense prophetic spirit may a year or two later be quite peaceful and declare himself "no longer troubled with religion."

I am sending one of the latest mimeographs ["The Long Hot Summer of Sixty-Seven"], a mere blowing off of steam. What I am more interested in: the poetry I am writing [Merton was working on *The Geography of Lograire*], which is not typed so far, including a Zulu piece which I may send one of these days.

To Jonathan Williams

Born in Asheville, North Carolina, in 1929, Jonathan Williams was educated at Princeton and studied painting at the Phillips Memorial Gallery and photography at Black Mountain College. Williams has distinguished himself as a poet and essayist and, since 1951, as publisher of The Jargon Society Books. Among Williams's best-known books of poetry are Blues & Roots Rue & Bluets: A Garland for the Southern Appalachians (2nd rev., 1985), An Ear in Bartram's Tree: Selected Poems, 1957–1967, Elite-Elate Poems 1971–1975, and Eight Days in Eire: or, Nothing So Urgent as Mañana (1990). He has also written introductions and texts for collections of photography. Jonathan Williams wrote that James Laughlin suggested he visit Merton while he was at the University of Kentucky "colporteuring" his "latest Orphic Snake-Oil Show for the proposed benefit of various snake-eyed undergraduates." Williams went to Gethsemani with Guy Davenport and Ralph Eugene Meatyard, a trio that Merton described as the "three kings from Lexington."

November 11, 1966

Good to get your letter. Bring the snake oil over this way. Afternoons are the best time, that is you can come and have dinner at the guesthouse (11:30) and I can be with you after that. Lexington is about an hour and a half from here. Bring Guy Davenport and if you like beer bring beer (I don't have any to offer you). If it is nice we can sit around in the woods somewhere . . . I will be very glad to have the [Ronald] Johnson book [*A Line of Poetry, A Row of Trees*] and maybe I could order a copy of the [Louis] Zukofsky you did and get someone to pay for it here. Got to support good cause . . .

I don't see much of what goes on I don't know what happens I don't hear what they say I don't get into any of their fights but I wish I saw more good poetry. Never never see *Jargon*. I see you speak of Stevie Smith: do you know her? I like her stuff immensely. You know maybe some time I could do a small volume of translations of some French or Spanish poet or Spanish American for your press. Let's think of that . . . I look forward to seeing you one of those afternoons: or in the evening if you can't make it afternoon though I am supposed to get to bed around seven or eight as the local sports club is up early in the basketball court. Like two a.m.

November 29, 1966

. . . Guy Davenport's long poem [*Flowers & Leaves*] is really beautiful, and holds up perfectly all the time, advancing in the stately way a long poem should and always very alive. I am enjoying it very much and the book is beautifully done. Thank you very much indeed for it.

Have just written a little piece on Zukofsky ["Paradise Bugged," which was also published under the title "Zukofsky: The Paradise Ear"] for a Catlick literary mag [*Critic*]. Won't do the Catlicks any harm to hear of some good poetry.

Are you in snow now? We are. Hills very gaunt and fine.

May 4, 1967

I am terribly sorry for the delay in writing. Doctors again, operation again, nonsense again, tests, inspections, inquisitions, visits of publishers, scrutinies of lawyers, quarrels of abbots, plagues of insects, bloody rain, dragons in the woods behind the house, well diggers pounding the earth, varmints scampering, St. Elmo's fire in abundance, northern lights in the bedroom, incidence of leprosy in the mind only but leprosy. Poems of leprosy have followed the St. Elmo's fire and the unquietness of the age. For all these reasons I have not thanked you for Ronald Johnson's book . . .

I now thank you for it, it is a beautiful book, good to have, good to converse with, good for meditation, good to sing, a fine book.

Now for Dahlberg, of course I will write for Dahlberg [Festschrift] and in fact here it is ["Ceremony for Edward Dahlberg"]. It is a second draft. I can't sit here drafting more drafts, I guess you can read this one all right.

I am glad to know where you are, where you have settled, come down and alighted. Keep in touch, tell me things that happen. I envy your collection of ancient postcards. You will see, I will roust out of some hole some even more fantastic ancient postcards of monasteries. You will see. I will send you almost invisible prints of the monks of Italian *chiostri* fermenting the juice of the juniper.

May 19, 1967

. . . I haven't been anchoritic enough these last weeks, and it culminated in a big flap in Louisville when an old friend of mine [Dan Walsh] was ordained priest at 60 in a sudden charismatic seizure of bishops. I went in and got stoned on champagne, which must have surprised the cult public. I am now hoping to get back into a little quiet, and meditation, and poetry. But meanwhile I have been held up in writing the current curriculum [vitae]. I am bad at writing these things, "born on a chimney top in Strasbourg in 1999" etc.) but you can select what you want from this one, there is plenty of choice.

Got a very good letter from Ron Johnson but so far no [*The Book of*] *Green Man*. I will agitate for it in the office where the mail gets lost. But I never had it and this is what I want most to have since seeing part of it. I will write him when I have the book in hand and have read some more.

I hope you are having more luck with the Festschrift contributions. I suppose it is understandable though that people rebel at making statements that might sound like blurbs. There are too many statements about everything, and I am lucky to be out of the blizzard thereof, so I can talk without embarrassment about liking, say, Dahlberg.

I just finished a piece ["The Shoshoneans"] on Ed Dorn's Indian book [*The Shoshoneans: The People of the Basin Plateau*], thought you might like it . . .

Curriculum vitae   Merton   May 1967

Born 1915 in Southern France a few miles from Catalonia so that I imagine myself by birth Catalan and am accepted as such in Barcelona where I have never been. Exiled therefore from Catalonia I came to New York, then went to Bermuda, then back to France, then to school at Montauban, then to school at Oakham in England, to Clare College Cambridge where my scholarship was taken away after a year of riotous living, to Columbia University New York where I earned two degrees of dullness and wrote a Master's thesis on Blake. Taught English among Franciscan football players at St. Bonaventure University, and then became a Trappist monk at Gethsemani Ky. in 1941. First published book of poems 1944. Autobiography 1948 created a general hallucination followed by too many pious books. Back to poetry in the fifties and sixties. Gradual backing away from the monastic institution until I now live alone in the woods not claiming to be anything, except of course a Catalan. But a Catalan in exile who would not return to Barcelona under any circumstances, never having been there. Recently published *Raids on the Un-*

speakable, Conjectures of a Guilty Bystander, Mystics and Zen Masters,
have translated work of poets like Vallejo, Alberti, Hernández, Nicanor
Parra etc. Proud of facial resemblance to Picasso and/or Jean Genet or
alternately Henry Miller (though not so much Miller).

June 9, 1967

You know, Ron Johnson's book (I mean now the *Green Man*) never
arrived. I tried to inquire about it, but got nowhere. I wonder what has
happened to it. Also a poem he said he was sending did not get here
either. The mail here of course is very strange, and everything goes
through the hands of people who if well meaning are often inefficient or
mixed up, or just don't pass everything on. I have got at some of these
people and am sure they would have passed the things on if they were
around here now. Hence one thinks of the General Postal Service which
is hardly better in many respects than the monastic . . .

Guy Davenport speaks of a new magazine in Lexington: *Kentucky
Review.* He and Gene [Meatyard] were over again a few weeks ago and
we had a time with much photography around an old house and a dead
pine tree.

I have finished a long poem series ["Edifying Cables"] and sent it
off to J. [Laughlin]. Am enjoying June, fighting allergy, working, reflecting
on how much Kafka's *Castle* has to say about the Church. Life is normal.

October 31, 1967

I'm off to a start. Here is a concrete poem I am working on. Right
away I am up against the new world of questions: I mean obviously there
is a certain amount of palaver with the editors before such a thing moves
on into print. Like in this one, I need my two O's, I need to dig up the
sort of typeface the two O's aren't yet in, and all like that. Maybe I need
a book of typefaces at my side every moment, who knows? But surely
every concrete poet doesn't have this. Well, anyway.

Then where can I get a copy of that magnificent book of concrete
poems you had there? I'd gladly review it even on my hands and
knees . . .

Merton sent Williams a copy of the following concrete poem, signed and dated:

(Concrete racegram of Pluto king of hell as he meets white foe in Gaol
while one or both is/are set free into the fair.)

PLU

TO	MET
O	FAY
IN	SIDE

TANK	2
O	PLU
TO	MET
RO	FAY
END	SIZE
O	TANK
UP	2
MY	PEN
TOE	FOE
PHASE	2

PLUTOT

TANK	OUT
END	UP
OUT	GRAM
TANK	SIDE
GRAM	SNOW
MOE	SAYS
LET	TELL
PIN	TOE
GOE	2

ALL
WELL
END

December 13, 1967

Many, many thanks for the Concrete Poets [an anthology]. Magnificent. Great to have and soak in. I see what you mean about my square effort. True does not connect at all. I look at these Brazilians. Wow.

Guess what. I am suddenly going into editing, temporarily. I want to put out four offset collections of poetry-prose from all good people. Just four collections. One brief magazine [Monks Pond] flash in the air and out, but four good collections. We have here our own offset press and I'd be crazy not to do this, we might as well put out something besides cheese ads for heavens sakes. Thus I want material for four good collections and how thick they'll be no one can say: no money involved one way or other give away the collections.

Can you please send me something of yours, poem, prose, published before or not no matter though preferably new, but good, saying what you most want to say. And can you ask Ron [Johnson] to send something, and maybe Dahlberg and so on. Only problem here is I forgot it has to be something the monks won't be shocked at. If you can think of someone else right around I wouldn't know, or something out of the past Mina Loy, or like that, get it sent. Translations too. Anything.

[Robert] Lax back in U.S. at Olean NY.

Jonathan Williams dispatched copies of Merton's letter of December 13 to colleagues, adding a note of his own encouraging contributions to Merton's new magazine.

April 12, 1968

I think I will use picture of you as harvest spirit with beer and thyrsus (Gene Meatyard) in next issue. Lots of good things coming in, very happy to have [Russell] Edson and Emmett Williams in next issue. And many others. Send more of your own and urge others to send stuff too. Happy Easter.

To William Carlos Williams

William Carlos Williams (1883–1963) lived all his life in Rutherford, New Jersey, combining a pediatric practice with work as a writer. Williams wrote novels, essays, and plays but is best known for his poetry, especially Paterson 1948–1956, *a poem originally published in five volumes and regarded as a distinctively American work. Merton began his brief exchange with Dr. Williams with a note expressing pleasure in his essay on Daniel Boone, published in* In the American Grain *in 1925. In reply, Williams suggested that Merton read Allen Ginsberg's poetry, especially* Kaddish and Other Poems 1958–1960, *published by City Lights in 1961.*

April 6, 1961

J. Laughlin—your publisher and mine—tells me you have been quite sick, a fact which I am sorry to hear. I hope you will be getting better soon & will be writing some more. From the thirties on I have been reading your poetry with great pleasure, and recently I opened up [*In the*] *American Grain* & came upon your fine essay on Daniel Boone. It moved me very much. I have a little house in the woods near the Abbey & all my neighbors are Boones & I guess I myself have become a Boone in my own way. What you said about D. Boone is profoundly meaningful, in a time when I get so sick of our infidelity to the original American grace that I no longer know what to do. Anyway Daniel Boone had it & I think you have kept it.

God bless you, & get well soon. May all things prosper with you.

July 11, 1961

It has taken me a long time to get to be able to follow your advice and read *Kaddish* [*and Other Poems*], because nobody sent me one. But finally Laughlin is out in SF and the City Lights Books sent me a copy. I agree with you about it. I think it is great and living poetry and certainly religious in its concern. In fact, who are more concerned with ultimates than the beats? Why do you think that just because I am a monk I should be likely to shrink from beats? Who am I to shrink from anyone, I am a monk, therefore by definition, as I understand it, the chief friend of beats and one who has no business reproving them. And why should I? Thank you for telling me about *Kaddish*. And I also liked very much the poem on Van Gogh's ear ["Death to Van Gogh's Ear!"]. I think this is one of the few people around who is saying anything. The others are in a bad way. I hope I can some time send you a long poem I think you may like. It ["Hagia Sophia"] is being printed by a friend of mine down the road here in Lexington.

God bless you. I liked two poems of yours that were in *Harper's*. I wish you all good things.

To Louis Zukofsky

Louis Zukofsky's poetry, like "all really valid poetry," is "a kind of recovery of paradise," Merton wrote in a review of All: The Collected Short Poems, 1956–1964. *Zukofsky's poems "spring from a ground of immense silence and love" (see "Louis Zukofsky—The Paradise Ear" in* The Literary Essays of Thomas Merton). *Touched by Merton's understanding of his work, Zukofsky wrote to thank Merton for the review and Merton responded with praise for Zukofsky's "A's." In the correspondence that ensued, it is obvious that the two took delight in each other as well as each other's work, offering helpful criticism of works in progress and words of advice on treatments for bursitis and other ills.*

Louis Zukofsky (1904–1978) was born in New York City, earned an M.A. at Columbia University, and taught English at several colleges and universities, including the Polytechnic Institute of Brooklyn, from which he retired in 1966. He began to publish poetry and literary criticism in the thirties and gained the admiration of poets like Ezra Pound and William Carlos Williams long before his work became more widely read in the sixties. Zukofsky's best-known work is "A," a long poem which he began in the twenties and completed in the seventies. A volume of all the "A's," containing previously published collections, appeared in 1978. Zukofsky's many other published writings include All: The Collected Short Poems, 1923–1964 *and* Bottom: On Shakespeare, *a two-volume work of criticism that includes a musical setting for Shakespeare's* Pericles *by Zukofsky's wife, Celia.*

March 11, 1967

Many thanks for your letter of nine days ago. The operation seems to have helped and has perhaps got rid of everything in that elbow (elbow included maybe). I agree with you about not wanting operations. The anesthetic is a terrible thing. Not bad this time though. I fought it off with everything—though can't take aspirin. Cortisone shots are very helpful. I made good use of hot-water bottles too. I need the arm to be all right so I can do a little work, keep my place swept, get in a little wood and so on. I live in a house in the woods near the monastery.

And now to your books [*Bottom: On Shakespeare; All: The Collected Short Poems, 1923–1958; "A" 1–12; "A" 9; and A Test of Poetry*]. What a happening. Really. Especially to have the superb volumes of *Bottom: On Shakespeare*—it's like getting *The Anatomy of Melancholy* from [Robert] Burton himself: a book into which everything has gone. It will be something to think about for years. I look at it with wonder as I move around my front room. Never having read the early "A's" it is they that I have begun on, and they are full of everything that is best. To begin with, this is the right way to read "A's" I think, not bit by bit here and there in magazines. One really gets into them.

"A" 7 is a most marvelous Easter fugue. You are in fact sacred music but as it should be, not just Church music. With the kind of secularity that is in Bach. And the compassion. The great Lenten compassion and sense of rising from the dead that must happen, that happens, that art is all about. The victory over death. This is the real witness to the world and you are the one who is saying it most clearly: which is probably one reason why as yet too few have heard it. I really get my breath knocked out of me completely by some of those "A's." The way in "A" 7 the perspectives fuse in and out of each other and the dead and the alive interchange and come into focus, and the echoes of the psalms in scorn of idols, the dead wood, the dead and living horses, oh my. Such praise.

I am glad to hear the second volume is coming. And look forward to *Prepositions*. A *Test* I am very glad to have too, and it will help much. Maybe with this stimulus I will at last begin to write some decent poetry myself. It is about time. There is not much that I am glad to have done and published. A few, not more.

I will send some books today, ones that for some reason I myself like. One is simply a matter of some versions based on Chuang Tzu [*The Way of Chuang Tzu*], nothing "original" but in a way the book of mine I like best. It is more the "finding" type of thing you mention. If you pass them on to someone else, that's fine too. The great struggle is against the invasion of paper first of all: though [there are] other more spiritual invasions and worse, now. The visions and noises. All the electric stuff. It is so good to be in contact with you: I wish I could be there sometime to hear you play music. When I get some questions about things in "A," I'll perhaps bother you for identifications.

April 15, 1967

Thanks for your wonderful appreciative letter of couple weeks back. And maybe you find *Conjectures* [*of a Guilty Bystander*] too quarrelsome:

most do. No matter, there are other things in it. But meanwhile I have fallen head first into a long poem of my own, swimming in its craziness, and trying other work and just walking in the sun. The operation did not really work I am afraid and so the arm is still a bit bad and the back is bad and all this making my typing a venture. But I am so convinced that none of these things matter. There is always the deep inner richness of a silence that comes up and meets and merges with the sunlight from the outside and all is one sun so who cares about whether work is done? Then the work does itself in its own freedom and if it is bad no matter. I think it will possibly be good.

The long Marxist section of "A" brought back the thirties as nothing else (though also a friend sent me a picture of Groucho Marx in the paper, another more influential Marxism of the thirties!) (Thought Groucho had gone to the Valhallas of laughter). "A" 10 is right up my alley as you will see from parts of *Conjectures* (though I do not write explicitly about the war). It is in a way Blake-like. So many good rich things. Especially the last long one. And now I read *Bottom*, too, when I am not writing my own: and the principle you lay down there is the one: that language comes up out of love in S. [Shakespeare] and in any valid poet. This is the truth we live for and by and there is no other (the Bible is full of the same). Also however, I read a Sufi, Ibn al Arabi, just getting into him, who says some remarkable things about the imagination: Abraham dreamed he must sacrifice Isaac but did not interpret his dream, so God had to interpret it for him showing him that he had a wrong notion of sacrifice: a literal notion. And it is true, we none of us interpret our dream: but you do in "A." It is a long, careful, valid, patient, humble, penetrating interpretation of your dream. It helps me to interpret my own. Praise God for giving us you.

This is just a note to give a sign of life, because next week comes the publisher [Naomi Burton Stone, Merton's editor and former literary agent] and I will be all tied up and won't be able to write . . .

All my very best to all of you, I wish I could be there or you here (maybe someday?).

May 5, 1967

Most grateful for yours of April 20th and for the parens in the Smithgirl poem ["A Round and a Hope for Smithgirls"]. You are certainly quite right in most cases, and I do not even question you: you have spotted useless words. Writing as I have alone in the woods for such a long time without anyone to make remarks, I have let too many useless sprouts grow out in all directions. The one I do doubt is "to surface"—somehow I wonder if that movement and coming into sight should not remain. I will think of it. And I have left "Look" perhaps because I have a weakness for saying "Look" (and perhaps that is the very reason why I should get rid of it). In any case, many thanks, you have helped the poem and the poet.

I just got from New Directions the selection of Charles Olson, whom I have hitherto not carefully read, and I see that I must. Especially his prose remarks on how you see things. This I think must contain a lot of important directions and suggestions. I have to read him slowly and carefully because his background is not quite mine and I have not situated him yet. What do you think about him? To what extent does your way of looking agree with his, would you say? I'd be interested to know. For my own part I have naturally grown up all full of myth and symbol and sound and explanation and elaboration, too much elaboration, but never allegory (except in worst moments of writing when I was not even present). In the long run I think one can have both the direct and continuous relation with the visible and also see it as symbol but not as containing a symbol that is something else and of something else. Hence what I really would like to do with Olson is reconcile his direct way with also a traditional symbol way that is properly understood, and after all there is Melville?! I must go into all this.

Back to Smithgirls: absolutely nothing from the papers which I do not read either, and I am not saluting them in some public event. A friend of mine [Amiya Chakravarty] who has been teaching Hindu philosophy there for a year (a disciple of Gandhi) has been reading them stuff of mine and they have got interested in it, finally sending some lovely reactions and happy remarks so that in return I wrote the poem, celebrating nothing more than that they were young and new and alive and new friends.

Letters have got far beyond me the last few weeks because I have had visiting publishers and am trying to catch up with the mail now . . .

Elbow is all right, back is all right (more or less), have allergies but who hasn't? All is well, and the May weather is perfect.

June 23, 1967

I don't know if I answered your last letter yet: your suggestion for the end of Smithgirls is fine and has been put into act. It is very hot here now and I have been busy finishing a small chore, a commentary on Camus's *The Plague* ["*The Plague* of Albert Camus: A Commentary and Introduction"]. Camus is a man for whom I have a lot of sympathy and he is one of the few people who can still preach and get away with it. Because he does it with much modesty . . .

What I have just read and highly recommend: Ronald Johnson's lovely poem *The Book of the Green Man* . . . It is really substantial and full of color, draftsmanship of a high order, sound, and memories most rich of things that have been forgotten to our cost, myths, and well-chosen people and places. It is one of the very finest things I have seen anywhere and I know you will like it if you have not liked it already.

Please excuse the very badly typed lepers and their lamentable rites.

July 18, 1967

The main purpose of my last letter was to thank you for *It Was* and so I didn't mention it! That, and the failure to answer fairly promptly yours of July 5th is some sign of the disarray I am and have been in for several weeks. Changes in my house, taking it all apart and putting it all back together, new shelves, new sink, running water that I can't dare drink, and then on top of that all the chickens (metaphorical ones) coming home to roost at once, reviews I have promised, people I have promised to see, all this has happened at once. And you are right, the mail is mad anyway and one has to wonder and worry about things like books: but I have *It Was* and in the uproar have read part of it, which is very much you and I am delighted to have it and see it in the context of everything else. I have not finished "Ferdinand" yet but it is what I like best—I have run ahead of the story a little to read the poem about the Cape Cod girls that have no combs and I like that very much. (The shanty. Now I will have to catch up with myself and find where it fits in.)

I am a fool to get involved in reviewing (in order to get still more books than I need) and as I have to do reviews for the magazine of the Order (no choice there!) I get hung up on books in German, which I read slowly and laboriously. More fun with Spanish and even lately Catalan (article on Catalan hermit movement and things like that!). But still, it is a deluge and who needs another deluge? We have deluges enough. The war in the Near East got me very upset and it was good it was soon "over," though is it over?

Take care of yourself and have a good summer, fair weather, peace, time to do the things you like. Blessings always, and my very best of everything.

August 30, 1967

Shouts from Kentucky. Reading "A" 18 . . . I can if I wish hold one "A" 18 in each hand and sing them. I have been ill. In bed with bad 'flu. "A" 18 the thing with also a little sunshine that has at last pulled me out. It has been good to be ill alone in the woods, one likes the woods better for it and is more suspicious of infirmaries. Back to "A" 18, everything so close, so clear, so new. Everything there even Rock well all shut up on yours and mine names day Aug. 25 St. Louis. That was when I got the flu. That p. 292 the whole thing flies beautifully and I too and trying like that especially like the top of the page. The big Buddhist fish is new to me and a portent: for the fish is Christ and if he shows his snozzle sure and the bloody Catlicks will bomb him. And the kids on the fence and the Gemini walker at the end of his cord. All the hot and cold, the fire and water. All Vietnam themes finely done and poor Roger La Porte etc. London's burning for sure, isn't it? Where did you get the Melanesian stuff? I am working that too: only a further development, the cargo cults. Yours sounds like [Bronislaw] Malinowski? I am getting into Claude Lévi-Strauss. Marvelous (Brazil mostly). "Let the mad dogs transports enjoy all success/ We are alone where they cannot exist alone / and alone our desire won't shadow their living." Just what I was coming out of it all with today, after being sick, after being oppressed by the spites etc. of so many competing operators (each day comes the mail and I am snowed with their goddam competitions). Even in the woods you cannot have quiet unless you determine not to have a shadow anymore and not to cast any. How? So many lovely things in "A" 18, I could see Chagall coming long before he appeared, announced pages ahead by Chagall fiddles, etc.

And also *Prepositions*. It finally reached me and I went to the Chaplin bit like iron filings to the magnet, remembering everything perfectly. But I have read it all, I do not get carried away by it like by the "A's."

I hope you are well and that you stay away from all flus and all competitions.

Some typography.

My old friend Victor Hammer died, too: great typographer and hand printer here in Lexington. It has been a hard summer.

December 28, 1967

Thanks for the letter and for the little bit of "A" 21 on the card—very moving. And now what do you think? I have become one of the million editors in the world and have decided upon starting a small magazine [*Monks Pond*] but it is only to run four issues and then goodbye. It will be a very simple offset thing, I hope and think, and can be done here without cost. No money involved anywhere. Poems, creative things, Asian texts, blues, koans, ghost dances, all to be crammed into four issues. Already have poets coming in with good stuff. And of course IF . . . well, editors assume all poets have thousands of poems tucked away somewhere. But if you do have some little piece of something, this will be an unusual magazine in many ways if only first of all because it is a monastic literary magazine—not many of those around! It would of course be marvelous to have something of yours in it, even something that has appeared elsewhere (preferably abroad!).

Failing that, if you have ideas about young poets with good things to dispose of, turn them this way. Or any other suggestions, poetry prose, ideas, people to waylay etc. I will try to see that everyone gets it who wants it (free).

Now I'm snowed in the hermitage and it is very quiet, with probably a lot more snow coming in the night. Otherwise the monastery down there is a bit unquiet, with a new abbot soon to be elected, and people fearing to get the wrong kind, someone afraid of anything good. I hope not. I'm out of it. I watch too much weather maybe.

New Year blessings to you and Celia and all of you. Joy and peace.

I think you might enjoy the little old piece on the Cell [see *Contemplation in a World of Action*] and as for the poem which does not really work, if you see the wrongs I'd be glad to hear them.

February 2, 1968

I know what you mean about the bronchial bug. I've had a wicked January, three or four days very sick indeed and the rest dragging around and coughing like a man who smokes three packs a day without having to go to the bother of smoking any.

Anyway I hope you are feeling better. It has been a bad 'flu and many of my friends have been hit hard by it.

The magazine has got off I think to a good start. First issue in the "press" and lots of material for the next two on hand. *Thanks to the Dictionary* has so much beautiful stuff in it. I will gladly accept your offer of the preface and ask also for more: could I add "Young David"? This in the second issue: and then especially the lovely bit "There was a horse its face bausond . . ." pp. 129–131? For another issue? And call it "David's Horse"? This little book is only 250 copies and who has seen it? The David and Michal section is also most sharp and lovely. Could I use all these, Louis? I would be most grateful and the people would see these things. And other poets being near them would be improved and helped.

Thanks for your remarks on my Cain poem which does indeed need more work. Part of a big long mixed-up thing [*The Geography of Lograire*] that will come together in time I hope. I need to soak in "A" again and deepen my understanding of how to get at such a venture.

I wonder why I started a magazine: but it has turned out to be a good idea and also I seem to find myself by it part of a family of brothers and sisters all likeminded though with different views all open and for the most part gentle and living around in remote places and in many ways monks.

Yes, I too am for statement: I wish though that my own made more sense. This one is not as clear as it could be (it presupposes that one has seen the things I refer to) but I think it is one I will not take back.

Acknowledgments

I am grateful to the members of the Thomas Merton Legacy Trust and to William H. Shannon, General Editor of the Merton Letters, for inviting me to select and edit Merton's letters to writers. It has been a privilege to read, firsthand, Merton's fascinating and challenging correspondence with writers all over the world. I hope that all who read this volume will find themselves drawn, by Merton's own voice, into the dialogue these letters represent and invite.

In my work I have enjoyed generous support and assistance. Robert E. Daggy and Brother Patrick Hart, each of whom edited a volume of Merton's letters, readily shared their editorial experience and expertise. I am especially grateful to Dr. Daggy, Director of the Thomas Merton Studies Center at Bellarmine College, for making archival materials and other resources of the center available to me and for welcoming me to Louisville, on numerous occasions, with graciousness and hospitality. Brother Patrick encouraged me throughout, made helpful suggestions, and even volunteered to read the galleys.

I also want to express my appreciation to Czeslaw Milosz for searching his files to find several letters Merton wrote to him; to Sally Brown, Curator of Literary Manuscripts at the British Library, for forwarding copies of Merton's letters to Evelyn Waugh; to Robert Menendes and Janet Casaverde for helping me translate letters Merton wrote in French and Spanish; to David D. Cooper for making available to me materials he gathered in work on Merton's letters; to Linda Loree and Geraldine Westcott for carefully typing various parts of the manuscript; and to my dear mother, Jane Spychalski Bochen, who kept me on task with frequent queries about my progress.

I am also grateful to Robert Giroux and the staff at Farrar, Straus and Giroux for the care they have taken with this volume. In addition to making suggestions that enhanced readability, Mr. Giroux shared with me his own memories of Thomas Merton, particularly concerning the publication of *The Seven Storey Mountain* and *The Sign of Jonas*.

Colleagues at Nazareth College have been thoughtful and supportive in many ways. I especially thank Dr. Rose Marie Beston, President, and Dr. Dennis Silva, Vice President for Academic Affairs, for granting me a sabbatical semester during which I was able to begin work on this volume. The staff of the Lorette Wilmot Library patiently fielded my many requests for interlibrary loans. Sheila A. Smyth, Associate Director of the Library, and Jennifer Burr, Reference Coordinator, drew on their professional expertise to help me ferret out numerous, sometimes obscure, biographical and bibliographical bits of information. Students in my classes on Thomas Merton, at Nazareth (and at St. Bernard's Institute), challenged my thinking and honed my understanding of Merton with their probing questions and insightful reading. I want my friends at Nazareth College, as well as in the International Thomas Merton Society and the Thomas Merton Society of Rochester, to know how very much I appreciate their unflagging interest in my work and their kind words of encouragement.

It should be noted here that several letters that are included in this volume have already appeared in print elsewhere. Merton's letters to Boris Pasternak appeared in a limited edition published by the King Library Press/University of Kentucky in 1973, under the title *Boris Pasternak–Thomas Merton: Six Letters*, with a foreword by Naomi Burton Stone and an introduction by Lydia Pasternak Slater. Merton's letters to Henry Miller, edited with an introduction by David D. Cooper, were published in *Helix* in 1984 as "Thomas Merton and Henry Miller: An Exchange of Letters." Merton himself selected several letters for publication as "Letters in a Time of Crisis" in *Seeds of Destruction*, published by Farrar, Straus and Giroux in 1964, including letters to Alceu Amoroso Lima, James Baldwin, Jacques Maritain, and Cintio Vitier.

Finally, and most especially, I want to express deep appreciation to my friend and colleague, William H. Shannon. From the day he first asked me to take on the work of this volume, he was available and supportive, whether offering constructive suggestions in a characteristically gentle and unobtrusive way, or helping me to decipher a seemingly illegible word or phrase written in Merton's own hand, or just sharing my excitement and, sometimes, my anxiety. He had a way of calling just when my energy was waning and, by talking with great enthusiasm about the Merton project he was working on at the time, reenergizing me. I appreciate his kindness, patience, confidence, scholarship, and ever good humor.

C.M.B.

Index